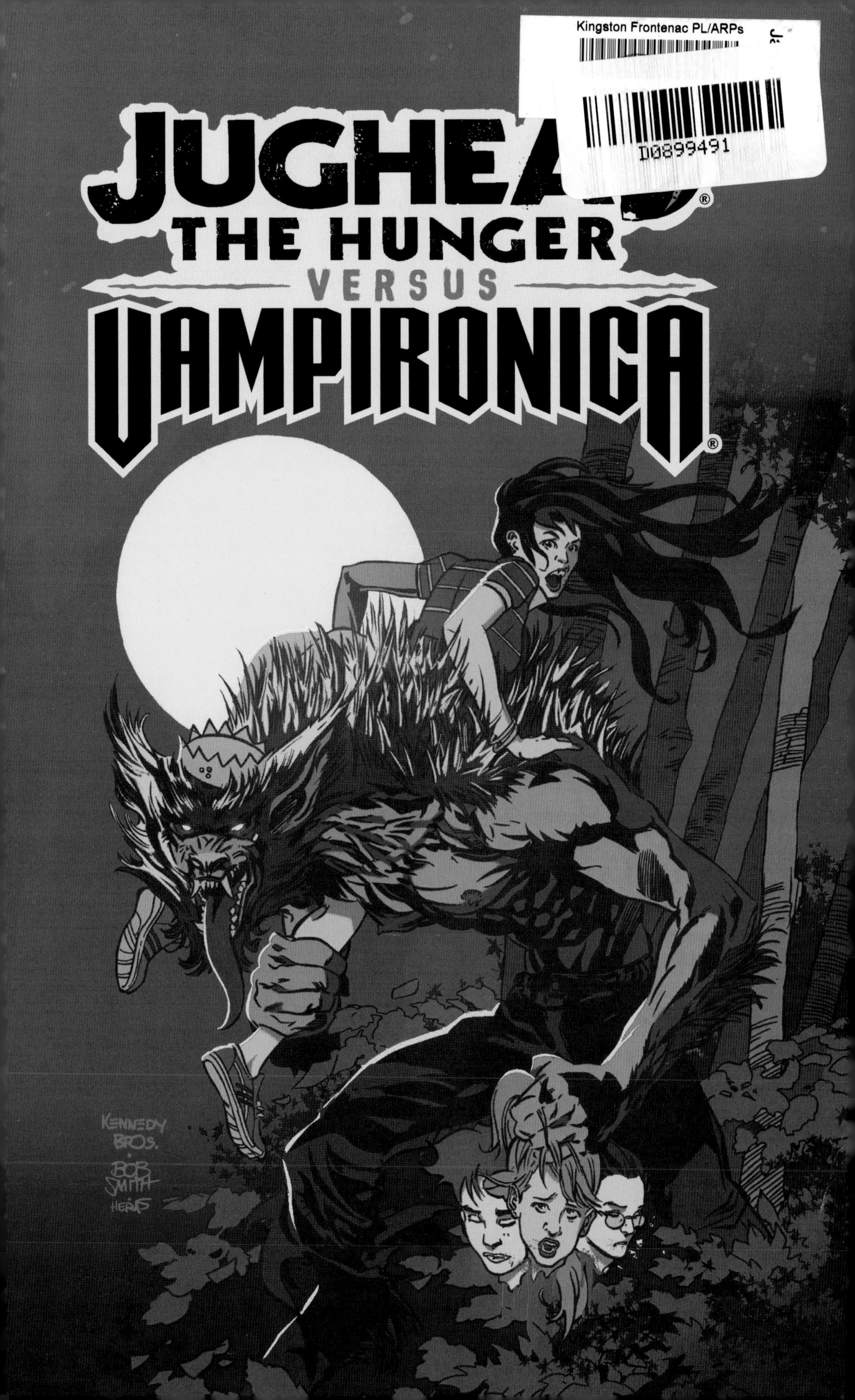
JUGHEAD®
THE HUNGER
VERSUS
VAMPIRONICA®
KENNEDY BROS.
BOB SMITH

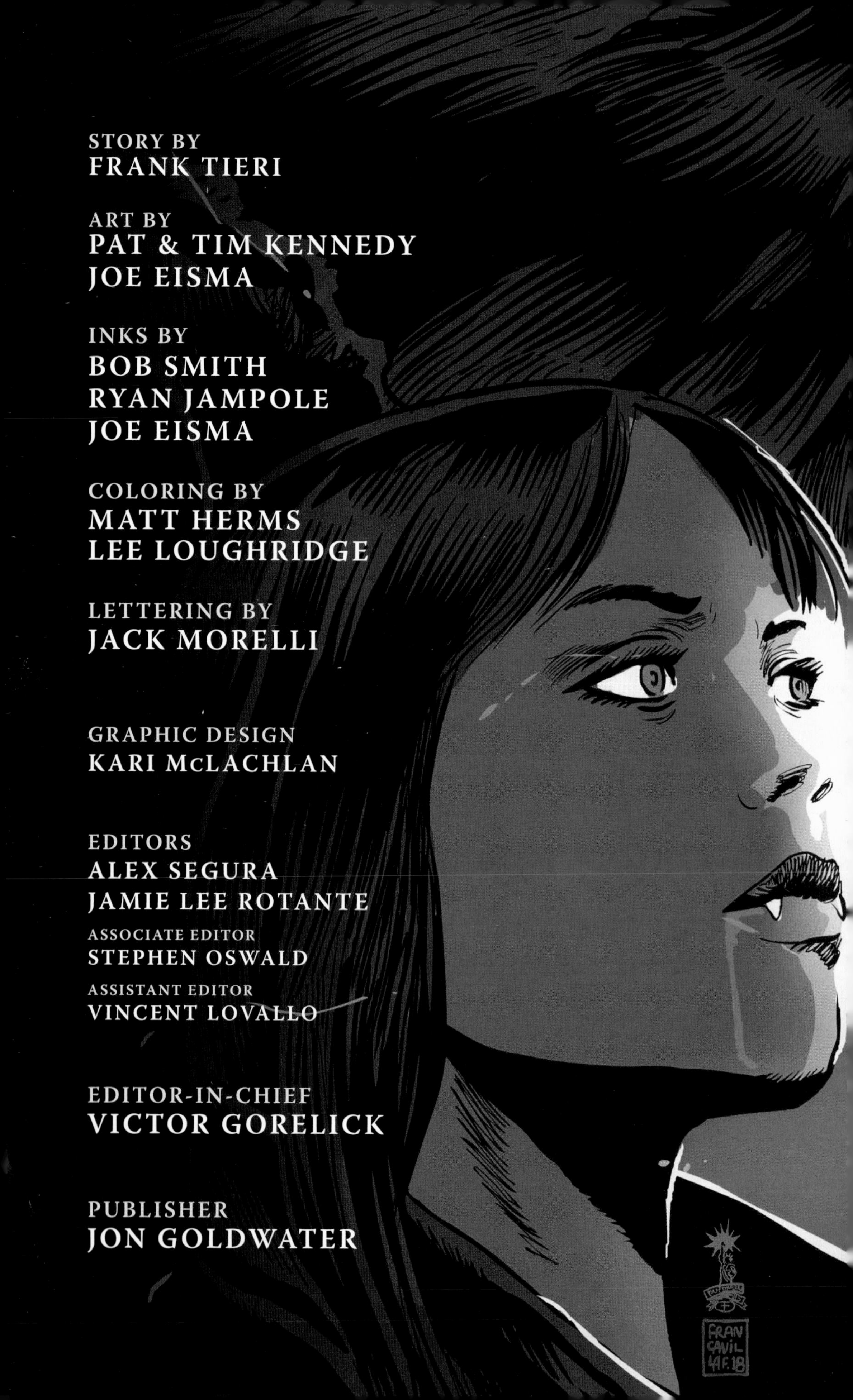

STORY BY
FRANK TIERI

ART BY
PAT & TIM KENNEDY
JOE EISMA

INKS BY
BOB SMITH
RYAN JAMPOLE
JOE EISMA

COLORING BY
MATT HERMS
LEE LOUGHRIDGE

LETTERING BY
JACK MORELLI

GRAPHIC DESIGN
KARI McLACHLAN

EDITORS
ALEX SEGURA
JAMIE LEE ROTANTE
ASSOCIATE EDITOR
STEPHEN OSWALD
ASSISTANT EDITOR
VINCENT LOVALLO

EDITOR-IN-CHIEF
VICTOR GORELICK

PUBLISHER
JON GOLDWATER

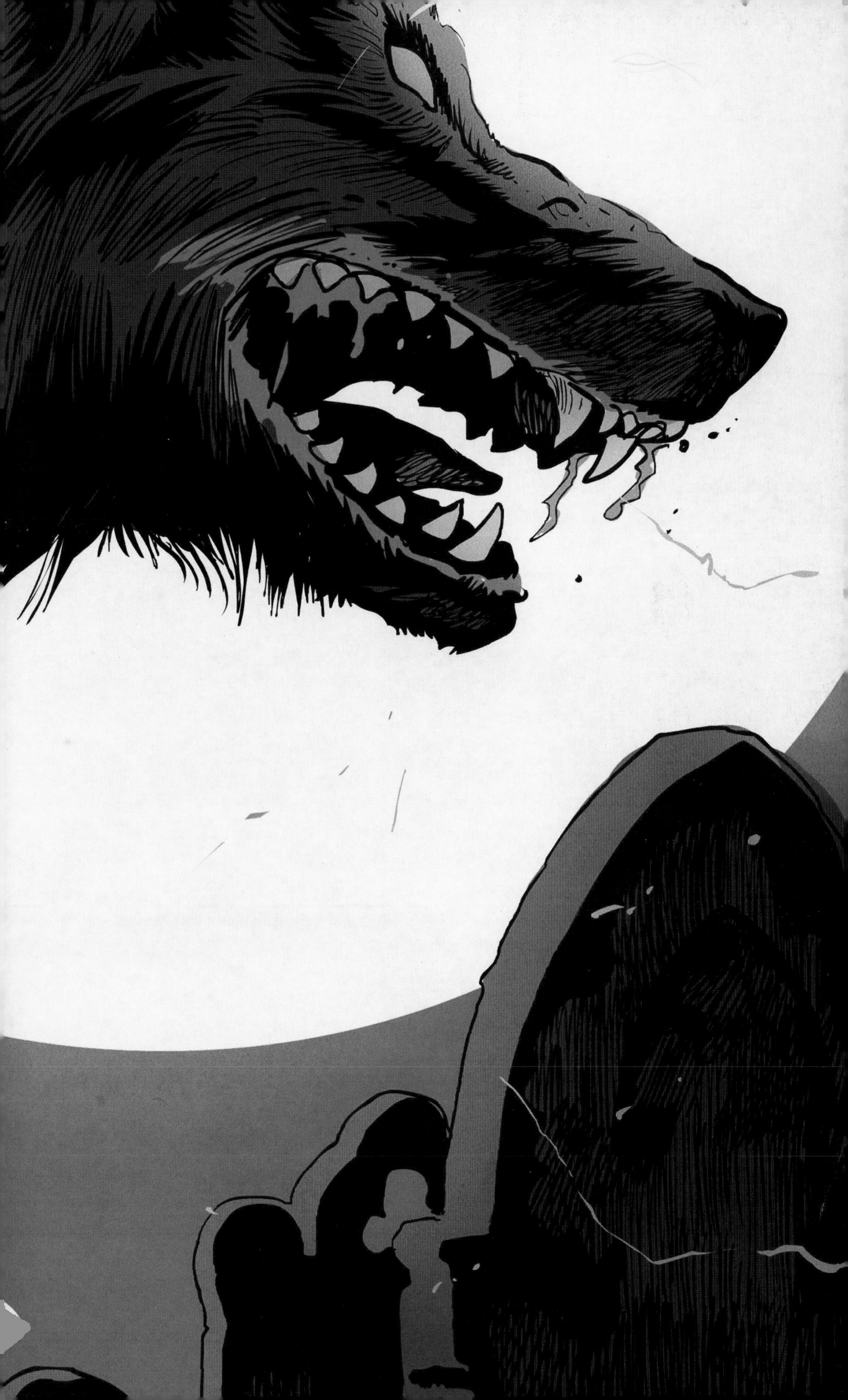

THE WORLD OF JUGHEAD THE HUNGER:

In his universe, **Jughead Jones** is more than just an ever-hungry teen, he's a **werewolf**! Jughead's dark family legacy has come to light after the teen unknowingly transformed and killed many helpless victims as the "Riverdale Ripper." Not one to put up with terror on her turf, werewolf hunter **Betty Cooper** set out for justice. With the help of **Archie Andrews**, the pair were able to use wolfsbane to cure Jughead's monstrous ways, albeit temporarily. Jughead skipped town, but not before leaving behind the bloodied corpse of local prankster **Reggie Mantle**.

While on the trail to track down Jughead, Betty and Archie meet with Betty's aunt, an experienced werewolf hunter named **Elena Cooper**, and her tough and intimidating cousin **Bo Cooper**. Elena explains of the centuries-long war between her family and the Joneses, leaving Betty with the uneasy choice of holding up her family legacy or helping her friend.

Meanwhile, Jughead teams up with his fellow Lycan cousin, **Bingo Wilkin**, to learn the ways of the werewolf. The pair are found by Betty and Archie, resulting in a fierce battle that leaves Jughead fatally wounded. Back in Riverdale, Reggie not only survives, but also learns that he has been turned into werewolf too. Reggie decides to turn **Veronica Lodge** and other Riverdale residents to form his own wolf pack and get revenge on Jughead by kidnapping his little sister, **Jellybean Jones**.

Jughead soon learns of his sister's abduction and discovers that Veronica killed his beloved pet **Hot Dog**. Together with Archie

and a reluctant Betty, the team forms a plan to fight off Reggie's band of werewolves and save Jellybean. Along the way, some unexpected help arrives as the Cooper clan assists in successfully fending off Reggie's wolfpack. Betty convinces the Coopers to spare the Jones siblings and makes the promise to keep an eye on them personally.

New mysteries begin to unfold as a series of grave robberies catch the eye of Betty. During her investigation, she learns that the robber is **Dilton Doiley**'s mad scientist cousin **Milton Doiley**! Milton has been resurrecting the deceased and turning them into monsters to do his bidding. Among them are his cousin Dilton and the monstrous **Moose Mason** (now known as **FrankenMoose**), who capture Betty. With a hostage in tow, Milton lures Jughead and Archie to his lair, where Wolfjug and FrankenMoose duke it out.

Jughead, Archie and Betty emerge somewhat victorious, reclaiming Jug's now-undead Hot Dog and putting an end to Milton's work. However, the true mastermind behind the scheme was really Veronica's father, **Mr. Lodge**, who has teamed up with Elena to take down the leader of the werewolves, Jughead's father **FP Jones**.

THE WORLD OF VAMPIRONICA:

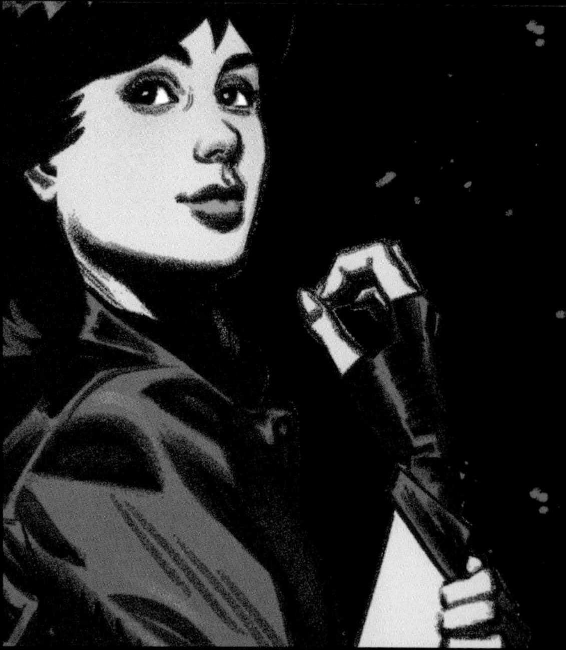

In her universe, **Veronica Lodge** is more than just beautiful, fashionable and rich... she's a vampire! Veronica descends from a long line of vampires, though her true form came to surface only after an encounter in her own home with an evil centuries-old vampire named **Ivan**! While Veronica narrowly escaped with her life, the same couldn't be said for her parents.

With the vicious vampire Ivan after her, Veronica took refuge in the basement of **Riverdale High School**. There she was discovered by her classmate and super genius

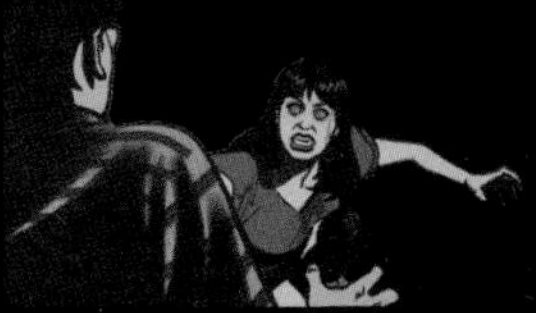

Dilton Doiley, who decided to help her learn about and eliminate the vampire threat.

Upon returning to her home to investigate, Veronica and Dilton found Veronica's parents were very much alive! But the reunion was not a happy one as **Mr. and Mrs. Lodge** were under the command of Ivan who was attempting to turn Veronica's crush **Archie Andrews** into a vampire

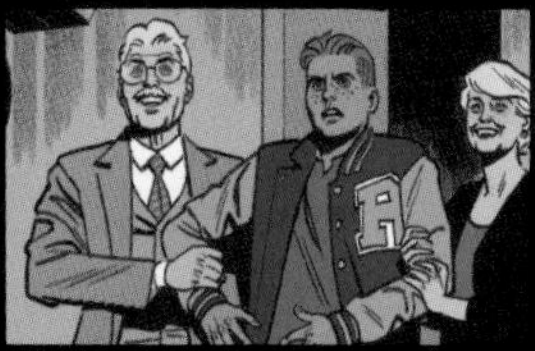

too! After saving the boy's life, Veronica and Dilton learned of Ivan's true goal to turn all of Riverdale into bloodsucking creatures of the night!

Together with her best friend **Betty Cooper**, Veronica, Dilton and Archie lead the fight against Ivan's vampire siege. Armed with water guns filled with holy water, the team was able to hold off the newly-turned vamps. But even after defeating Ivan, the curse was not broken. It was then that Veronica realized that there was another master vampire pulling the strings back at **Lodge Mansion**. After facing horrible traps and illusions, Veronica heroically defeated the master vampire and saved the town!

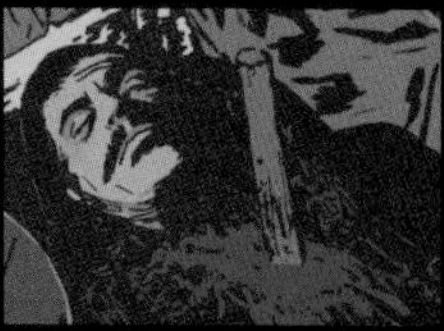

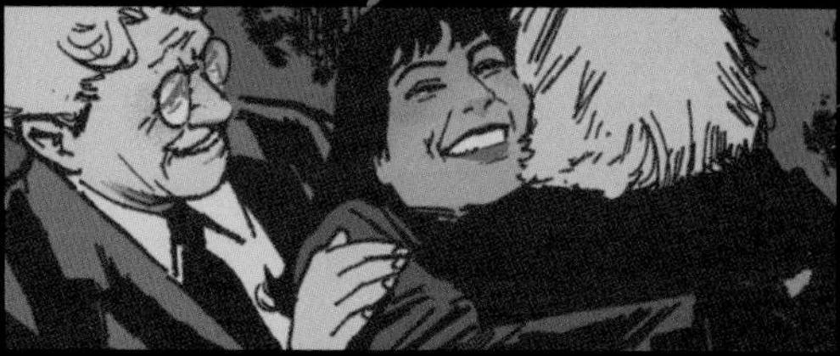

TWO WORLDS, ONE DESTINY:

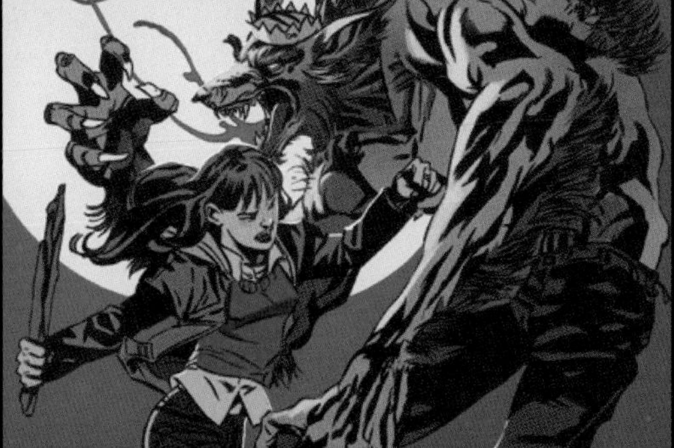

In the world of JUGHEAD THE HUNGER, there are no vampires, having been wiped out in their great war with the werewolves. In the world of VAMPIRONICA, the opposite is the case, as it was the vampires who were the victors. So what happens when these two eternal enemies are brought together again? Whatever it is, it can't be good for poor ol' Jug and Vampironica, you can count on that much...

CHAPTER ONE

COVER ART BY **PAT & TIM KENNEDY**
WITH **BOB SMITH** AND **MATT HERMS**

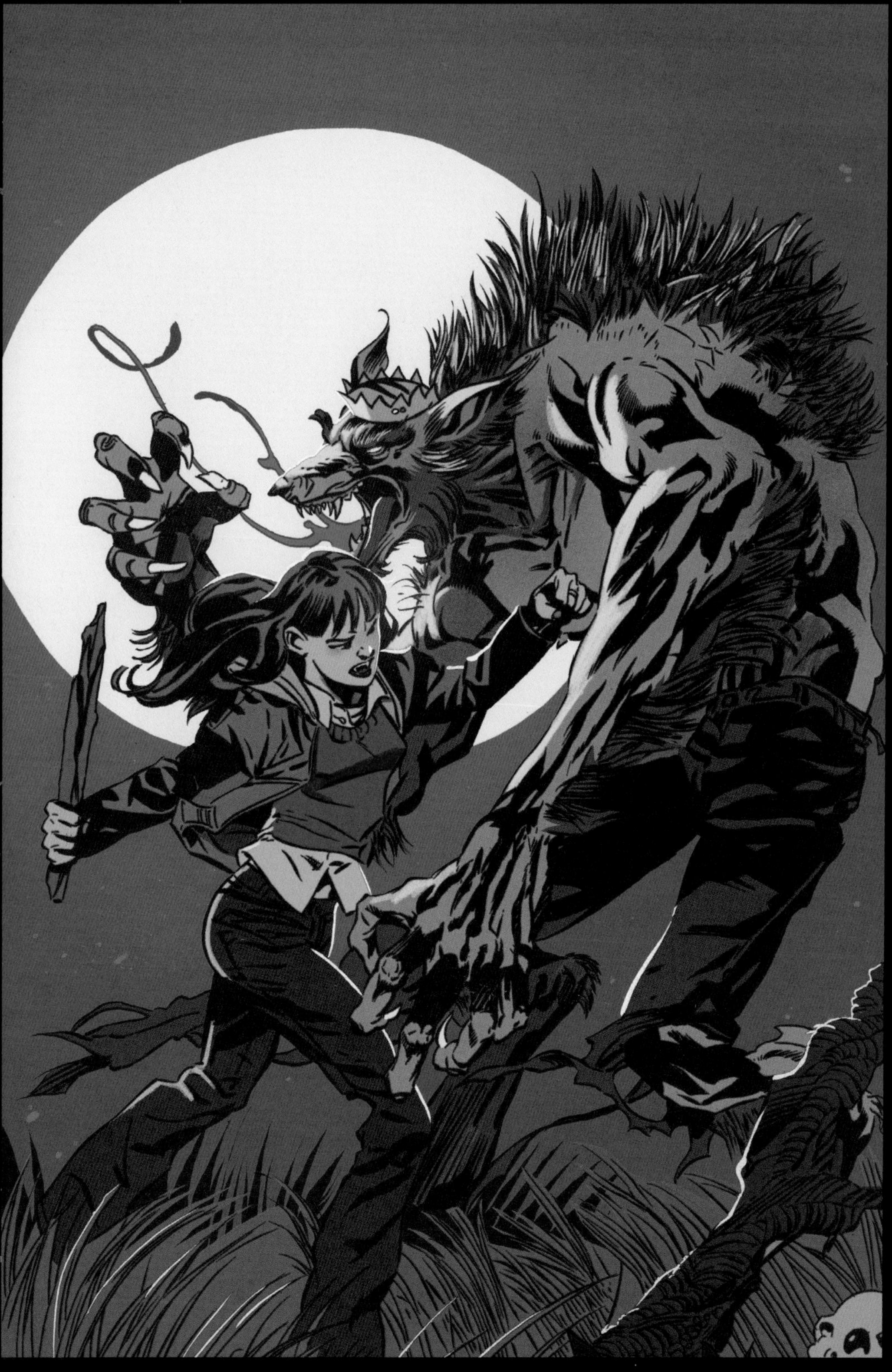

STORY BY **FRANK TIERI**
ART BY **PAT & TIM KENNEDY** (p.1-15) **JOE EISMA** (p.16-20)
INKS BY **BOB SMITH** (p.1-9,11,13-15) **RYAN JAMPOLE** (p.10,12,14)
COLORING BY **MATT HERMS** LETTERING BY **JACK MORELLI**

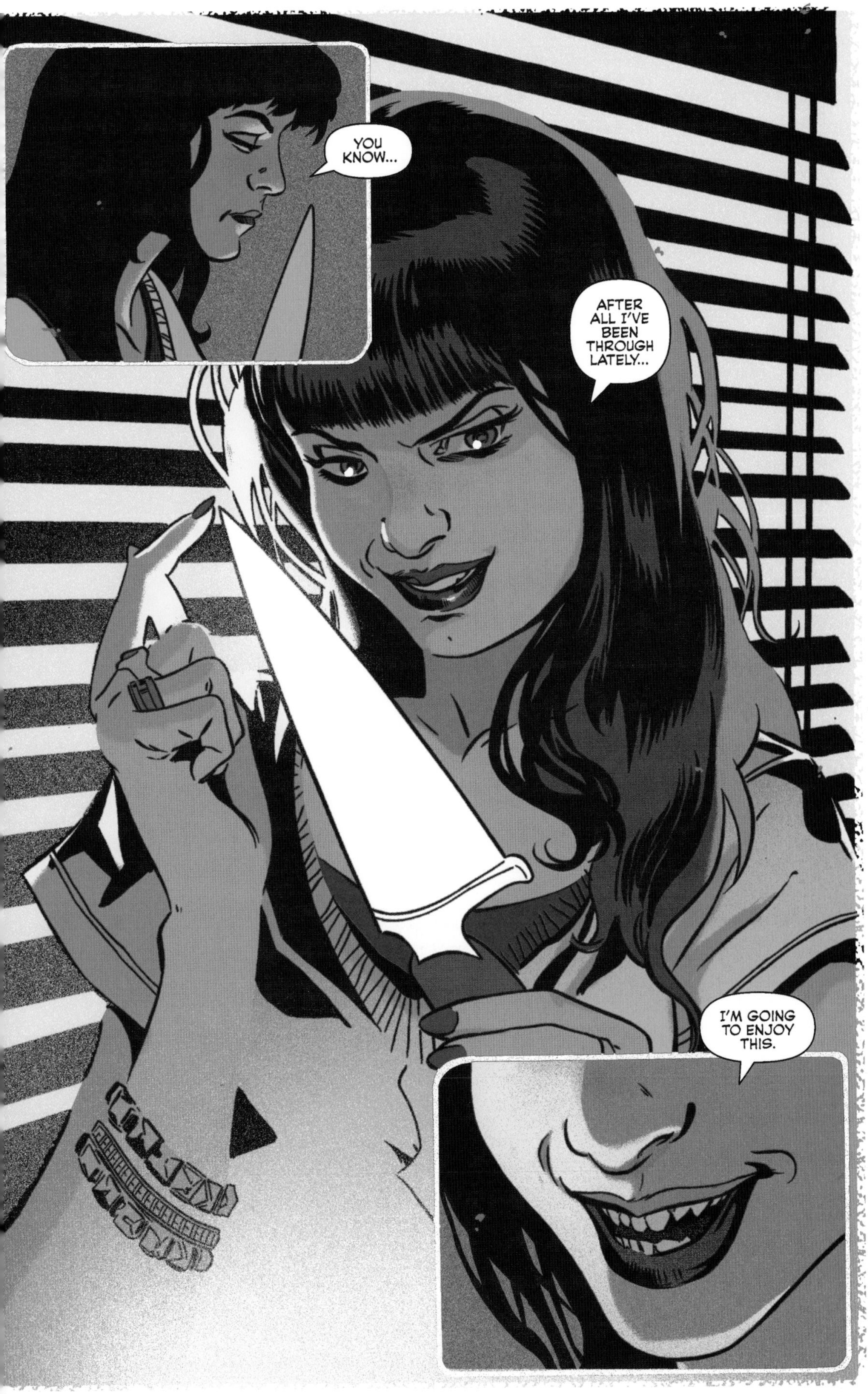
YOU KNOW...
AFTER ALL I'VE BEEN THROUGH LATELY...
I'M GOING TO ENJOY THIS.

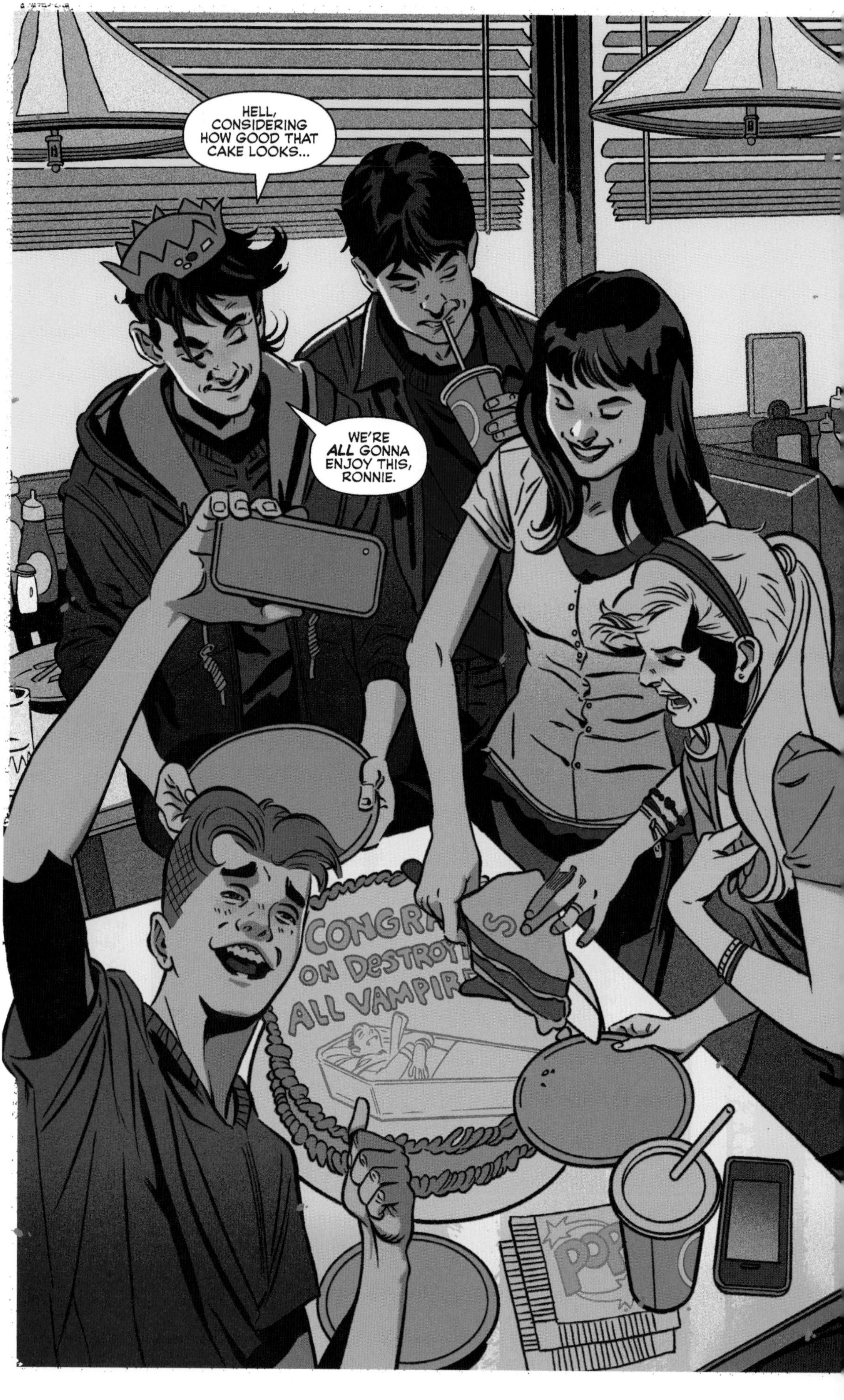
HELL, CONSIDERING HOW GOOD THAT CAKE LOOKS...
WE'RE ALL GONNA ENJOY THIS, RONNIE.
CONGRA S ON DESTROYI ALL VAMPIRE
POP

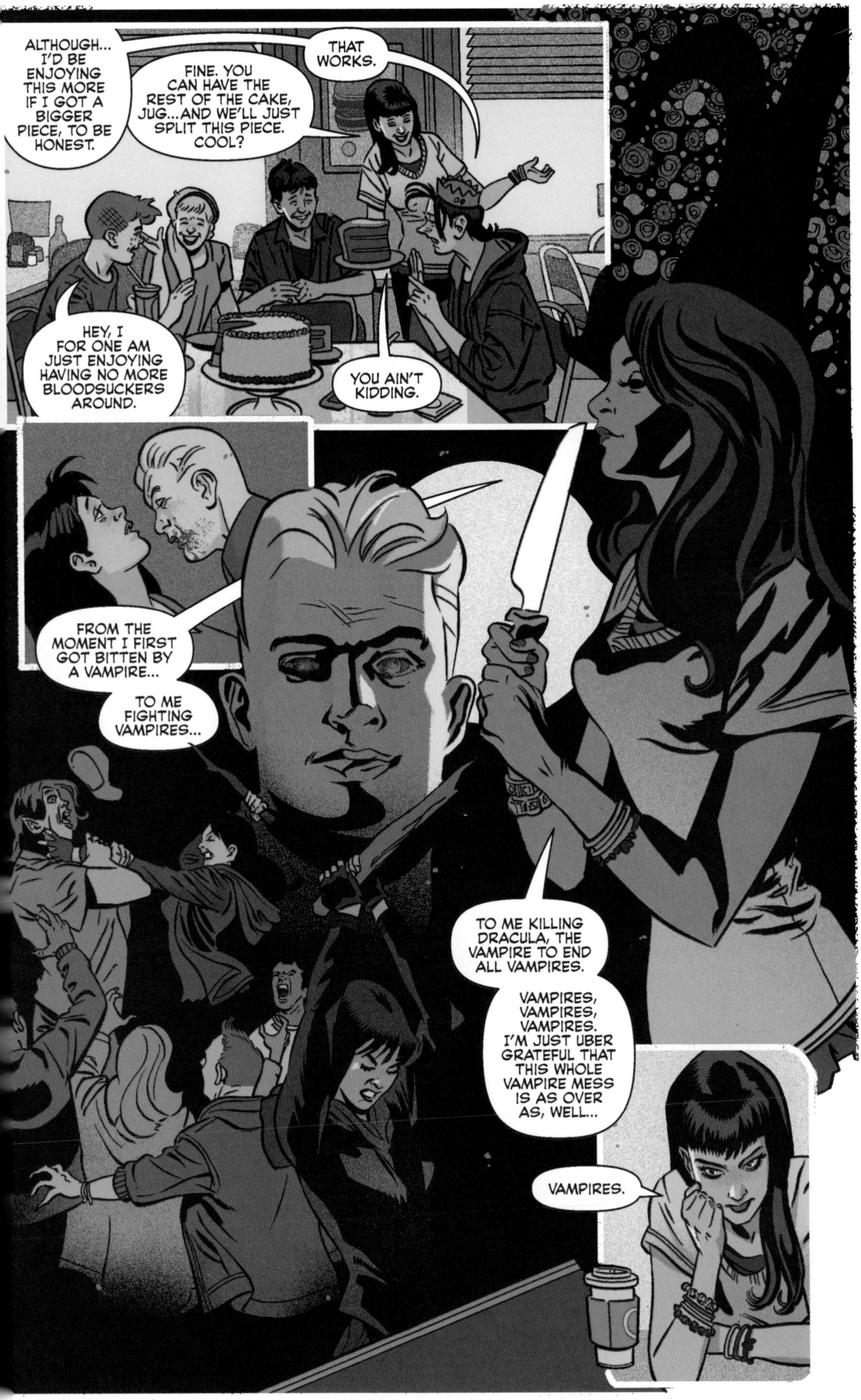

ALTHOUGH... I'D BE ENJOYING THIS MORE IF I GOT A BIGGER PIECE, TO BE HONEST.
FINE. YOU CAN HAVE THE REST OF THE CAKE, JUG...AND WE'LL JUST SPLIT THIS PIECE. COOL?
THAT WORKS.
HEY, I FOR ONE AM JUST ENJOYING HAVING NO MORE BLOODSUCKERS AROUND.
YOU AIN'T KIDDING.
FROM THE MOMENT I FIRST GOT BITTEN BY A VAMPIRE...
TO ME FIGHTING VAMPIRES...
TO ME KILLING DRACULA, THE VAMPIRE TO END ALL VAMPIRES.
VAMPIRES, VAMPIRES, VAMPIRES. I'M JUST UBER GRATEFUL THAT THIS WHOLE VAMPIRE MESS IS AS OVER AS, WELL...
VAMPIRES.

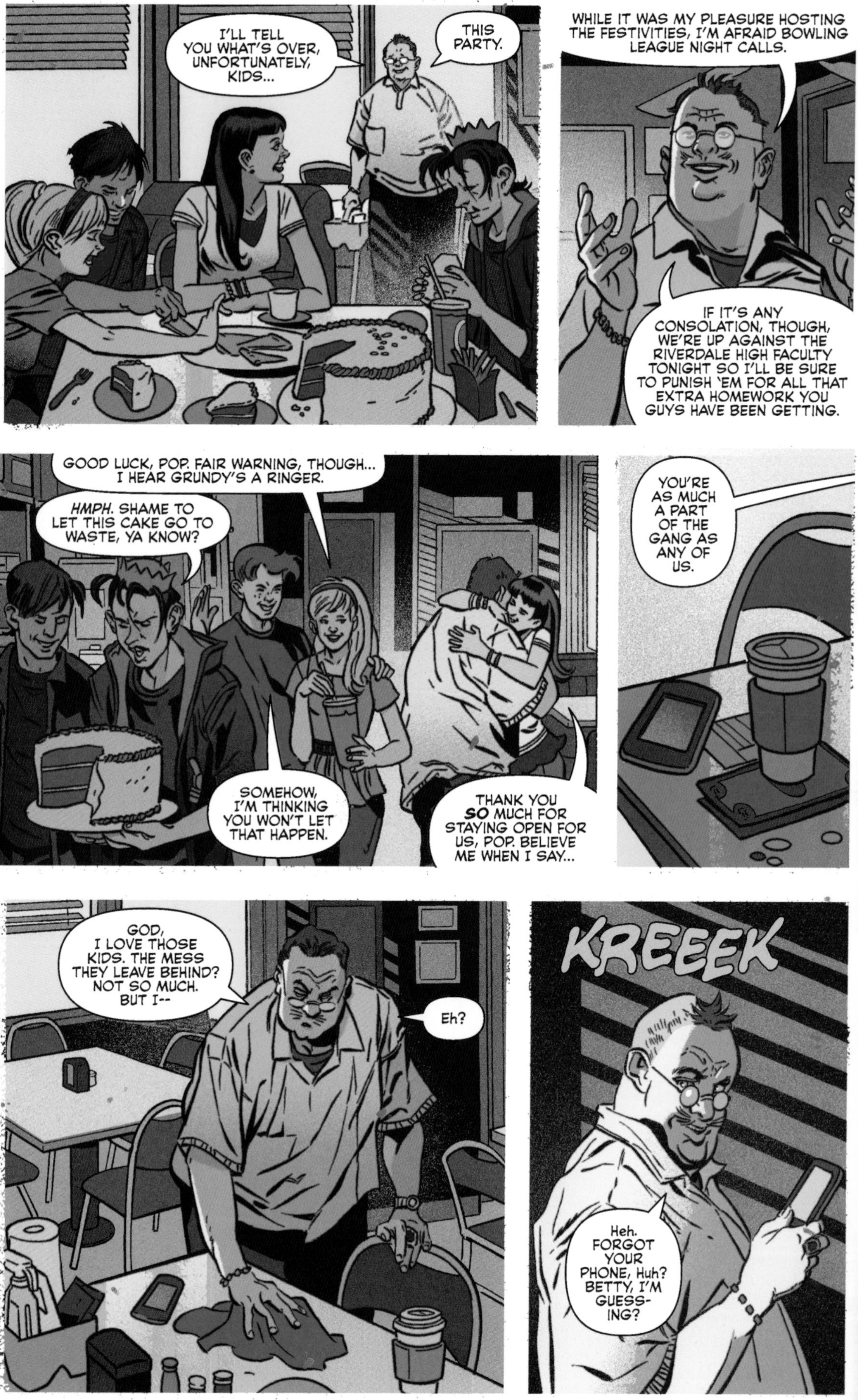
I'LL TELL YOU WHAT'S OVER, UNFORTUNATELY, KIDS...
THIS PARTY.
WHILE IT WAS MY PLEASURE HOSTING THE FESTIVITIES, I'M AFRAID BOWLING LEAGUE NIGHT CALLS.
IF IT'S ANY CONSOLATION, THOUGH, WE'RE UP AGAINST THE RIVERDALE HIGH FACULTY TONIGHT SO I'LL BE SURE TO PUNISH 'EM FOR ALL THAT EXTRA HOMEWORK YOU GUYS HAVE BEEN GETTING.
GOOD LUCK, POP. FAIR WARNING, THOUGH... I HEAR GRUNDY'S A RINGER.
HMPH. SHAME TO LET THIS CAKE GO TO WASTE, YA KNOW?
SOMEHOW, I'M THINKING YOU WON'T LET THAT HAPPEN.
THANK YOU **SO** MUCH FOR STAYING OPEN FOR US, POP. BELIEVE ME WHEN I SAY...
YOU'RE AS MUCH A PART OF THE GANG AS ANY OF US.
GOD, I LOVE THOSE KIDS. THE MESS THEY LEAVE BEHIND? NOT SO MUCH. BUT I--
Eh?
KREEEK
Heh. FORGOT YOUR PHONE, Huh? BETTY, I'M GUESS-ING?

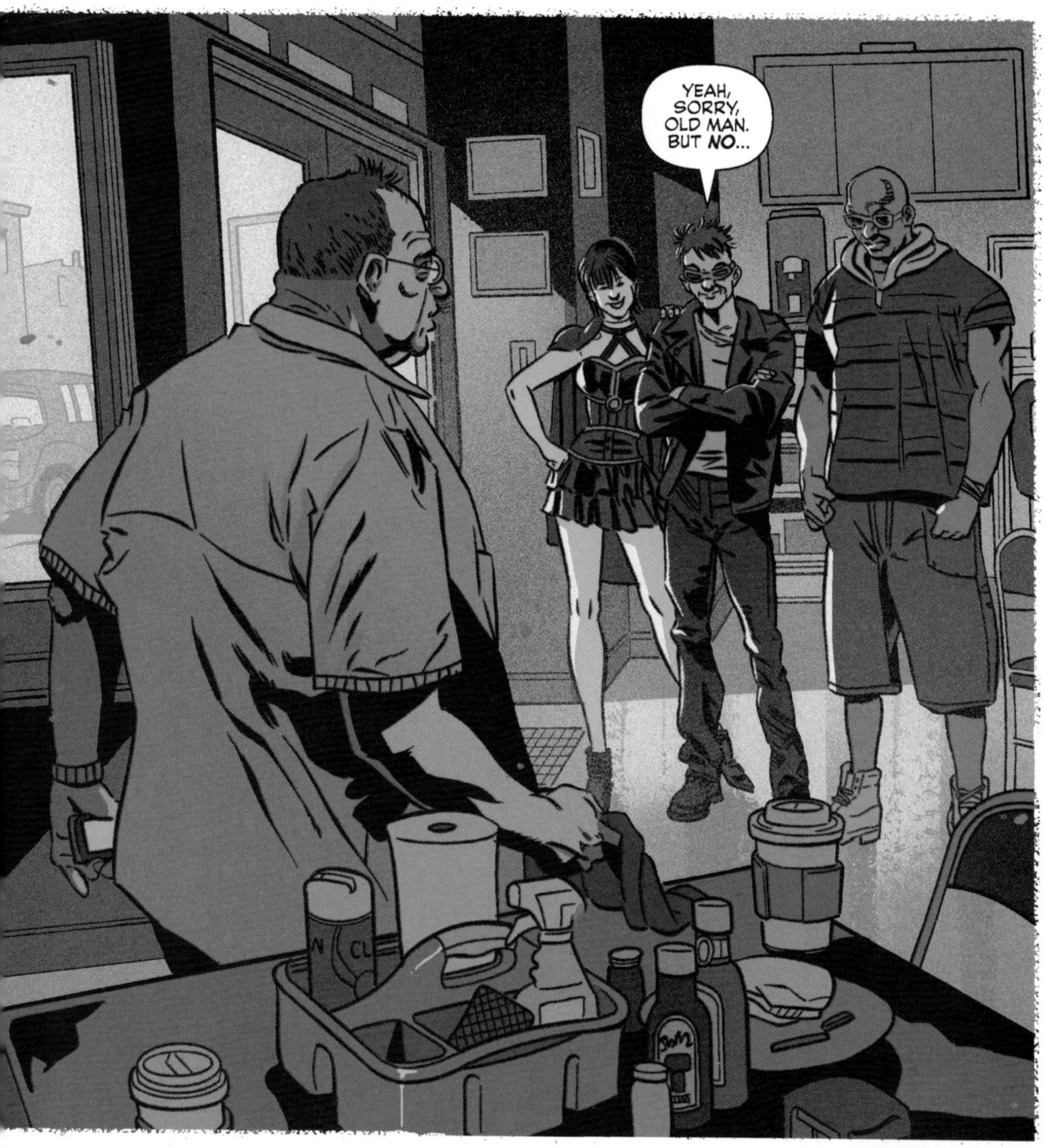
YEAH, SORRY, OLD MAN. BUT NO...

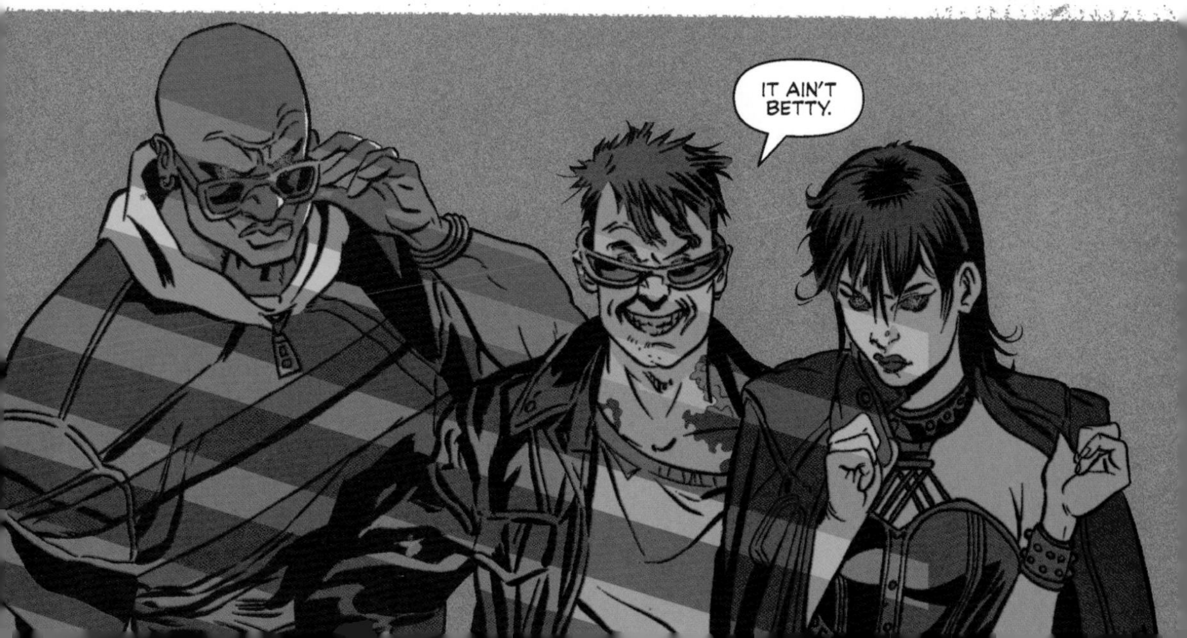
IT AIN'T BETTY.

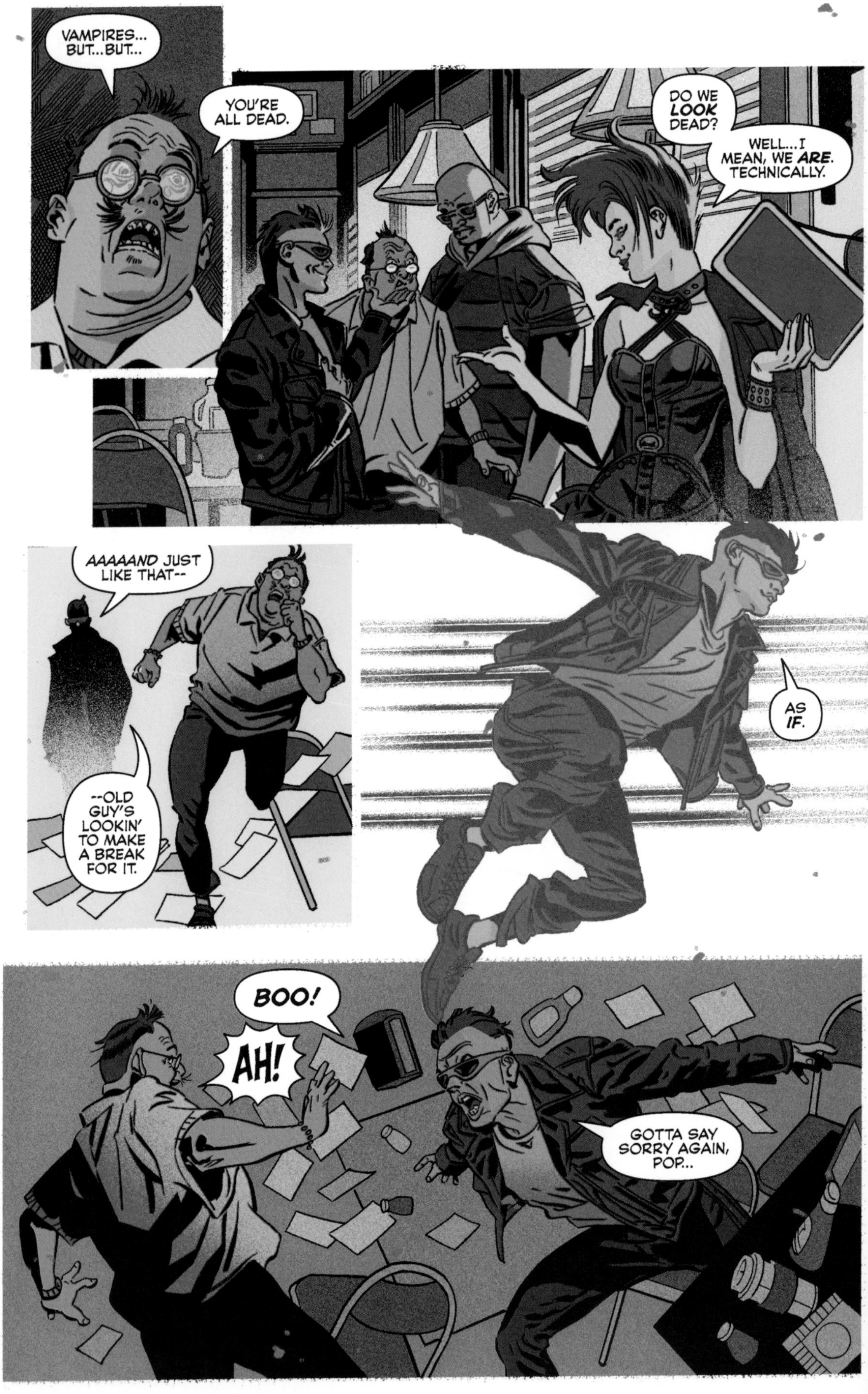
VAMPIRES... BUT...BUT...
YOU'RE ALL DEAD.
DO WE LOOK DEAD?
WELL...I MEAN, WE ARE. TECHNICALLY.
AAAAAND JUST LIKE THAT--
--OLD GUY'S LOOKIN' TO MAKE A BREAK FOR IT.
AS IF.
BOO!
AH!
GOTTA SAY SORRY AGAIN, POP...

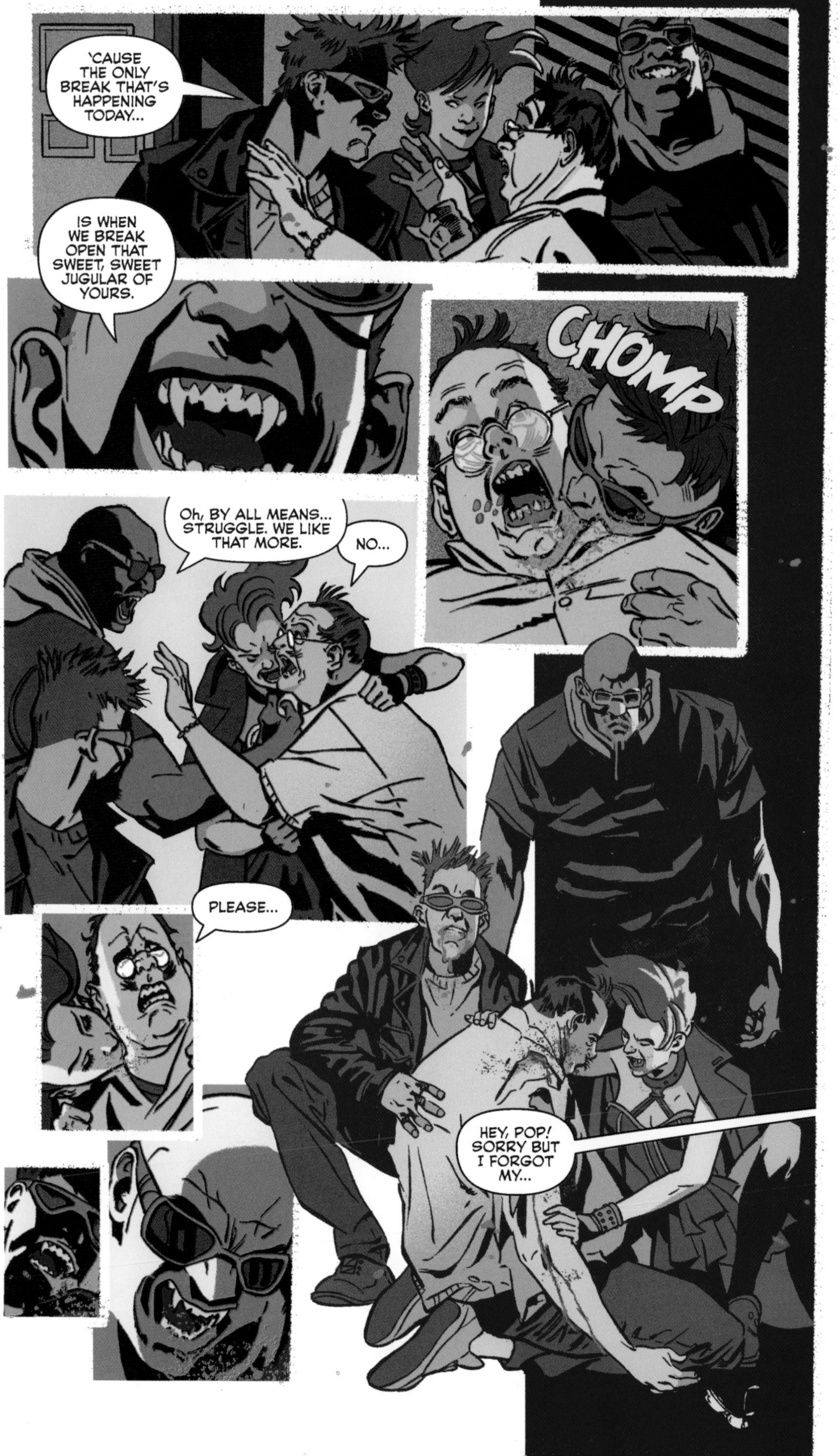
'CAUSE THE ONLY BREAK THAT'S HAPPENING TODAY...
IS WHEN WE BREAK OPEN THAT SWEET, SWEET JUGULAR OF YOURS.
CHOMP
Oh, BY ALL MEANS... STRUGGLE. WE LIKE THAT MORE.
NO...
PLEASE...
HEY, POP! SORRY BUT I FORGOT MY...

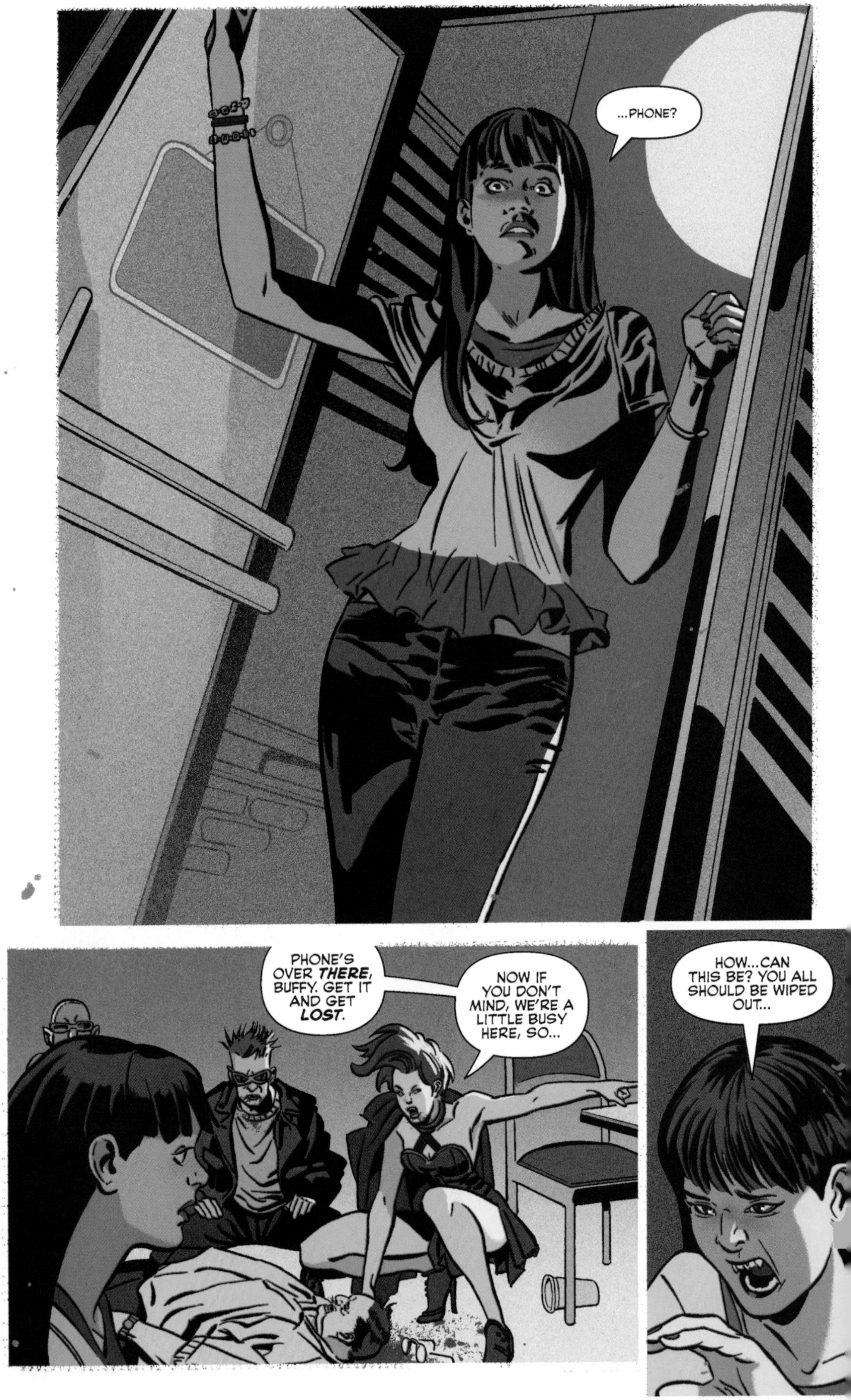
...PHONE?
PHONE'S OVER ***THERE***, BUFFY. GET IT AND GET ***LOST***.
NOW IF YOU DON'T MIND, WE'RE A LITTLE BUSY HERE, SO...
HOW...CAN THIS BE? YOU ALL SHOULD BE WIPED OUT...

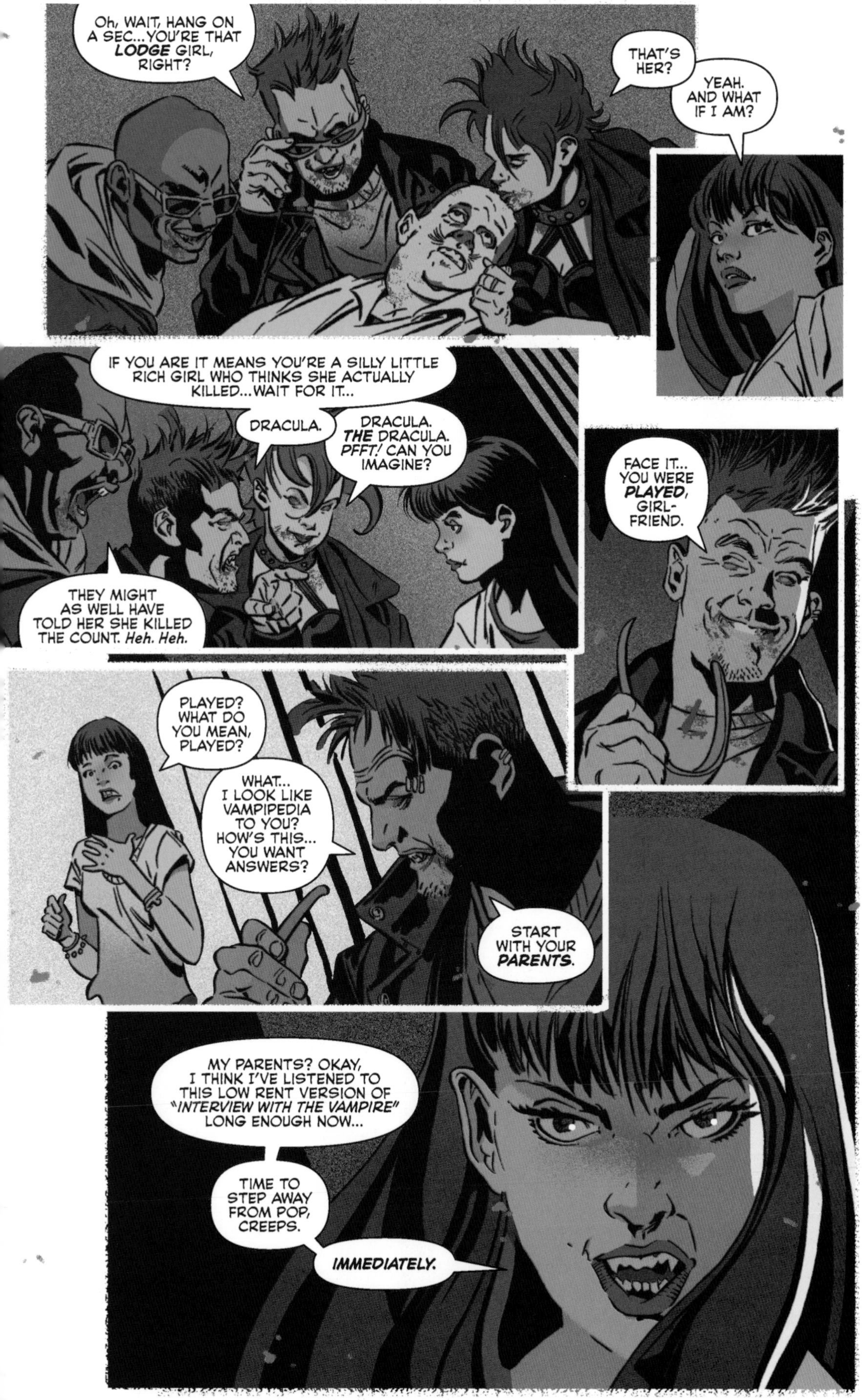

Oh, WAIT, HANG ON A SEC...YOU'RE THAT LODGE GIRL, RIGHT?
THAT'S HER?
YEAH. AND WHAT IF I AM?
IF YOU ARE IT MEANS YOU'RE A SILLY LITTLE RICH GIRL WHO THINKS SHE ACTUALLY KILLED...WAIT FOR IT...
DRACULA.
DRACULA. THE DRACULA. PFFT! CAN YOU IMAGINE?
THEY MIGHT AS WELL HAVE TOLD HER SHE KILLED THE COUNT. Heh. Heh.
FACE IT... YOU WERE PLAYED, GIRL-FRIEND.
PLAYED? WHAT DO YOU MEAN, PLAYED?
WHAT... I LOOK LIKE VAMPIPEDIA TO YOU? HOW'S THIS... YOU WANT ANSWERS?
START WITH YOUR PARENTS.
MY PARENTS? OKAY, I THINK I'VE LISTENED TO THIS LOW RENT VERSION OF "INTERVIEW WITH THE VAMPIRE" LONG ENOUGH NOW...
TIME TO STEP AWAY FROM POP, CREEPS.
IMMEDIATELY.

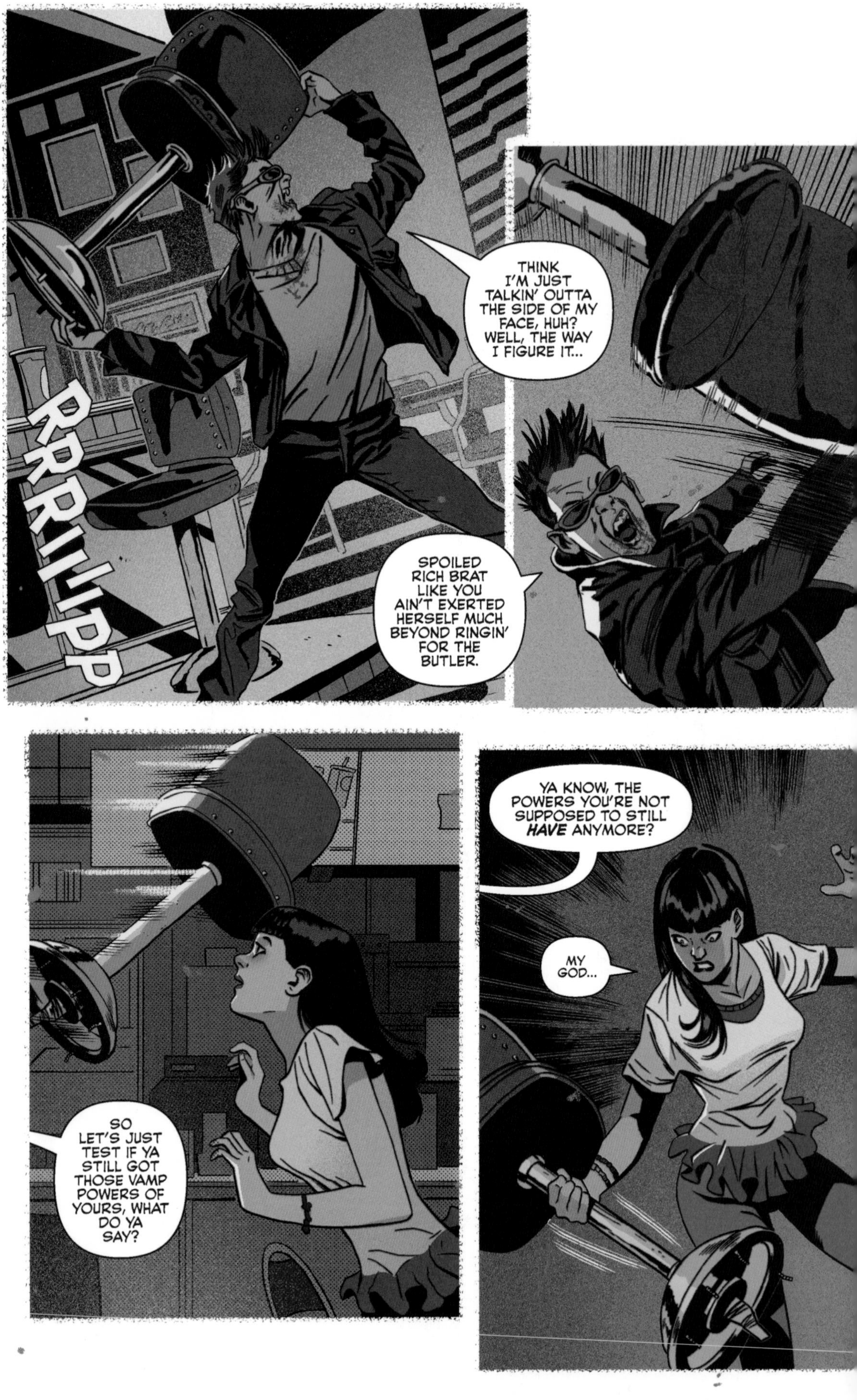
THINK I'M JUST TALKIN' OUTTA THE SIDE OF MY FACE, HUH? WELL, THE WAY I FIGURE IT...
RRRIIIPP
SPOILED RICH BRAT LIKE YOU AIN'T EXERTED HERSELF MUCH BEYOND RINGIN' FOR THE BUTLER.
SO LET'S JUST TEST IF YA STILL GOT THOSE VAMP POWERS OF YOURS, WHAT DO YA SAY?
YA KNOW, THE POWERS YOU'RE NOT SUPPOSED TO STILL *HAVE* ANYMORE?
MY GOD...

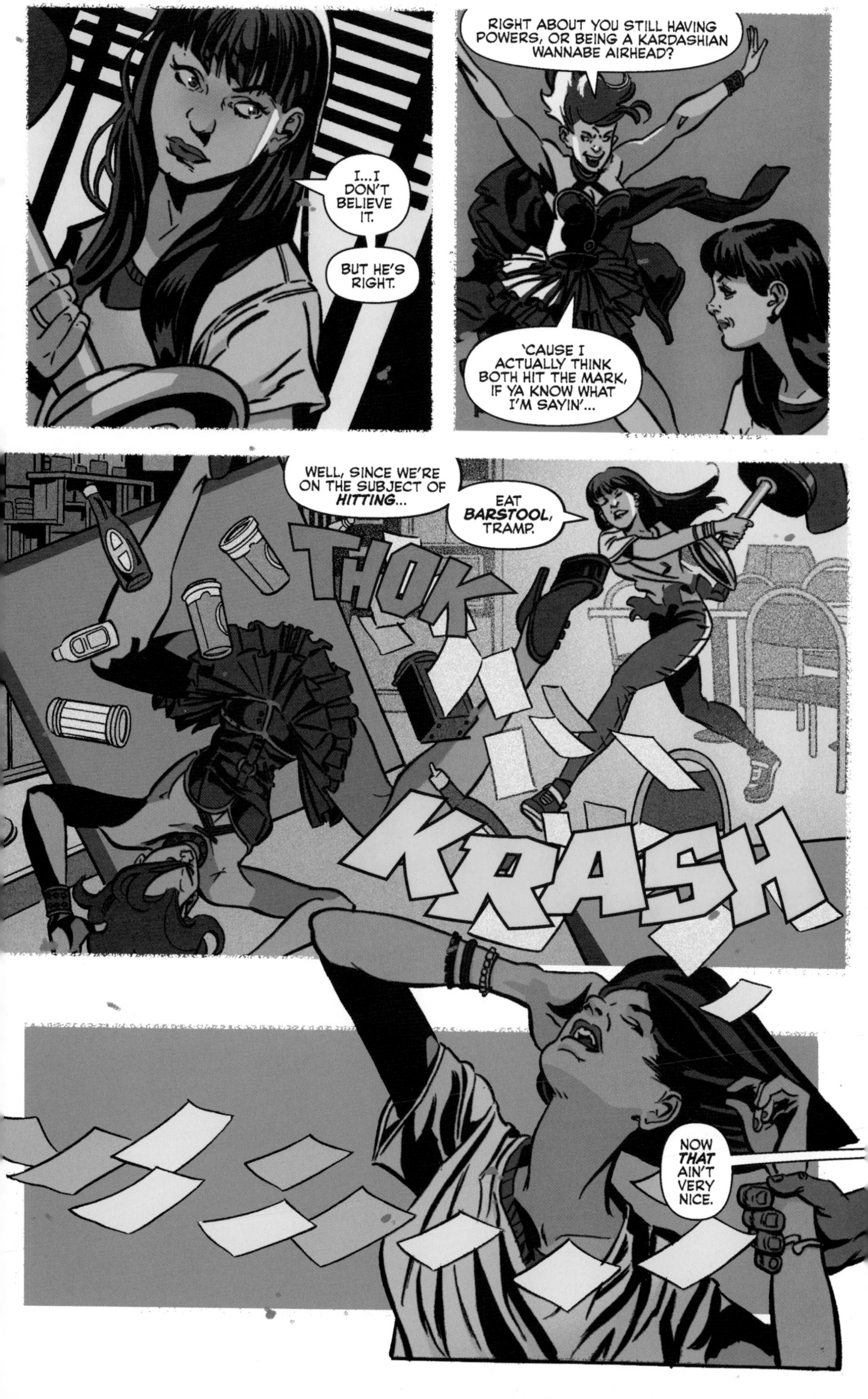
I...I DON'T BELIEVE IT.
BUT HE'S RIGHT.
RIGHT ABOUT YOU STILL HAVING POWERS, OR BEING A KARDASHIAN WANNABE AIRHEAD?
'CAUSE I ACTUALLY THINK BOTH HIT THE MARK, IF YA KNOW WHAT I'M SAYIN'...
WELL, SINCE WE'RE ON THE SUBJECT OF *HITTING*...
EAT *BARSTOOL*, TRAMP.
THOK
KRASH
NOW *THAT* AIN'T VERY NICE.

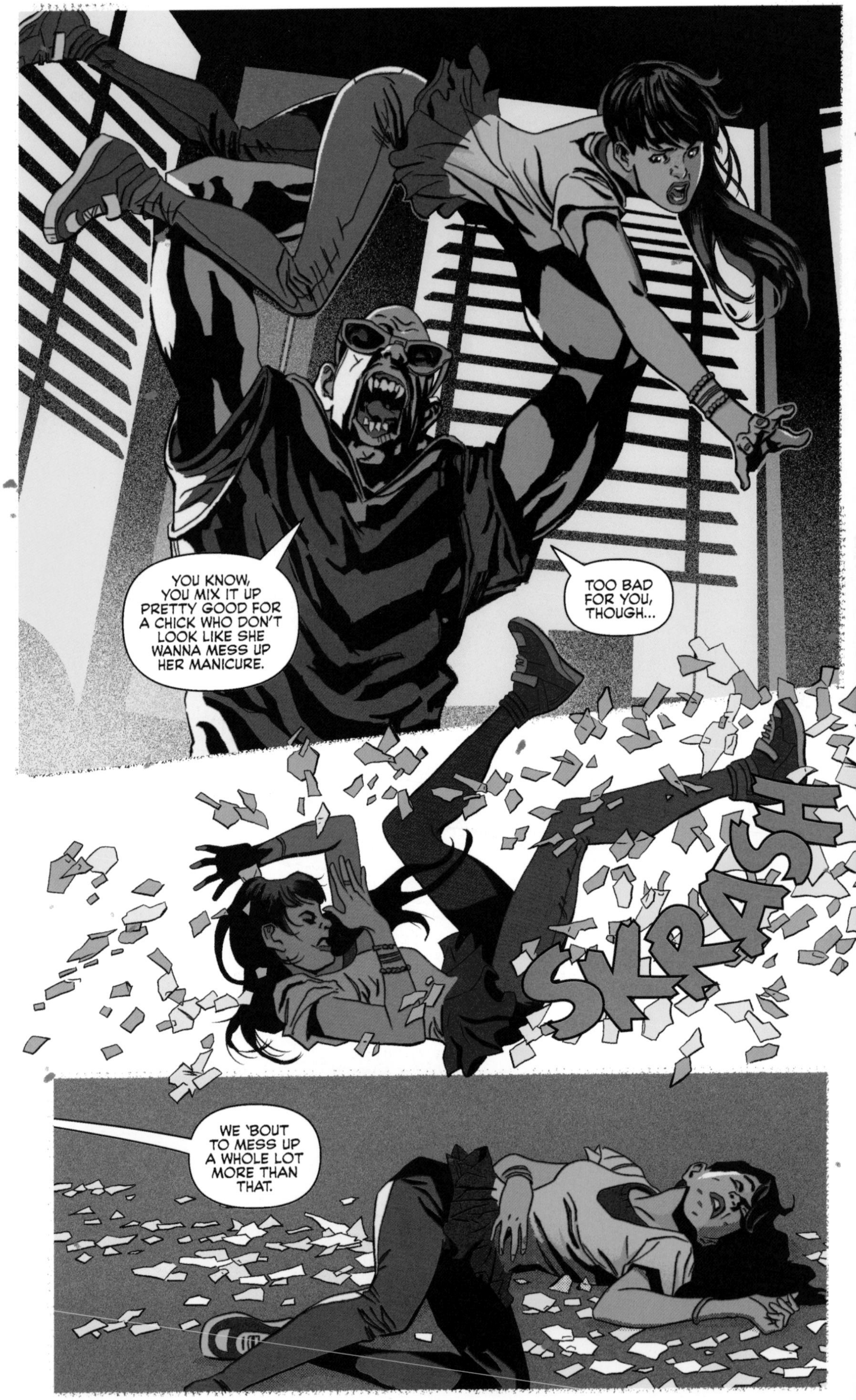
YOU KNOW, YOU MIX IT UP PRETTY GOOD FOR A CHICK WHO DON'T LOOK LIKE SHE WANNA MESS UP HER MANICURE.
TOO BAD FOR YOU, THOUGH...
SKRASH
WE 'BOUT TO MESS UP A WHOLE LOT MORE THAN THAT.

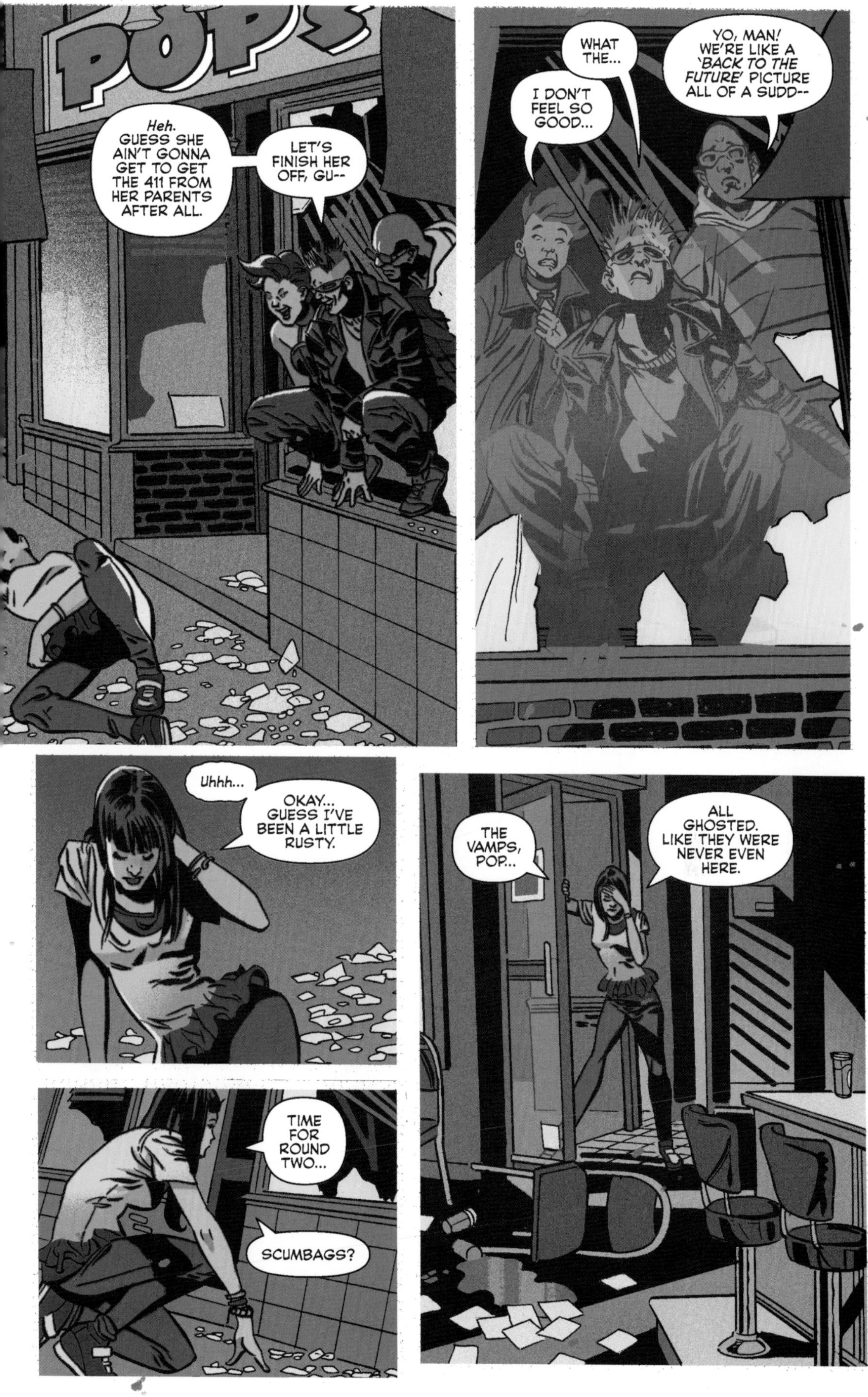
POPS
Heh. GUESS SHE AIN'T GONNA GET TO GET THE 411 FROM HER PARENTS AFTER ALL.
LET'S FINISH HER OFF, GU--
WHAT THE...
I DON'T FEEL SO GOOD...
YO, MAN! WE'RE LIKE A '*BACK TO THE FUTURE*' PICTURE ALL OF A SUDD--
Uhhh...
OKAY... GUESS I'VE BEEN A LITTLE RUSTY.
TIME FOR ROUND TWO...
SCUMBAGS?
THE VAMPS, POP...
ALL GHOSTED. LIKE THEY WERE NEVER EVEN HERE.

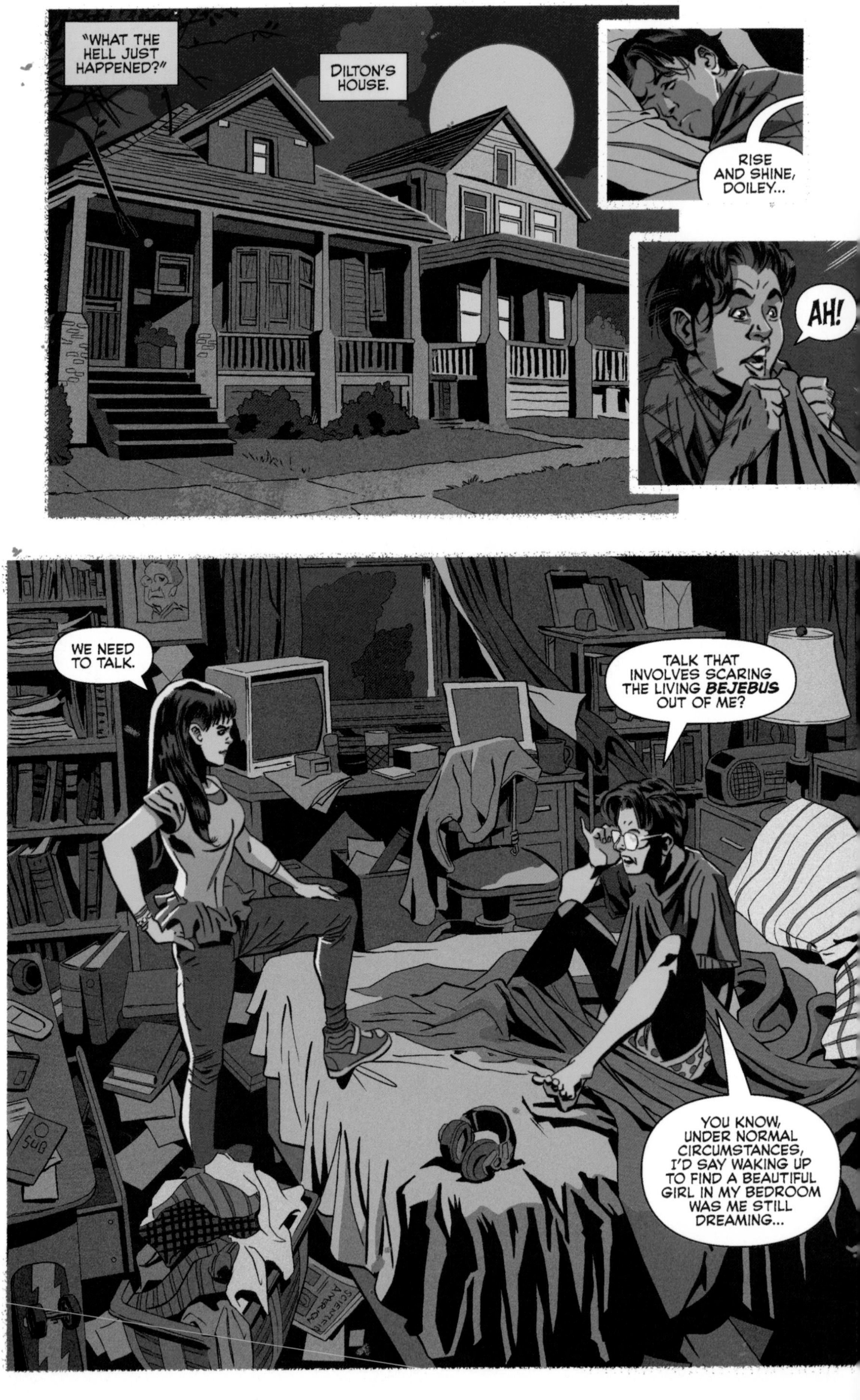
"WHAT THE HELL JUST HAPPENED?"
DILTON'S HOUSE.
RISE AND SHINE, DOILEY...
AH!
WE NEED TO TALK.
TALK THAT INVOLVES SCARING THE LIVING *BEJEBUS* OUT OF ME?
YOU KNOW, UNDER NORMAL CIRCUMSTANCES, I'D SAY WAKING UP TO FIND A BEAUTIFUL GIRL IN MY BEDROOM WAS ME STILL DREAMING...

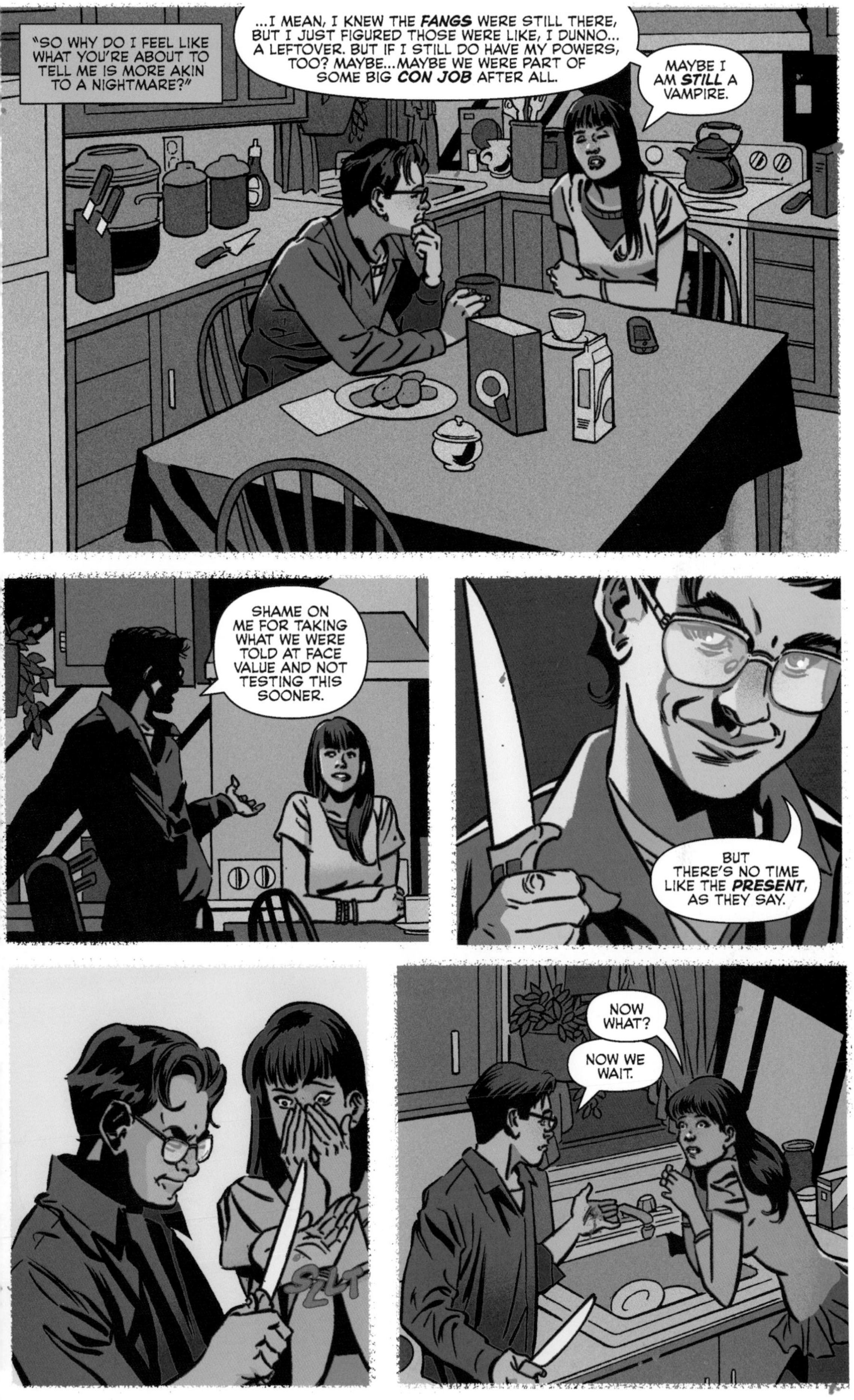
"SO WHY DO I FEEL LIKE WHAT YOU'RE ABOUT TO TELL ME IS MORE AKIN TO A NIGHTMARE?"
...I MEAN, I KNEW THE **FANGS** WERE STILL THERE, BUT I JUST FIGURED THOSE WERE LIKE, I DUNNO... A LEFTOVER. BUT IF I STILL DO HAVE MY POWERS, TOO? MAYBE...MAYBE WE WERE PART OF SOME BIG **CON JOB** AFTER ALL.
MAYBE I AM ***STILL*** A VAMPIRE.
SHAME ON ME FOR TAKING WHAT WE WERE TOLD AT FACE VALUE AND NOT TESTING THIS SOONER.
BUT THERE'S NO TIME LIKE THE ***PRESENT***, AS THEY SAY.
SZLT
NOW WHAT?
NOW WE WAIT.

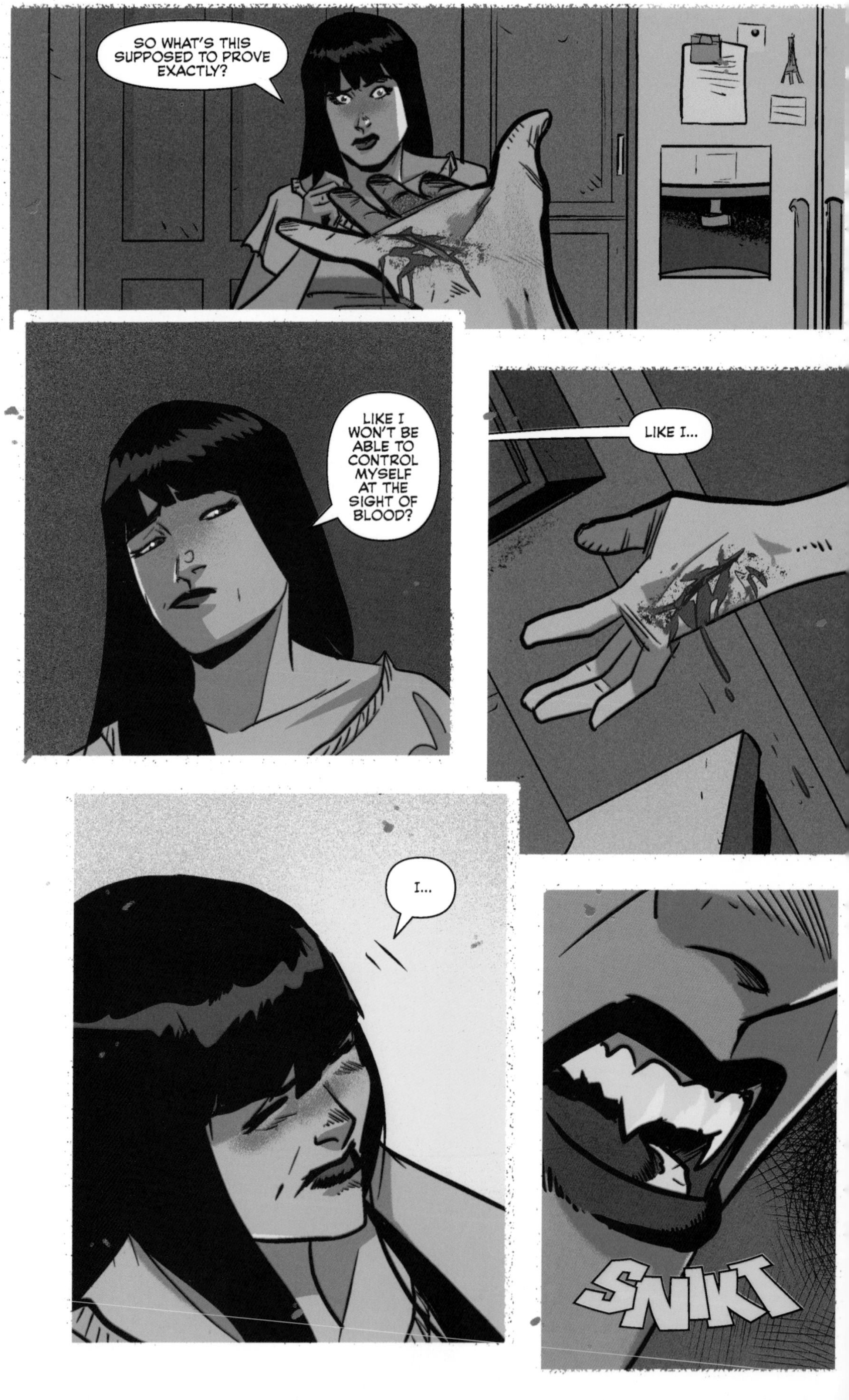
SO WHAT'S THIS SUPPOSED TO PROVE EXACTLY?
LIKE I WON'T BE ABLE TO CONTROL MYSELF AT THE SIGHT OF BLOOD?
LIKE I...
I...
SNIKT

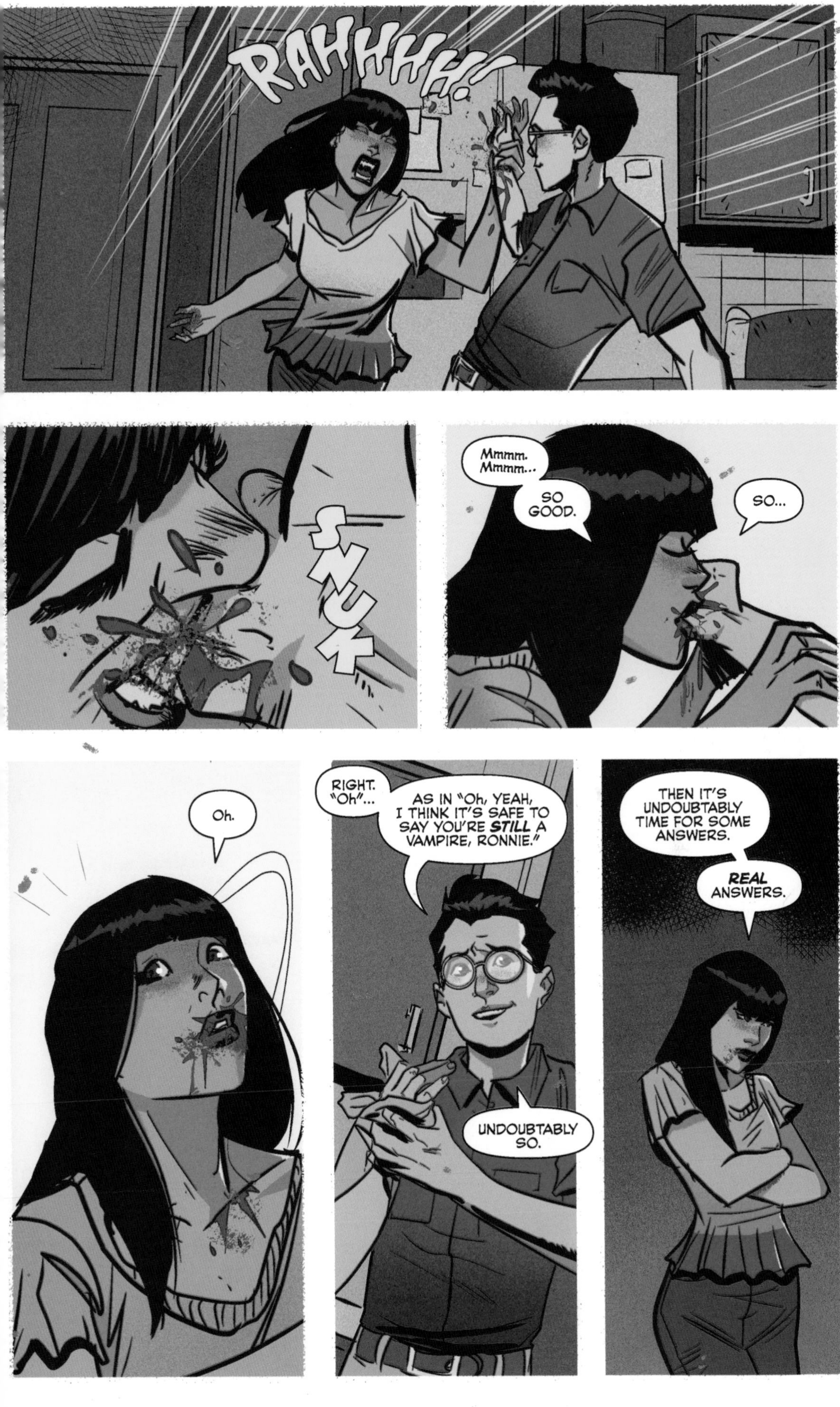
RAHHHH!
SNUK
Mmmm.
Mmmm...
SO GOOD.
SO...
Oh.
RIGHT. "Oh"...
AS IN "Oh, YEAH, I THINK IT'S SAFE TO SAY YOU'RE STILL A VAMPIRE, RONNIE."
UNDOUBTABLY SO.
THEN IT'S UNDOUBTABLY TIME FOR SOME ANSWERS.
REAL ANSWERS.

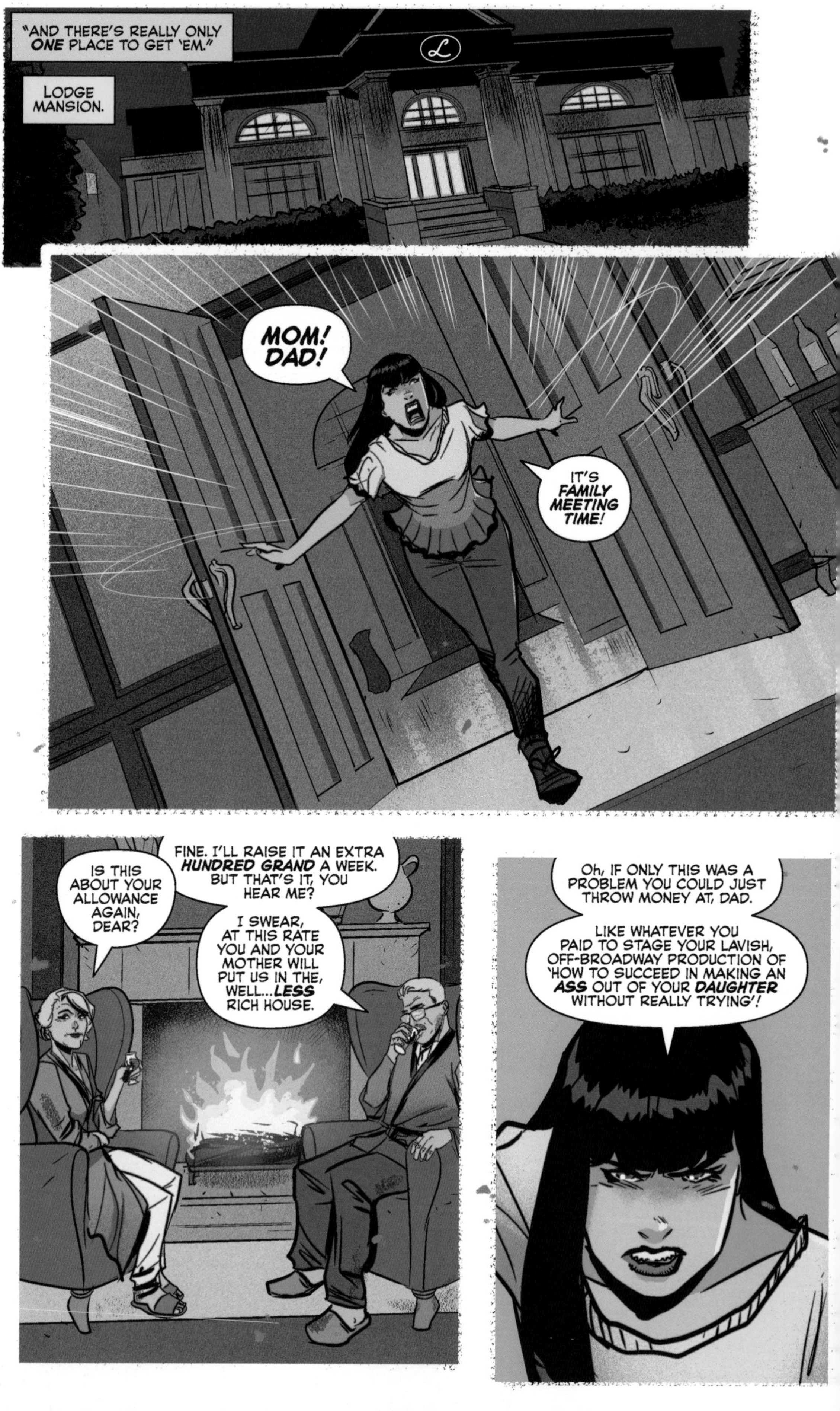
"AND THERE'S REALLY ONLY ONE PLACE TO GET 'EM."
LODGE MANSION.
MOM! DAD!
IT'S FAMILY MEETING TIME!
IS THIS ABOUT YOUR ALLOWANCE AGAIN, DEAR?
FINE. I'LL RAISE IT AN EXTRA HUNDRED GRAND A WEEK. BUT THAT'S IT, YOU HEAR ME?
I SWEAR, AT THIS RATE YOU AND YOUR MOTHER WILL PUT US IN THE, WELL...LESS RICH HOUSE.
Oh, IF ONLY THIS WAS A PROBLEM YOU COULD JUST THROW MONEY AT, DAD.
LIKE WHATEVER YOU PAID TO STAGE YOUR LAVISH, OFF-BROADWAY PRODUCTION OF 'HOW TO SUCCEED IN MAKING AN ASS OUT OF YOUR DAUGHTER WITHOUT REALLY TRYING'!

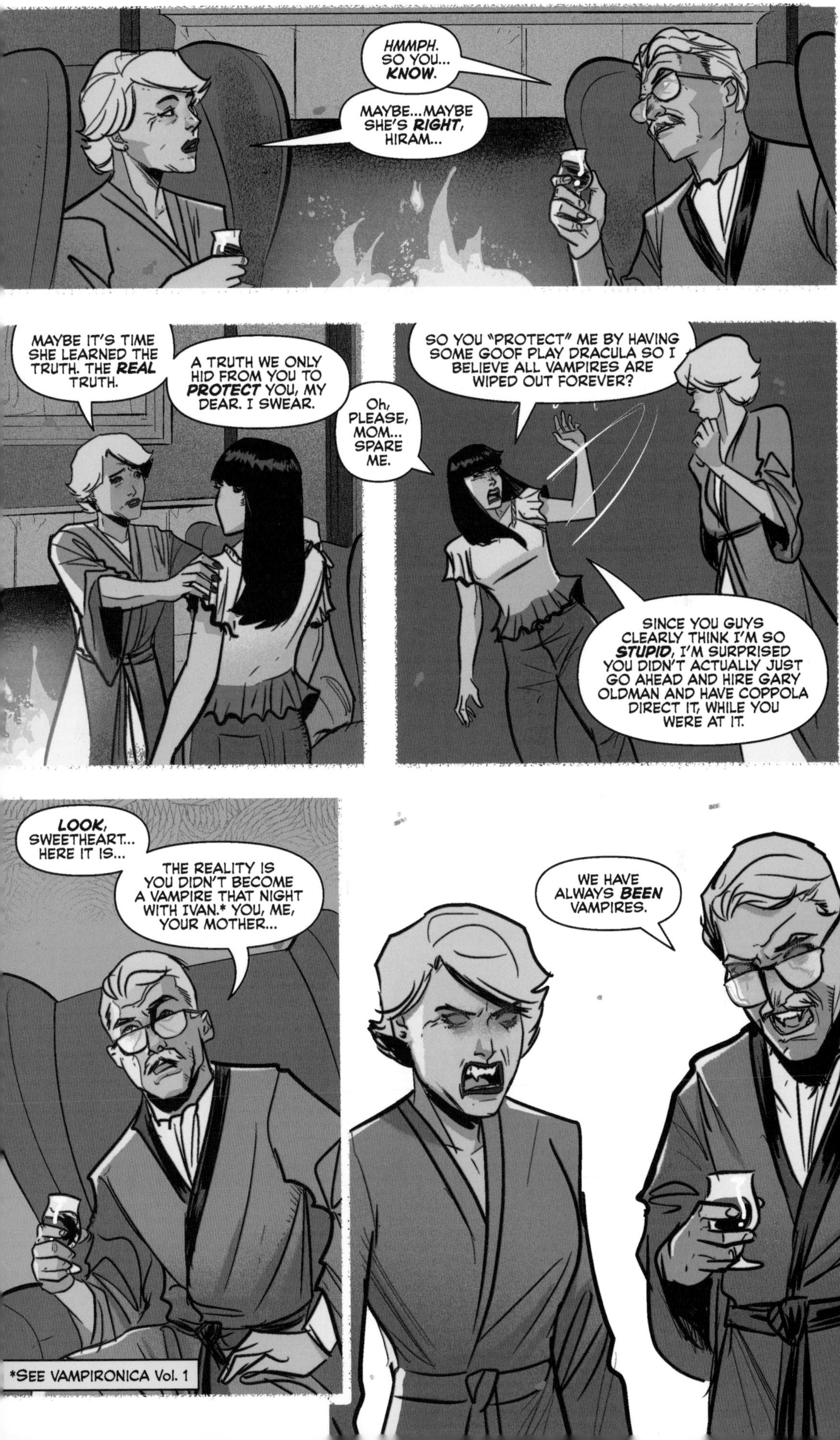
HMMPH. SO YOU... KNOW.
MAYBE...MAYBE SHE'S RIGHT, HIRAM...
MAYBE IT'S TIME SHE LEARNED THE TRUTH. THE REAL TRUTH.
A TRUTH WE ONLY HID FROM YOU TO PROTECT YOU, MY DEAR. I SWEAR.
Oh, PLEASE, MOM... SPARE ME.
SO YOU "PROTECT" ME BY HAVING SOME GOOF PLAY DRACULA SO I BELIEVE ALL VAMPIRES ARE WIPED OUT FOREVER?
SINCE YOU GUYS CLEARLY THINK I'M SO STUPID, I'M SURPRISED YOU DIDN'T ACTUALLY JUST GO AHEAD AND HIRE GARY OLDMAN AND HAVE COPPOLA DIRECT IT, WHILE YOU WERE AT IT.
LOOK, SWEETHEART... HERE IT IS...
THE REALITY IS YOU DIDN'T BECOME A VAMPIRE THAT NIGHT WITH IVAN.* YOU, ME, YOUR MOTHER...
*SEE VAMPIRONICA Vol. 1
WE HAVE ALWAYS BEEN VAMPIRES.

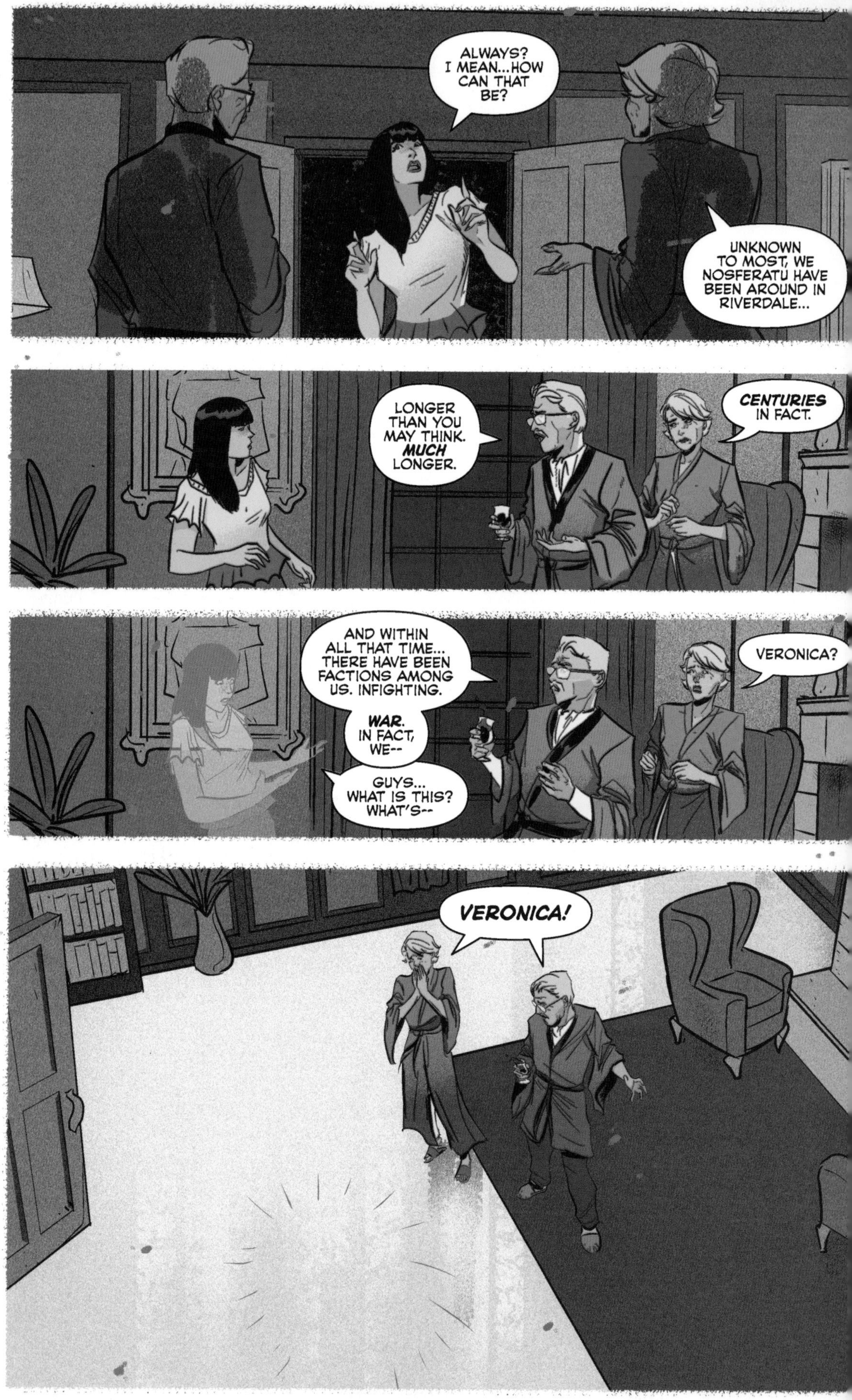
ALWAYS? I MEAN...HOW CAN THAT BE?
UNKNOWN TO MOST, WE NOSFERATU HAVE BEEN AROUND IN RIVERDALE...
LONGER THAN YOU MAY THINK. MUCH LONGER.
CENTURIES IN FACT.
AND WITHIN ALL THAT TIME... THERE HAVE BEEN FACTIONS AMONG US. INFIGHTING.
WAR. IN FACT, WE--
VERONICA?
GUYS... WHAT IS THIS? WHAT'S--
VERONICA!

CHAPTER TWO

COVER ART BY **PAT & TIM KENNEDY**
WITH **BOB SMITH** AND **MATT HERMS**

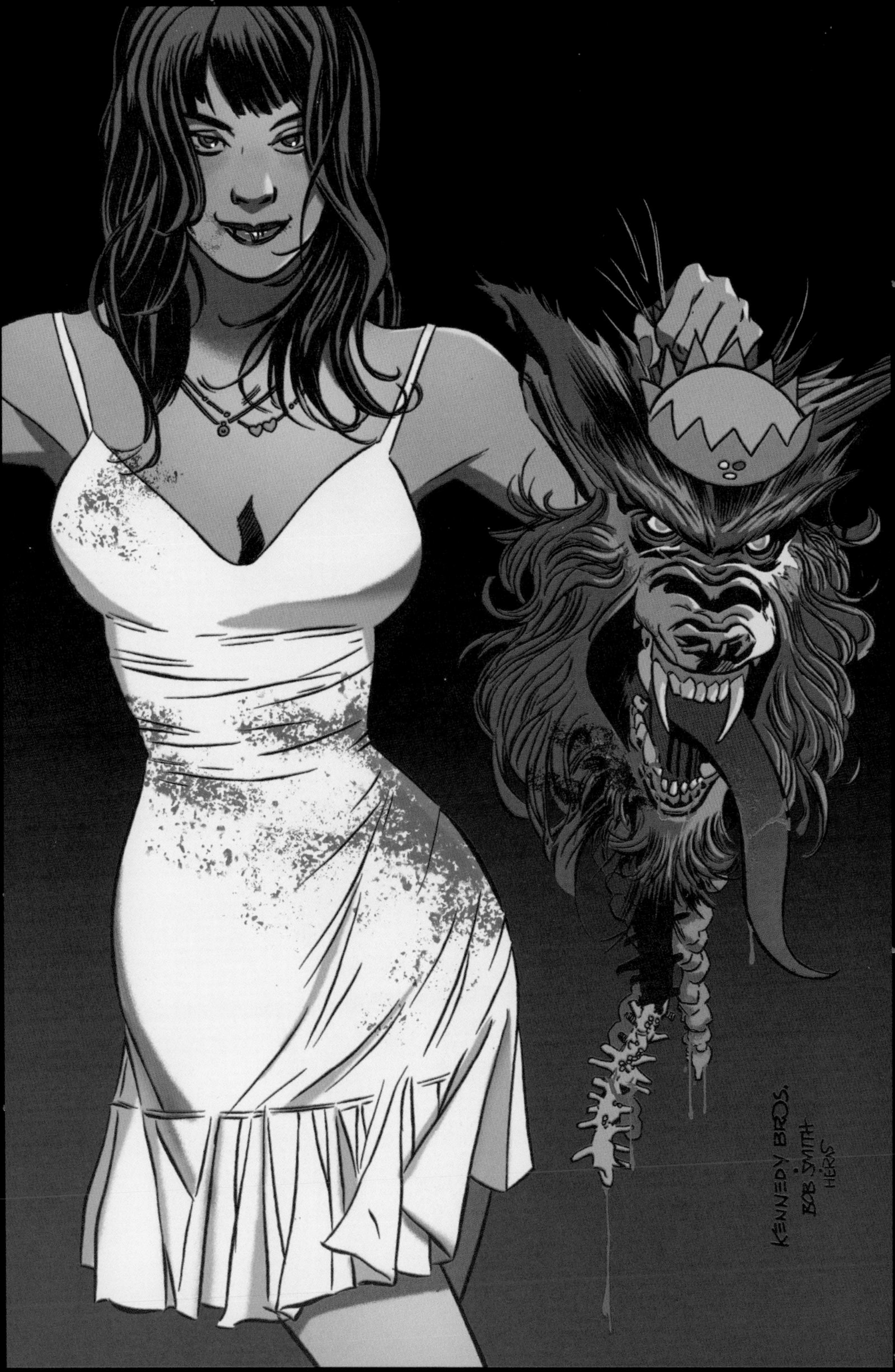
KENNEDY BROS.
BOB SMITH
HERMS

STORY BY **FRANK TIERI**
ART BY **PAT & TIM KENNEDY** (p.1-14,17) **JOE EISMA** (p.15-16,18-20)
INKS BY **BOB SMITH** (p.1-5,7,9,11,12,17) **RYAN JAMPOLE** (p.6,8,10,13,14)
COLORING BY **MATT HERMS** LETTERING BY **JACK MORELLI**

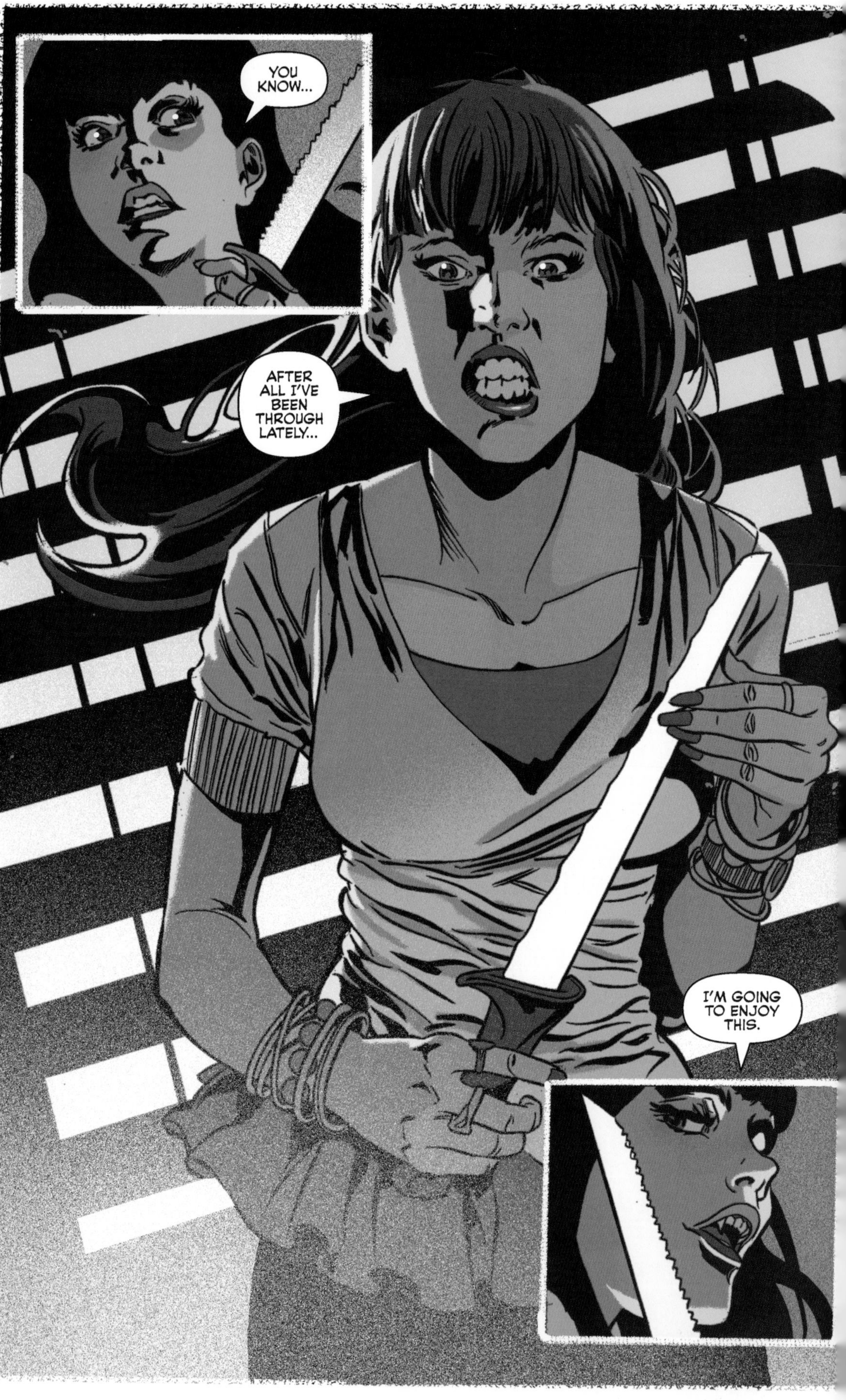
YOU KNOW...
AFTER ALL I'VE BEEN THROUGH LATELY...
I'M GOING TO ENJOY THIS.

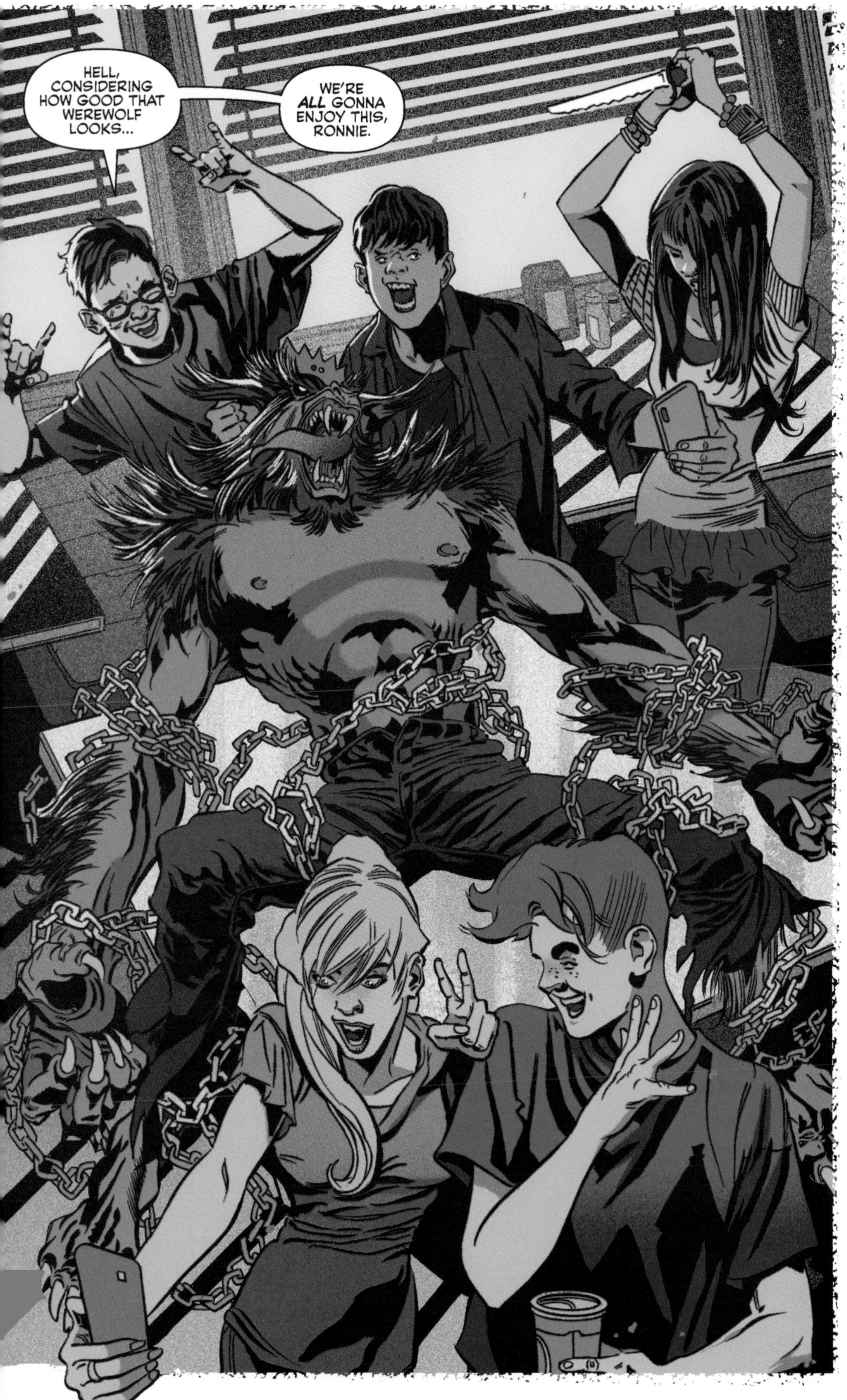
HELL, CONSIDERING HOW GOOD THAT WEREWOLF LOOKS...
WE'RE *ALL* GONNA ENJOY THIS, RONNIE.

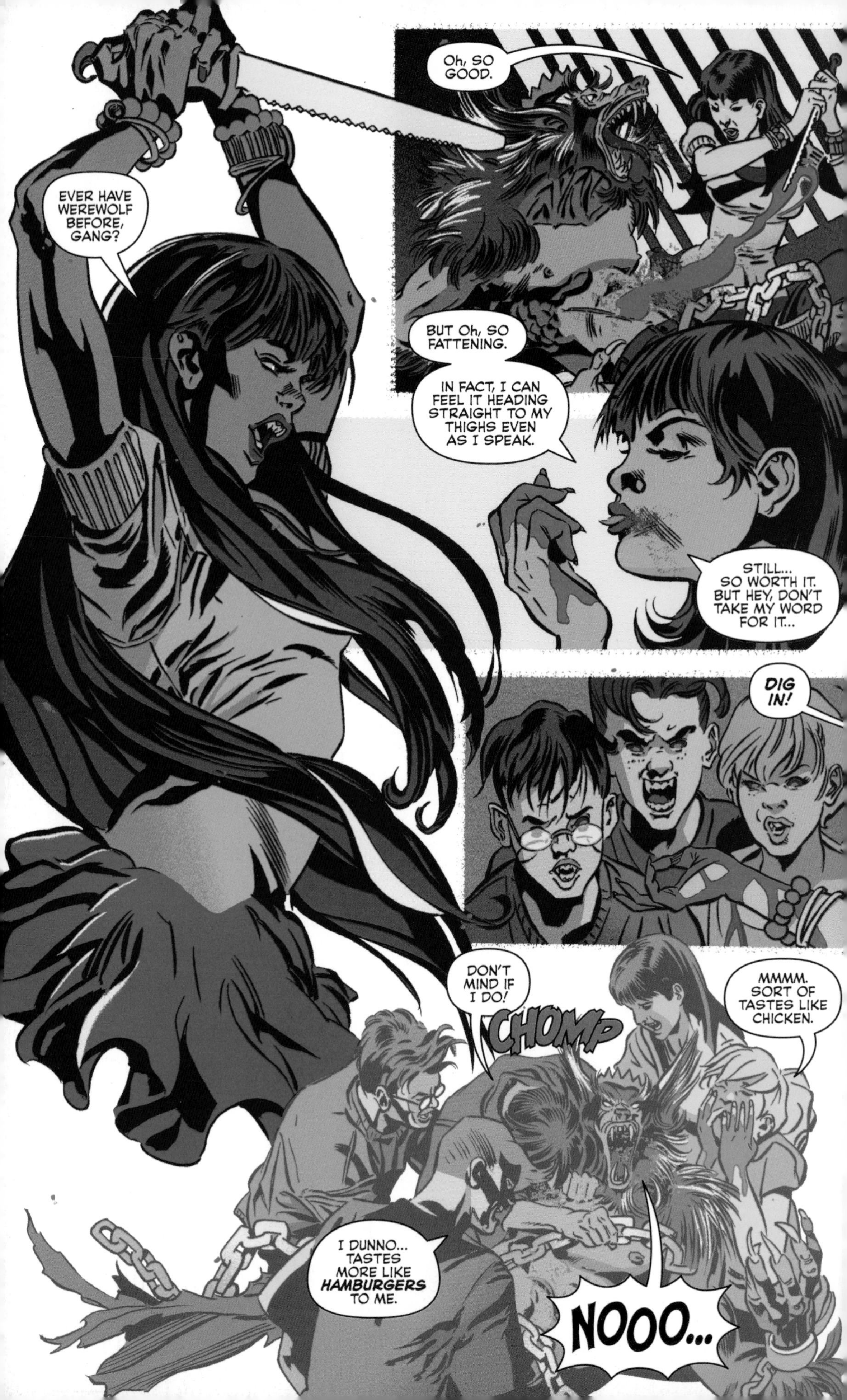
EVER HAVE WEREWOLF BEFORE, GANG?
Oh, SO GOOD.
BUT Oh, SO FATTENING.
IN FACT, I CAN FEEL IT HEADING STRAIGHT TO MY THIGHS EVEN AS I SPEAK.
STILL... SO WORTH IT. BUT HEY, DON'T TAKE MY WORD FOR IT...
DIG IN!
DON'T MIND IF I DO!
CHOMP
MMMM. SORT OF TASTES LIKE CHICKEN.
I DUNNO... TASTES MORE LIKE HAMBURGERS TO ME.
NOOO...

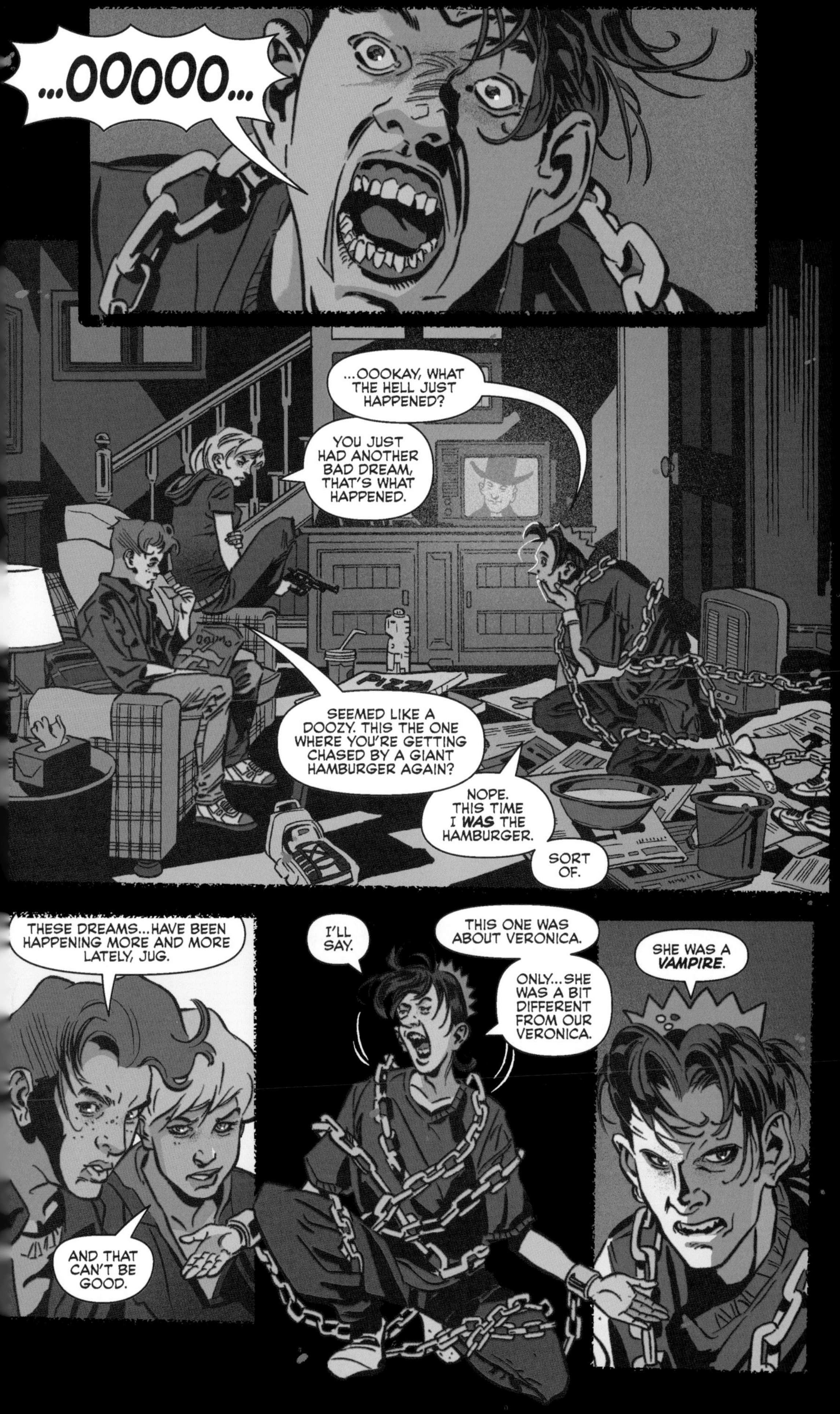
...OOOOO...
...OOOKAY, WHAT THE HELL JUST HAPPENED?
YOU JUST HAD ANOTHER BAD DREAM, THAT'S WHAT HAPPENED.
SEEMED LIKE A DOOZY. THIS THE ONE WHERE YOU'RE GETTING CHASED BY A GIANT HAMBURGER AGAIN?
NOPE. THIS TIME I **WAS** THE HAMBURGER.
SORT OF.
THESE DREAMS...HAVE BEEN HAPPENING MORE AND MORE LATELY, JUG.
AND THAT CAN'T BE GOOD.
I'LL SAY.
THIS ONE WAS ABOUT VERONICA.
ONLY...SHE WAS A BIT DIFFERENT FROM OUR VERONICA.
SHE WAS A ***VAMPIRE***.

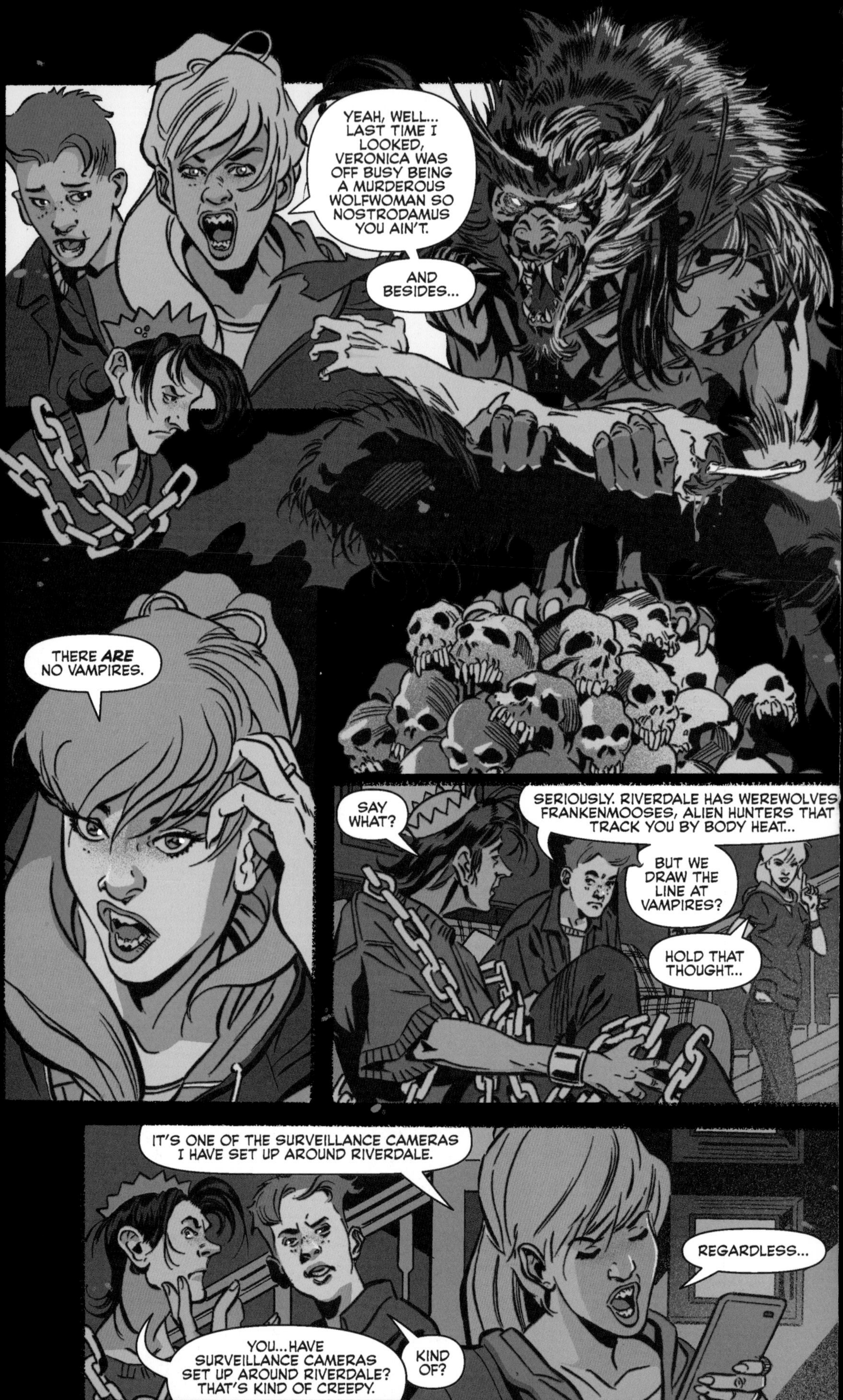
YEAH, WELL... LAST TIME I LOOKED, VERONICA WAS OFF BUSY BEING A MURDEROUS WOLFWOMAN SO NOSTRODAMUS YOU AIN'T.
AND BESIDES...
THERE *ARE* NO VAMPIRES.
SAY WHAT?
SERIOUSLY. RIVERDALE HAS WEREWOLVES, FRANKENMOOSES, ALIEN HUNTERS THAT TRACK YOU BY BODY HEAT...
BUT WE DRAW THE LINE AT VAMPIRES?
HOLD THAT THOUGHT...
IT'S ONE OF THE SURVEILLANCE CAMERAS I HAVE SET UP AROUND RIVERDALE.
REGARDLESS...
YOU...HAVE SURVEILLANCE CAMERAS SET UP AROUND RIVERDALE? THAT'S KIND OF CREEPY.
KIND OF?

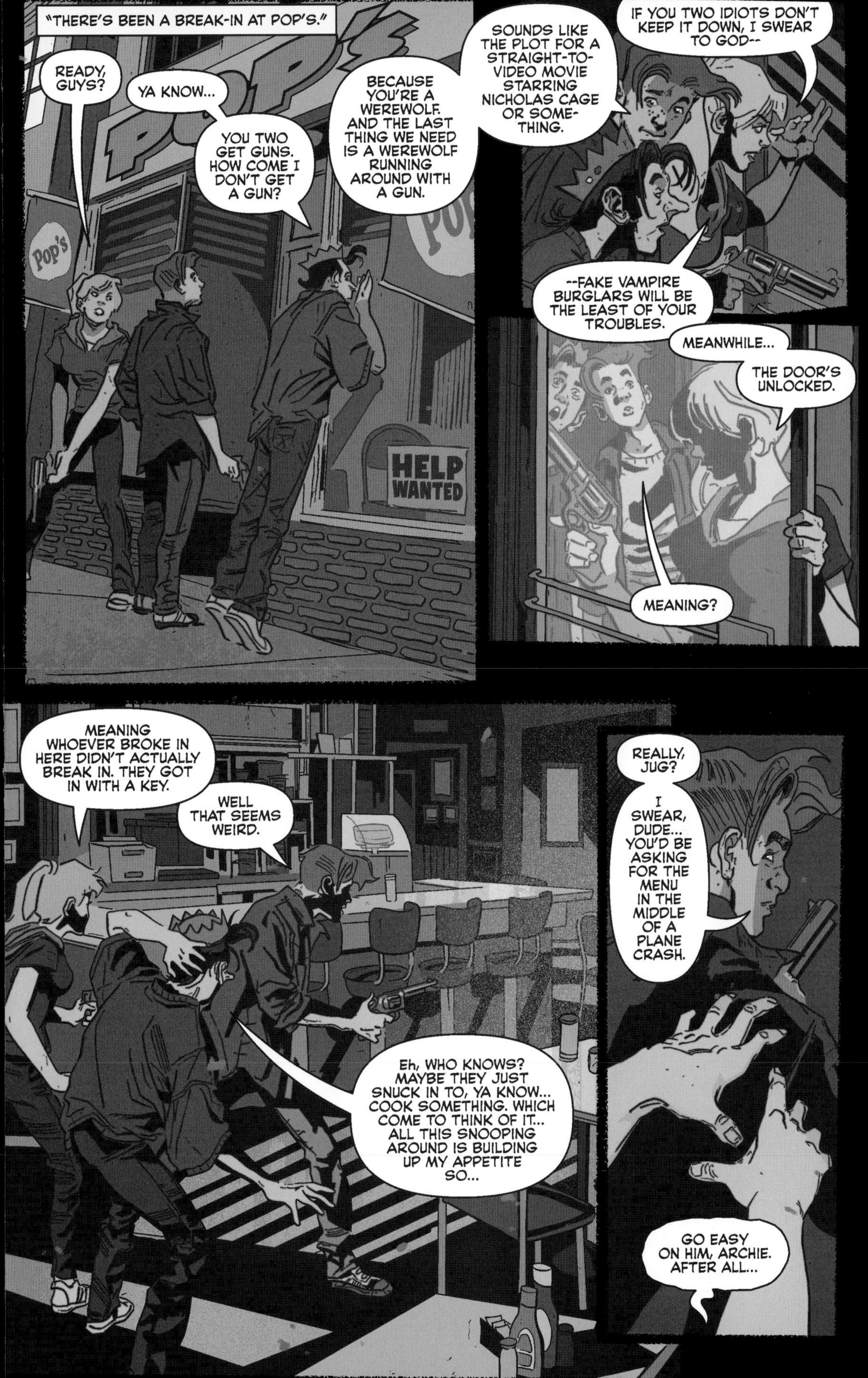
"THERE'S BEEN A BREAK-IN AT POP'S."
POP'S
READY, GUYS?
YA KNOW...
YOU TWO GET GUNS. HOW COME I DON'T GET A GUN?
BECAUSE YOU'RE A WEREWOLF. AND THE LAST THING WE NEED IS A WEREWOLF RUNNING AROUND WITH A GUN.
SOUNDS LIKE THE PLOT FOR A STRAIGHT-TO-VIDEO MOVIE STARRING NICHOLAS CAGE OR SOMETHING.
IF YOU TWO IDIOTS DON'T KEEP IT DOWN, I SWEAR TO GOD--
--FAKE VAMPIRE BURGLARS WILL BE THE LEAST OF YOUR TROUBLES.
Pop's
HELP WANTED
MEANWHILE...
THE DOOR'S UNLOCKED.
MEANING?
MEANING WHOEVER BROKE IN HERE DIDN'T ACTUALLY BREAK IN. THEY GOT IN WITH A KEY.
WELL THAT SEEMS WEIRD.
Eh, WHO KNOWS? MAYBE THEY JUST SNUCK IN TO, YA KNOW... COOK SOMETHING. WHICH COME TO THINK OF IT... ALL THIS SNOOPING AROUND IS BUILDING UP MY APPETITE SO...
REALLY, JUG?
I SWEAR, DUDE... YOU'D BE ASKING FOR THE MENU IN THE MIDDLE OF A PLANE CRASH.
GO EASY ON HIM, ARCHIE. AFTER ALL...

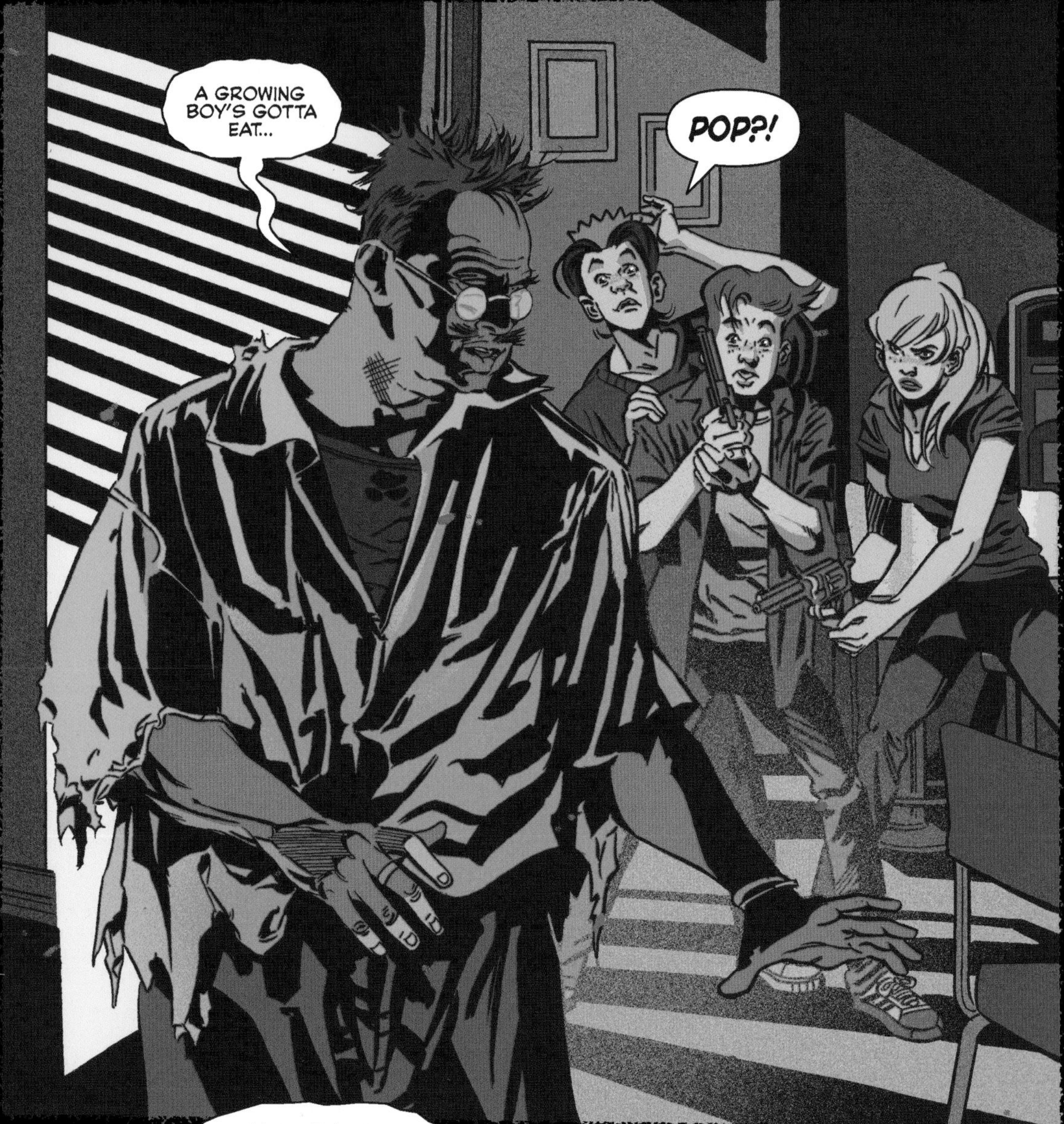
A GROWING BOY'S GOTTA EAT...
POP?!

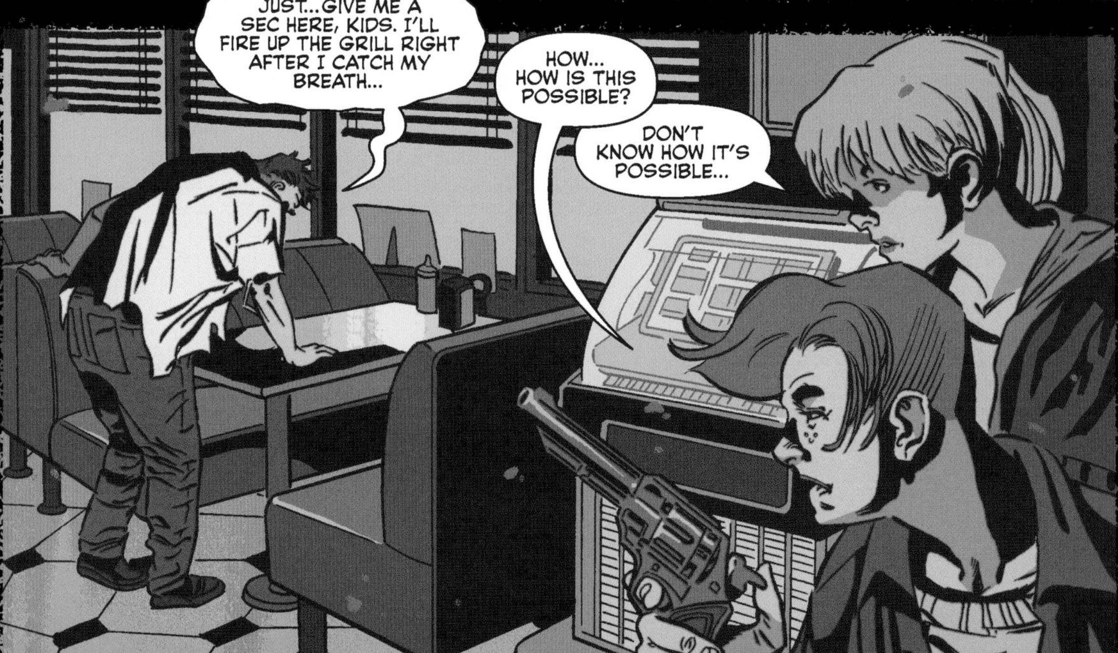
JUST...GIVE ME A SEC HERE, KIDS. I'LL FIRE UP THE GRILL RIGHT AFTER I CATCH MY BREATH...
HOW... HOW IS THIS POSSIBLE?
DON'T KNOW HOW IT'S POSSIBLE...

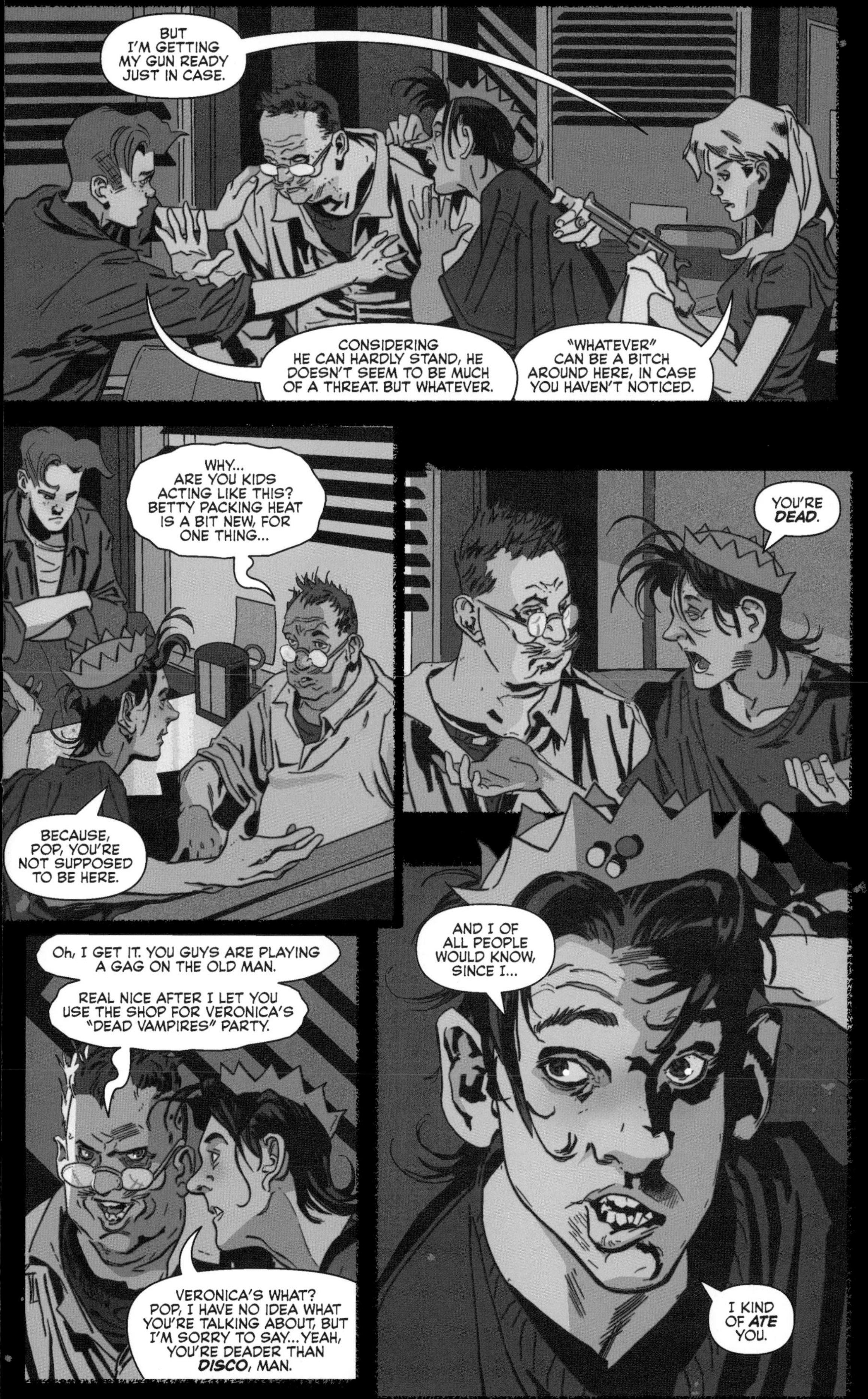
BUT I'M GETTING MY GUN READY JUST IN CASE.
CONSIDERING HE CAN HARDLY STAND, HE DOESN'T SEEM TO BE MUCH OF A THREAT. BUT WHATEVER.
"WHATEVER" CAN BE A BITCH AROUND HERE, IN CASE YOU HAVEN'T NOTICED.
WHY... ARE YOU KIDS ACTING LIKE THIS? BETTY PACKING HEAT IS A BIT NEW, FOR ONE THING...
BECAUSE, POP, YOU'RE NOT SUPPOSED TO BE HERE.
YOU'RE *DEAD*.
Oh, I GET IT. YOU GUYS ARE PLAYING A GAG ON THE OLD MAN.
REAL NICE AFTER I LET YOU USE THE SHOP FOR VERONICA'S "DEAD VAMPIRES" PARTY.
VERONICA'S WHAT? POP, I HAVE NO IDEA WHAT YOU'RE TALKING ABOUT, BUT I'M SORRY TO SAY... YEAH, YOU'RE DEADER THAN *DISCO*, MAN.
AND I OF ALL PEOPLE WOULD KNOW, SINCE I...
I KIND OF *ATE* YOU.

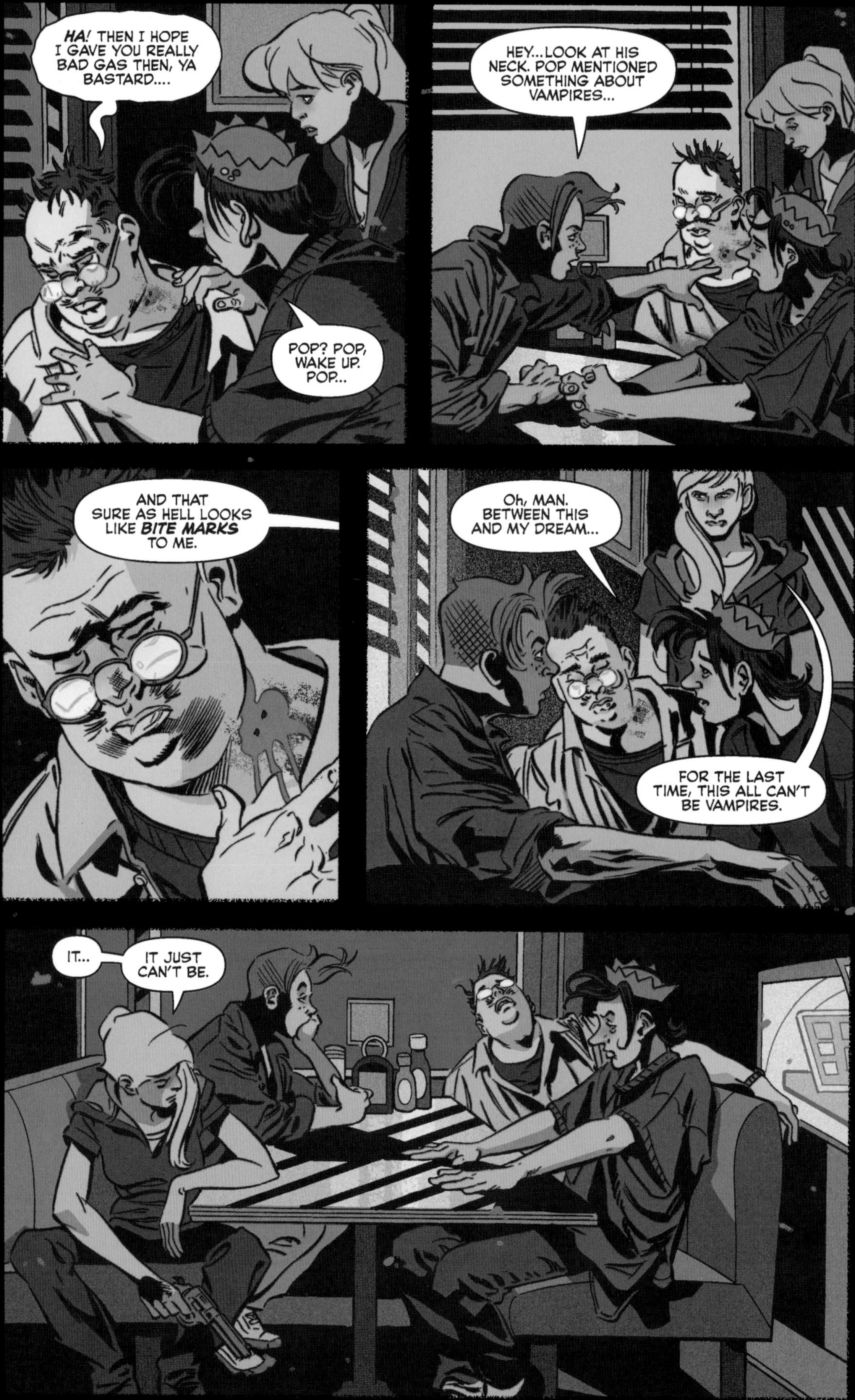

HA! THEN I HOPE I GAVE YOU REALLY BAD GAS THEN, YA BASTARD....
POP? POP, WAKE UP. POP...
HEY...LOOK AT HIS NECK. POP MENTIONED SOMETHING ABOUT VAMPIRES...
AND THAT SURE AS HELL LOOKS LIKE BITE MARKS TO ME.
Oh, MAN. BETWEEN THIS AND MY DREAM...
FOR THE LAST TIME, THIS ALL CAN'T BE VAMPIRES.
IT...
IT JUST CAN'T BE.

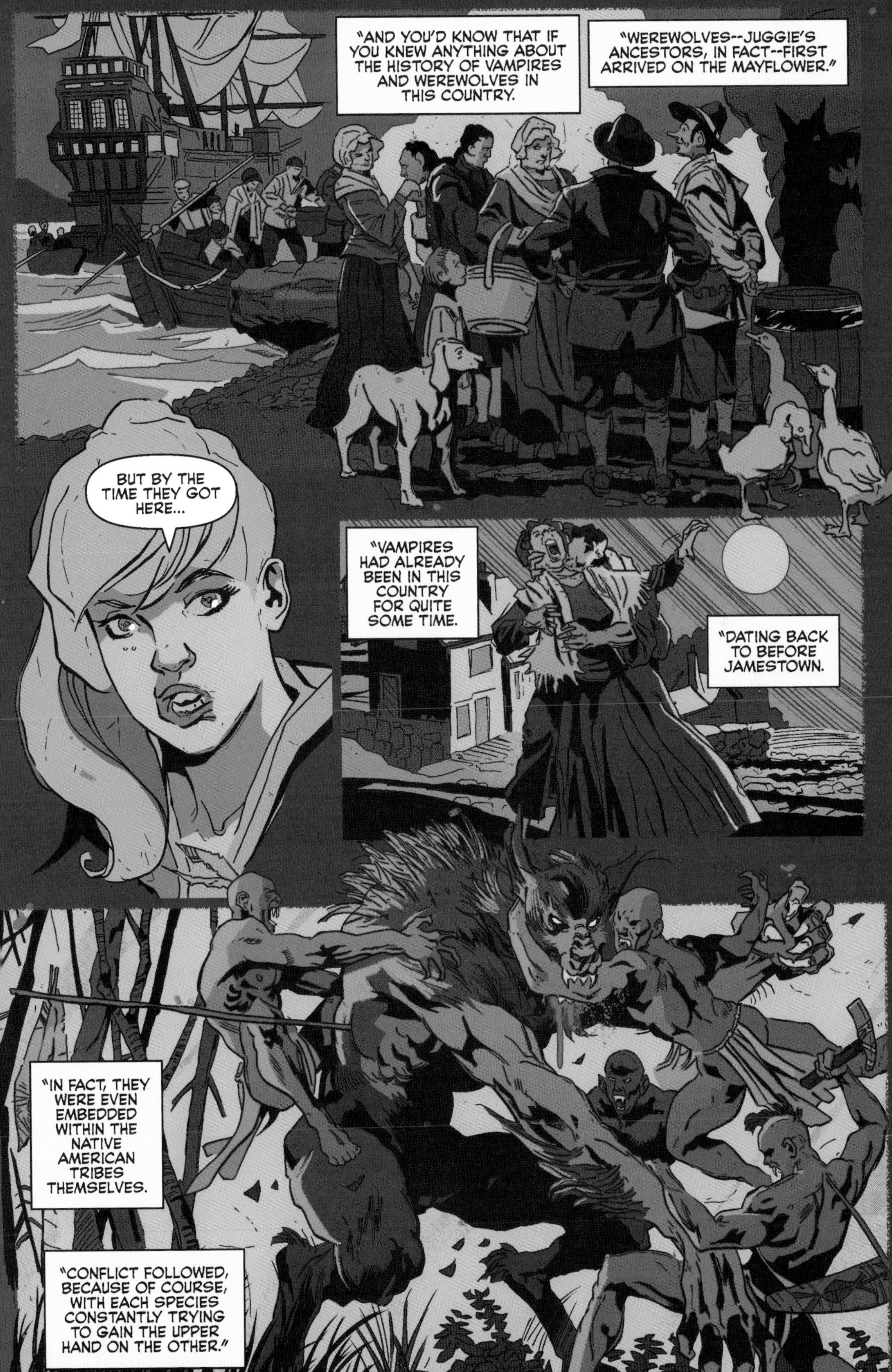
"AND YOU'D KNOW THAT IF YOU KNEW ANYTHING ABOUT THE HISTORY OF VAMPIRES AND WEREWOLVES IN THIS COUNTRY.
"WEREWOLVES--JUGGIE'S ANCESTORS, IN FACT--FIRST ARRIVED ON THE MAYFLOWER."
BUT BY THE TIME THEY GOT HERE...
"VAMPIRES HAD ALREADY BEEN IN THIS COUNTRY FOR QUITE SOME TIME.
"DATING BACK TO BEFORE JAMESTOWN.
"IN FACT, THEY WERE EVEN EMBEDDED WITHIN THE NATIVE AMERICAN TRIBES THEMSELVES.
"CONFLICT FOLLOWED, BECAUSE OF COURSE, WITH EACH SPECIES CONSTANTLY TRYING TO GAIN THE UPPER HAND ON THE OTHER."

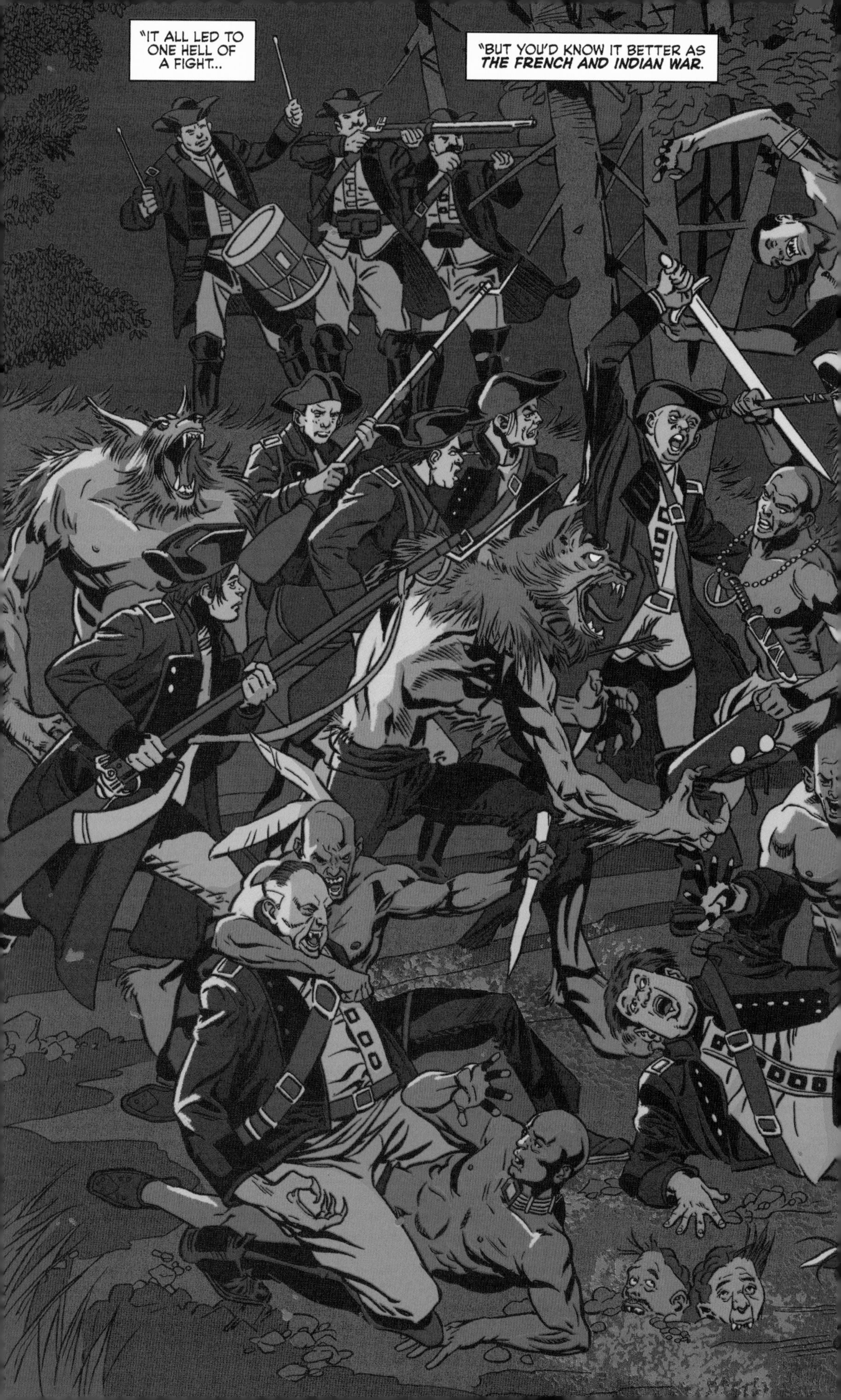
"IT ALL LED TO ONE HELL OF A FIGHT...
"BUT YOU'D KNOW IT BETTER AS ***THE FRENCH AND INDIAN WAR***.

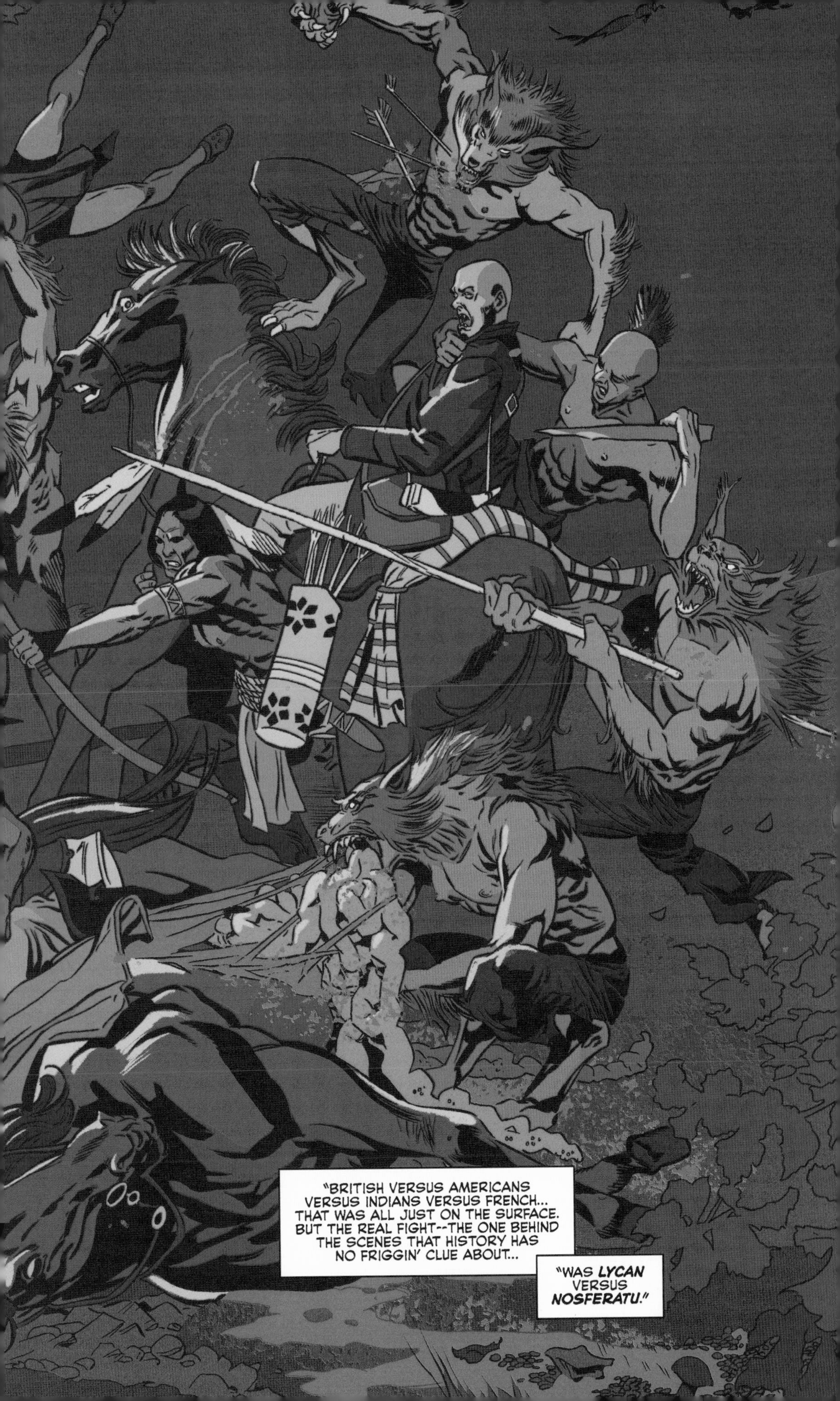
"BRITISH VERSUS AMERICANS VERSUS INDIANS VERSUS FRENCH... THAT WAS ALL JUST ON THE SURFACE. BUT THE REAL FIGHT--THE ONE BEHIND THE SCENES THAT HISTORY HAS NO FRIGGIN' CLUE ABOUT...
"WAS **LYCAN** VERSUS **NOSFERATU.**"

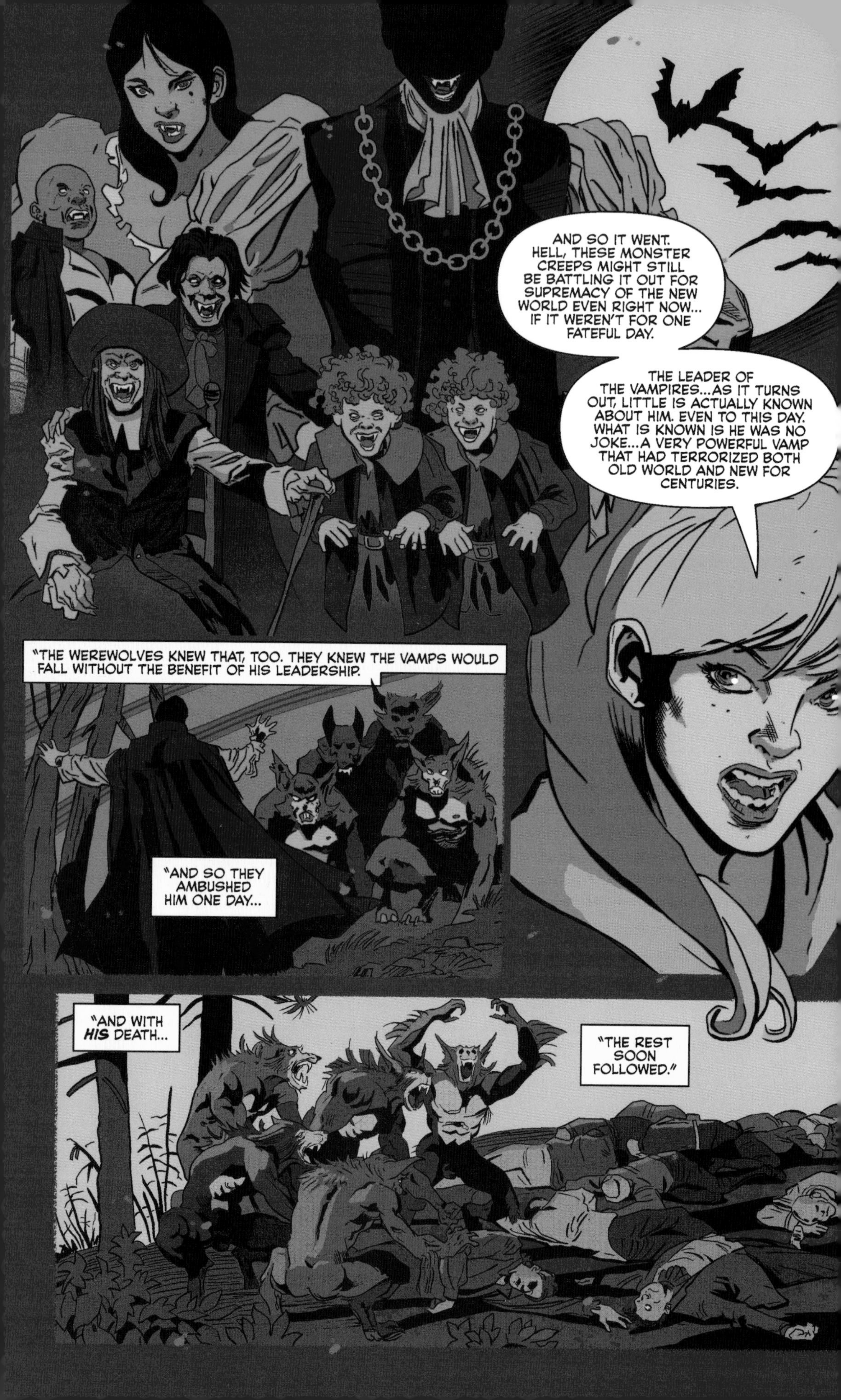
AND SO IT WENT. HELL, THESE MONSTER CREEPS MIGHT STILL BE BATTLING IT OUT FOR SUPREMACY OF THE NEW WORLD EVEN RIGHT NOW... IF IT WEREN'T FOR ONE FATEFUL DAY.
THE LEADER OF THE VAMPIRES...AS IT TURNS OUT, LITTLE IS ACTUALLY KNOWN ABOUT HIM. EVEN TO THIS DAY. WHAT IS KNOWN IS HE WAS NO JOKE...A VERY POWERFUL VAMP THAT HAD TERRORIZED BOTH OLD WORLD AND NEW FOR CENTURIES.
"THE WEREWOLVES KNEW THAT, TOO. THEY KNEW THE VAMPS WOULD FALL WITHOUT THE BENEFIT OF HIS LEADERSHIP.
"AND SO THEY AMBUSHED HIM ONE DAY...
"AND WITH HIS DEATH...
"THE REST SOON FOLLOWED."

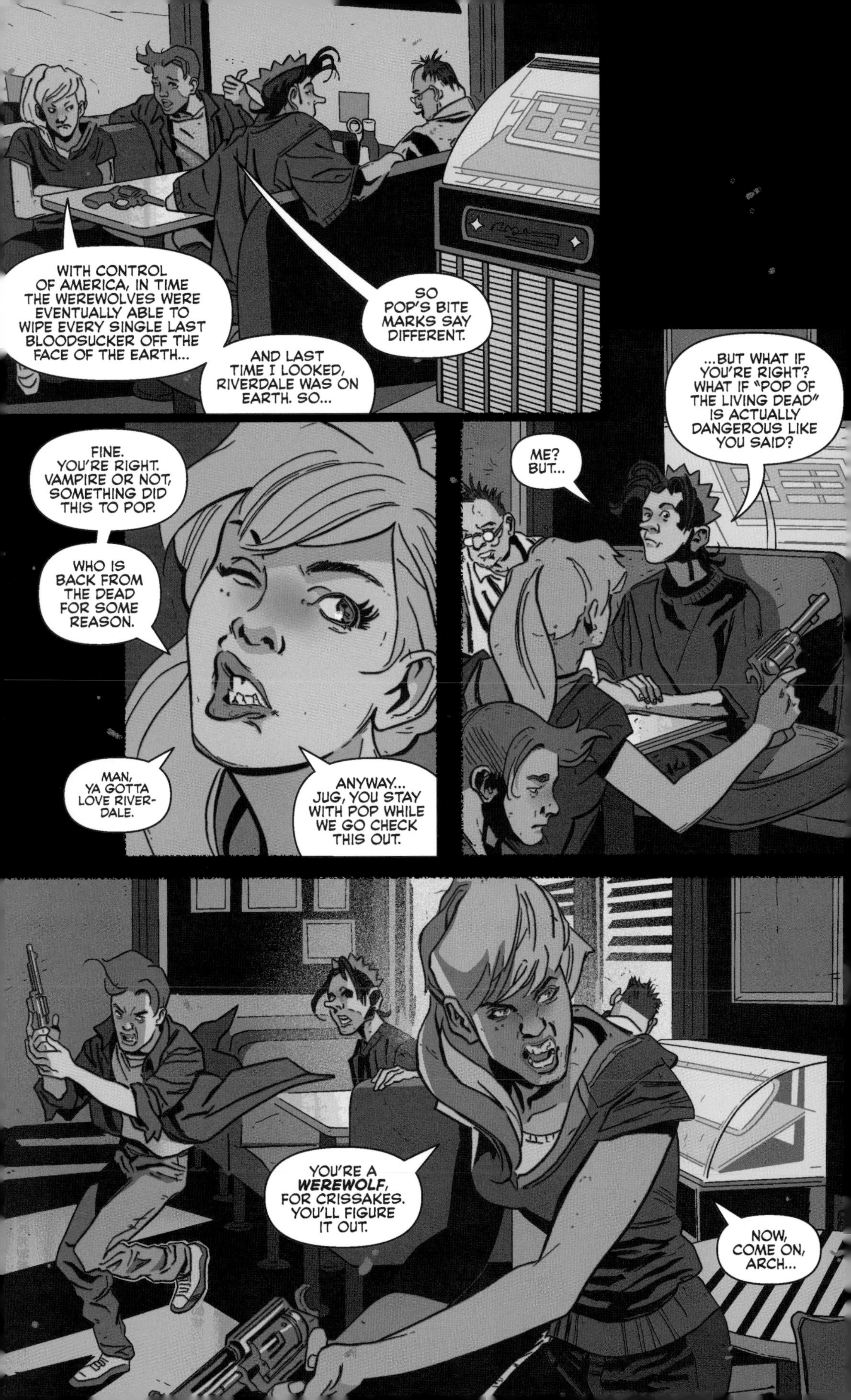
WITH CONTROL OF AMERICA, IN TIME THE WEREWOLVES WERE EVENTUALLY ABLE TO WIPE EVERY SINGLE LAST BLOODSUCKER OFF THE FACE OF THE EARTH...
AND LAST TIME I LOOKED, RIVERDALE WAS ON EARTH. SO...
SO POP'S BITE MARKS SAY DIFFERENT.
...BUT WHAT IF YOU'RE RIGHT? WHAT IF "POP OF THE LIVING DEAD" IS ACTUALLY DANGEROUS LIKE YOU SAID?
ME? BUT...
FINE. YOU'RE RIGHT. VAMPIRE OR NOT, SOMETHING DID THIS TO POP.
WHO IS BACK FROM THE DEAD FOR SOME REASON.
MAN, YA GOTTA LOVE RIVER-DALE.
ANYWAY... JUG, YOU STAY WITH POP WHILE WE GO CHECK THIS OUT.
YOU'RE A ***WEREWOLF***, FOR CRISSAKES. YOU'LL FIGURE IT OUT.
NOW, COME ON, ARCH...

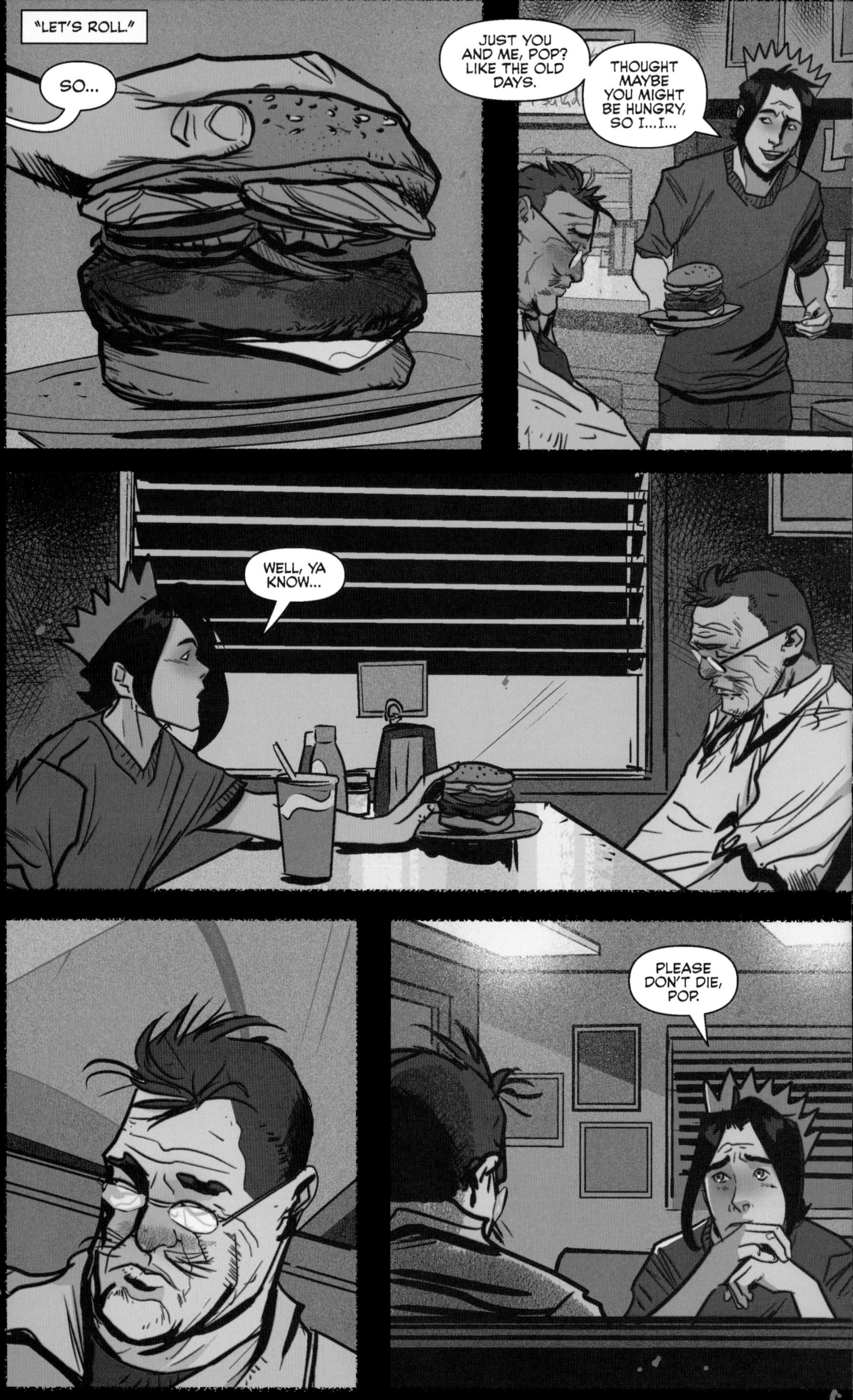
"LET'S ROLL."
SO...
JUST YOU AND ME, POP? LIKE THE OLD DAYS.
THOUGHT MAYBE YOU MIGHT BE HUNGRY, SO I...I...
WELL, YA KNOW...
PLEASE DON'T DIE, POP.

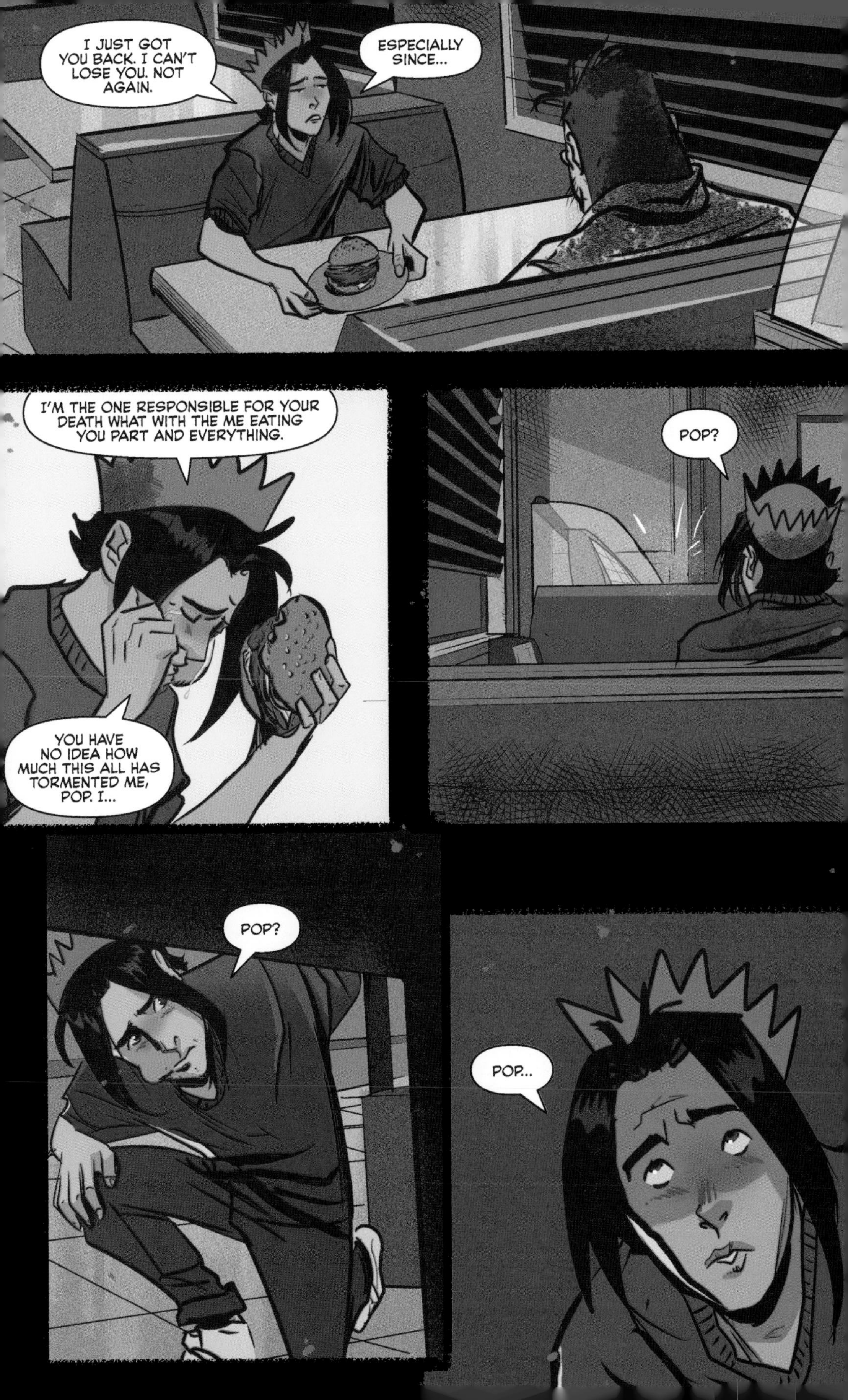
I JUST GOT YOU BACK. I CAN'T LOSE YOU. NOT AGAIN.
ESPECIALLY SINCE...
I'M THE ONE RESPONSIBLE FOR YOUR DEATH WHAT WITH THE ME EATING YOU PART AND EVERYTHING.
YOU HAVE NO IDEA HOW MUCH THIS ALL HAS TORMENTED ME, POP. I...
POP?
POP?
POP...

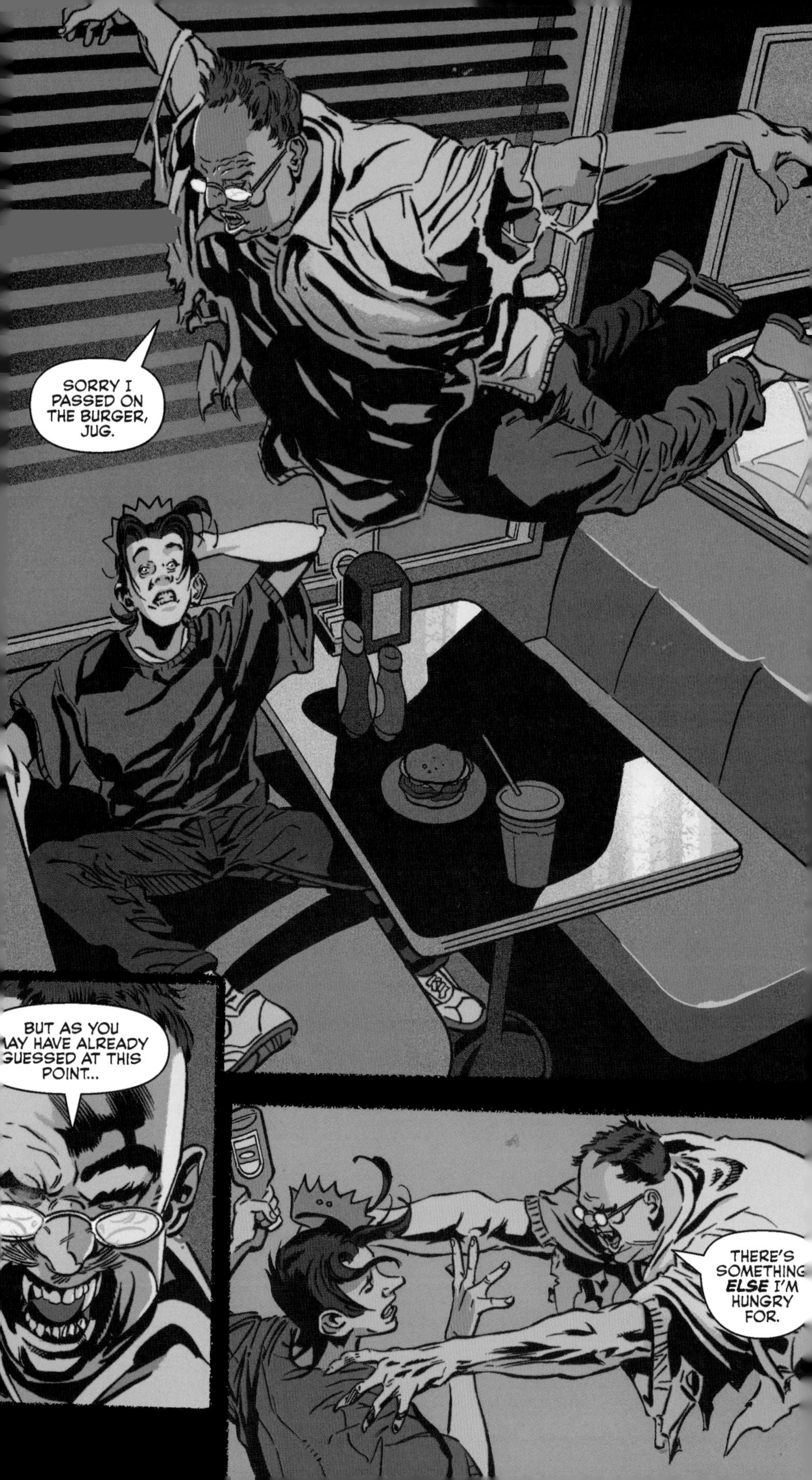
SORRY I PASSED ON THE BURGER, JUG.
BUT AS YOU MAY HAVE ALREADY GUESSED AT THIS POINT...
THERE'S SOMETHING ELSE I'M HUNGRY FOR.

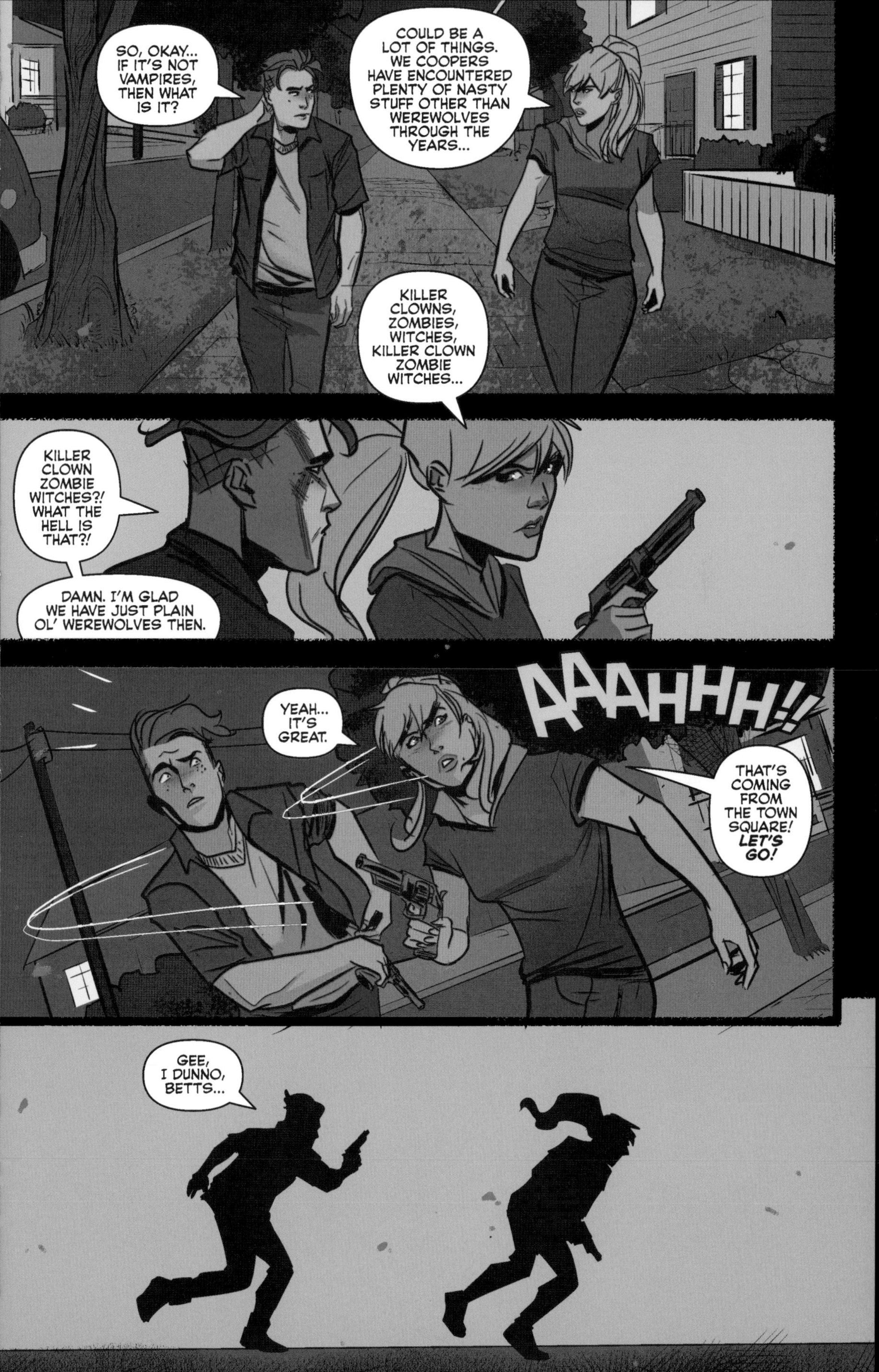
SO, OKAY... IF IT'S NOT VAMPIRES, THEN WHAT IS IT?
COULD BE A LOT OF THINGS. WE COOPERS HAVE ENCOUNTERED PLENTY OF NASTY STUFF OTHER THAN WEREWOLVES THROUGH THE YEARS...
KILLER CLOWNS, ZOMBIES, WITCHES, KILLER CLOWN ZOMBIE WITCHES...
KILLER CLOWN ZOMBIE WITCHES?! WHAT THE HELL IS THAT?!
DAMN. I'M GLAD WE HAVE JUST PLAIN OL' WEREWOLVES THEN.
YEAH... IT'S GREAT.
AAAHHH!!
THAT'S COMING FROM THE TOWN SQUARE! ***LET'S GO!***
GEE, I DUNNO, BETTS...

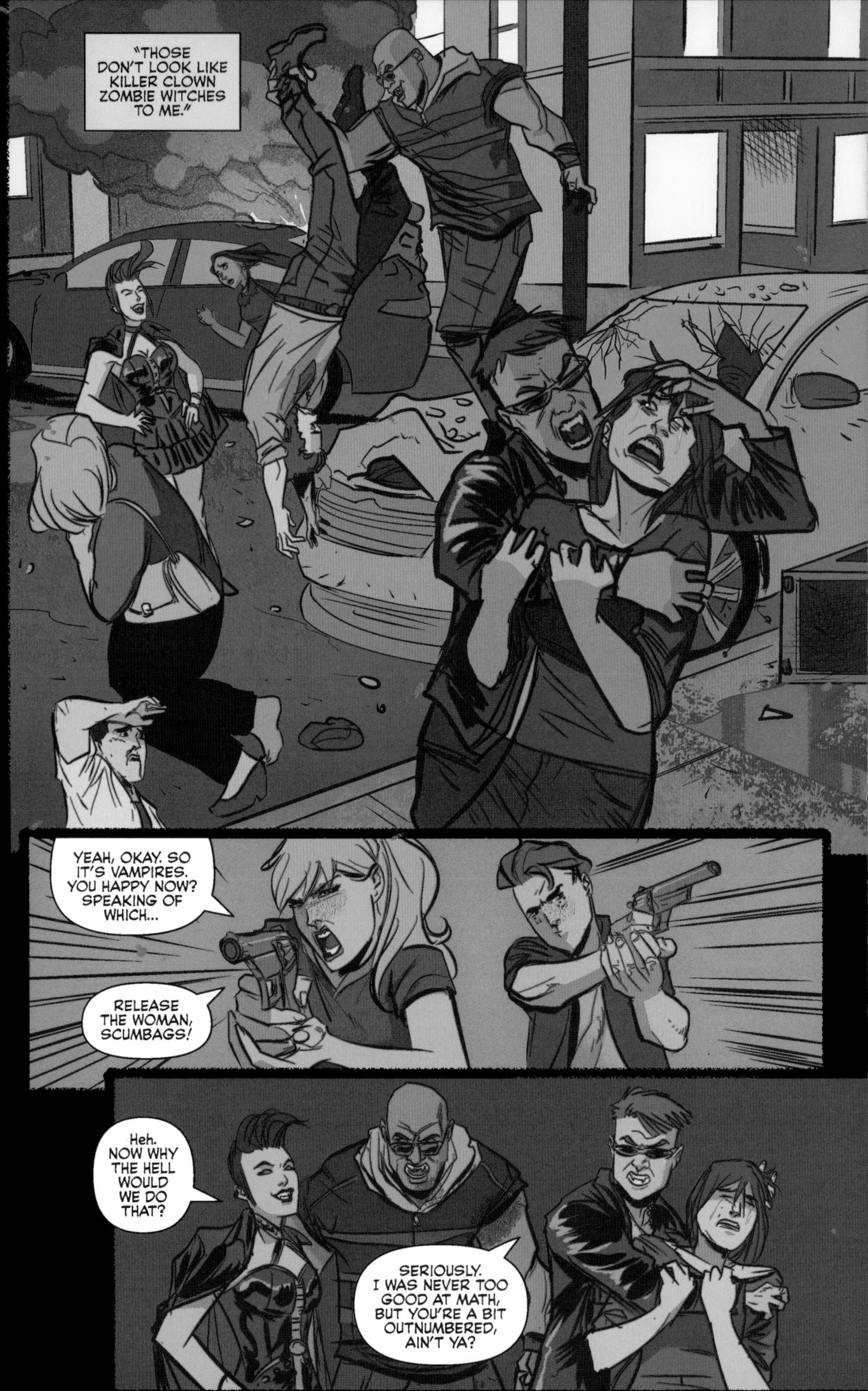
"THOSE DON'T LOOK LIKE KILLER CLOWN ZOMBIE WITCHES TO ME."
YEAH, OKAY. SO IT'S VAMPIRES. YOU HAPPY NOW? SPEAKING OF WHICH...
RELEASE THE WOMAN, SCUMBAGS!
Heh. NOW WHY THE HELL WOULD WE DO THAT?
SERIOUSLY. I WAS NEVER TOO GOOD AT MATH, BUT YOU'RE A BIT OUTNUMBERED, AIN'T YA?

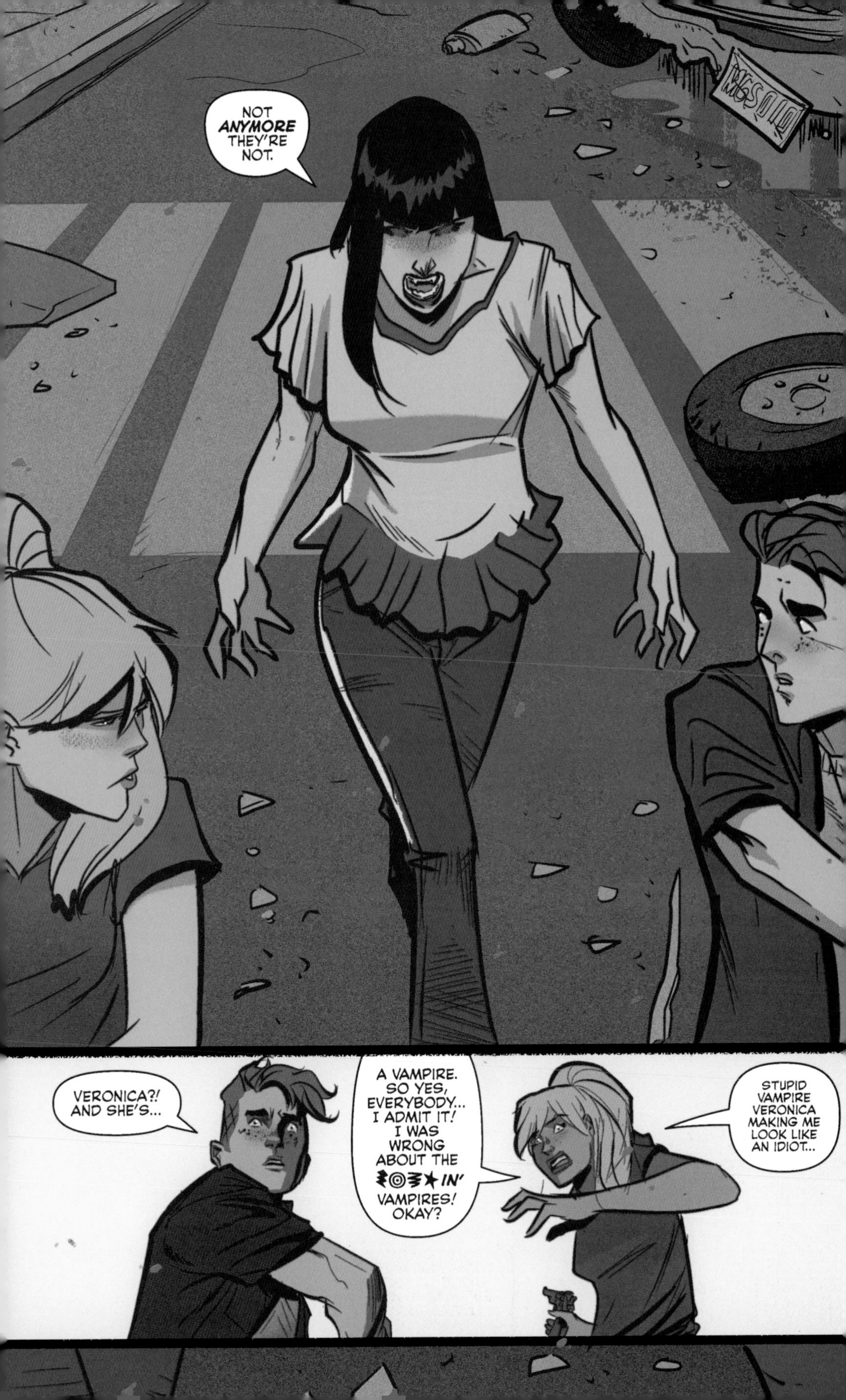
NOT ANYMORE THEY'RE NOT.
VERONICA?! AND SHE'S...
A VAMPIRE. SO YES, EVERYBODY... I ADMIT IT! I WAS WRONG ABOUT THE ≷◎≶★IN' VAMPIRES! OKAY?
STUPID VAMPIRE VERONICA MAKING ME LOOK LIKE AN IDIOT...

CHAPTER THREE

COVER ART BY **PAT & TIM KENNEDY**
WITH **BOB SMITH** AND **MATT HERMS**

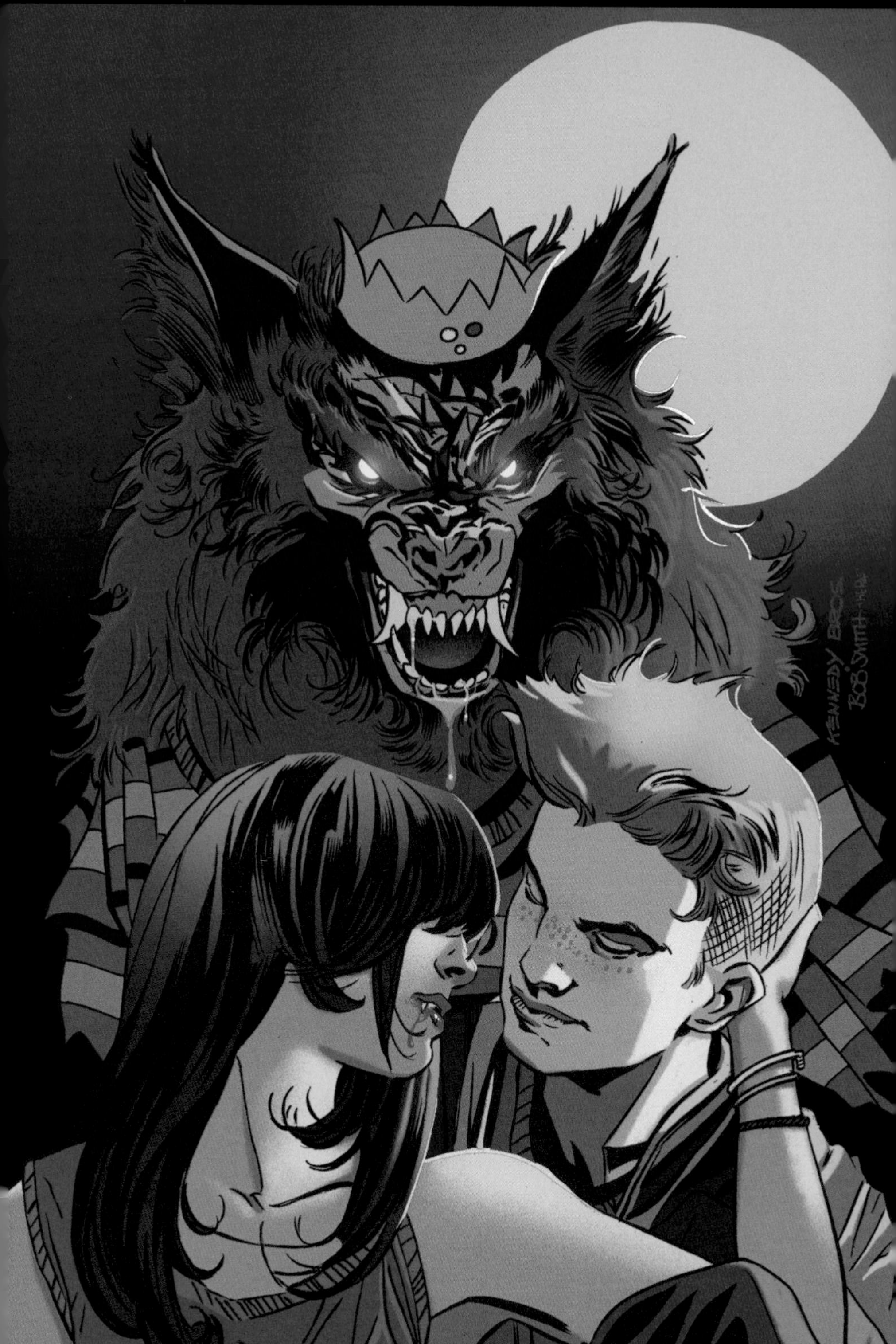

STORY BY **FRANK TIERI**
ART BY **PAT & TIM KENNEDY** (p.1-9,12) **JOE EISMA** (p.10-11,13-20)
INKS BY **BOB SMITH** (p.1-7) **RYAN JAMPOLE** (p.8,12) **JOE EISMA** (p.9)
COLORING BY **MATT HERMS** & **LEE LOUGHRIDGE** (p.1-3,5 rendering)
LETTERING BY **JACK MORELLI**

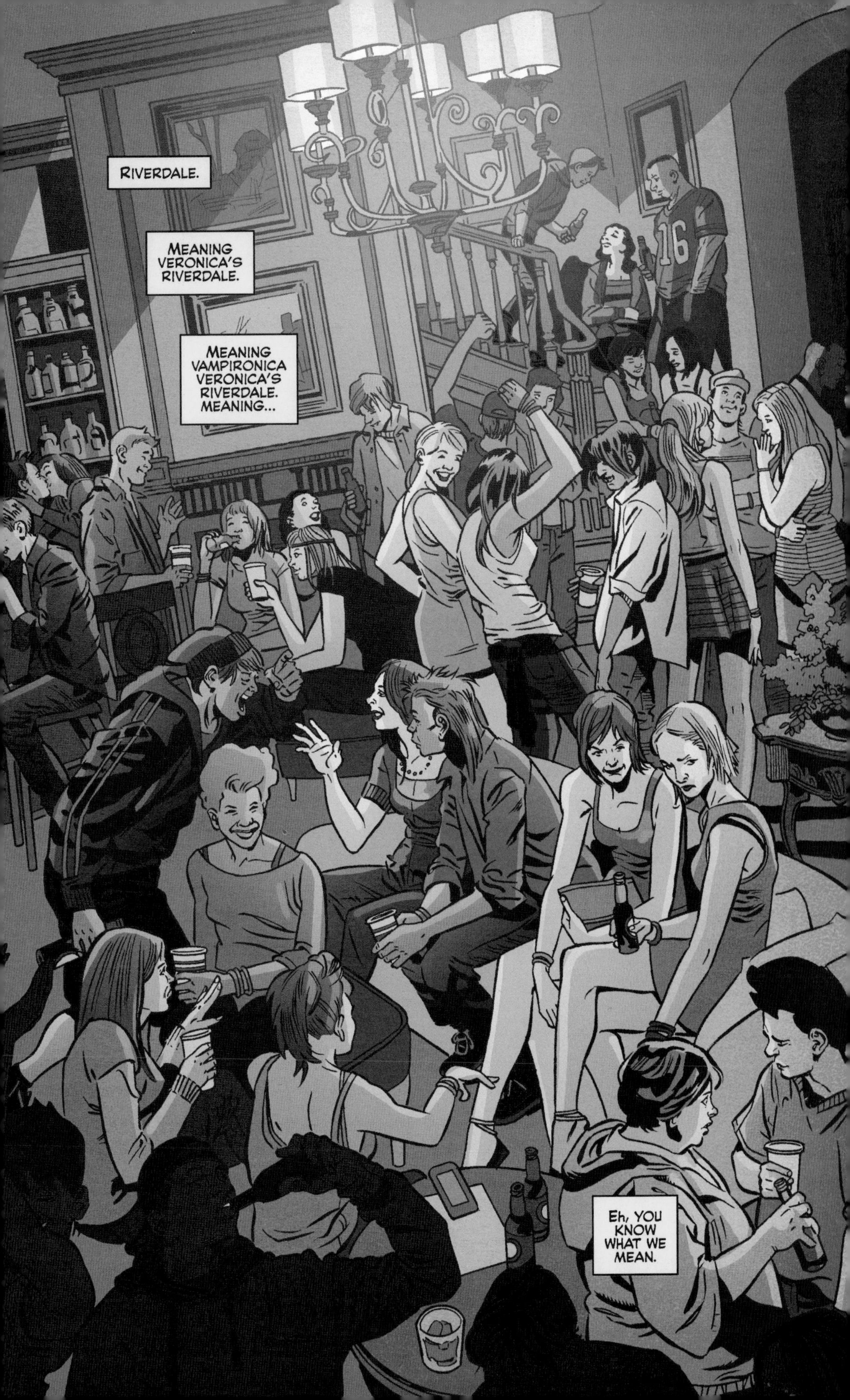
RIVERDALE.
MEANING VERONICA'S RIVERDALE.
MEANING VAMPIRONICA VERONICA'S RIVERDALE. MEANING...
Eh, YOU KNOW WHAT WE MEAN.

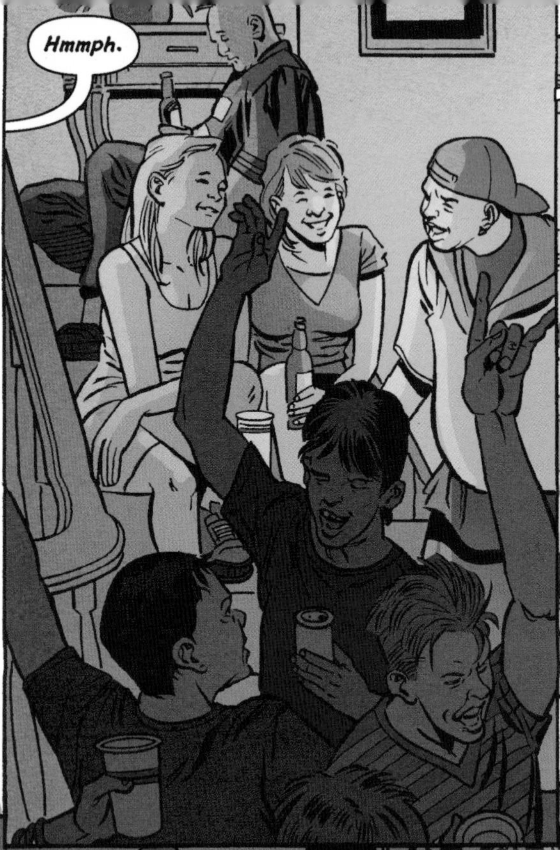
Hmmph.

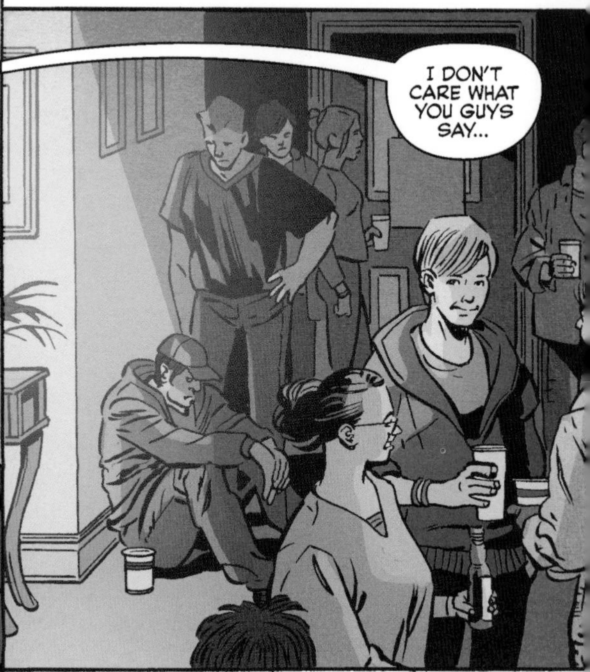
I DON'T CARE WHAT YOU GUYS SAY...

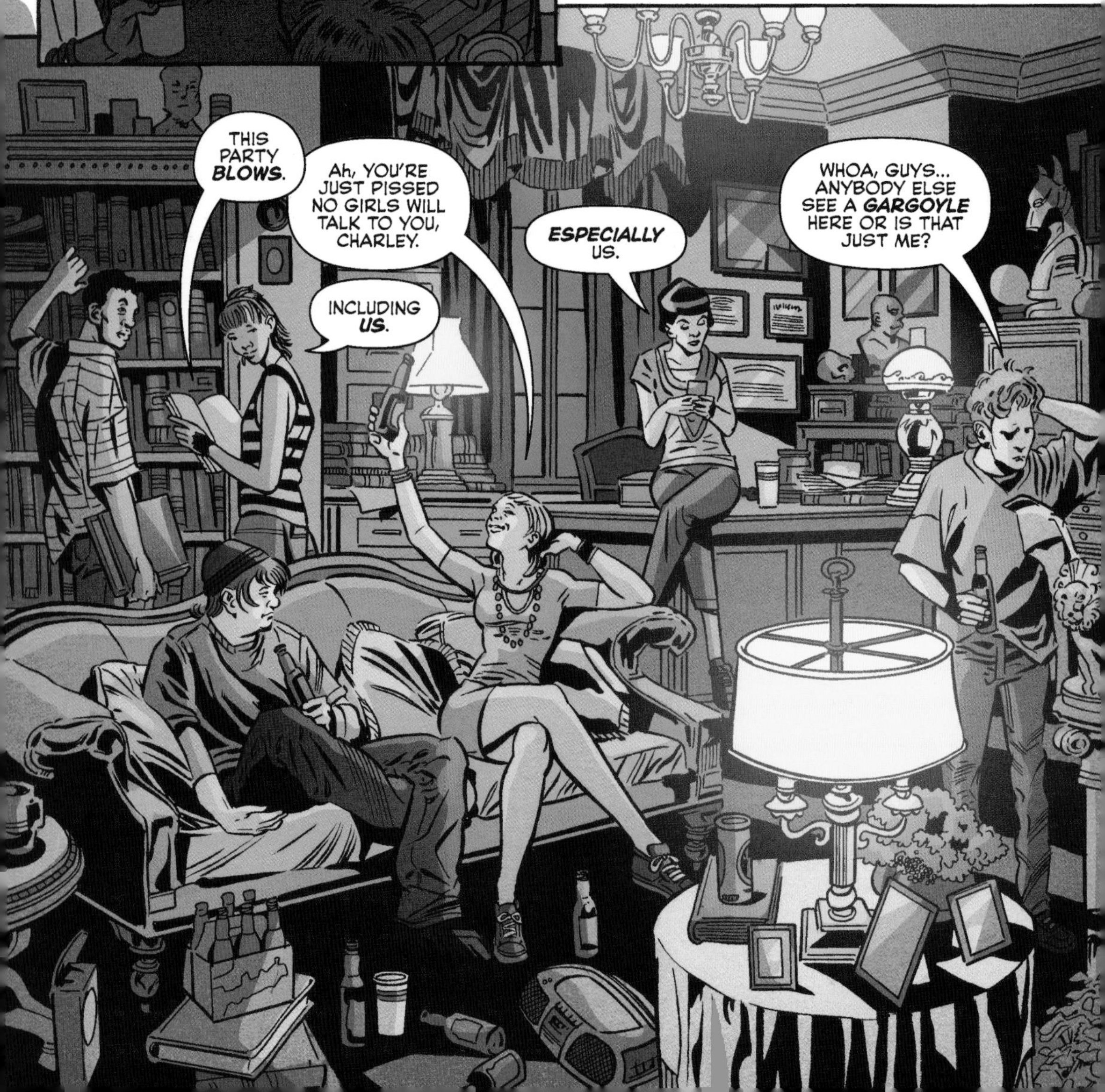
THIS PARTY **BLOWS**.
Ah, YOU'RE JUST PISSED NO GIRLS WILL TALK TO YOU, CHARLEY.
INCLUDING **US**.
ESPECIALLY US.
WHOA, GUYS... ANYBODY ELSE SEE A **GARGOYLE** HERE OR IS THAT JUST ME?

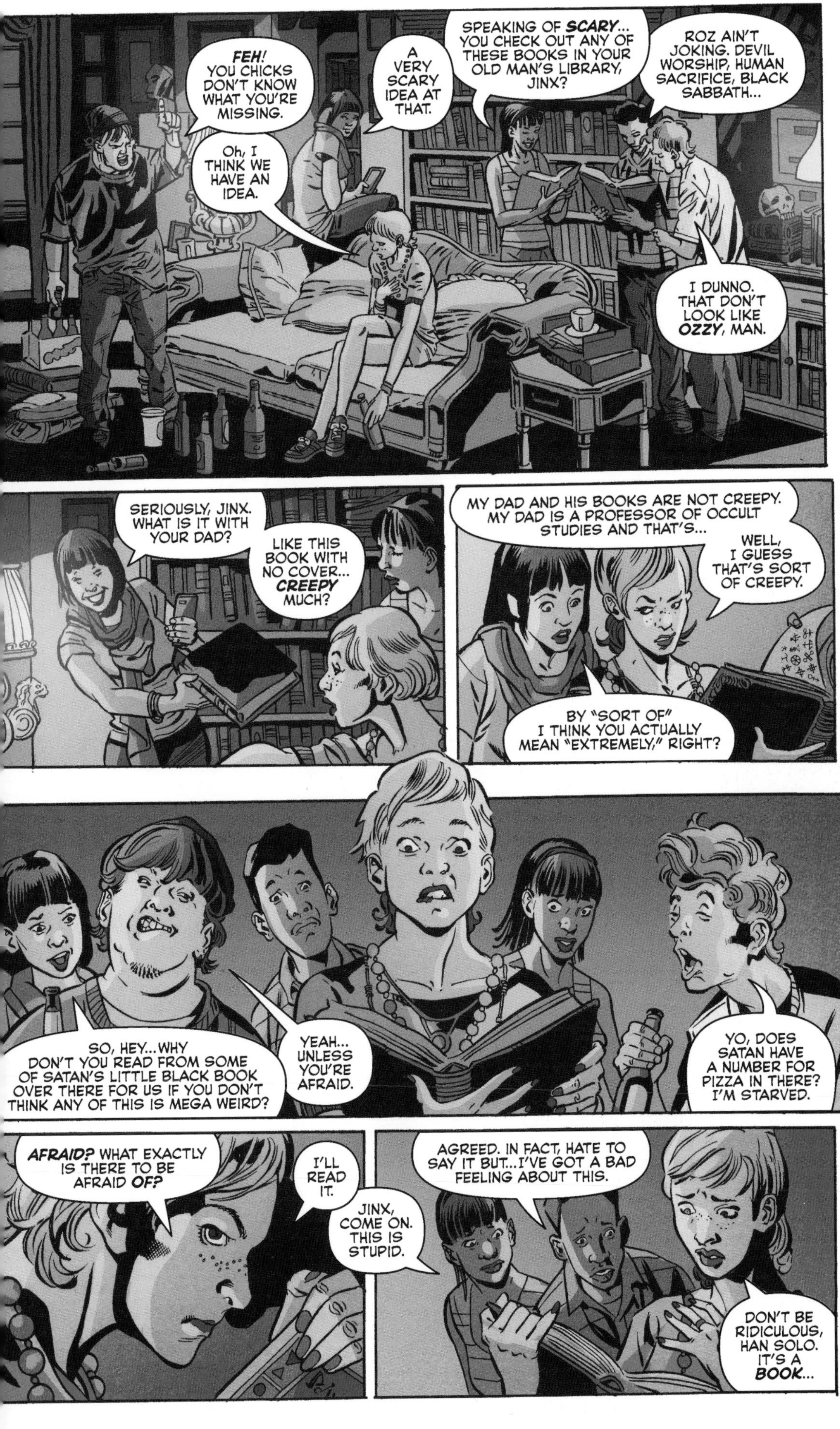
FEH! YOU CHICKS DON'T KNOW WHAT YOU'RE MISSING.
Oh, I THINK WE HAVE AN IDEA.
A VERY SCARY IDEA AT THAT.
SPEAKING OF SCARY... YOU CHECK OUT ANY OF THESE BOOKS IN YOUR OLD MAN'S LIBRARY, JINX?
ROZ AIN'T JOKING. DEVIL WORSHIP, HUMAN SACRIFICE, BLACK SABBATH...
I DUNNO. THAT DON'T LOOK LIKE OZZY, MAN.
SERIOUSLY, JINX. WHAT IS IT WITH YOUR DAD?
LIKE THIS BOOK WITH NO COVER... CREEPY MUCH?
MY DAD AND HIS BOOKS ARE NOT CREEPY. MY DAD IS A PROFESSOR OF OCCULT STUDIES AND THAT'S...
WELL, I GUESS THAT'S SORT OF CREEPY.
BY "SORT OF" I THINK YOU ACTUALLY MEAN "EXTREMELY," RIGHT?
SO, HEY...WHY DON'T YOU READ FROM SOME OF SATAN'S LITTLE BLACK BOOK OVER THERE FOR US IF YOU DON'T THINK ANY OF THIS IS MEGA WEIRD?
YEAH... UNLESS YOU'RE AFRAID.
YO, DOES SATAN HAVE A NUMBER FOR PIZZA IN THERE? I'M STARVED.
AFRAID? WHAT EXACTLY IS THERE TO BE AFRAID OF?
I'LL READ IT.
JINX, COME ON. THIS IS STUPID.
AGREED. IN FACT, HATE TO SAY IT BUT...I'VE GOT A BAD FEELING ABOUT THIS.
DON'T BE RIDICULOUS, HAN SOLO. IT'S A BOOK...

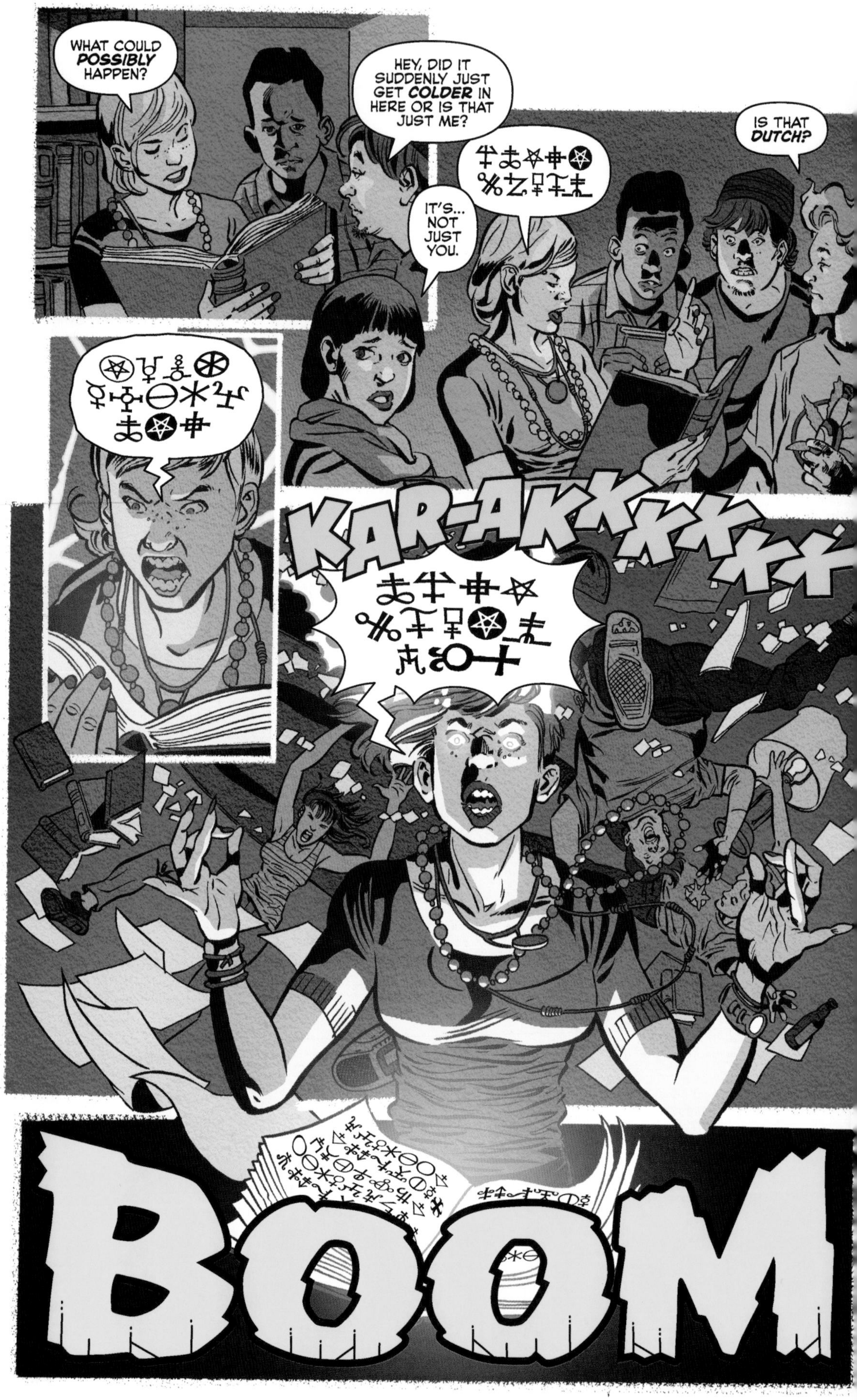
WHAT COULD POSSIBLY HAPPEN?
HEY, DID IT SUDDENLY JUST GET COLDER IN HERE OR IS THAT JUST ME?
IT'S... NOT JUST YOU.
IS THAT DUTCH?
KAR-AKKKKKK
BOOM

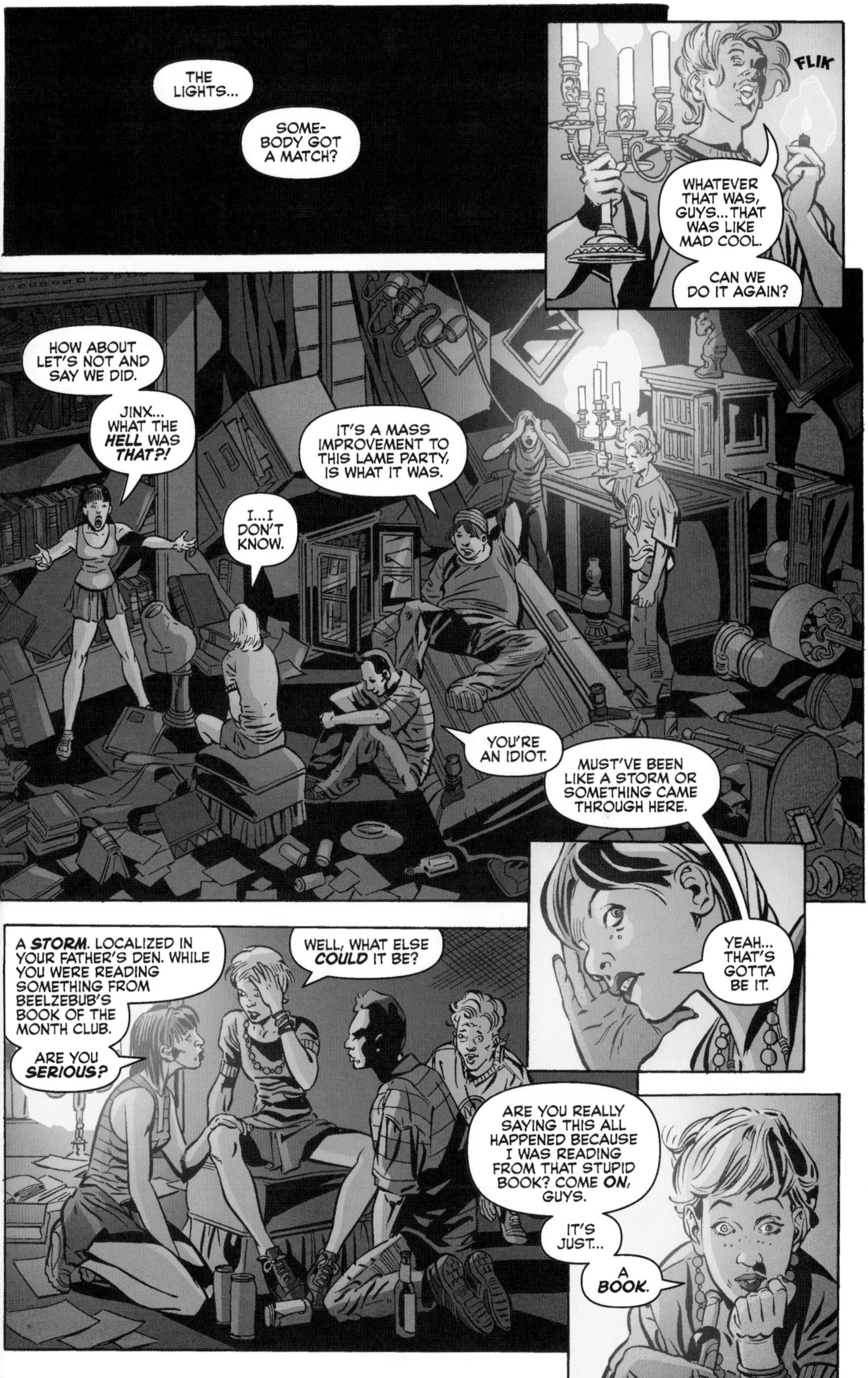
THE LIGHTS...
SOME-BODY GOT A MATCH?
FLIK
WHATEVER THAT WAS, GUYS...THAT WAS LIKE MAD COOL.
CAN WE DO IT AGAIN?
HOW ABOUT LET'S NOT AND SAY WE DID.
JINX... WHAT THE **HELL** WAS **THAT?!**
IT'S A MASS IMPROVEMENT TO THIS LAME PARTY, IS WHAT IT WAS.
I...I DON'T KNOW.
YOU'RE AN IDIOT.
MUST'VE BEEN LIKE A STORM OR SOMETHING CAME THROUGH HERE.
YEAH... THAT'S GOTTA BE IT.
A **STORM**. LOCALIZED IN YOUR FATHER'S DEN. WHILE YOU WERE READING SOMETHING FROM BEELZEBUB'S BOOK OF THE MONTH CLUB.
ARE YOU **SERIOUS?**
WELL, WHAT ELSE **COULD** IT BE?
ARE YOU REALLY SAYING THIS ALL HAPPENED BECAUSE I WAS READING FROM THAT STUPID BOOK? COME **ON**, GUYS.
IT'S JUST...
A **BOOK**.

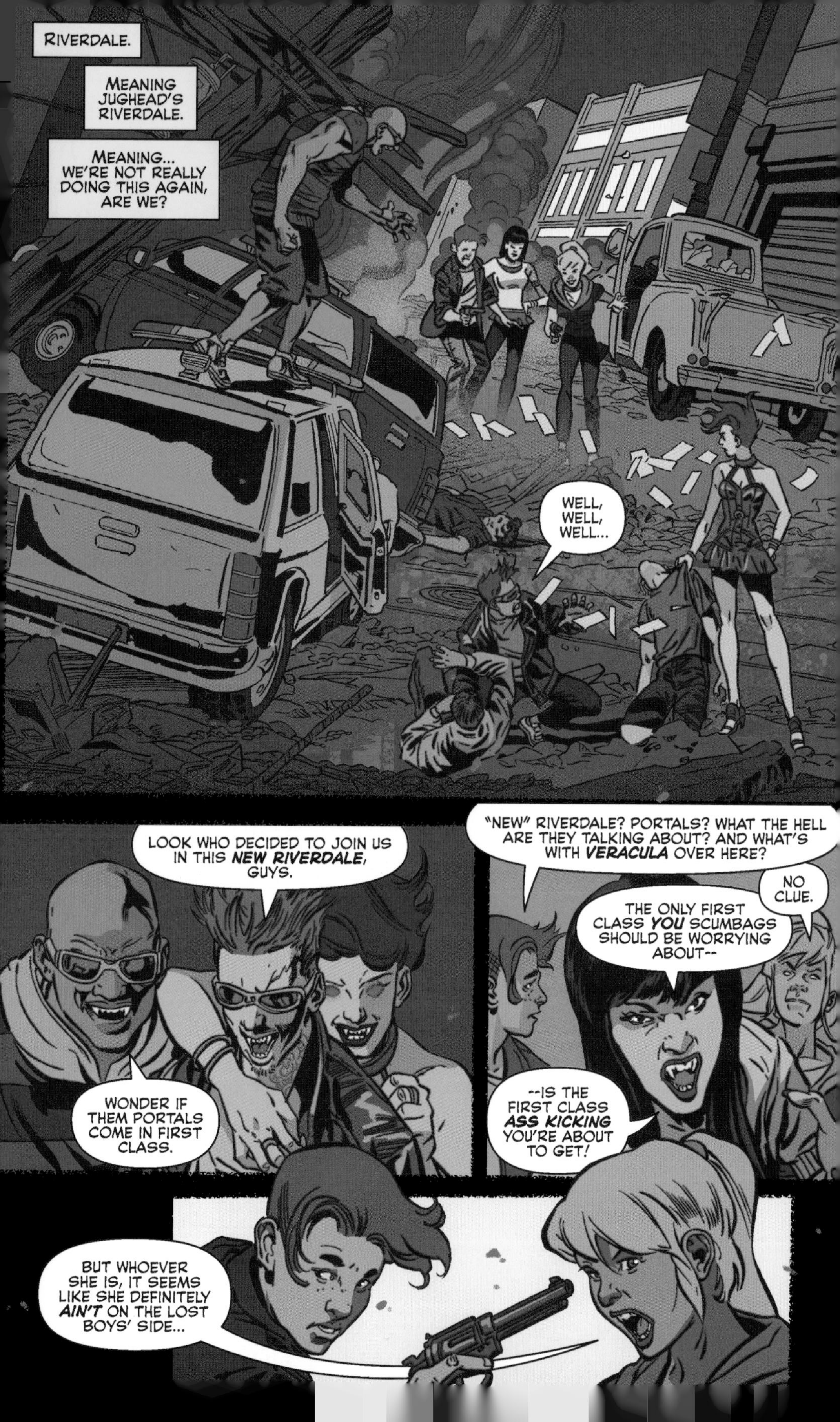
RIVERDALE.
MEANING JUGHEAD'S RIVERDALE.
MEANING... WE'RE NOT REALLY DOING THIS AGAIN, ARE WE?
WELL, WELL, WELL...
LOOK WHO DECIDED TO JOIN US IN THIS NEW RIVERDALE, GUYS.
WONDER IF THEM PORTALS COME IN FIRST CLASS.
"NEW" RIVERDALE? PORTALS? WHAT THE HELL ARE THEY TALKING ABOUT? AND WHAT'S WITH VERACULA OVER HERE?
NO CLUE.
THE ONLY FIRST CLASS YOU SCUMBAGS SHOULD BE WORRYING ABOUT--
--IS THE FIRST CLASS ASS KICKING YOU'RE ABOUT TO GET!
BUT WHOEVER SHE IS, IT SEEMS LIKE SHE DEFINITELY AIN'T ON THE LOST BOYS' SIDE...

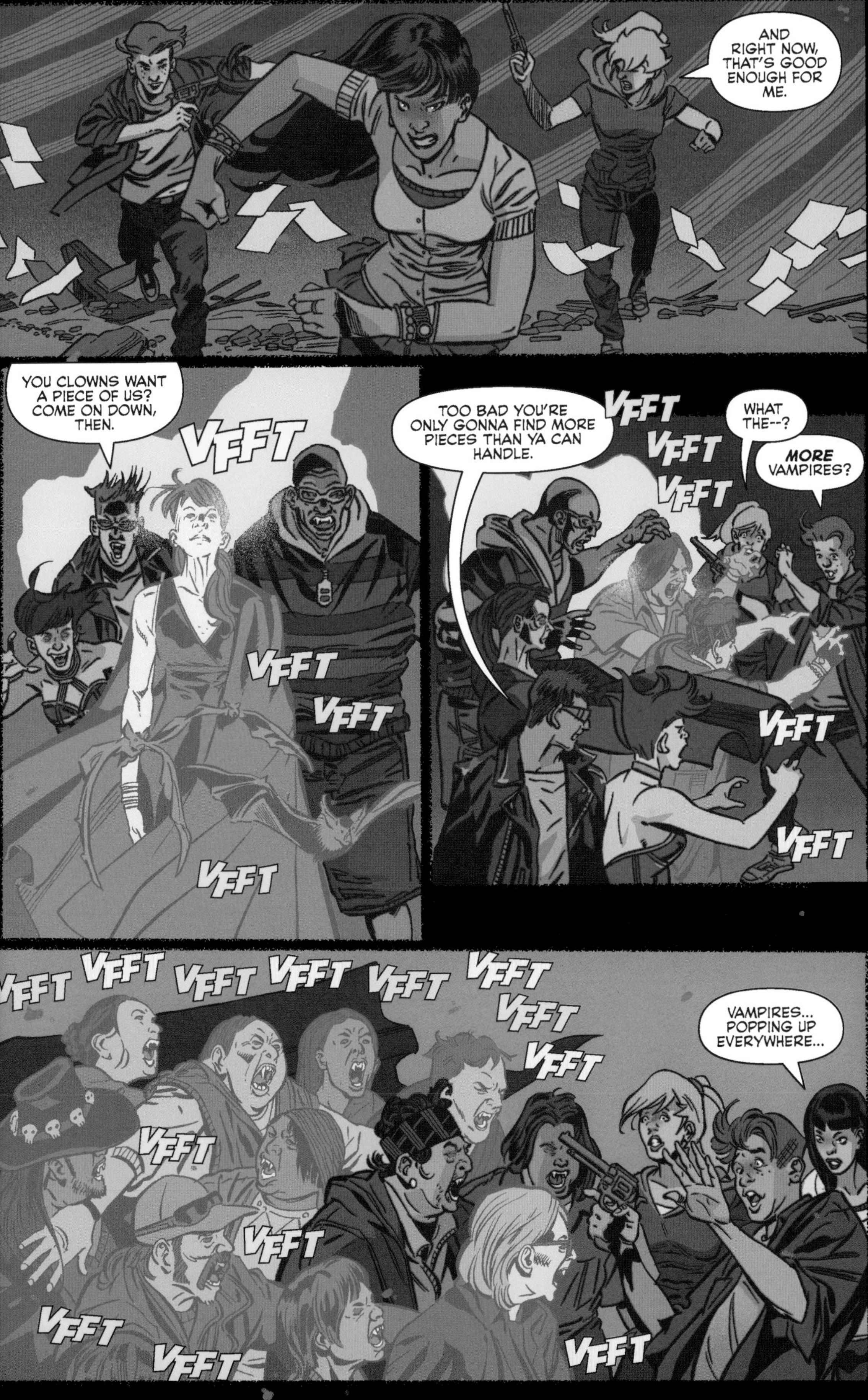
AND RIGHT NOW, THAT'S GOOD ENOUGH FOR ME.
YOU CLOWNS WANT A PIECE OF US? COME ON DOWN, THEN.
VFFT
VFFT
VFFT
VFFT
TOO BAD YOU'RE ONLY GONNA FIND MORE PIECES THAN YA CAN HANDLE.
VFFT
VFFT
VFFT
WHAT THE--?
MORE VAMPIRES?
VFFT
VFFT
VFFT VFFT VFFT VFFT VFFT VFFT
VFFT
VFFT
VAMPIRES... POPPING UP EVERYWHERE...
VFFT
VFFT
VFFT
VFFT
VFFT

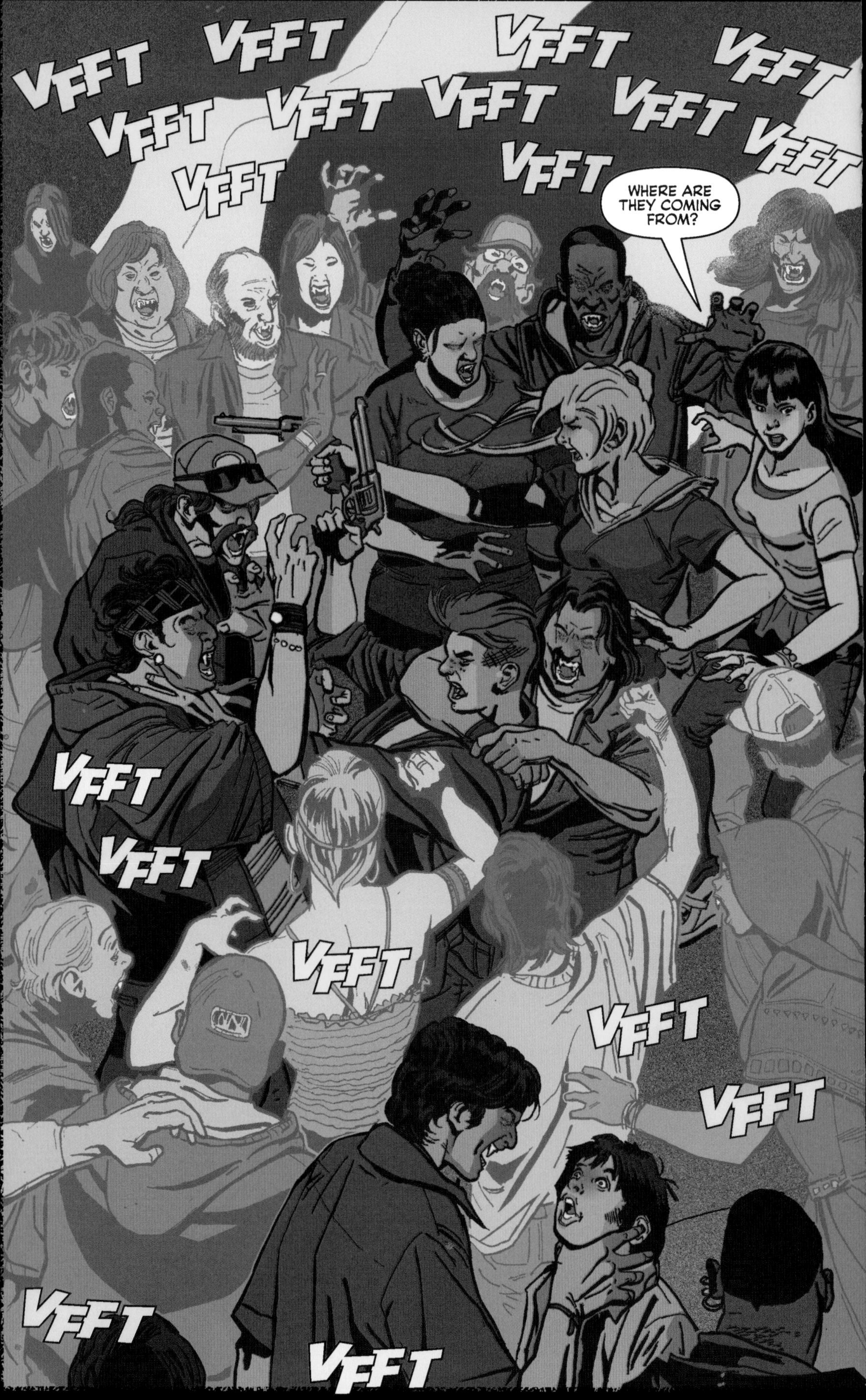
VFFT
VFFT
VFFT
VFFT
VFFT
VFFT
VFFT
VFFT
VFFT
VFFT
VFFT
WHERE ARE THEY COMING FROM?
VFFT
VFFT
VFFT
VFFT
VFFT
VFFT
VFFT

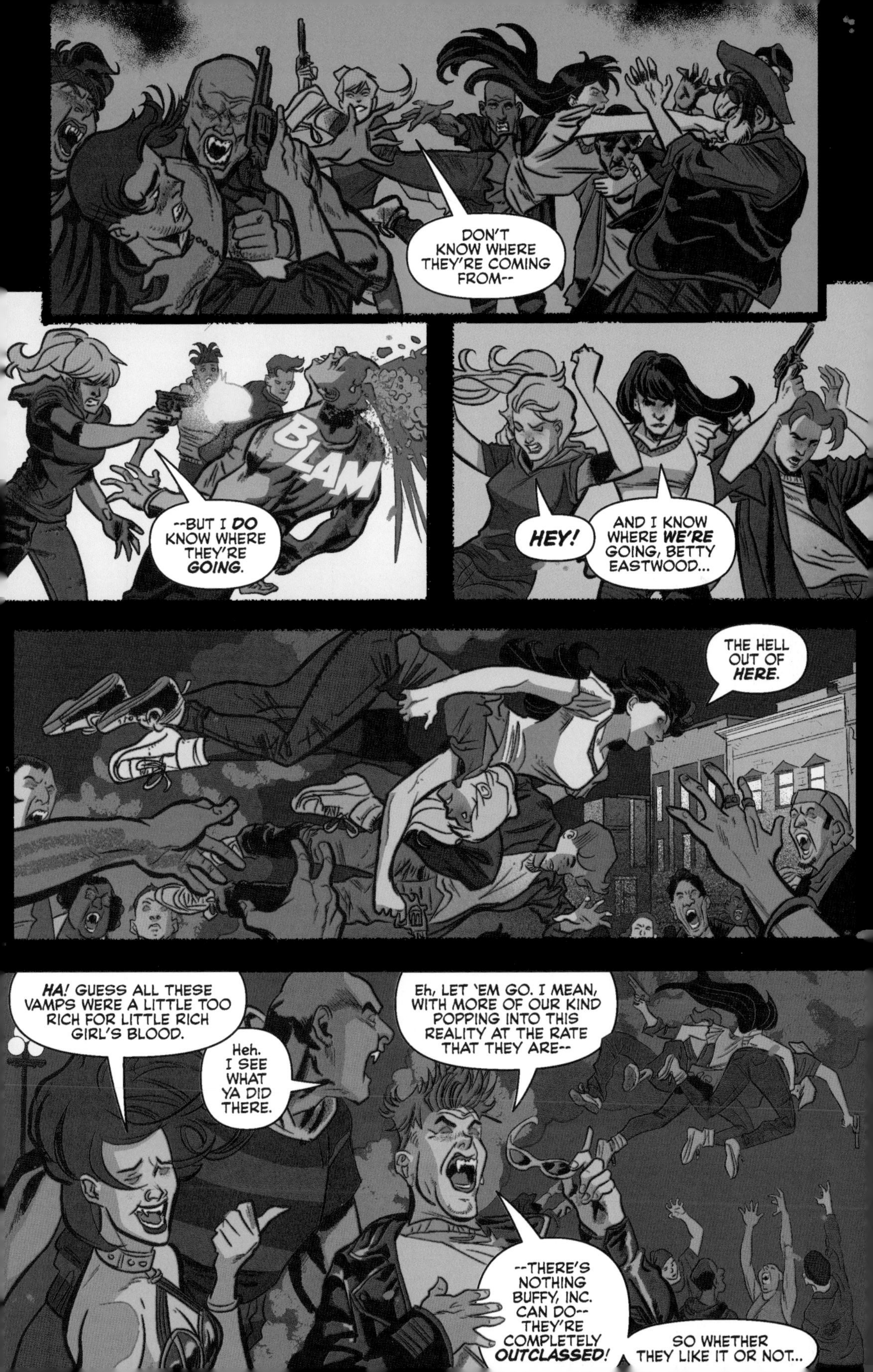
DON'T KNOW WHERE THEY'RE COMING FROM--
BLAM
--BUT I **DO** KNOW WHERE THEY'RE **GOING**.
HEY!
AND I KNOW WHERE **WE'RE** GOING, BETTY EASTWOOD...
THE HELL OUT OF **HERE**.
HA! GUESS ALL THESE VAMPS WERE A LITTLE TOO RICH FOR LITTLE RICH GIRL'S BLOOD.
Heh. I SEE WHAT YA DID THERE.
Eh, LET 'EM GO. I MEAN, WITH MORE OF OUR KIND POPPING INTO THIS REALITY AT THE RATE THAT THEY ARE--
--THERE'S NOTHING BUFFY, INC. CAN DO-- THEY'RE COMPLETELY **OUTCLASSED!**
SO WHETHER THEY LIKE IT OR NOT...

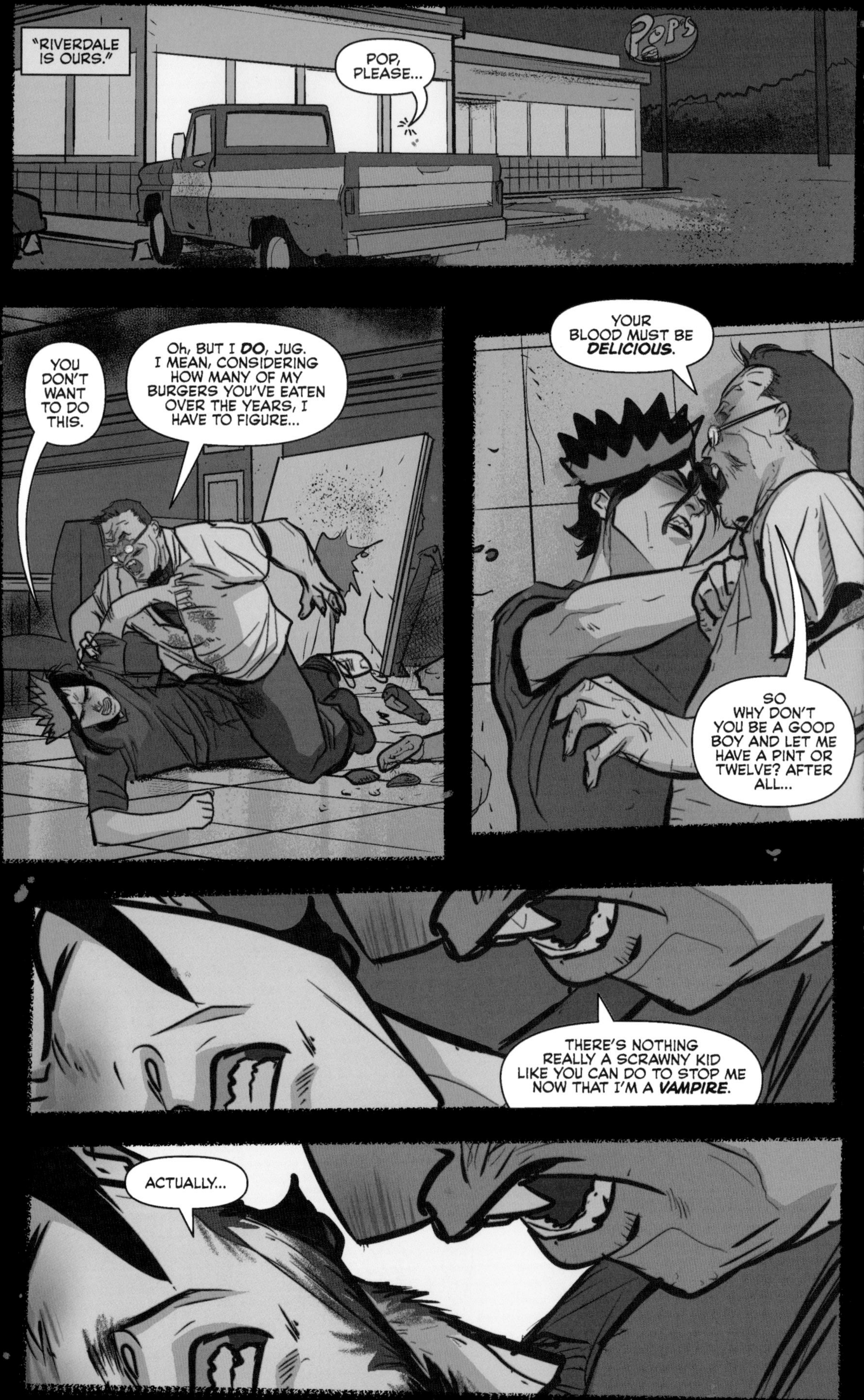
"RIVERDALE IS OURS."
POP, PLEASE...
YOU DON'T WANT TO DO THIS.
Oh, BUT I **DO**, JUG. I MEAN, CONSIDERING HOW MANY OF MY BURGERS YOU'VE EATEN OVER THE YEARS, I HAVE TO FIGURE...
YOUR BLOOD MUST BE **DELICIOUS**.
SO WHY DON'T YOU BE A GOOD BOY AND LET ME HAVE A PINT OR TWELVE? AFTER ALL...
THERE'S NOTHING REALLY A SCRAWNY KID LIKE YOU CAN DO TO STOP ME NOW THAT I'M A ***VAMPIRE***.
ACTUALLY...

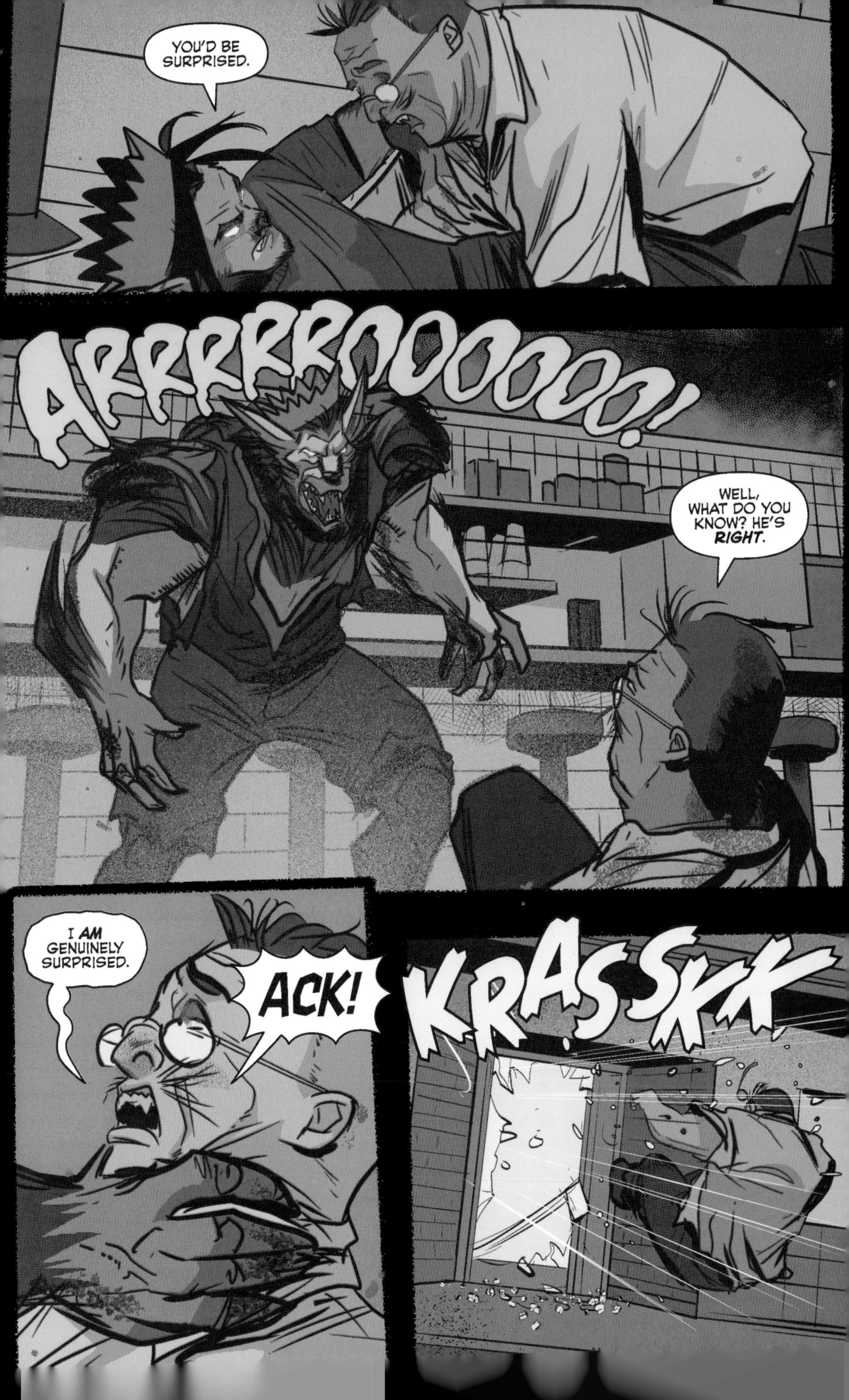
YOU'D BE SURPRISED.
ARRRRROOOOOO!
WELL, WHAT DO YOU KNOW? HE'S RIGHT.
I AM GENUINELY SURPRISED.
ACK!
KRASSKK

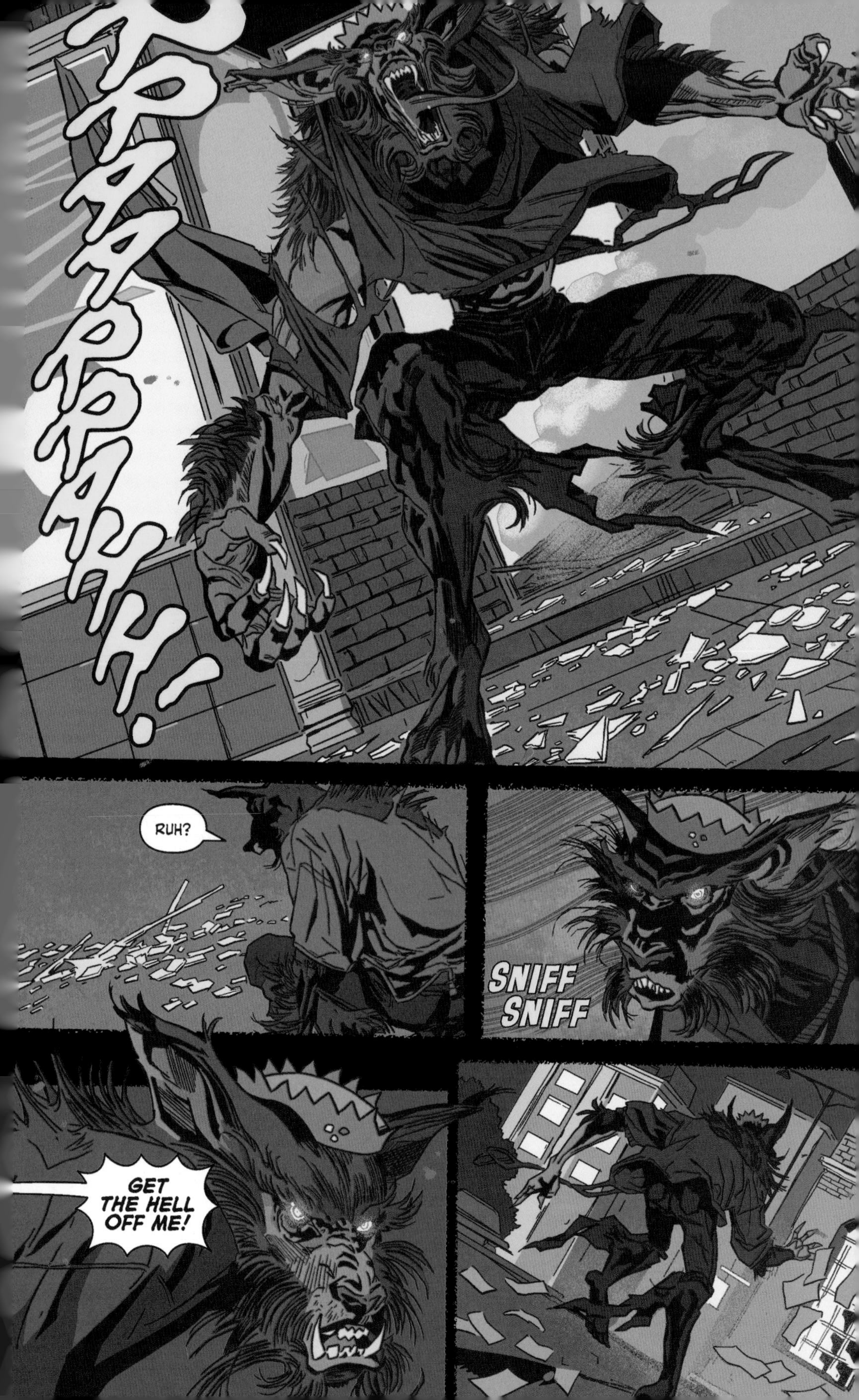
RRRAAAAAH!
RUH?
SNIFF
SNIFF
GET THE HELL OFF ME!

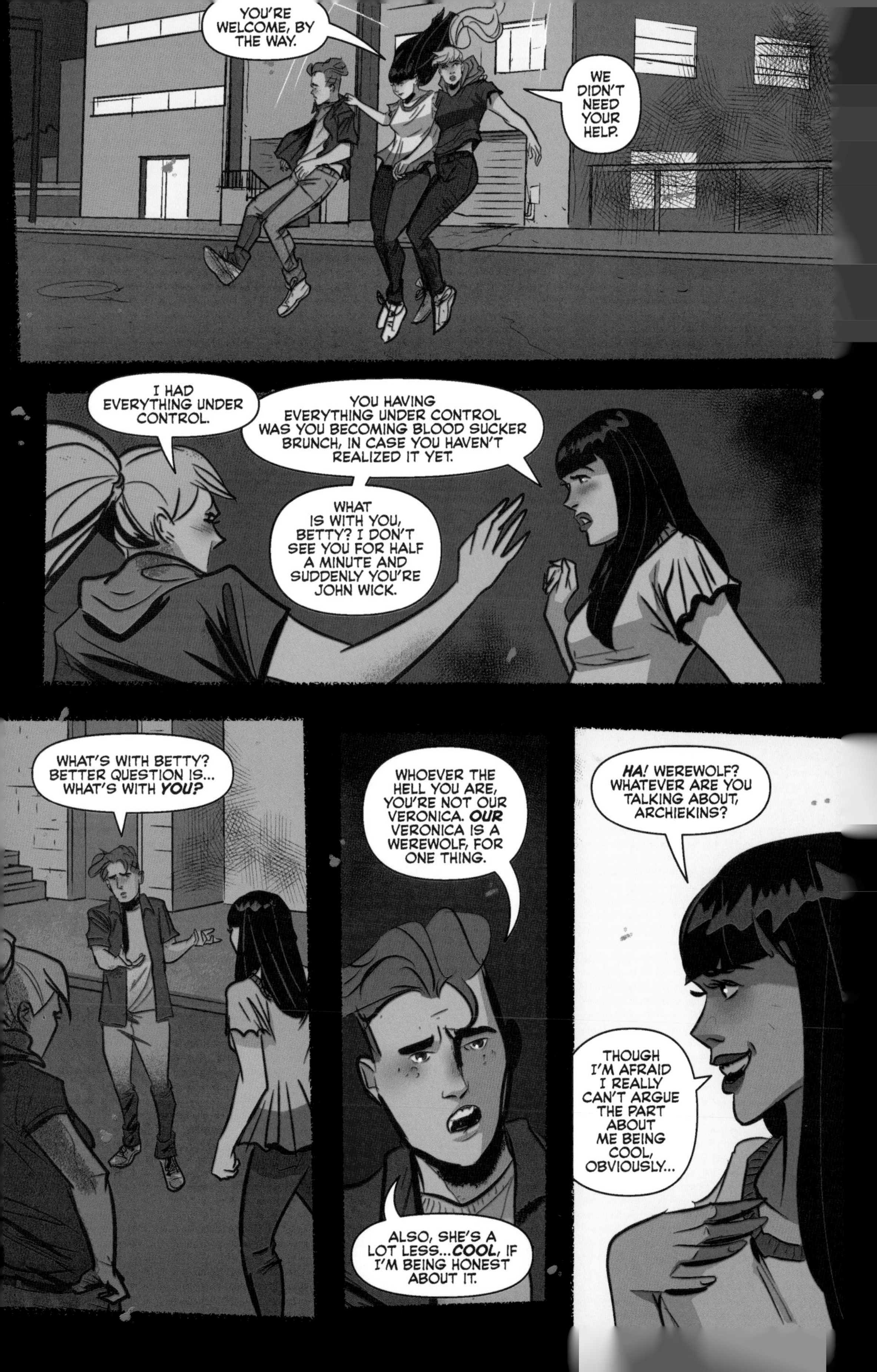
YOU'RE WELCOME, BY THE WAY.
WE DIDN'T NEED YOUR HELP.
I HAD EVERYTHING UNDER CONTROL.
YOU HAVING EVERYTHING UNDER CONTROL WAS YOU BECOMING BLOOD SUCKER BRUNCH, IN CASE YOU HAVEN'T REALIZED IT YET.
WHAT IS WITH YOU, BETTY? I DON'T SEE YOU FOR HALF A MINUTE AND SUDDENLY YOU'RE JOHN WICK.
WHAT'S WITH BETTY? BETTER QUESTION IS... WHAT'S WITH *YOU?*
WHOEVER THE HELL YOU ARE, YOU'RE NOT OUR VERONICA. ***OUR*** VERONICA IS A WEREWOLF, FOR ONE THING.
ALSO, SHE'S A LOT LESS...***COOL***, IF I'M BEING HONEST ABOUT IT.
HA! WEREWOLF? WHATEVER ARE YOU TALKING ABOUT, ARCHIEKINS?
THOUGH I'M AFRAID I REALLY CAN'T ARGUE THE PART ABOUT ME BEING COOL, OBVIOUSLY...

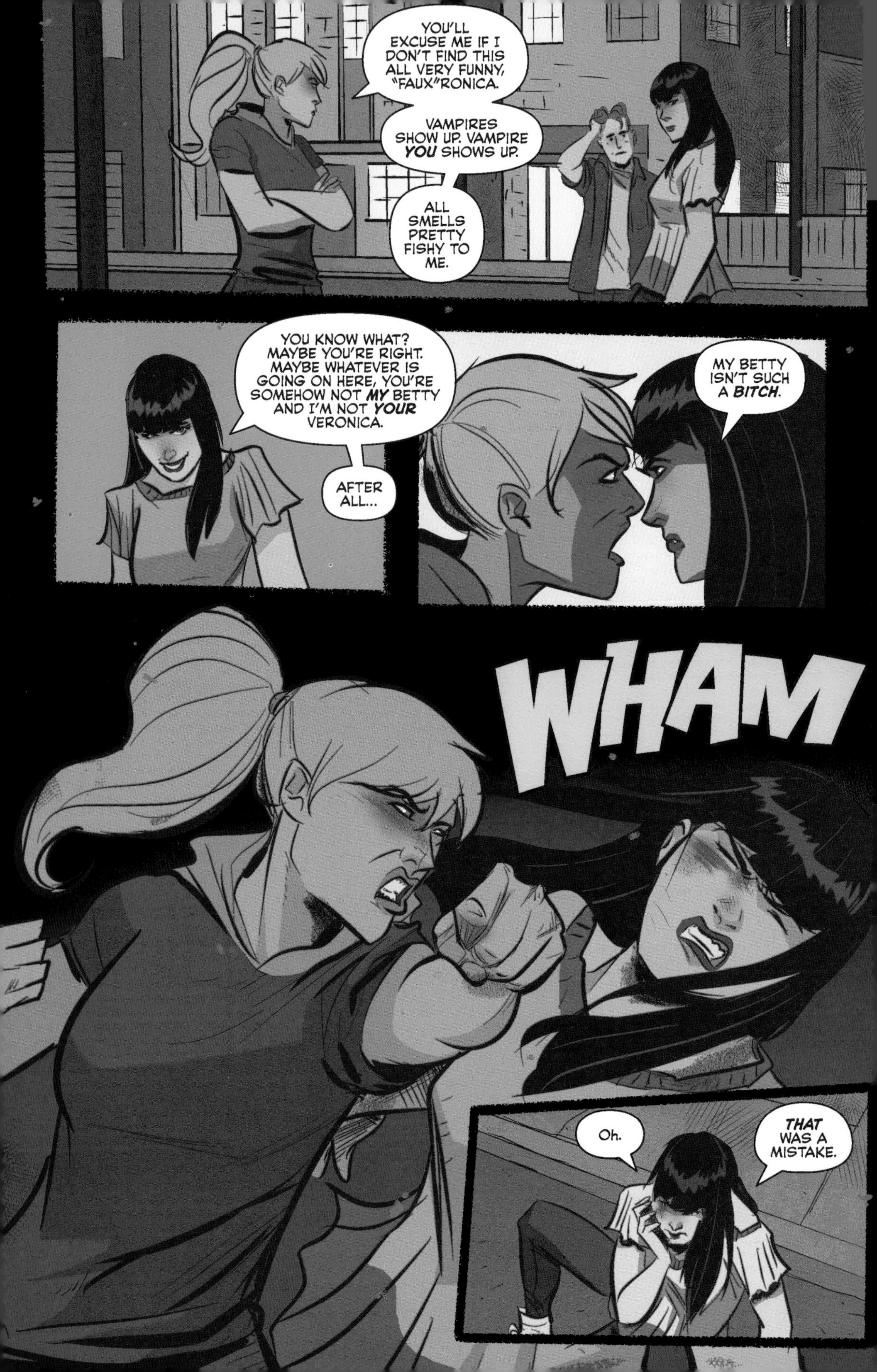
YOU'LL EXCUSE ME IF I DON'T FIND THIS ALL VERY FUNNY, "FAUX"RONICA.
VAMPIRES SHOW UP. VAMPIRE *YOU* SHOWS UP.
ALL SMELLS PRETTY FISHY TO ME.
YOU KNOW WHAT? MAYBE YOU'RE RIGHT. MAYBE WHATEVER IS GOING ON HERE, YOU'RE SOMEHOW NOT *MY* BETTY AND I'M NOT *YOUR* VERONICA.
AFTER ALL...
MY BETTY ISN'T SUCH A *BITCH*.
WHAM
Oh.
THAT WAS A MISTAKE.

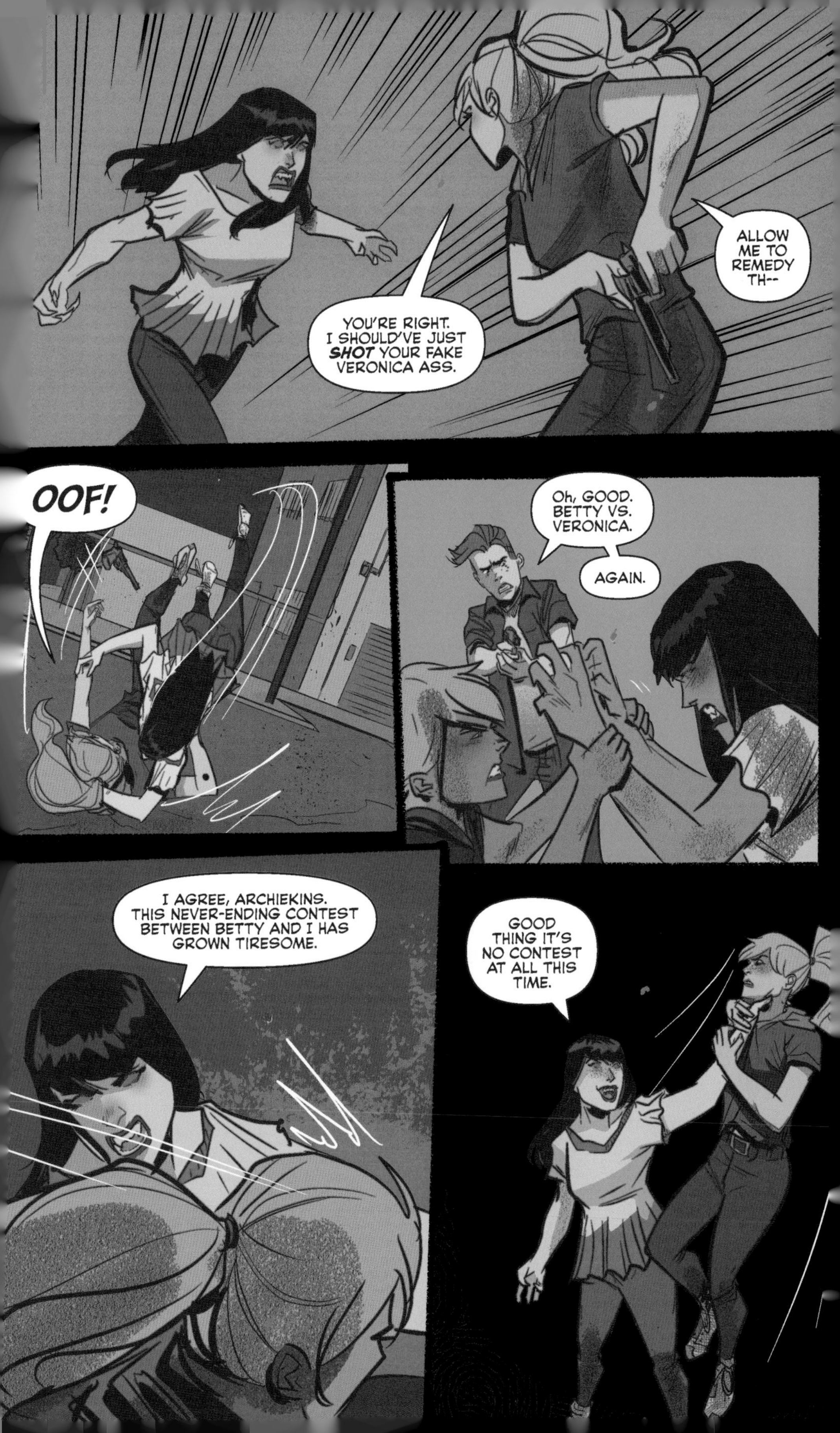
YOU'RE RIGHT. I SHOULD'VE JUST SHOT YOUR FAKE VERONICA ASS.
ALLOW ME TO REMEDY TH--
OOF!
Oh, GOOD. BETTY VS. VERONICA.
AGAIN.
I AGREE, ARCHIEKINS. THIS NEVER-ENDING CONTEST BETWEEN BETTY AND I HAS GROWN TIRESOME.
GOOD THING IT'S NO CONTEST AT ALL THIS TIME.

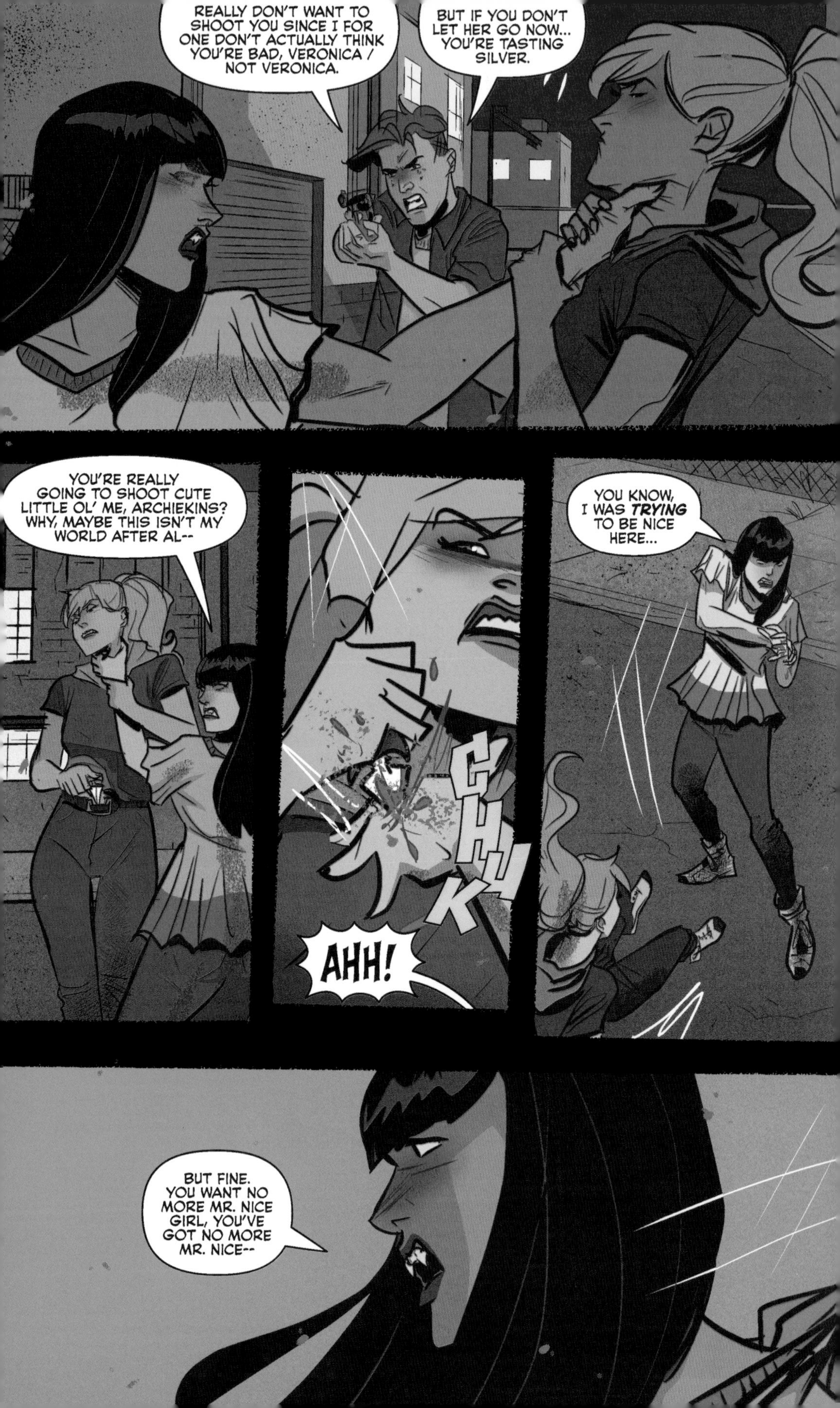
REALLY DON'T WANT TO SHOOT YOU SINCE I FOR ONE DON'T ACTUALLY THINK YOU'RE BAD, VERONICA / NOT VERONICA.
BUT IF YOU DON'T LET HER GO NOW... YOU'RE TASTING SILVER.
YOU'RE REALLY GOING TO SHOOT CUTE LITTLE OL' ME, ARCHIEKINS? WHY, MAYBE THIS ISN'T MY WORLD AFTER AL--
CHHUK
AHH!
YOU KNOW, I WAS *TRYING* TO BE NICE HERE...
BUT FINE. YOU WANT NO MORE MR. NICE GIRL, YOU'VE GOT NO MORE MR. NICE--

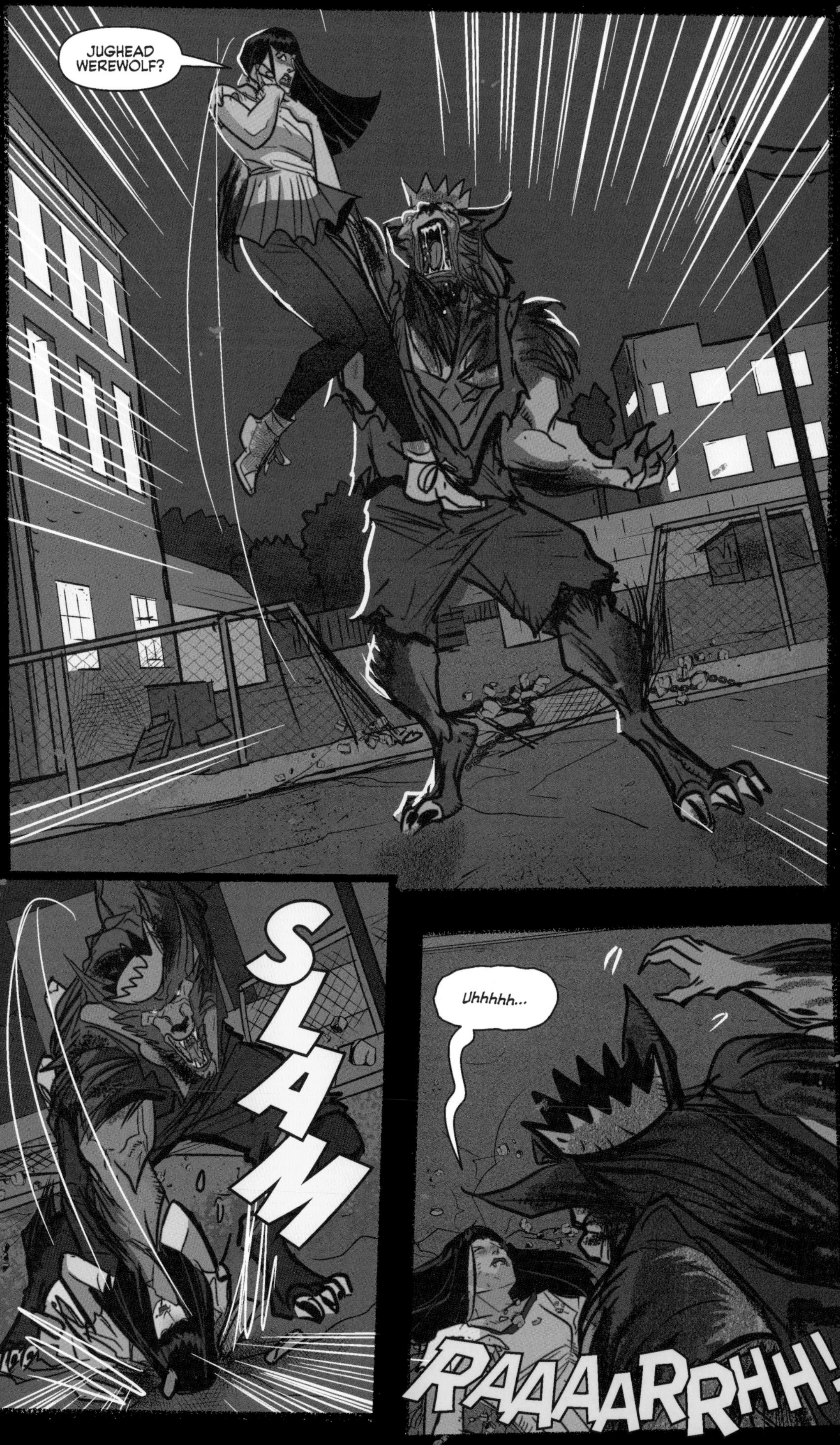
JUGHEAD WEREWOLF?
SLAM
Uhhhhh...
RAAAARRHH!

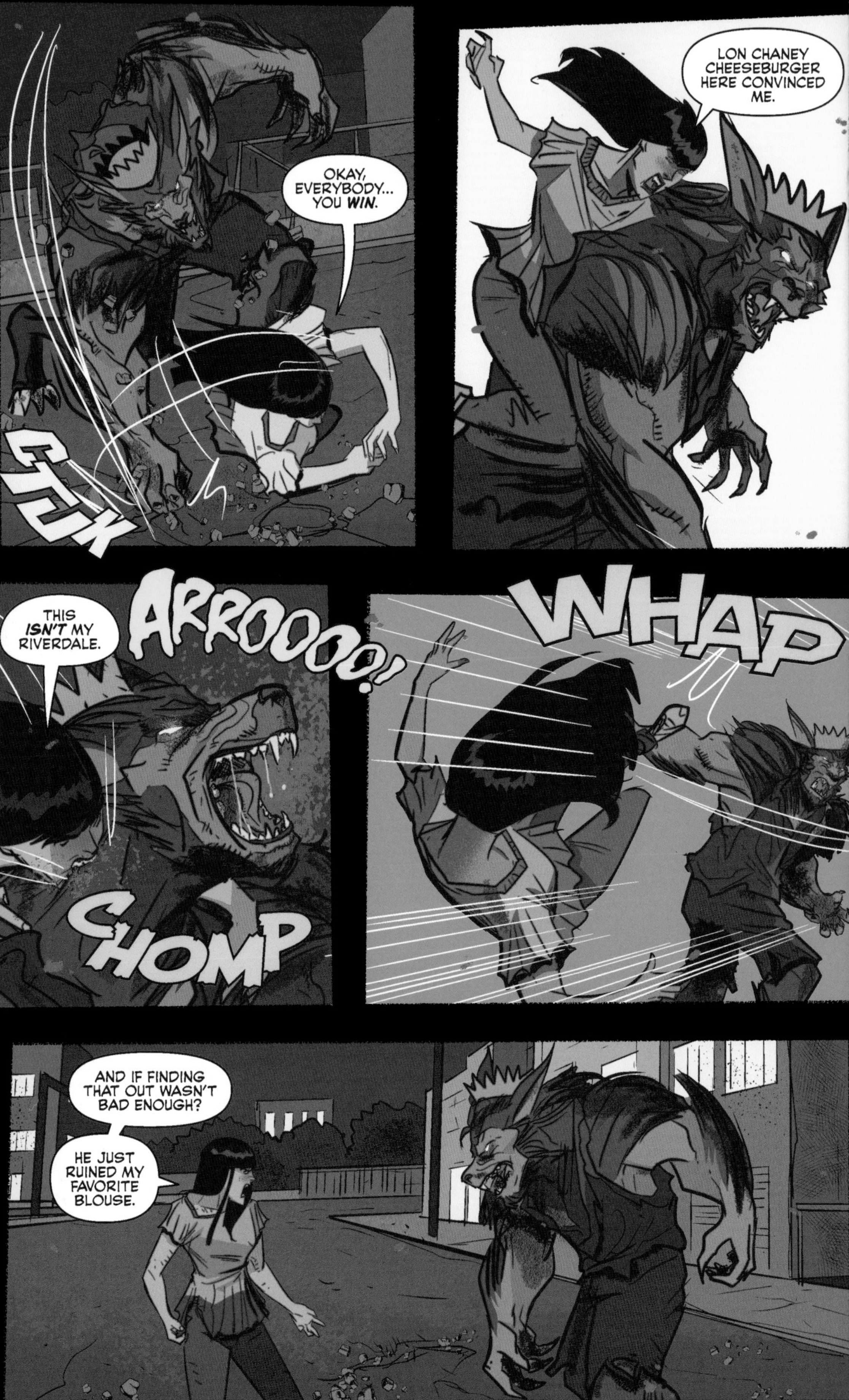
OKAY, EVERYBODY... YOU WIN.
CTJK
LON CHANEY CHEESEBURGER HERE CONVINCED ME.
THIS ISN'T MY RIVERDALE.
ARROOOO!!
CHOMP
WHAP
AND IF FINDING THAT OUT WASN'T BAD ENOUGH?
HE JUST RUINED MY FAVORITE BLOUSE.

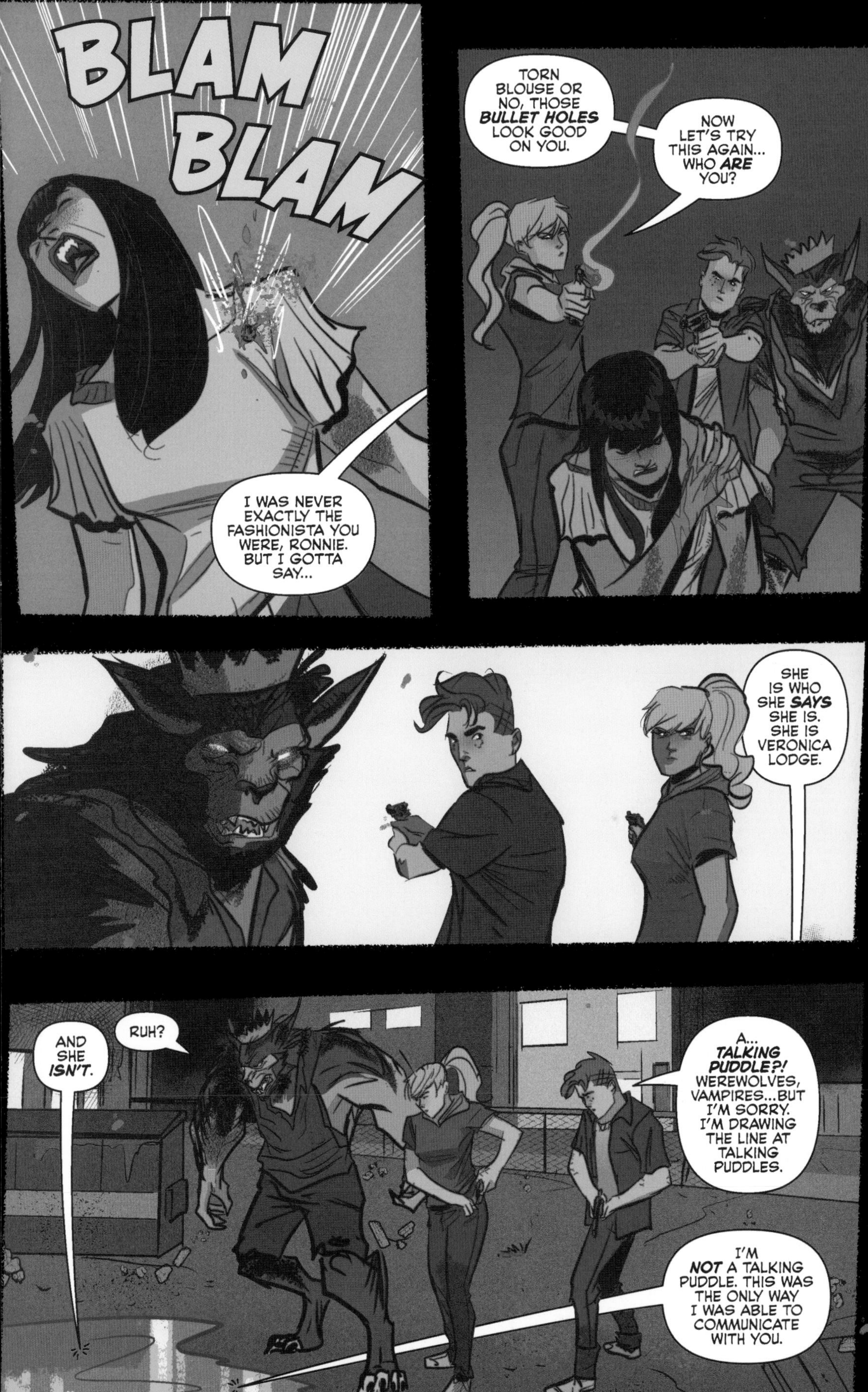
BLAM BLAM
I WAS NEVER EXACTLY THE FASHIONISTA YOU WERE, RONNIE. BUT I GOTTA SAY...
TORN BLOUSE OR NO, THOSE BULLET HOLES LOOK GOOD ON YOU.
NOW LET'S TRY THIS AGAIN... WHO ARE YOU?
SHE IS WHO SHE SAYS SHE IS. SHE IS VERONICA LODGE.
AND SHE ISN'T.
RUH?
A... TALKING PUDDLE?! WEREWOLVES, VAMPIRES...BUT I'M SORRY. I'M DRAWING THE LINE AT TALKING PUDDLES.
I'M NOT A TALKING PUDDLE. THIS WAS THE ONLY WAY I WAS ABLE TO COMMUNICATE WITH YOU.

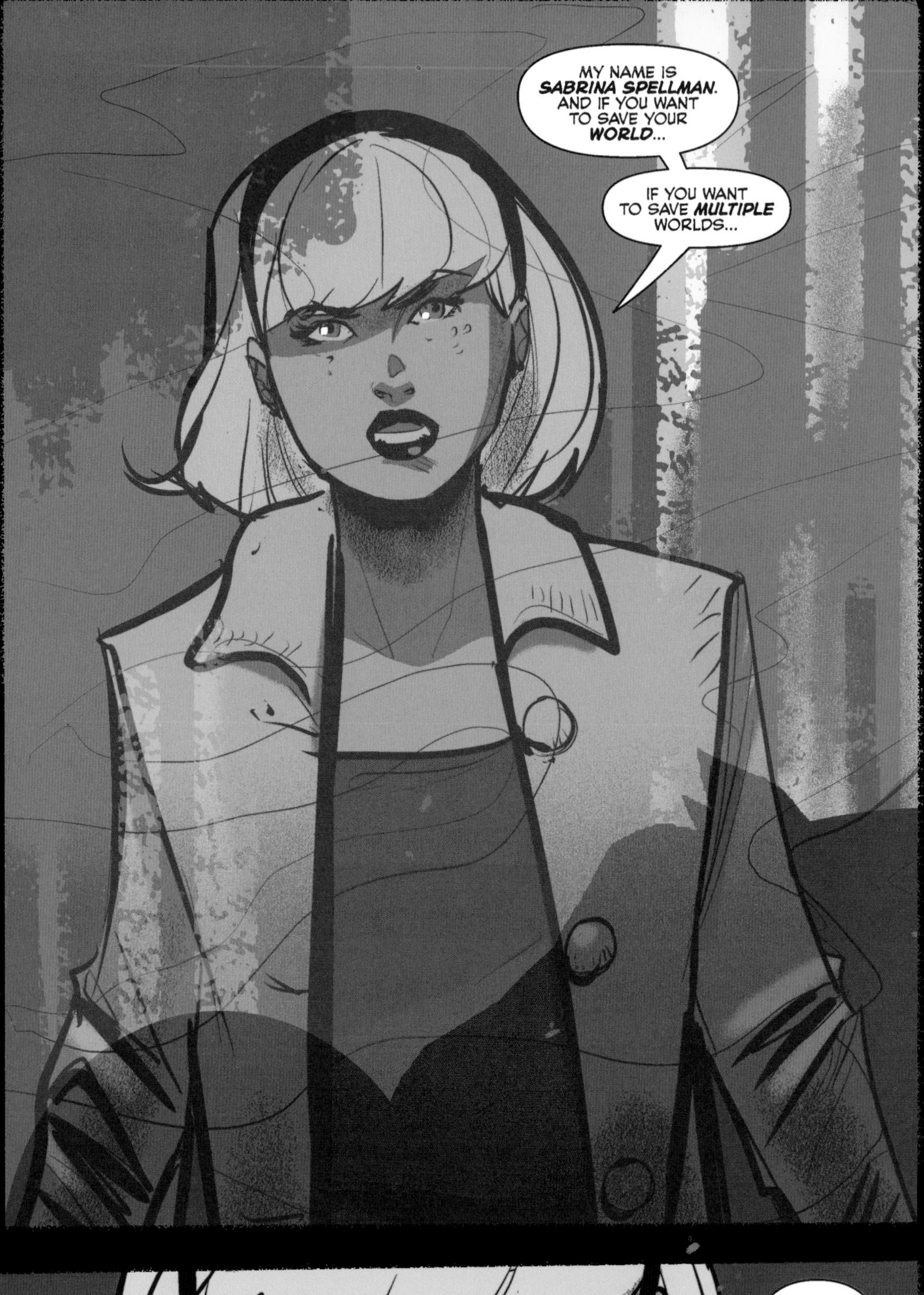
MY NAME IS SABRINA SPELLMAN. AND IF YOU WANT TO SAVE YOUR WORLD...
IF YOU WANT TO SAVE MULTIPLE WORLDS...

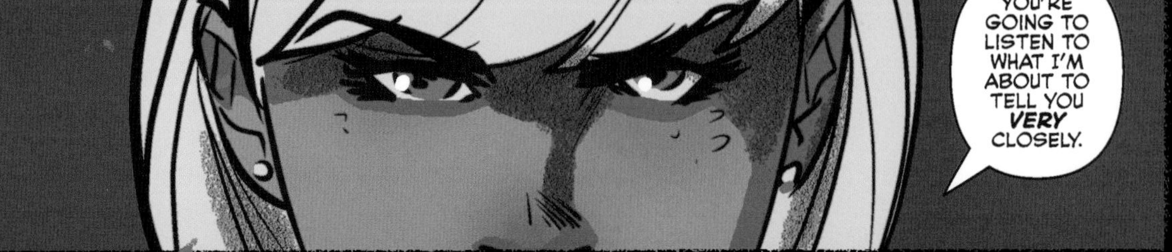
YOU'RE GOING TO LISTEN TO WHAT I'M ABOUT TO TELL YOU VERY CLOSELY.

CHAPTER FOUR

COVER ART BY **PAT & TIM KENNEDY**
WITH **BOB SMITH** AND **MATT HERMS**

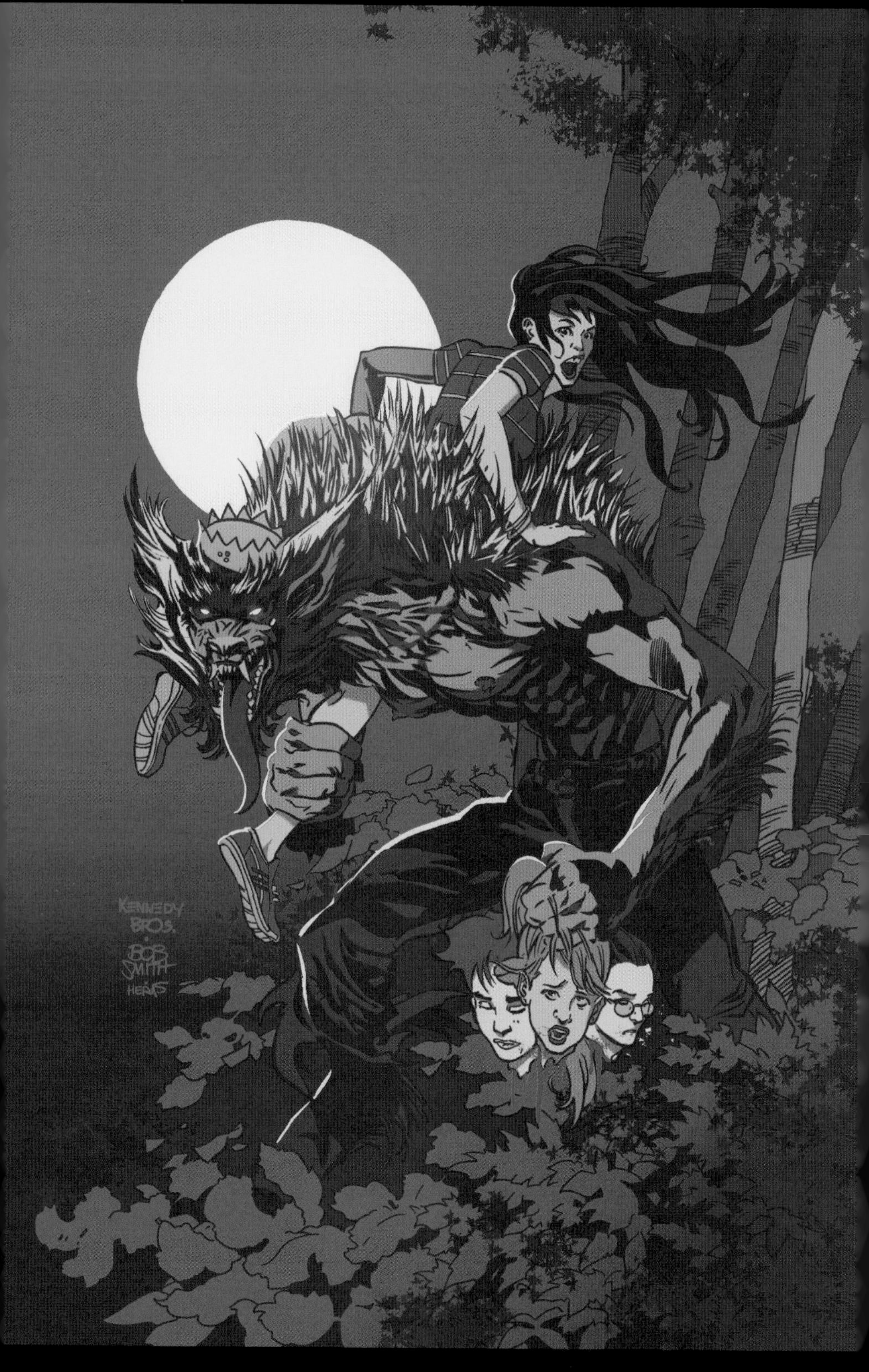

STORY BY **FRANK TIERI**
ART BY **PAT & TIM KENNEDY** (p.1-15) **JOE EISMA** (p.16-20)
INKS BY **BOB SMITH** (p.1-10,12-14) **JOE EISMA** (p.11,15)
COLORING BY **LEE LOUGHRIDGE** LETTERING BY **JACK MORELLI**

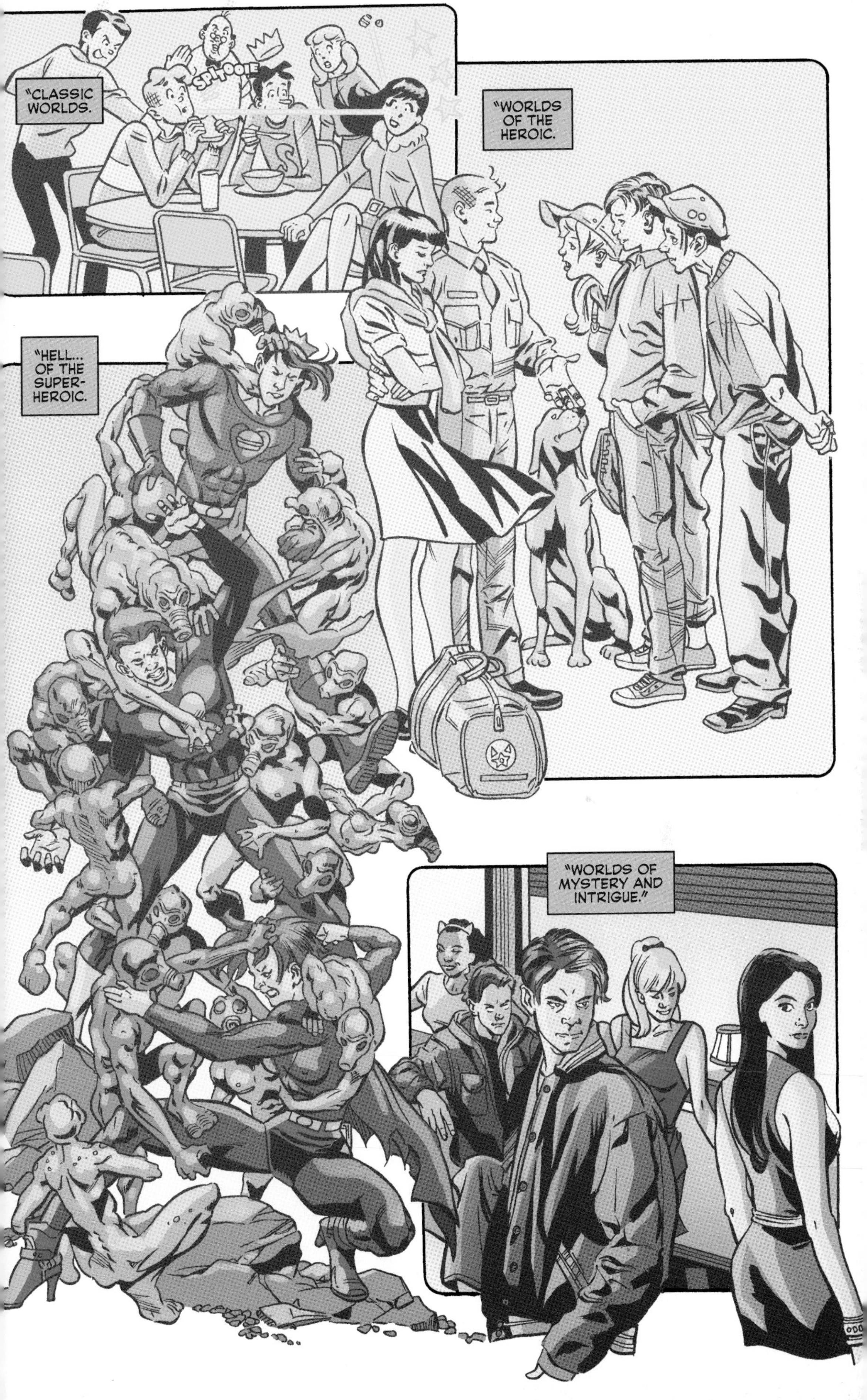
"CLASSIC WORLDS.
SPLOOIE
"WORLDS OF THE HEROIC.
"HELL... OF THE SUPER-HEROIC.
"WORLDS OF MYSTERY AND INTRIGUE."

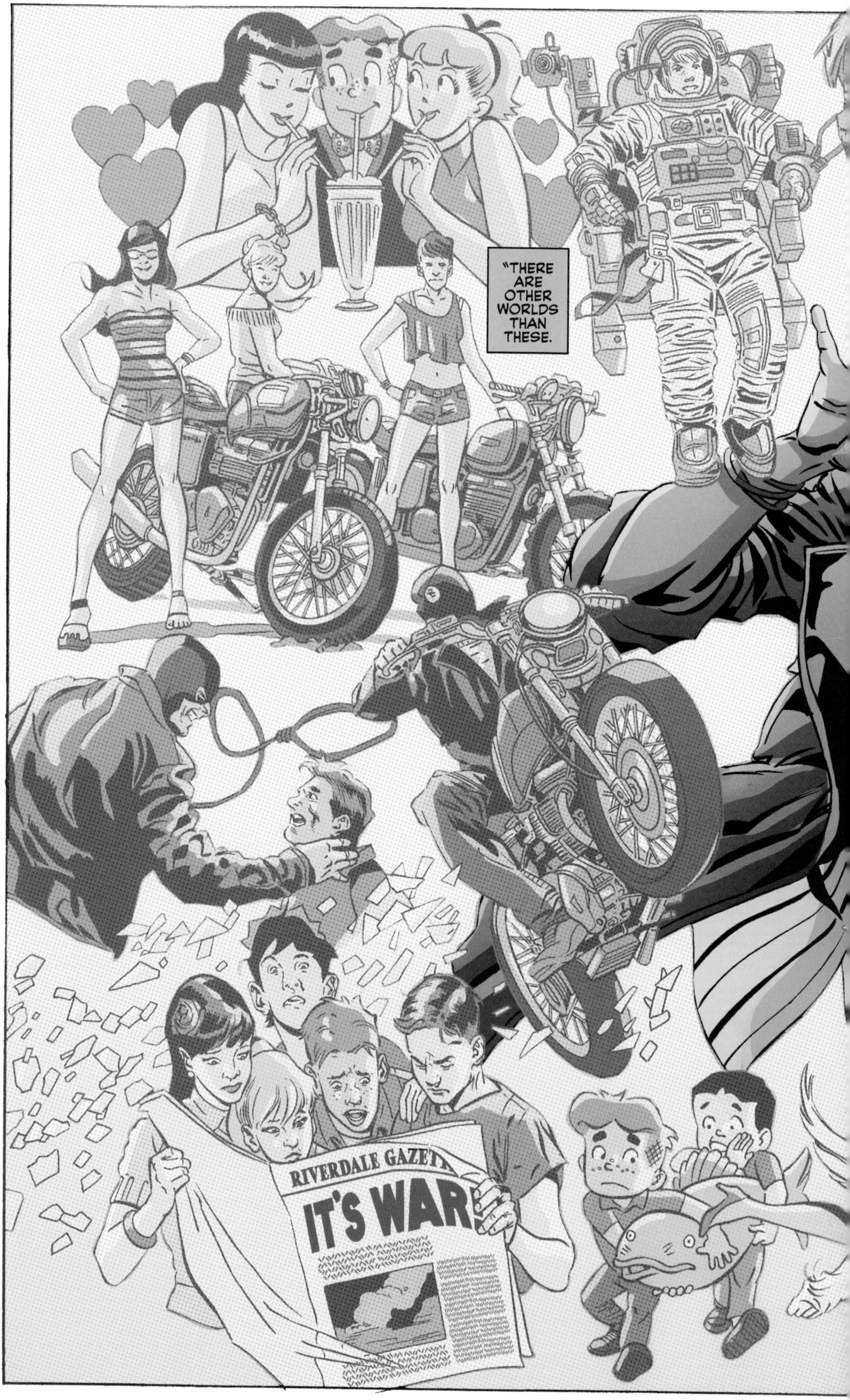
"THERE ARE OTHER WORLDS THAN THESE.
RIVERDALE GAZETT
IT'S WAR

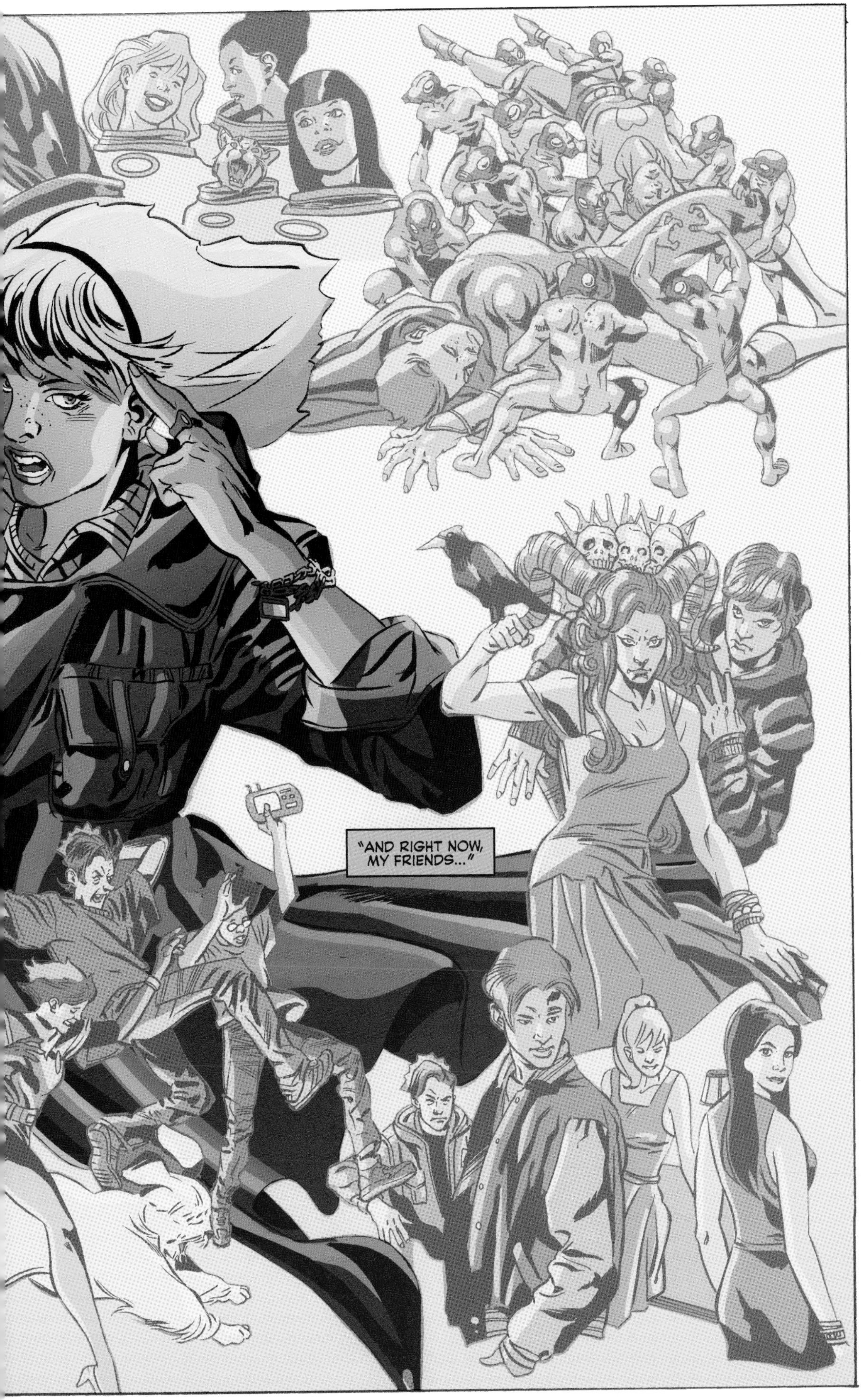
"AND RIGHT NOW, MY FRIENDS..."

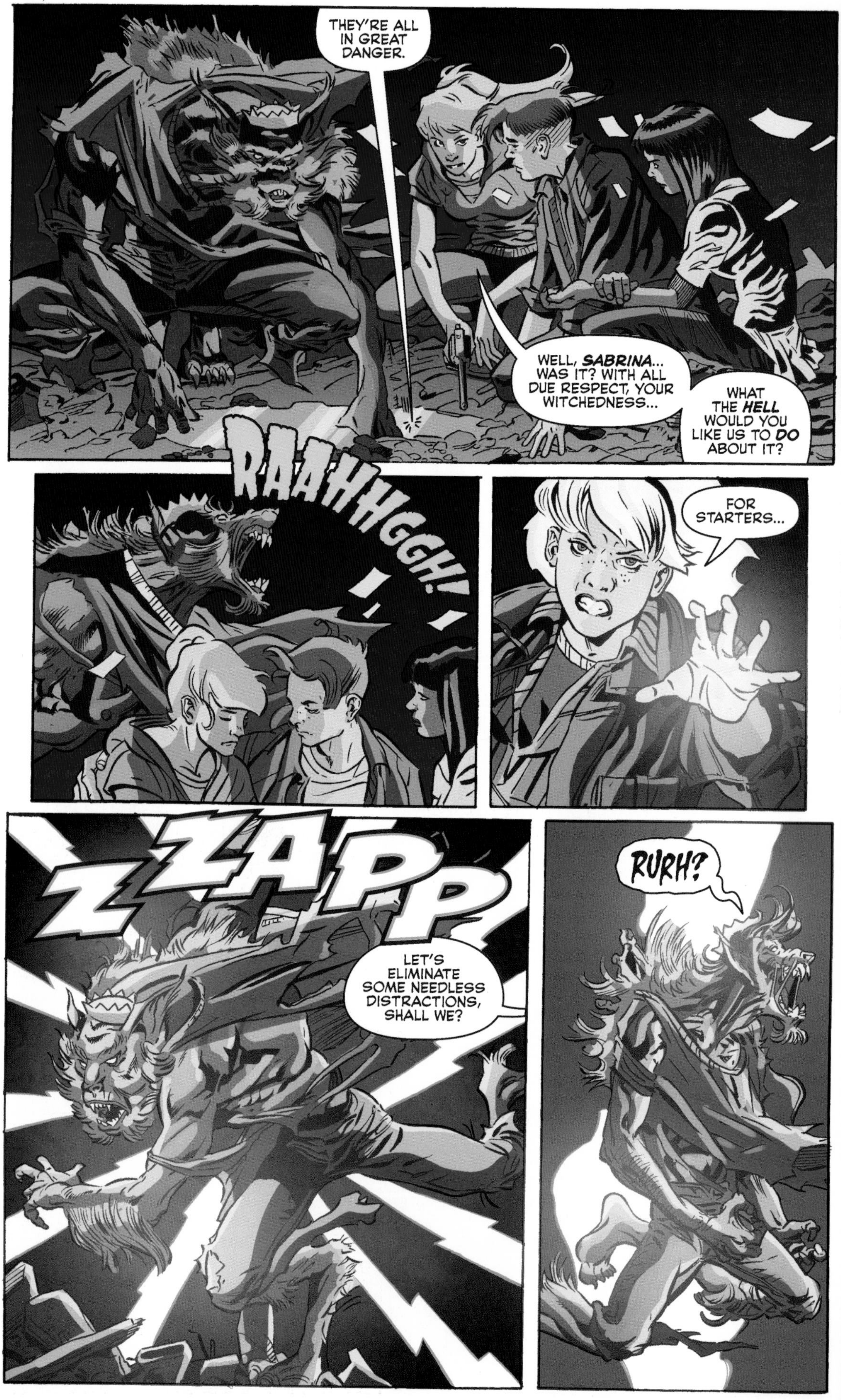
THEY'RE ALL IN GREAT DANGER.
WELL, SABRINA... WAS IT? WITH ALL DUE RESPECT, YOUR WITCHEDNESS...
WHAT THE HELL WOULD YOU LIKE US TO DO ABOUT IT?
RAAHHGGH!
FOR STARTERS...
ZZAPP
LET'S ELIMINATE SOME NEEDLESS DISTRACTIONS, SHALL WE?
RURH?

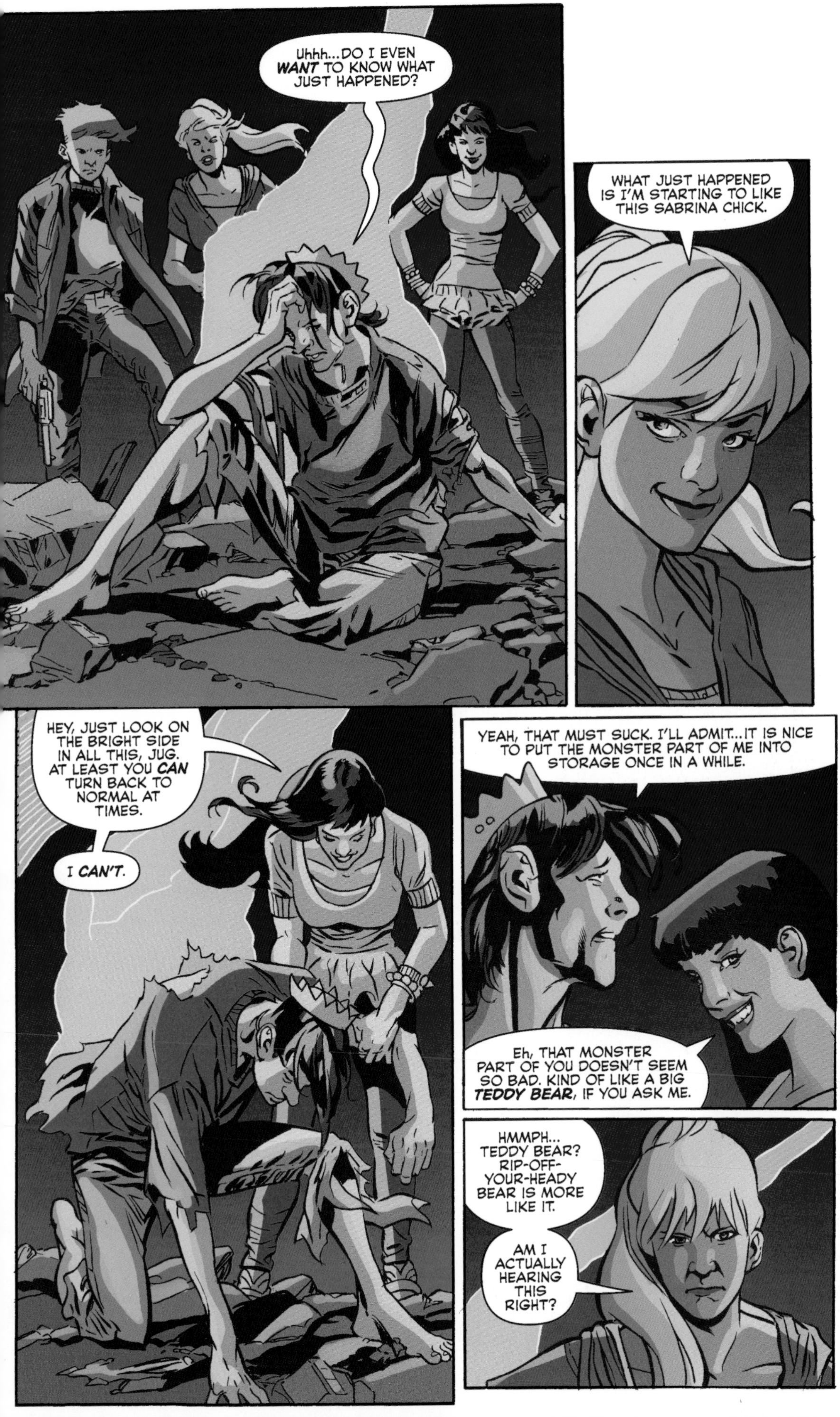
Uhhh...DO I EVEN WANT TO KNOW WHAT JUST HAPPENED?
WHAT JUST HAPPENED IS I'M STARTING TO LIKE THIS SABRINA CHICK.
HEY, JUST LOOK ON THE BRIGHT SIDE IN ALL THIS, JUG. AT LEAST YOU CAN TURN BACK TO NORMAL AT TIMES.
I CAN'T.
YEAH, THAT MUST SUCK. I'LL ADMIT...IT IS NICE TO PUT THE MONSTER PART OF ME INTO STORAGE ONCE IN A WHILE.
Eh, THAT MONSTER PART OF YOU DOESN'T SEEM SO BAD. KIND OF LIKE A BIG TEDDY BEAR, IF YOU ASK ME.
HMMPH... TEDDY BEAR? RIP-OFF-YOUR-HEADY BEAR IS MORE LIKE IT.
AM I ACTUALLY HEARING THIS RIGHT?

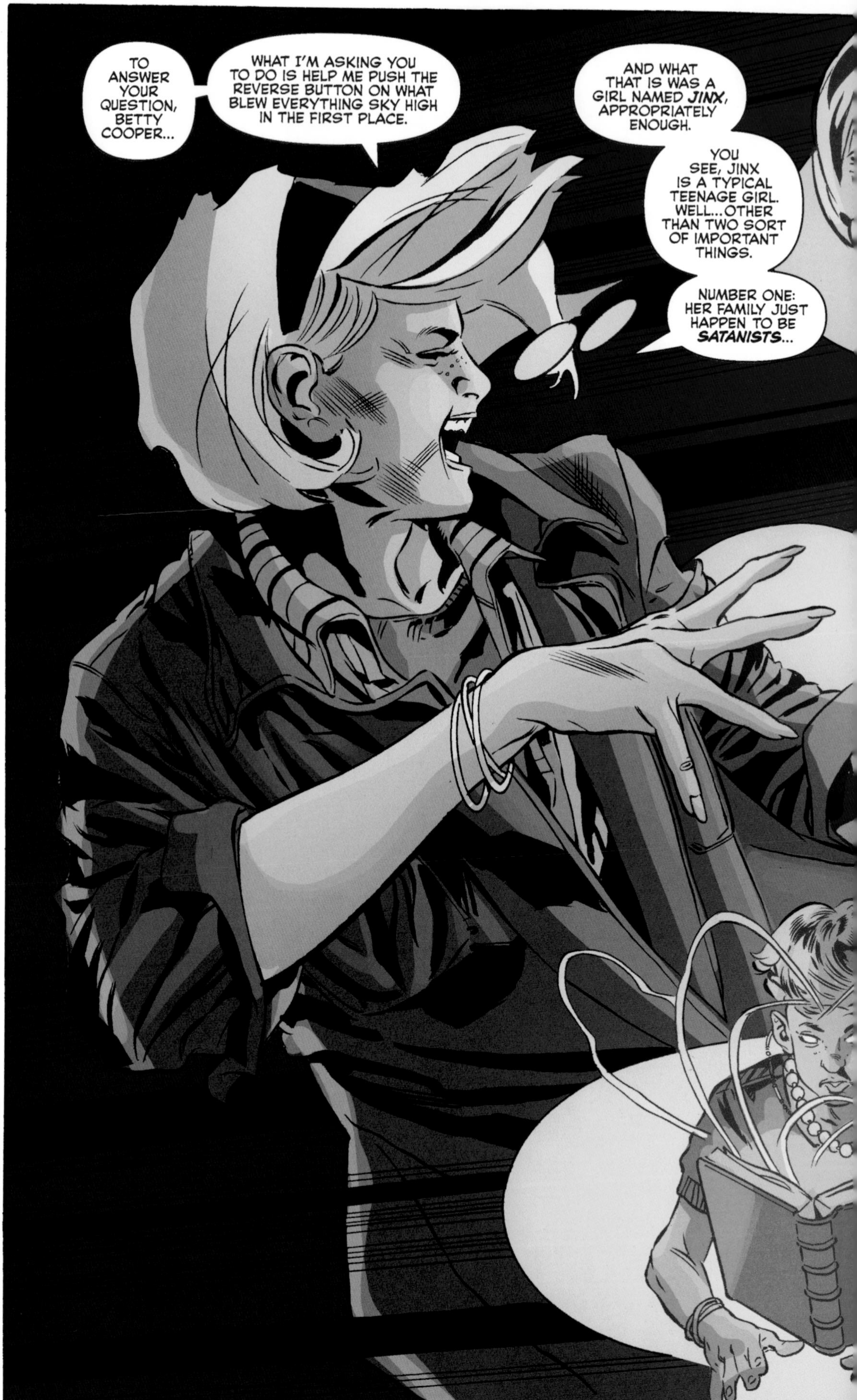
TO ANSWER YOUR QUESTION, BETTY COOPER...
WHAT I'M ASKING YOU TO DO IS HELP ME PUSH THE REVERSE BUTTON ON WHAT BLEW EVERYTHING SKY HIGH IN THE FIRST PLACE.
AND WHAT THAT IS WAS A GIRL NAMED *JINX*, APPROPRIATELY ENOUGH.
YOU SEE, JINX IS A TYPICAL TEENAGE GIRL. WELL...OTHER THAN TWO SORT OF IMPORTANT THINGS.
NUMBER ONE: HER FAMILY JUST HAPPEN TO BE ***SATANISTS***...

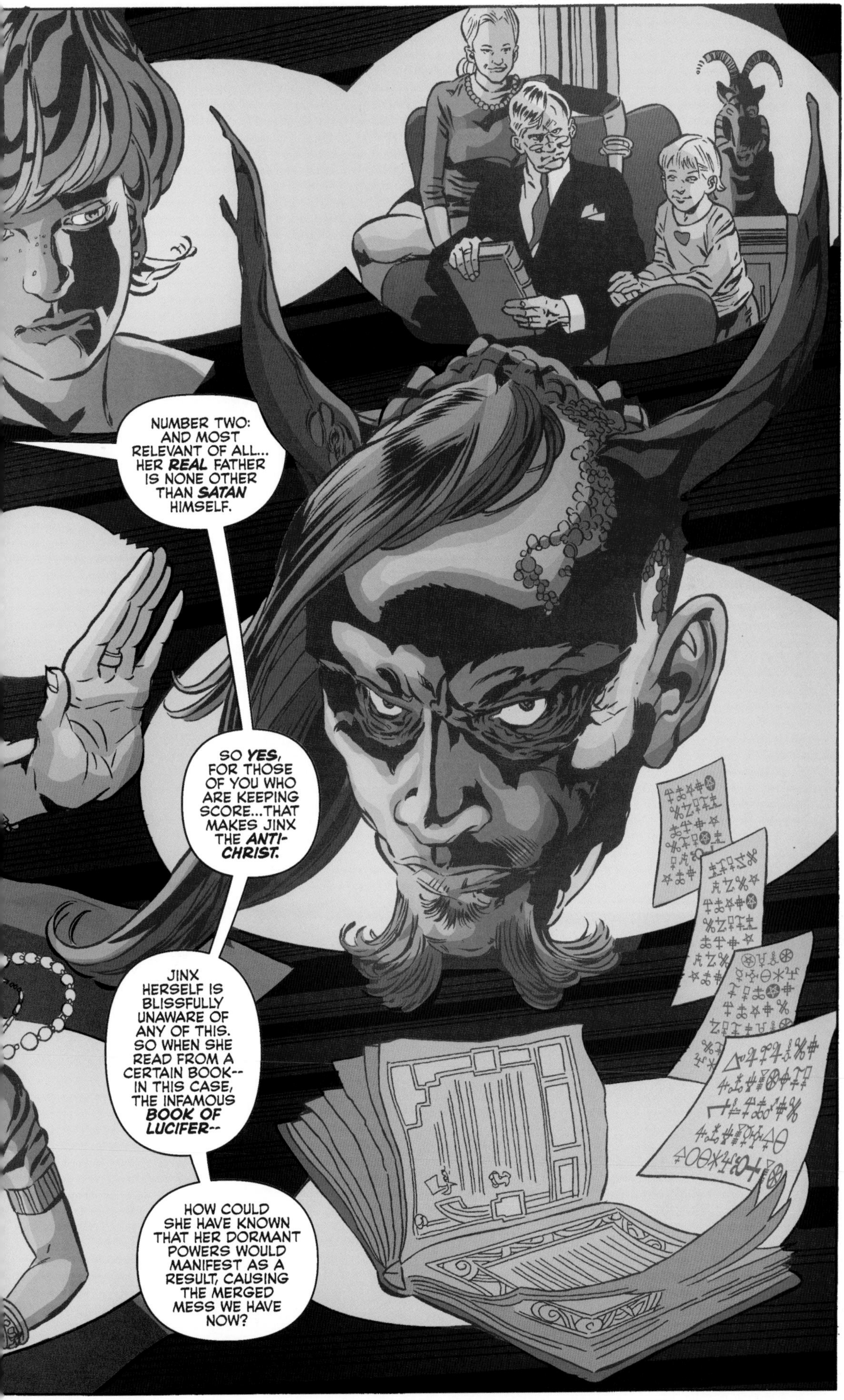

NUMBER TWO: AND MOST RELEVANT OF ALL... HER **REAL** FATHER IS NONE OTHER THAN **SATAN** HIMSELF.
SO **YES**, FOR THOSE OF YOU WHO ARE KEEPING SCORE...THAT MAKES JINX THE **ANTI-CHRIST.**
JINX HERSELF IS BLISSFULLY UNAWARE OF ANY OF THIS. SO WHEN SHE READ FROM A CERTAIN BOOK-- IN THIS CASE, THE INFAMOUS **BOOK OF LUCIFER**--
HOW COULD SHE HAVE KNOWN THAT HER DORMANT POWERS WOULD MANIFEST AS A RESULT, CAUSING THE MERGED MESS WE HAVE NOW?

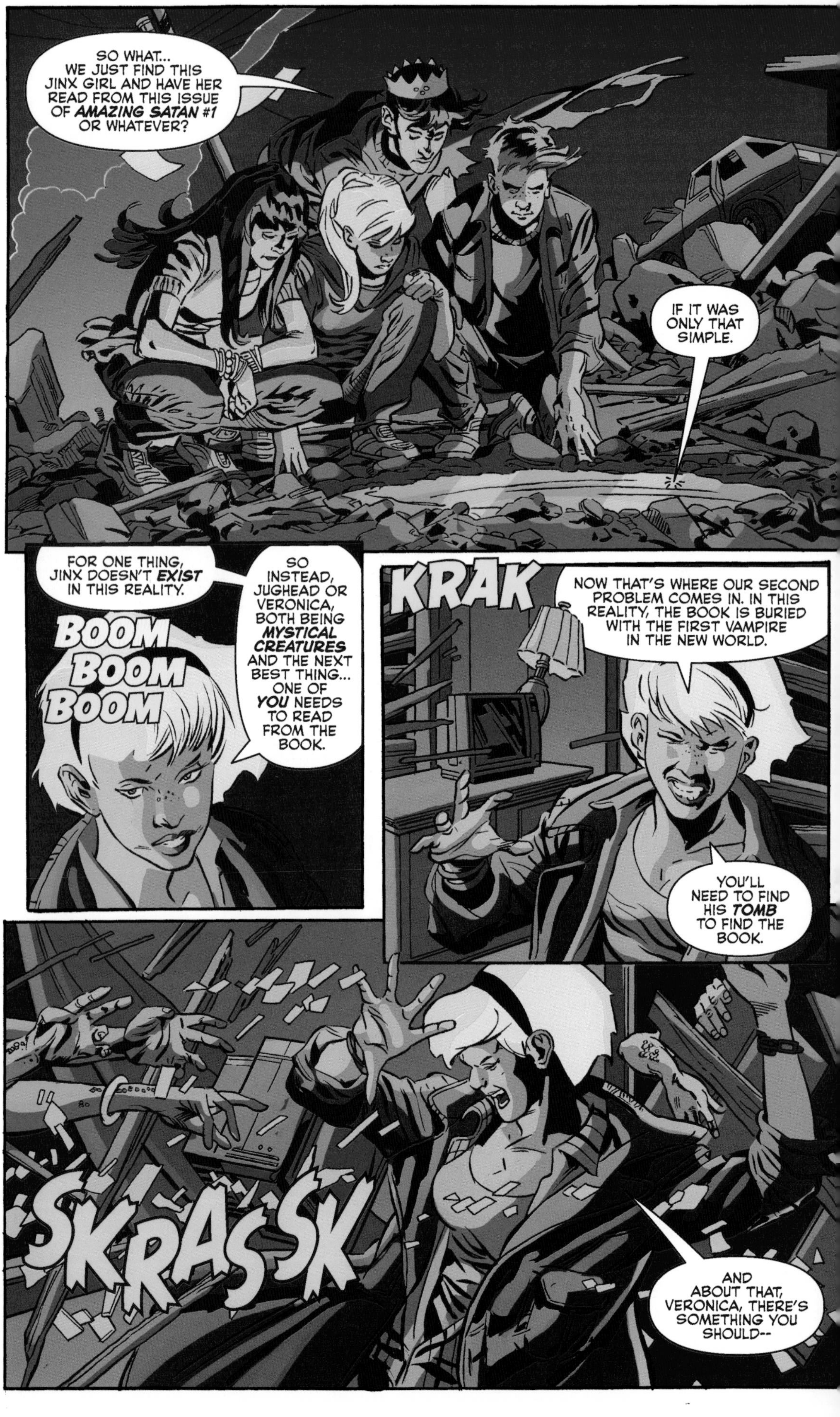

SO WHAT... WE JUST FIND THIS JINX GIRL AND HAVE HER READ FROM THIS ISSUE OF *AMAZING SATAN #1* OR WHATEVER?
IF IT WAS ONLY THAT SIMPLE.
FOR ONE THING, JINX DOESN'T *EXIST* IN THIS REALITY.
SO INSTEAD, JUGHEAD OR VERONICA, BOTH BEING *MYSTICAL CREATURES* AND THE NEXT BEST THING... ONE OF *YOU* NEEDS TO READ FROM THE BOOK.
BOOM BOOM BOOM
KRAK
NOW THAT'S WHERE OUR SECOND PROBLEM COMES IN. IN THIS REALITY, THE BOOK IS BURIED WITH THE FIRST VAMPIRE IN THE NEW WORLD.
YOU'LL NEED TO FIND HIS *TOMB* TO FIND THE BOOK.
SKRASSK
AND ABOUT THAT, VERONICA, THERE'S SOMETHING YOU SHOULD--

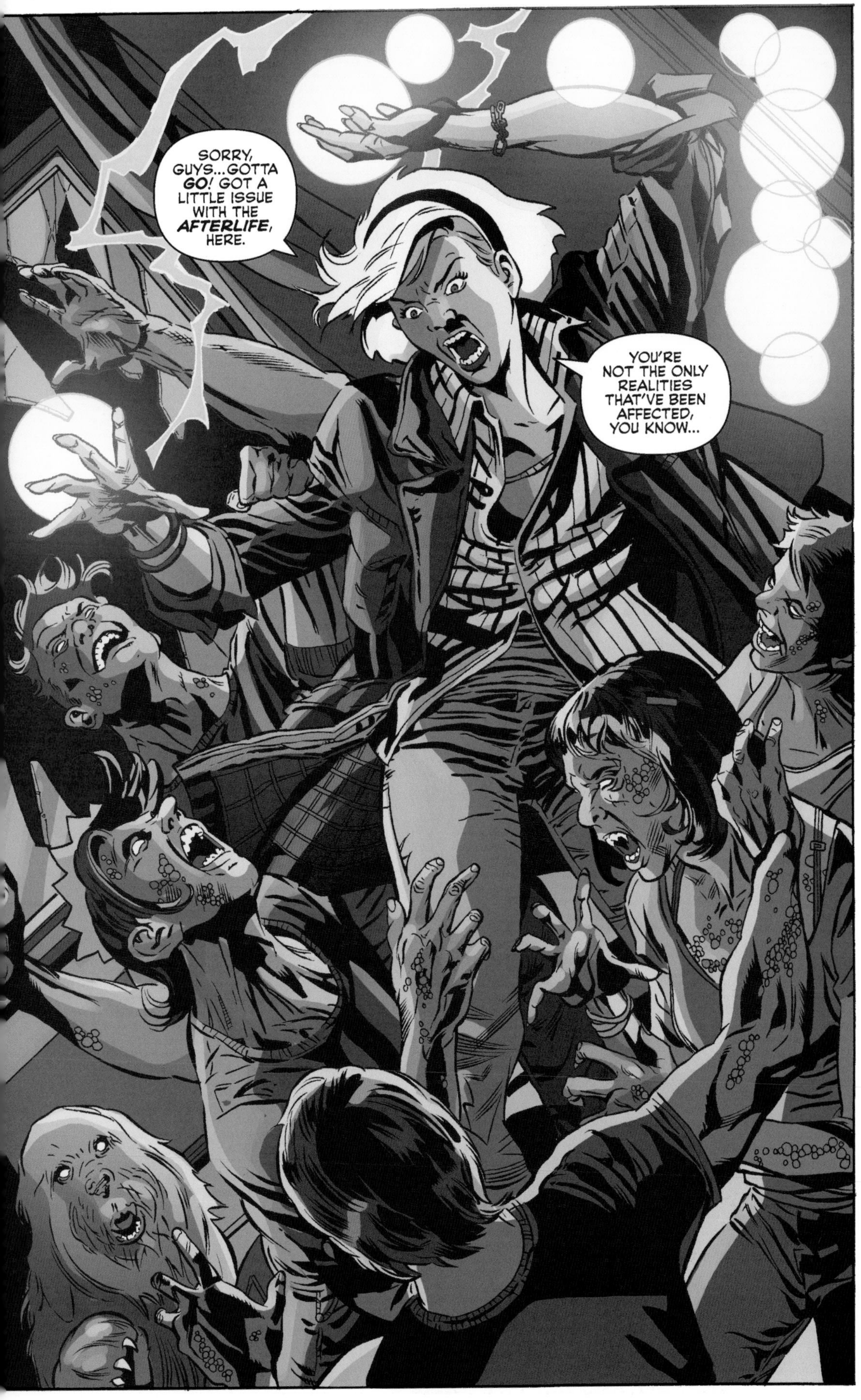
SORRY, GUYS...GOTTA GO! GOT A LITTLE ISSUE WITH THE AFTERLIFE, HERE.
YOU'RE NOT THE ONLY REALITIES THAT'VE BEEN AFFECTED, YOU KNOW...

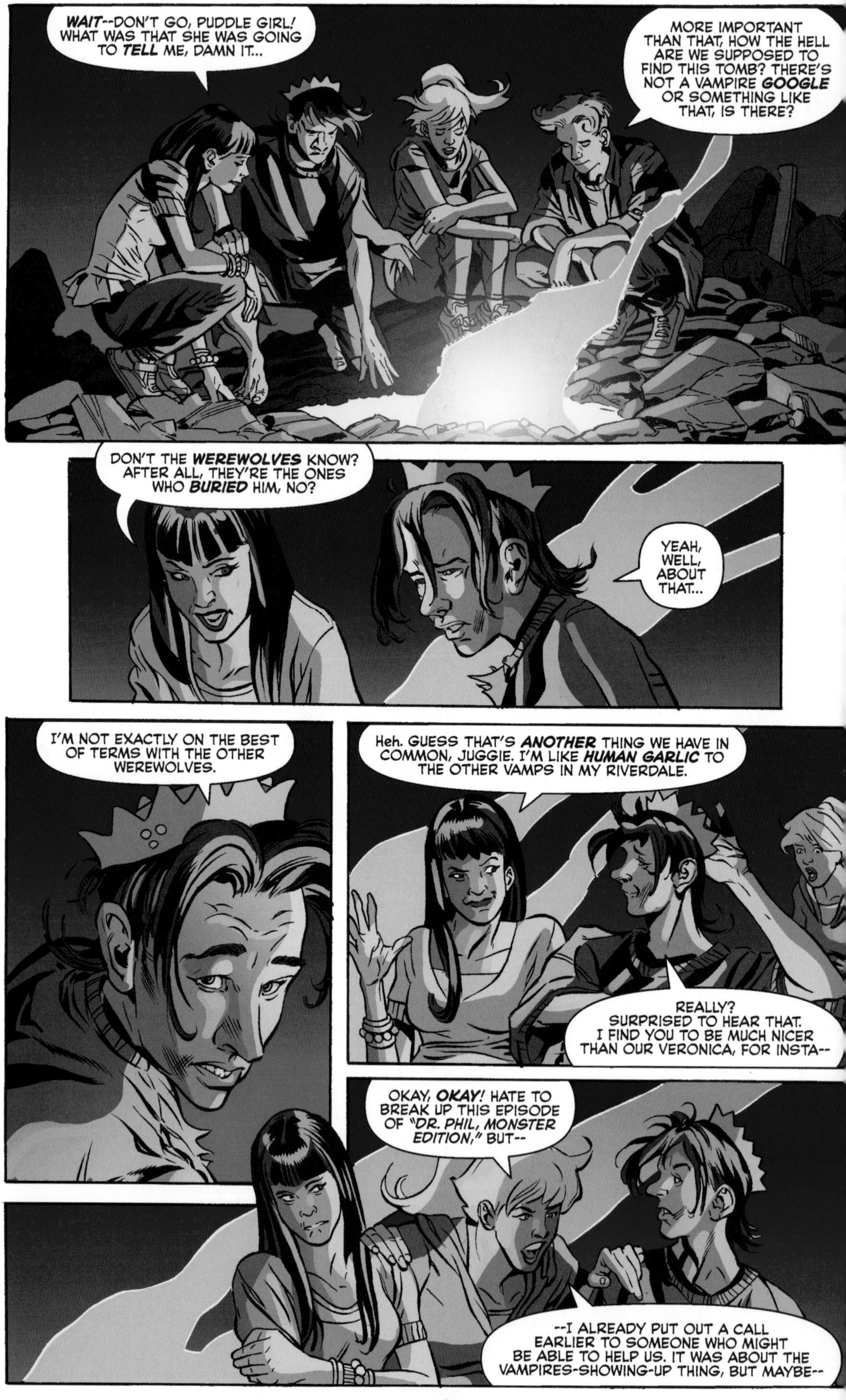
WAIT--DON'T GO, PUDDLE GIRL! WHAT WAS THAT SHE WAS GOING TO TELL ME, DAMN IT...
MORE IMPORTANT THAN THAT, HOW THE HELL ARE WE SUPPOSED TO FIND THIS TOMB? THERE'S NOT A VAMPIRE GOOGLE OR SOMETHING LIKE THAT, IS THERE?
DON'T THE WEREWOLVES KNOW? AFTER ALL, THEY'RE THE ONES WHO BURIED HIM, NO?
YEAH, WELL, ABOUT THAT...
I'M NOT EXACTLY ON THE BEST OF TERMS WITH THE OTHER WEREWOLVES.
Heh. GUESS THAT'S ANOTHER THING WE HAVE IN COMMON, JUGGIE. I'M LIKE HUMAN GARLIC TO THE OTHER VAMPS IN MY RIVERDALE.
REALLY? SURPRISED TO HEAR THAT. I FIND YOU TO BE MUCH NICER THAN OUR VERONICA, FOR INSTA--
OKAY, OKAY! HATE TO BREAK UP THIS EPISODE OF "DR. PHIL, MONSTER EDITION," BUT--
--I ALREADY PUT OUT A CALL EARLIER TO SOMEONE WHO MIGHT BE ABLE TO HELP US. IT WAS ABOUT THE VAMPIRES-SHOWING-UP THING, BUT MAYBE--

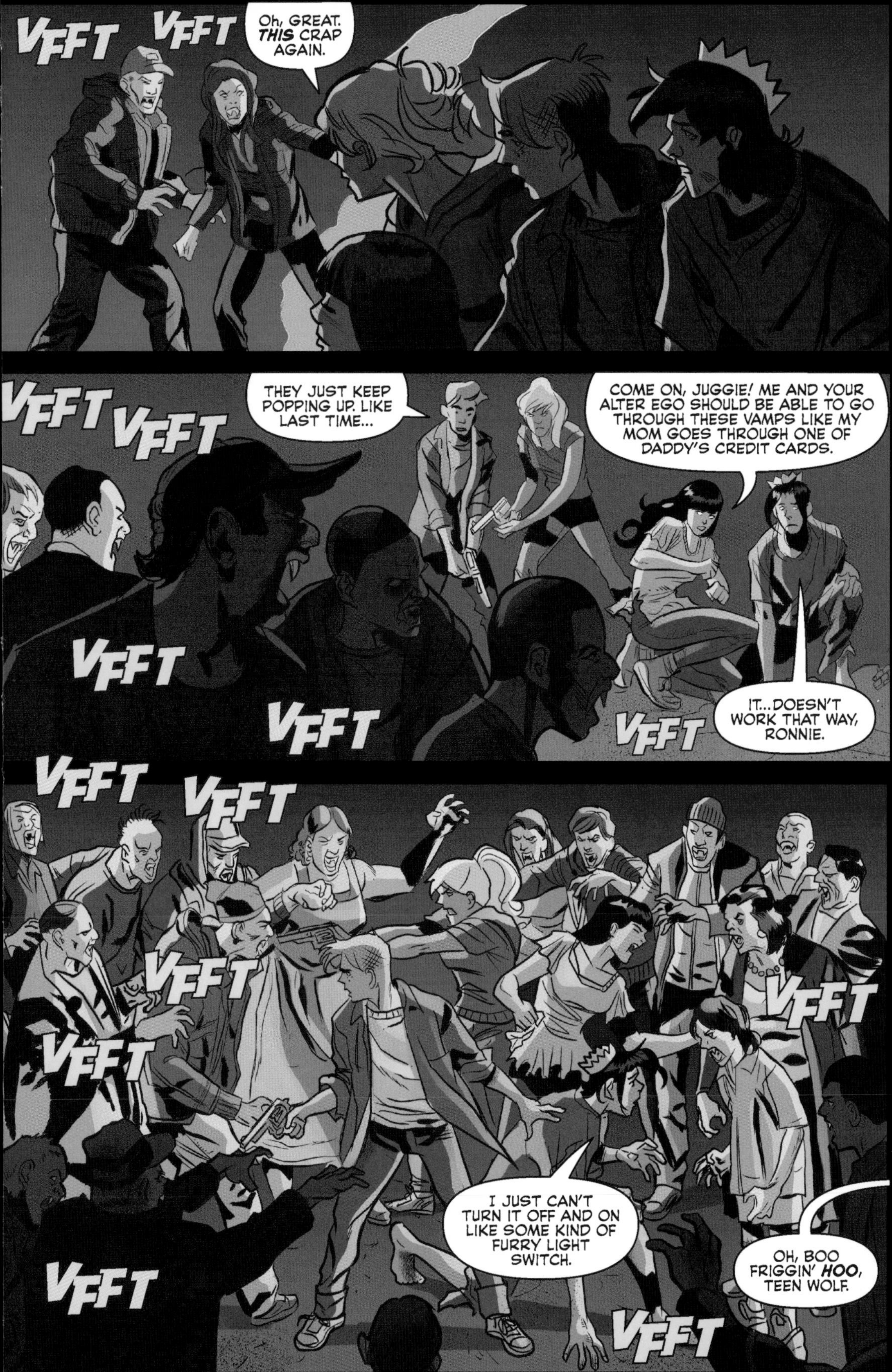
VFFT VFFT
Oh, GREAT. THIS CRAP AGAIN.
VFFT VFFT
THEY JUST KEEP POPPING UP. LIKE LAST TIME...
COME ON, JUGGIE! ME AND YOUR ALTER EGO SHOULD BE ABLE TO GO THROUGH THESE VAMPS LIKE MY MOM GOES THROUGH ONE OF DADDY'S CREDIT CARDS.
VFFT
VFFT
VFFT
IT...DOESN'T WORK THAT WAY, RONNIE.
VFFT VFFT
VFFT
VFFT
VFFT
I JUST CAN'T TURN IT OFF AND ON LIKE SOME KIND OF FURRY LIGHT SWITCH.
OH, BOO FRIGGIN' HOO, TEEN WOLF.
VFFT
VFFT

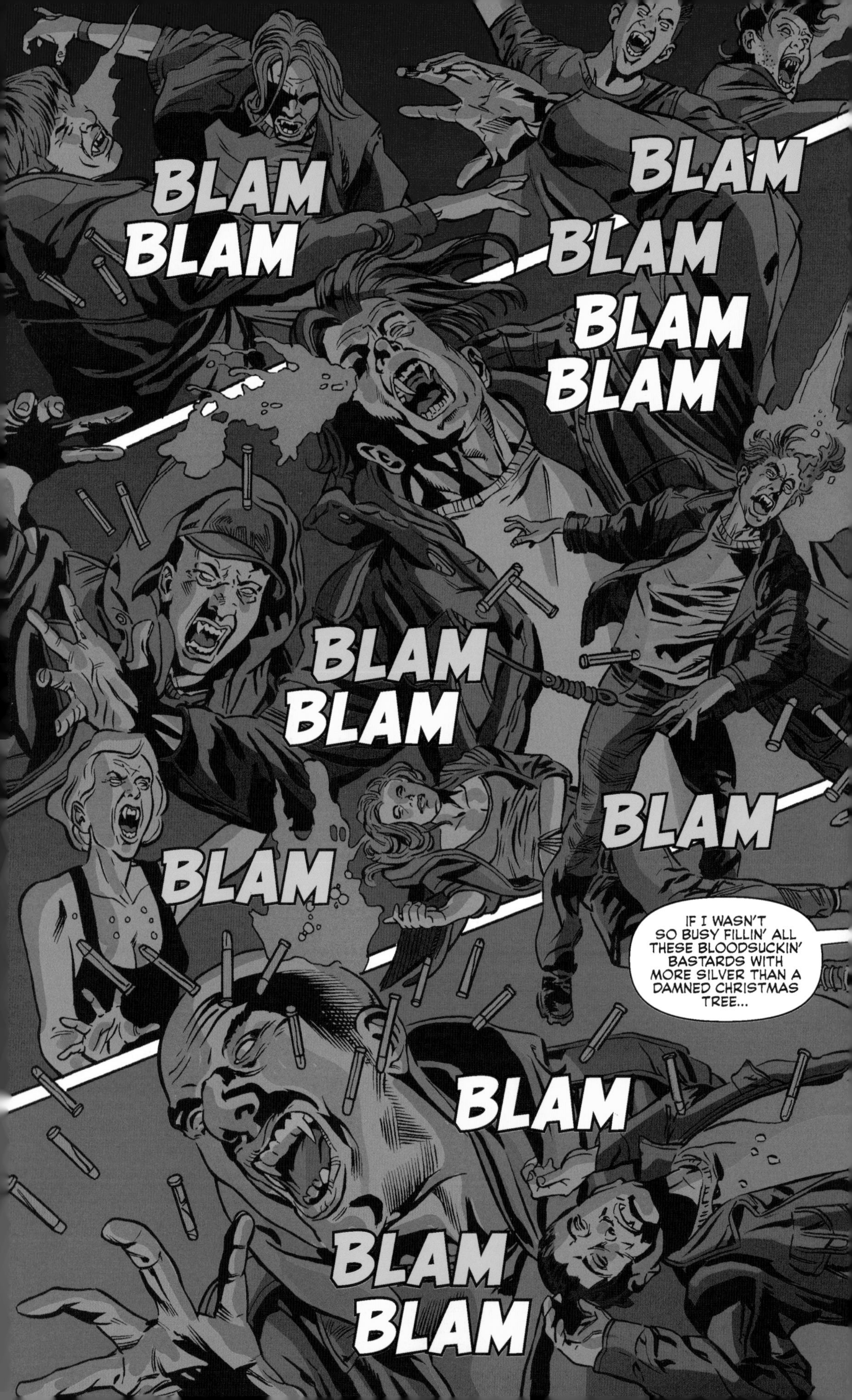
BLAM
BLAM
BLAM
BLAM
BLAM
BLAM
BLAM
BLAM
BLAM
BLAM
IF I WASN'T SO BUSY FILLIN' ALL THESE BLOODSUCKIN' BASTARDS WITH MORE SILVER THAN A DAMNED CHRISTMAS TREE...
BLAM
BLAM
BLAM

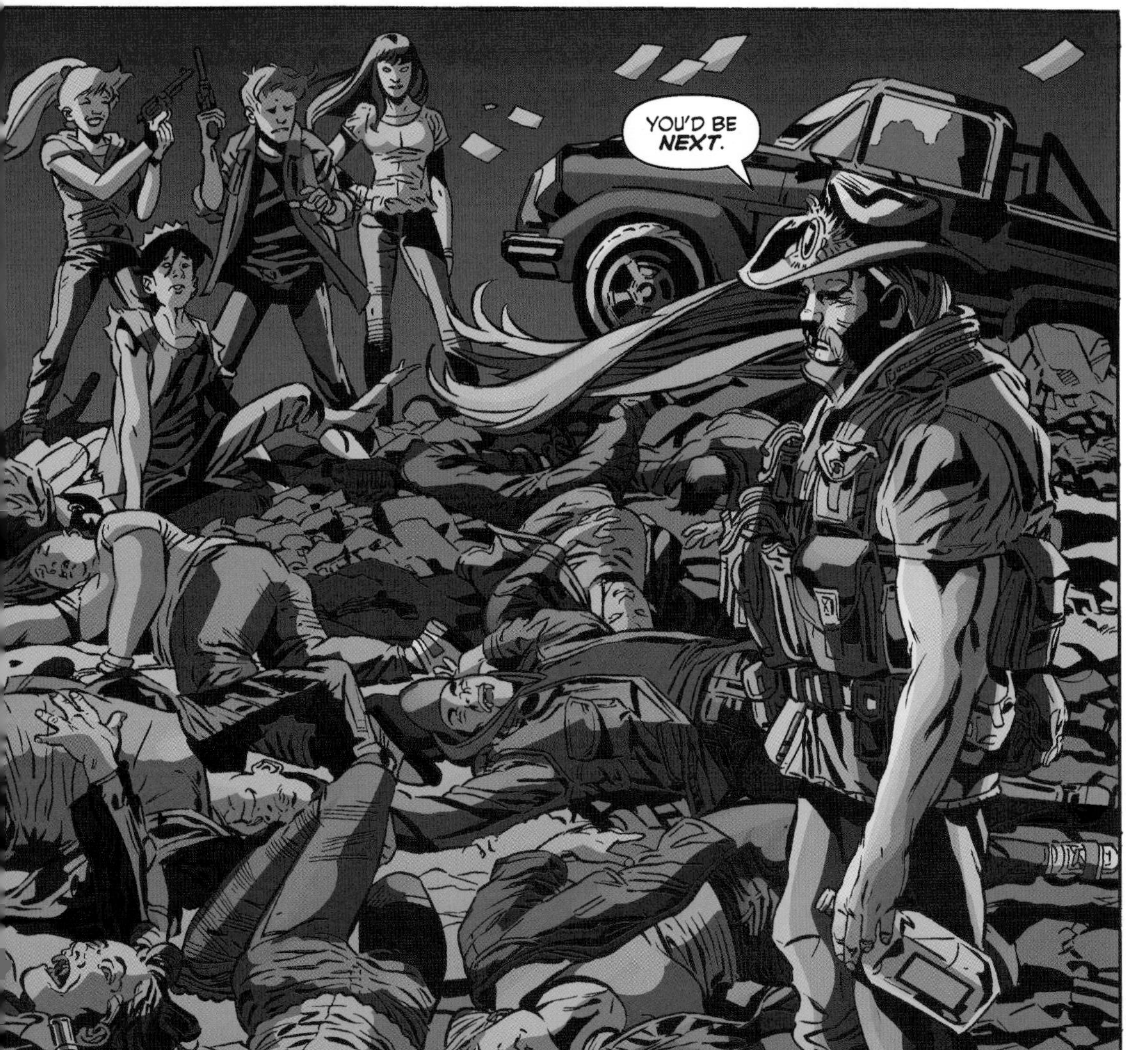
YOU'D BE NEXT.
AND HE CAN STILL BE, BETTS. I LOST COUNT BUT I MIGHT HAVE A COUPLE LEFT IN THIS BAD BOY.

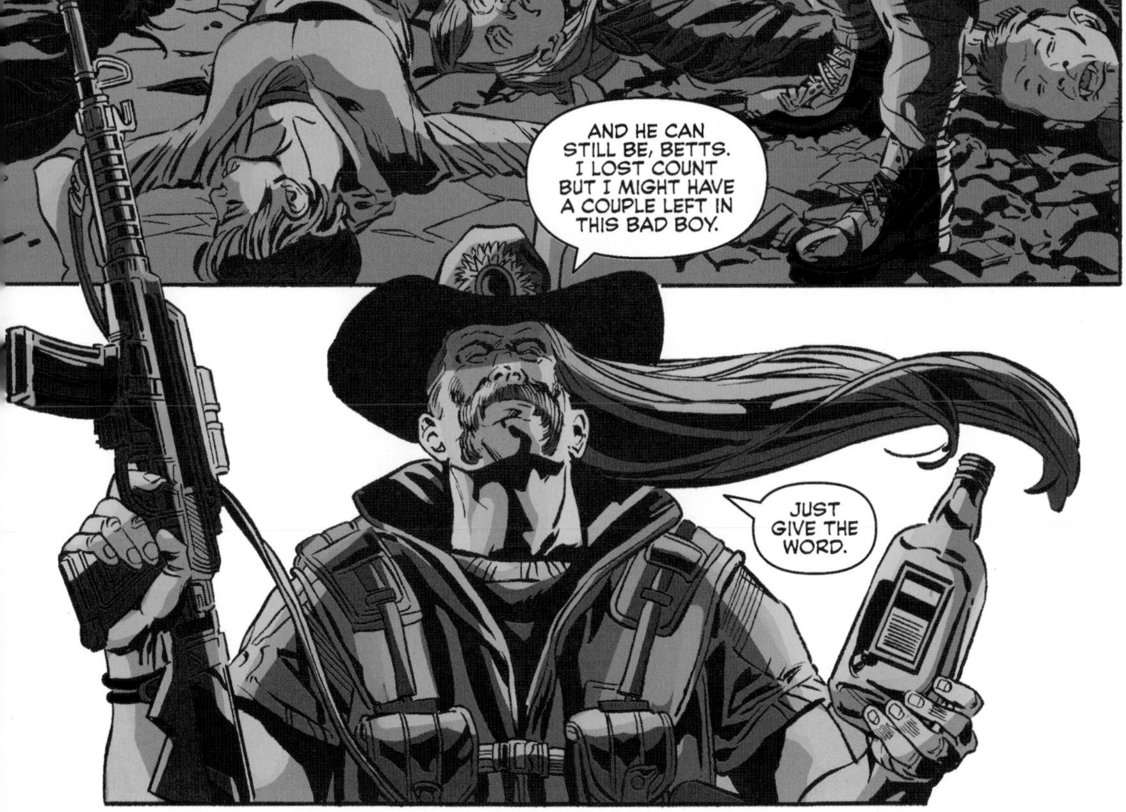
JUST GIVE THE WORD.

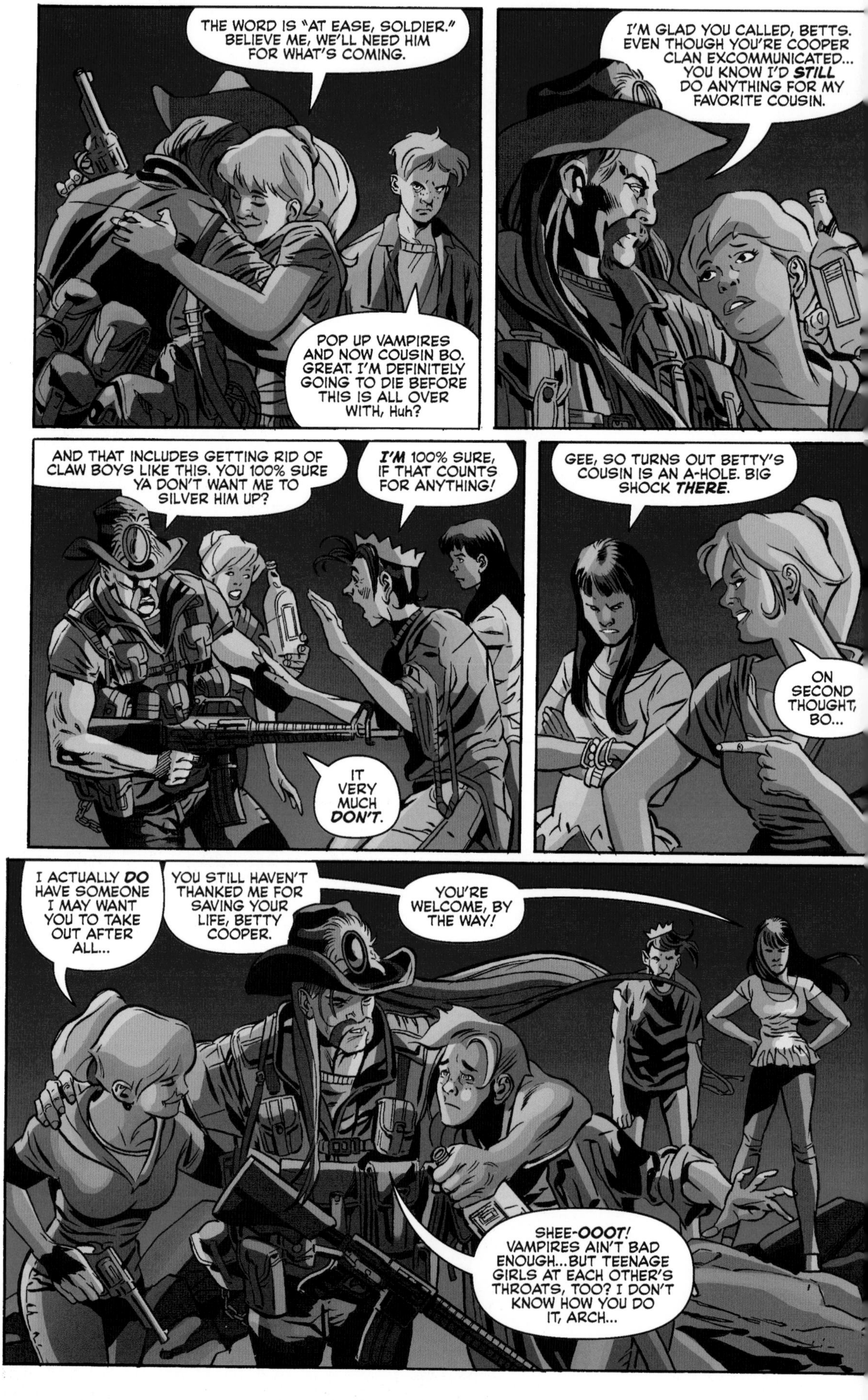
THE WORD IS "AT EASE, SOLDIER." BELIEVE ME, WE'LL NEED HIM FOR WHAT'S COMING.
POP UP VAMPIRES AND NOW COUSIN BO. GREAT. I'M DEFINITELY GOING TO DIE BEFORE THIS IS ALL OVER WITH, Huh?
I'M GLAD YOU CALLED, BETTS. EVEN THOUGH YOU'RE COOPER CLAN EXCOMMUNICATED... YOU KNOW I'D STILL DO ANYTHING FOR MY FAVORITE COUSIN.
AND THAT INCLUDES GETTING RID OF CLAW BOYS LIKE THIS. YOU 100% SURE YA DON'T WANT ME TO SILVER HIM UP?
I'M 100% SURE, IF THAT COUNTS FOR ANYTHING!
IT VERY MUCH DON'T.
GEE, SO TURNS OUT BETTY'S COUSIN IS AN A-HOLE. BIG SHOCK THERE.
ON SECOND THOUGHT, BO...
I ACTUALLY DO HAVE SOMEONE I MAY WANT YOU TO TAKE OUT AFTER ALL...
YOU STILL HAVEN'T THANKED ME FOR SAVING YOUR LIFE, BETTY COOPER.
YOU'RE WELCOME, BY THE WAY!
SHEE-OOOT! VAMPIRES AIN'T BAD ENOUGH...BUT TEENAGE GIRLS AT EACH OTHER'S THROATS, TOO? I DON'T KNOW HOW YOU DO IT, ARCH...

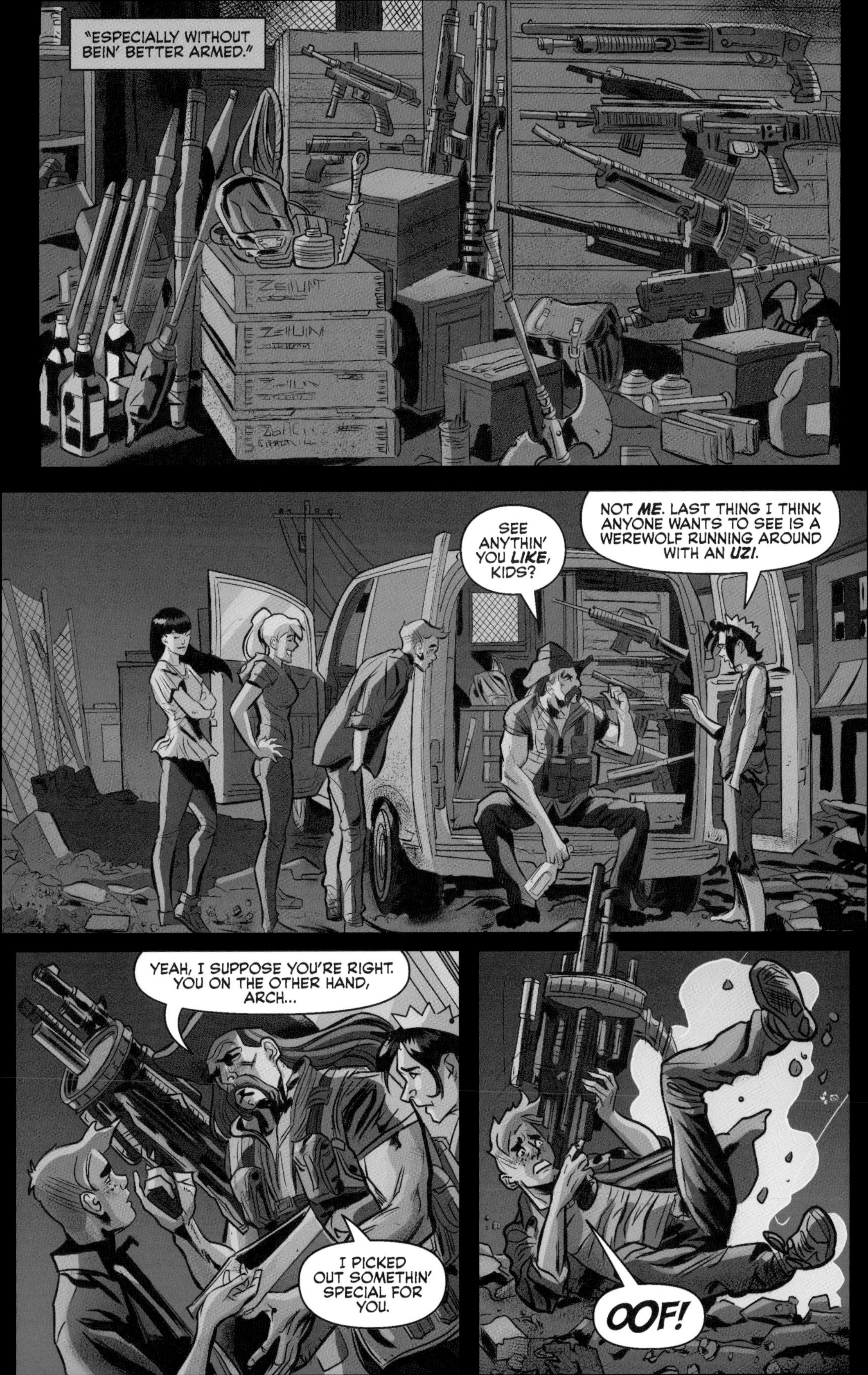
"ESPECIALLY WITHOUT BEIN' BETTER ARMED."
SEE ANYTHIN' YOU LIKE, KIDS?
NOT ME. LAST THING I THINK ANYONE WANTS TO SEE IS A WEREWOLF RUNNING AROUND WITH AN UZI.
YEAH, I SUPPOSE YOU'RE RIGHT. YOU ON THE OTHER HAND, ARCH...
I PICKED OUT SOMETHIN' SPECIAL FOR YOU.
OOF!

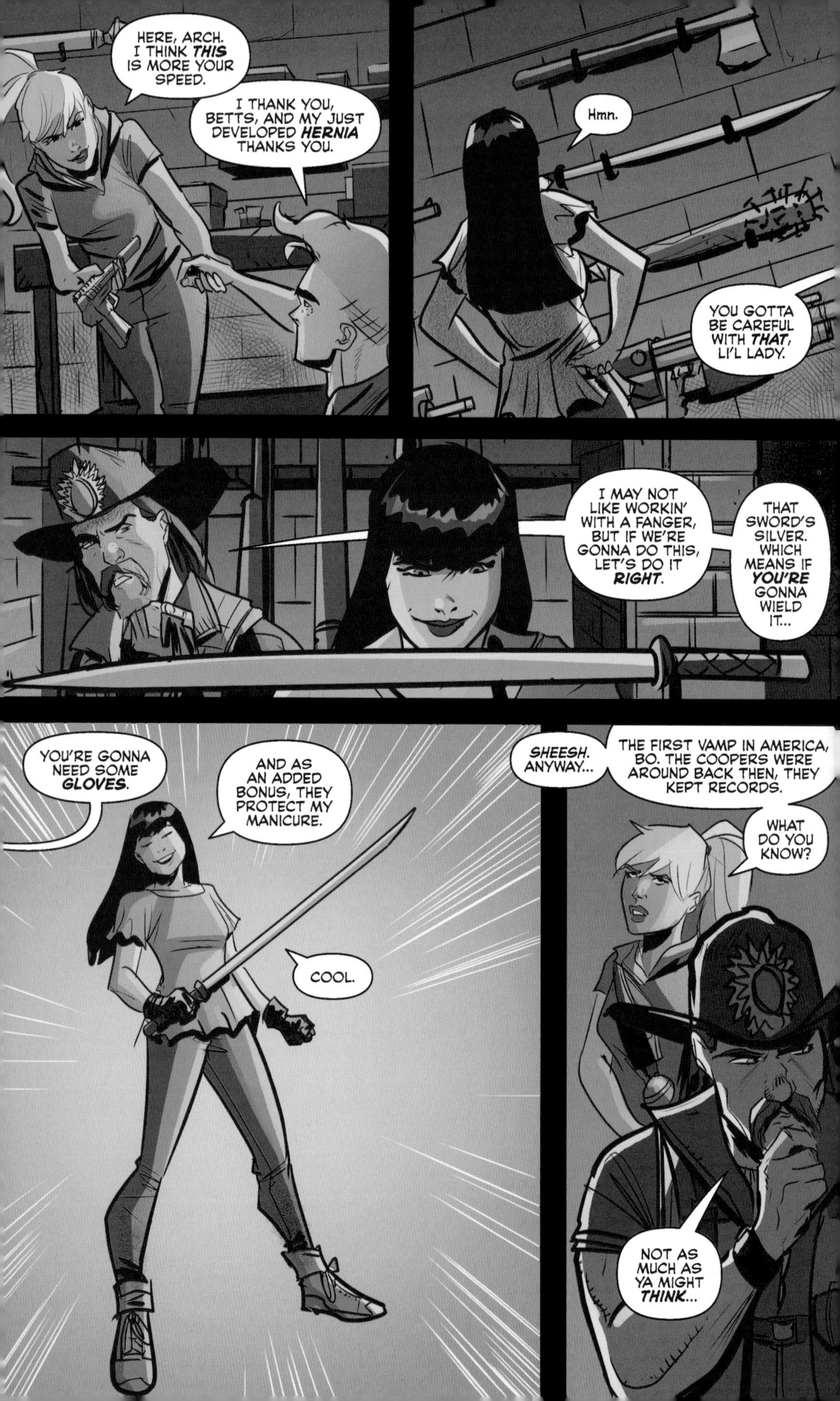
HERE, ARCH. I THINK THIS IS MORE YOUR SPEED.
I THANK YOU, BETTS, AND MY JUST DEVELOPED HERNIA THANKS YOU.
Hmn.
YOU GOTTA BE CAREFUL WITH THAT, LI'L LADY.
I MAY NOT LIKE WORKIN' WITH A FANGER, BUT IF WE'RE GONNA DO THIS, LET'S DO IT RIGHT.
THAT SWORD'S SILVER. WHICH MEANS IF YOU'RE GONNA WIELD IT...
YOU'RE GONNA NEED SOME GLOVES.
AND AS AN ADDED BONUS, THEY PROTECT MY MANICURE.
COOL.
SHEESH. ANYWAY...
THE FIRST VAMP IN AMERICA, BO. THE COOPERS WERE AROUND BACK THEN, THEY KEPT RECORDS.
WHAT DO YOU KNOW?
NOT AS MUCH AS YA MIGHT THINK...

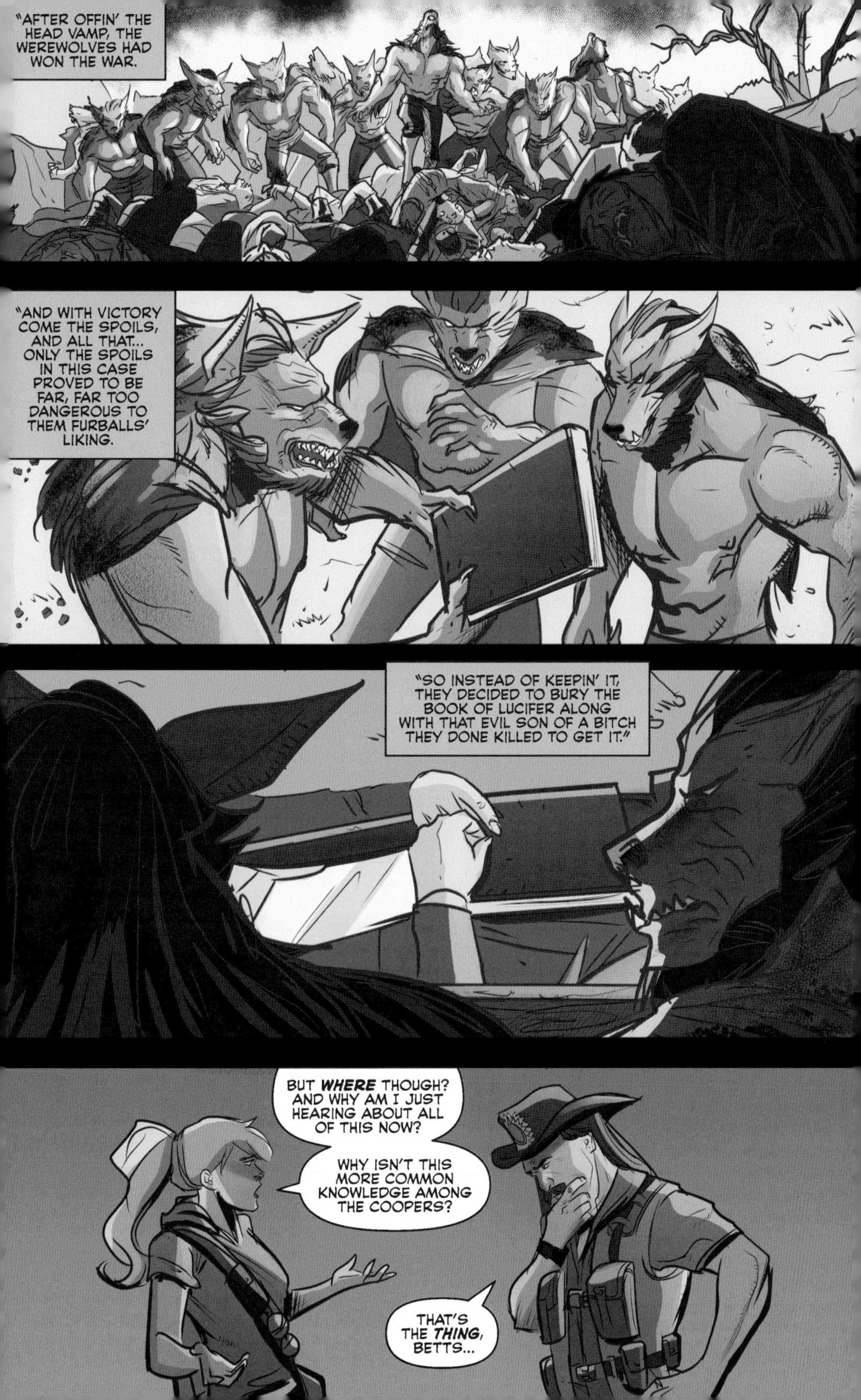
"AFTER OFFIN' THE HEAD VAMP, THE WEREWOLVES HAD WON THE WAR.
"AND WITH VICTORY COME THE SPOILS, AND ALL THAT... ONLY THE SPOILS IN THIS CASE PROVED TO BE FAR, FAR TOO DANGEROUS TO THEM FURBALLS' LIKING.
"SO INSTEAD OF KEEPIN' IT, THEY DECIDED TO BURY THE BOOK OF LUCIFER ALONG WITH THAT EVIL SON OF A BITCH THEY DONE KILLED TO GET IT."
BUT ***WHERE*** THOUGH? AND WHY AM I JUST HEARING ABOUT ALL OF THIS NOW?
WHY ISN'T THIS MORE COMMON KNOWLEDGE AMONG THE COOPERS?
THAT'S THE ***THING***, BETTS...

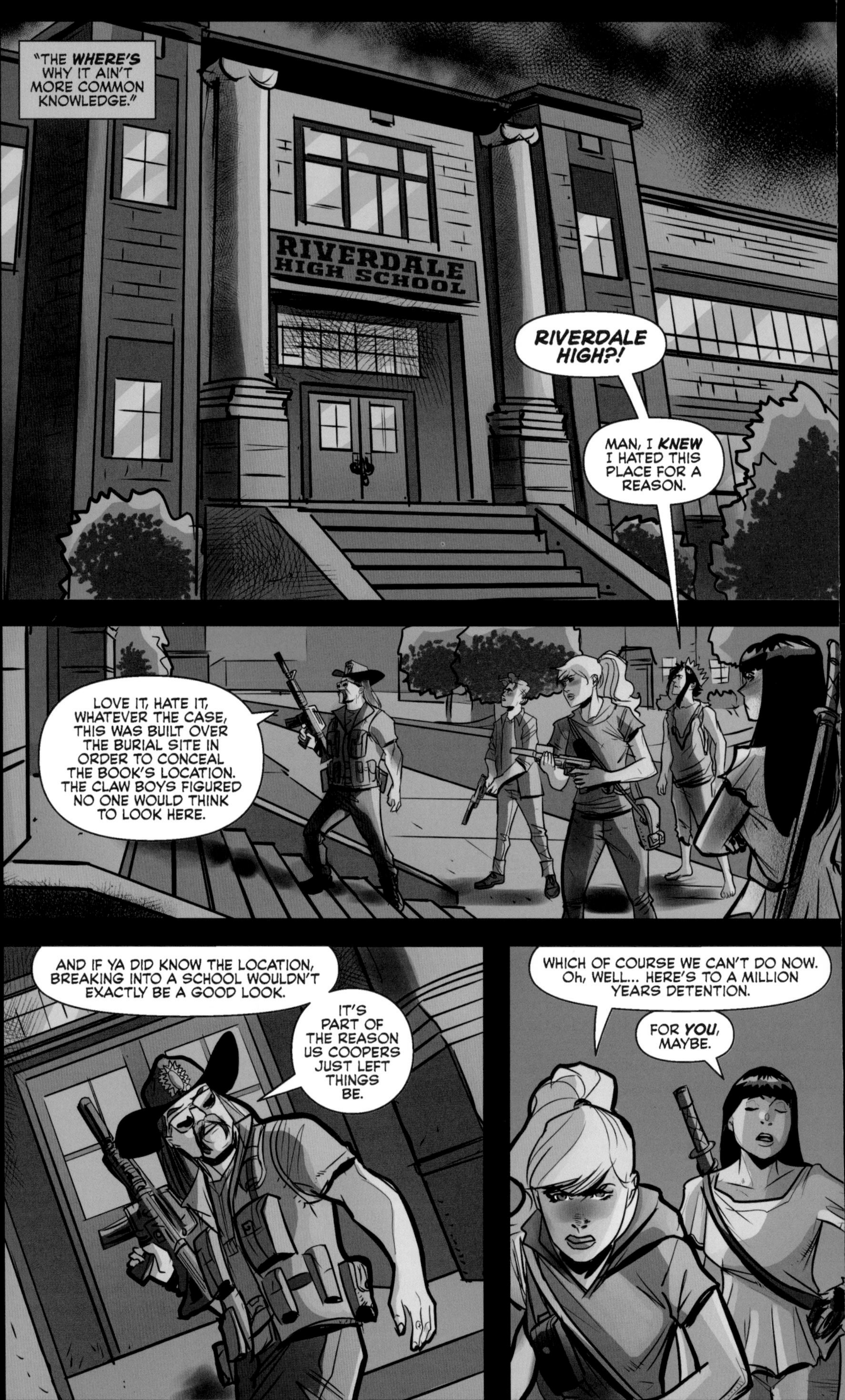
"THE WHERE'S WHY IT AIN'T MORE COMMON KNOWLEDGE."
RIVERDALE HIGH SCHOOL
RIVERDALE HIGH?!
MAN, I KNEW I HATED THIS PLACE FOR A REASON.
LOVE IT, HATE IT, WHATEVER THE CASE, THIS WAS BUILT OVER THE BURIAL SITE IN ORDER TO CONCEAL THE BOOK'S LOCATION. THE CLAW BOYS FIGURED NO ONE WOULD THINK TO LOOK HERE.
AND IF YA DID KNOW THE LOCATION, BREAKING INTO A SCHOOL WOULDN'T EXACTLY BE A GOOD LOOK.
IT'S PART OF THE REASON US COOPERS JUST LEFT THINGS BE.
WHICH OF COURSE WE CAN'T DO NOW. Oh, WELL... HERE'S TO A MILLION YEARS DETENTION.
FOR YOU, MAYBE.

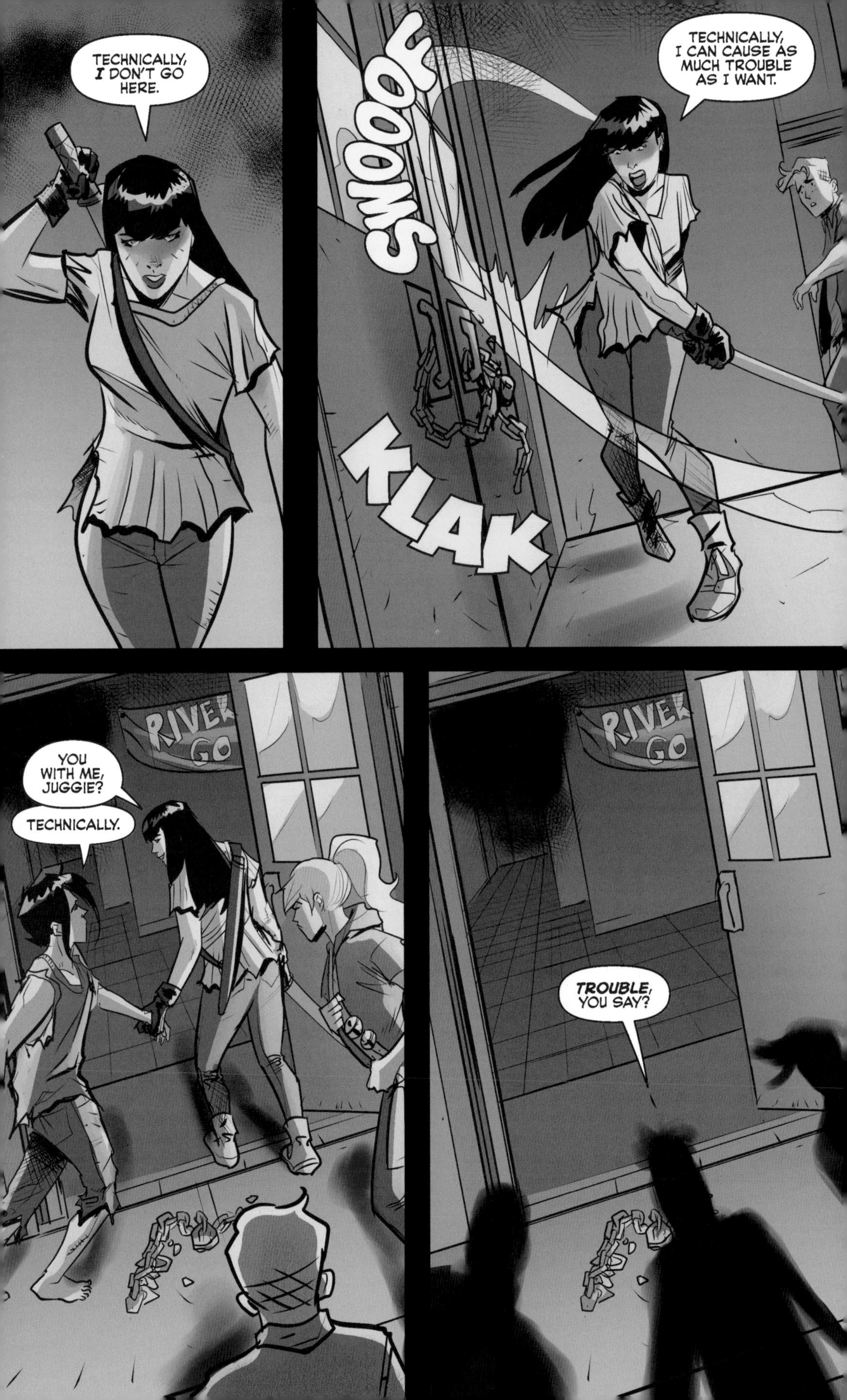
TECHNICALLY, *I* DON'T GO HERE.
SWOOOF
KLAK
TECHNICALLY, I CAN CAUSE AS MUCH TROUBLE AS I WANT.
RIVER GO
YOU WITH ME, JUGGIE?
TECHNICALLY.
RIVER GO
TROUBLE, YOU SAY?

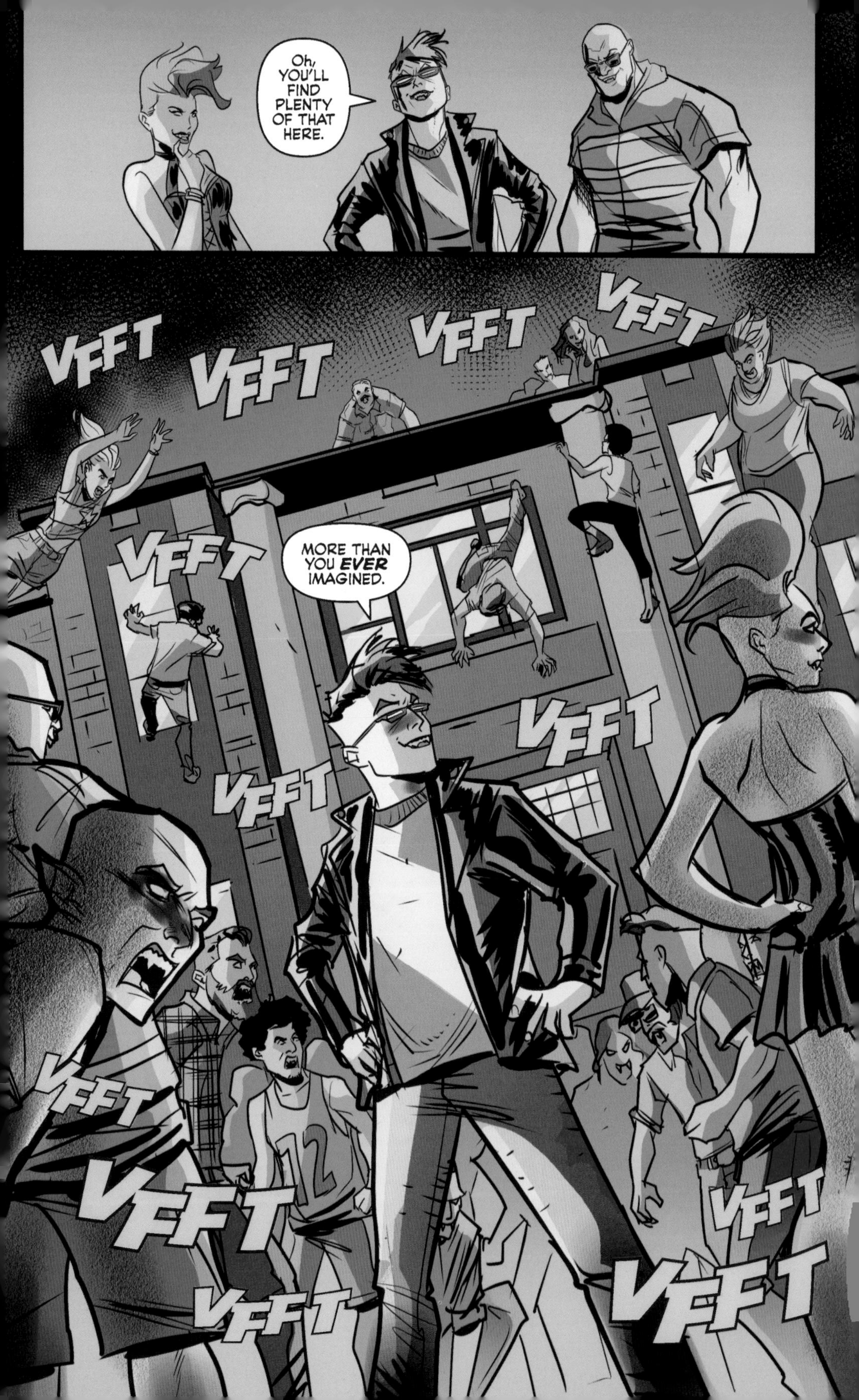
Oh, YOU'LL FIND PLENTY OF THAT HERE.
VFFT
VFFT
VFFT
VFFT
VFFT
MORE THAN YOU *EVER* IMAGINED.
VFFT
VFFT
VFFT
VFFT
VFFT
VFFT
VFFT

CHAPTER FIVE

COVER ART BY PAT & TIM KENNEDY
WITH BOB SMITH AND MATT HERMS

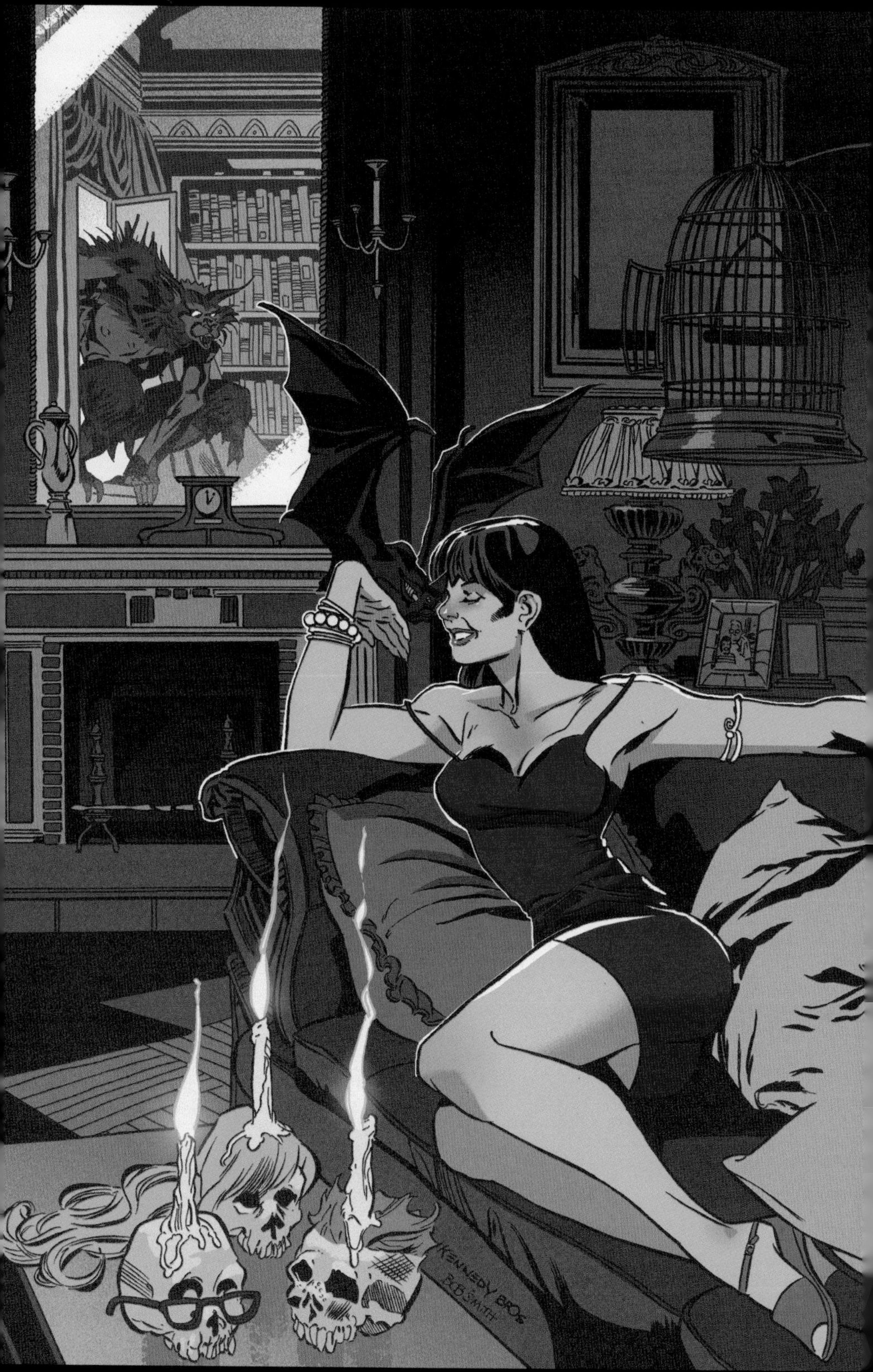

STORY BY FRANK TIERI
RT BY PAT & TIM KENNEDY (p.1-3,6-12,15,17) JOE EISMA (p.4-5,13-14,16,18-20)
INKS BY BOB SMITH (p.1-3,6-10,15,17) JOE EISMA (p.11-12)
COLORING BY MATT HERMS LETTERING BY JACK MORELLI

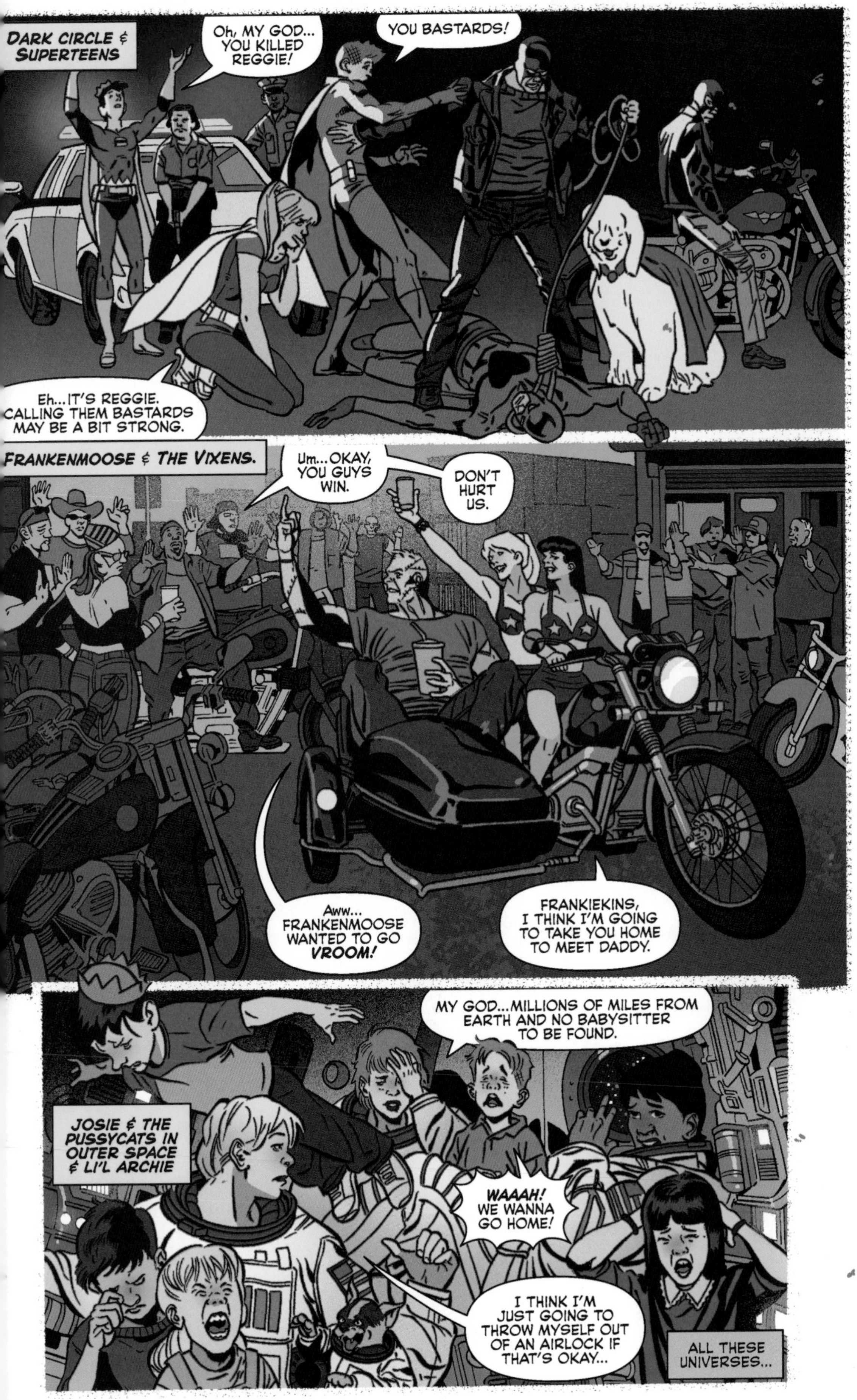
DARK CIRCLE & SUPERTEENS
Oh, MY GOD... YOU KILLED REGGIE!
YOU BASTARDS!
Eh...IT'S REGGIE. CALLING THEM BASTARDS MAY BE A BIT STRONG.
FRANKENMOOSE & THE VIXENS.
Um...OKAY, YOU GUYS WIN.
DON'T HURT US.
Aww... FRANKENMOOSE WANTED TO GO VROOM!
FRANKIEKINS, I THINK I'M GOING TO TAKE YOU HOME TO MEET DADDY.
MY GOD...MILLIONS OF MILES FROM EARTH AND NO BABYSITTER TO BE FOUND.
JOSIE & THE PUSSYCATS IN OUTER SPACE & LI'L ARCHIE
WAAAH! WE WANNA GO HOME!
I THINK I'M JUST GOING TO THROW MYSELF OUT OF AN AIRLOCK IF THAT'S OKAY...
ALL THESE UNIVERSES...

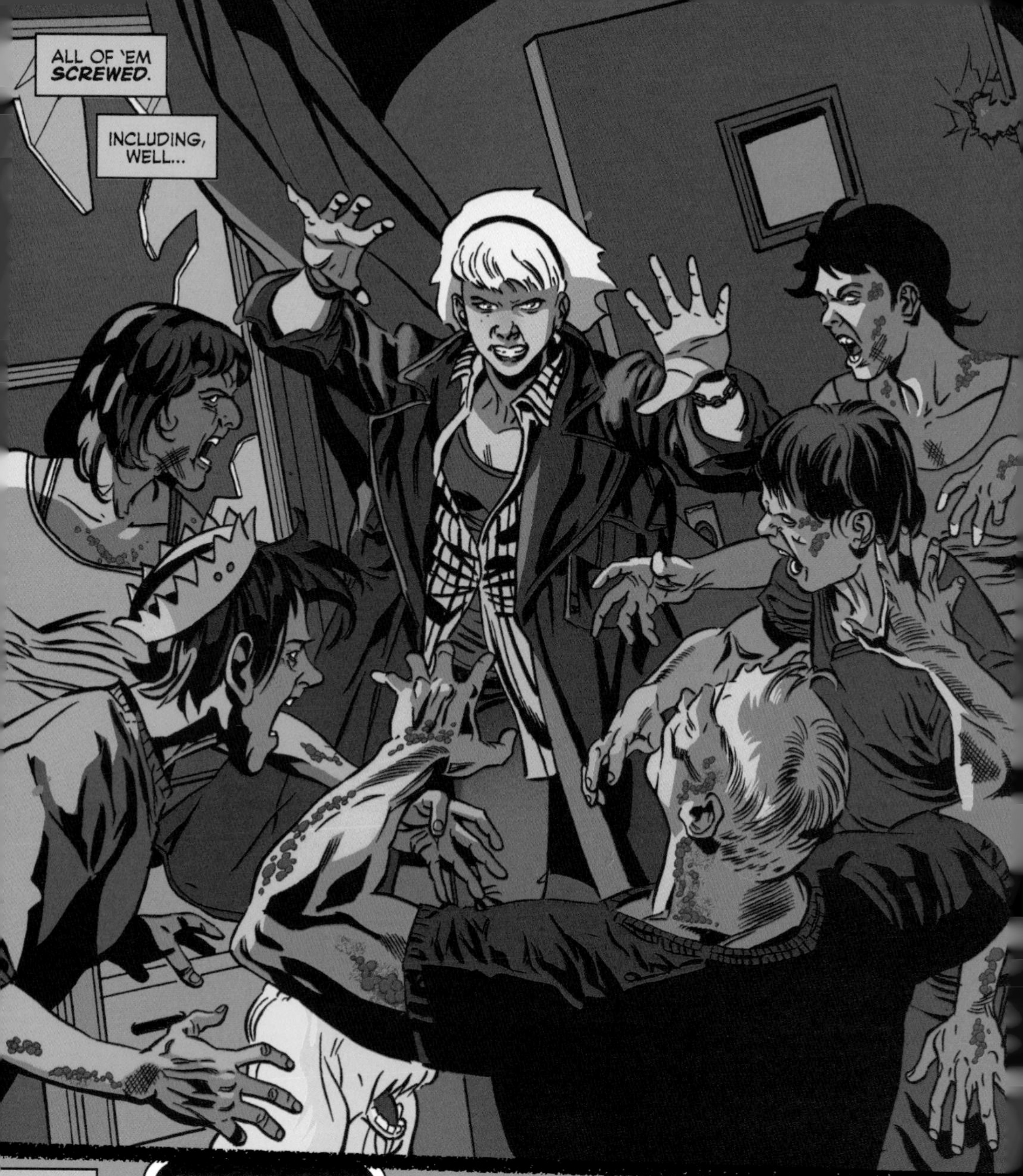
ALL OF 'EM SCREWED.
INCLUDING, WELL...

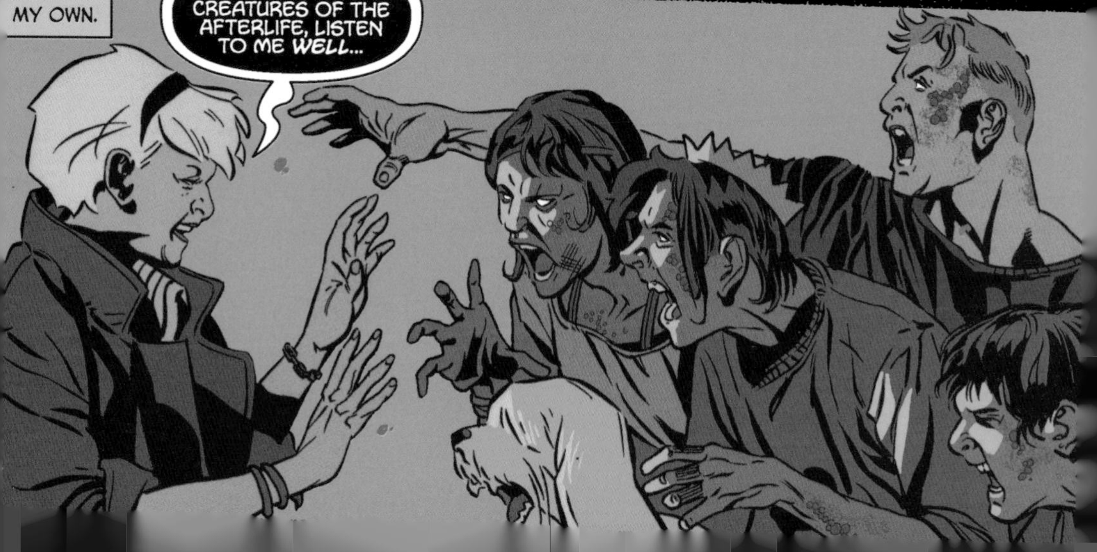
MY OWN.
CREATURES OF THE AFTERLIFE, LISTEN TO ME WELL...

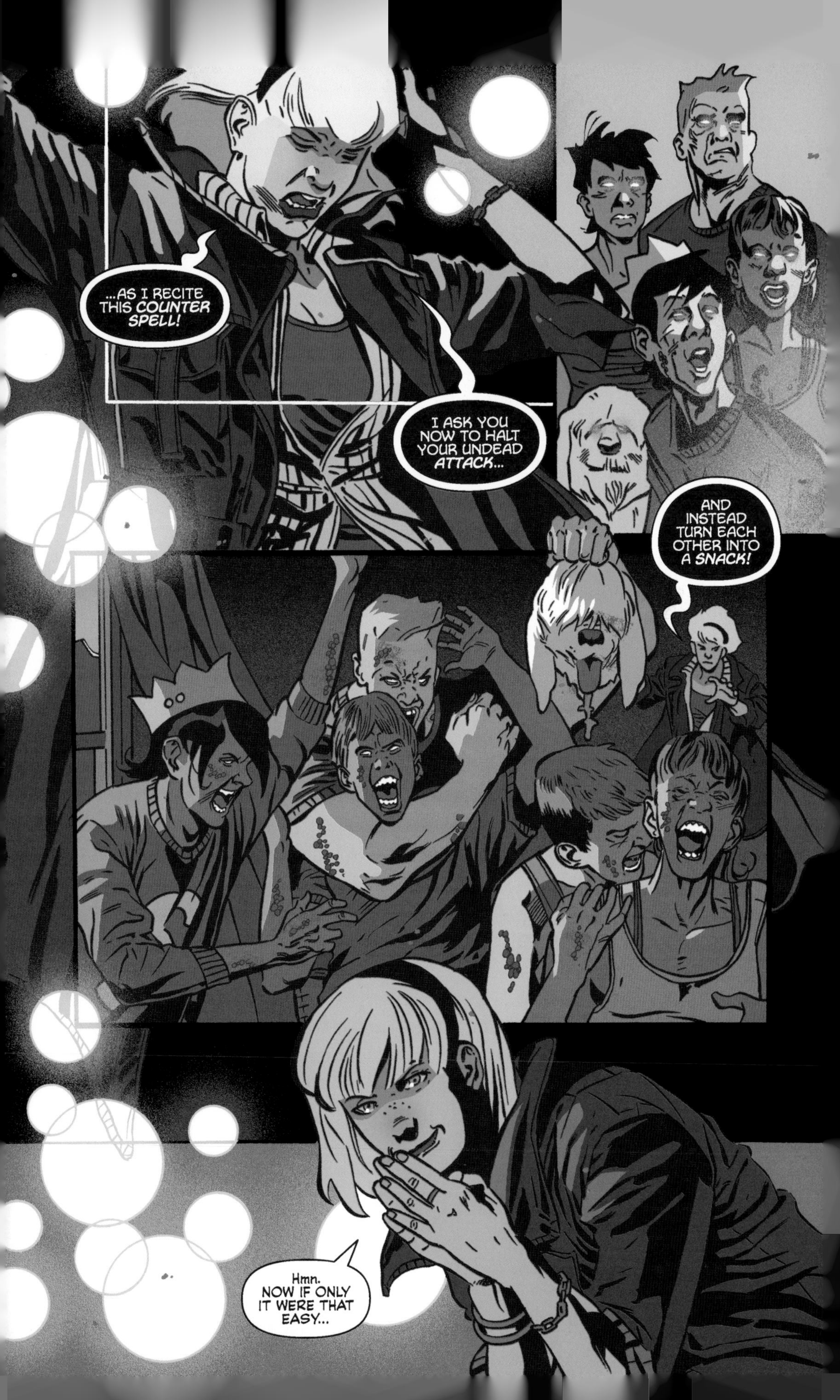
...AS I RECITE THIS COUNTER SPELL!
I ASK YOU NOW TO HALT YOUR UNDEAD ATTACK...
AND INSTEAD TURN EACH OTHER INTO A SNACK!
Hmn. NOW IF ONLY IT WERE THAT EASY...

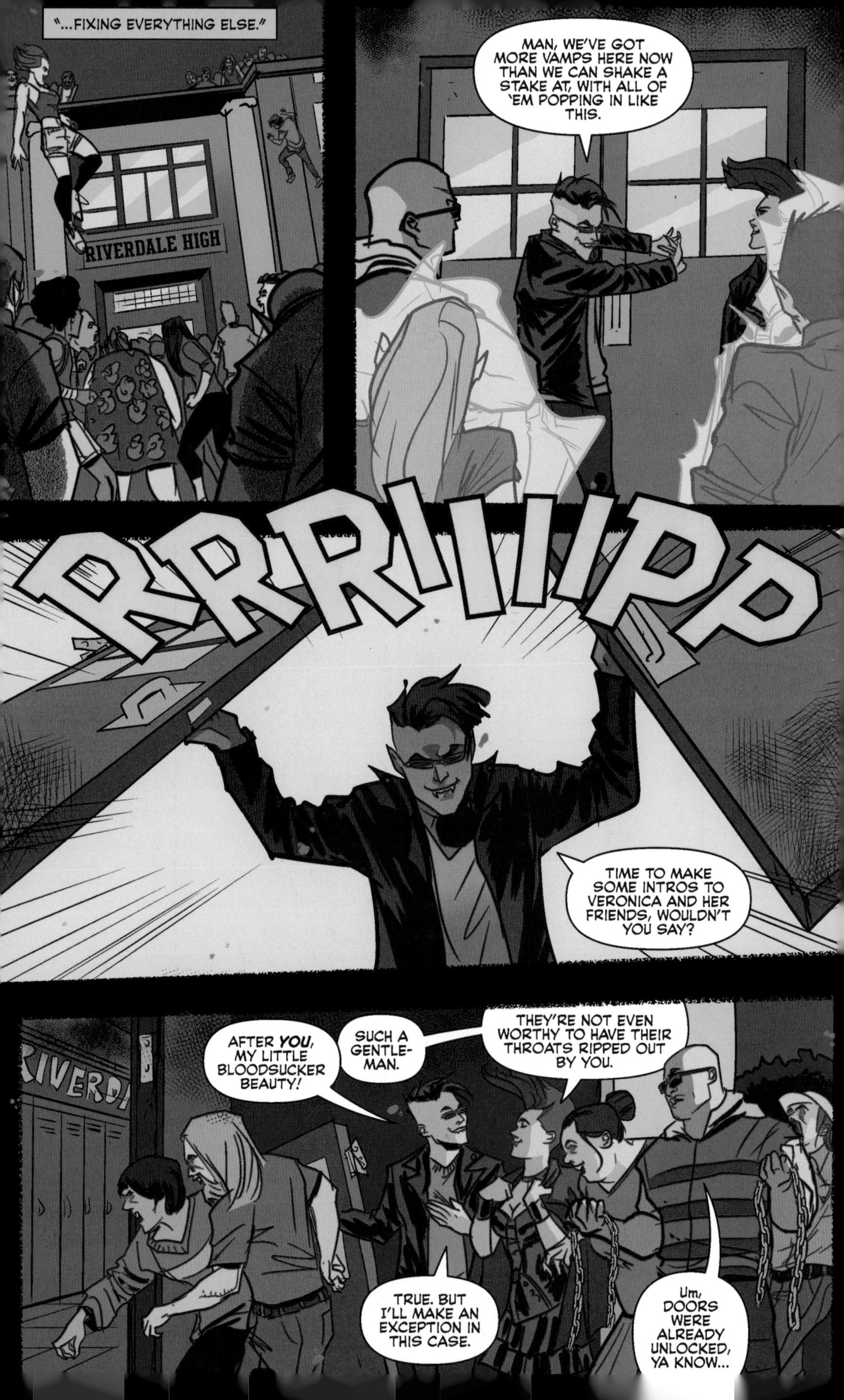

"...FIXING EVERYTHING ELSE."
RIVERDALE HIGH
MAN, WE'VE GOT MORE VAMPS HERE NOW THAN WE CAN SHAKE A STAKE AT, WITH ALL OF 'EM POPPING IN LIKE THIS.
RRRIIIIPP
TIME TO MAKE SOME INTROS TO VERONICA AND HER FRIENDS, WOULDN'T YOU SAY?
RIVERD
AFTER YOU, MY LITTLE BLOODSUCKER BEAUTY!
SUCH A GENTLE-MAN.
THEY'RE NOT EVEN WORTHY TO HAVE THEIR THROATS RIPPED OUT BY YOU.
TRUE. BUT I'LL MAKE AN EXCEPTION IN THIS CASE.
Um, DOORS WERE ALREADY UNLOCKED, YA KNOW...

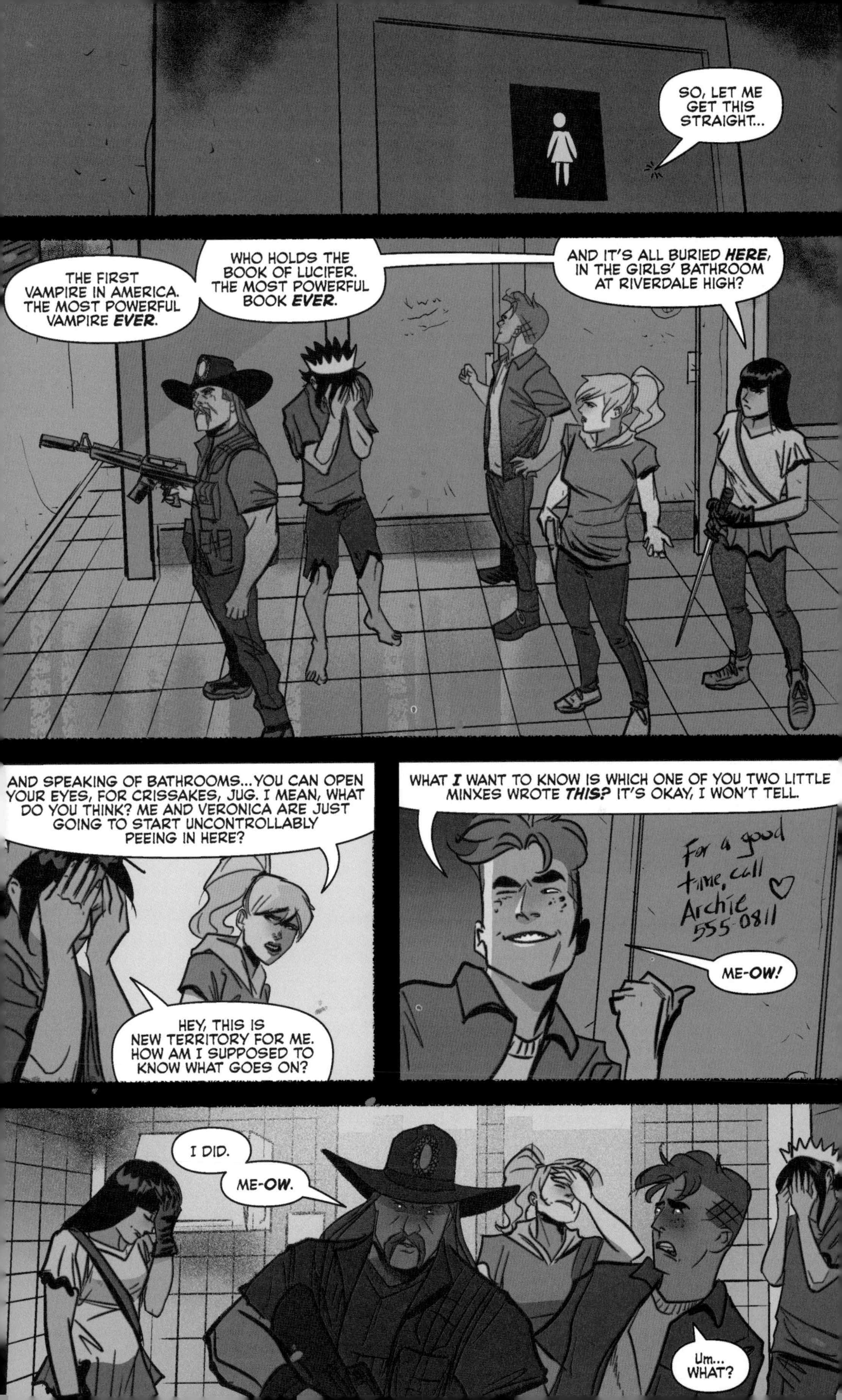
SO, LET ME GET THIS STRAIGHT...
THE FIRST VAMPIRE IN AMERICA. THE MOST POWERFUL VAMPIRE EVER.
WHO HOLDS THE BOOK OF LUCIFER. THE MOST POWERFUL BOOK EVER.
AND IT'S ALL BURIED HERE, IN THE GIRLS' BATHROOM AT RIVERDALE HIGH?
AND SPEAKING OF BATHROOMS...YOU CAN OPEN YOUR EYES, FOR CRISSAKES, JUG. I MEAN, WHAT DO YOU THINK? ME AND VERONICA ARE JUST GOING TO START UNCONTROLLABLY PEEING IN HERE?
HEY, THIS IS NEW TERRITORY FOR ME. HOW AM I SUPPOSED TO KNOW WHAT GOES ON?
WHAT I WANT TO KNOW IS WHICH ONE OF YOU TWO LITTLE MINXES WROTE THIS? IT'S OKAY, I WON'T TELL.
For a good time, call Archie 555-0811
ME-OW!
I DID.
ME-OW.
Um... WHAT?

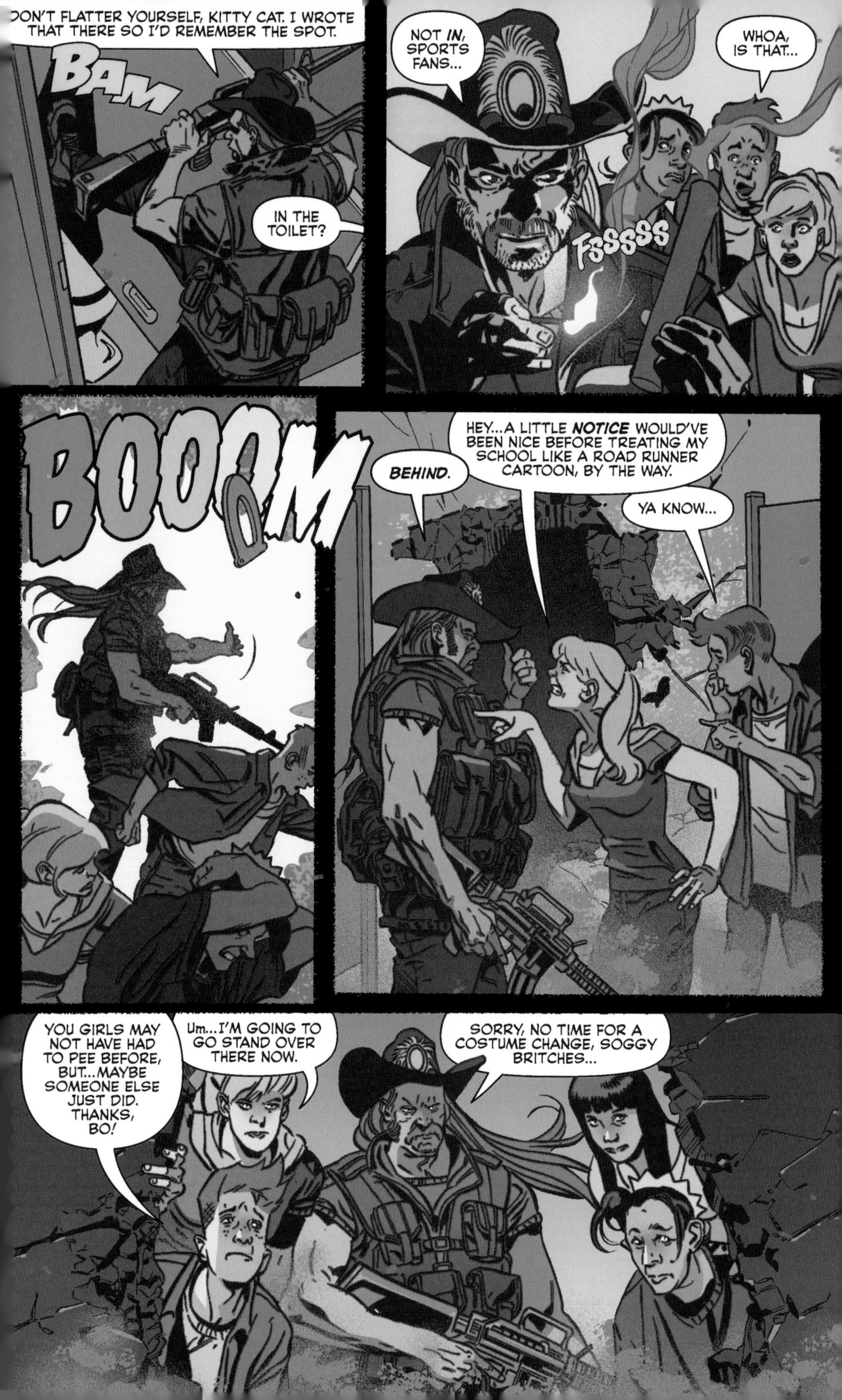
DON'T FLATTER YOURSELF, KITTY CAT. I WROTE THAT THERE SO I'D REMEMBER THE SPOT.
BAM
IN THE TOILET?
NOT IN, SPORTS FANS...
WHOA, IS THAT...
FSSSSS
BOOOM
BEHIND.
HEY...A LITTLE NOTICE WOULD'VE BEEN NICE BEFORE TREATING MY SCHOOL LIKE A ROAD RUNNER CARTOON, BY THE WAY.
YA KNOW...
YOU GIRLS MAY NOT HAVE HAD TO PEE BEFORE, BUT...MAYBE SOMEONE ELSE JUST DID. THANKS, BO!
Um...I'M GOING TO GO STAND OVER THERE NOW.
SORRY, NO TIME FOR A COSTUME CHANGE, SOGGY BRITCHES...

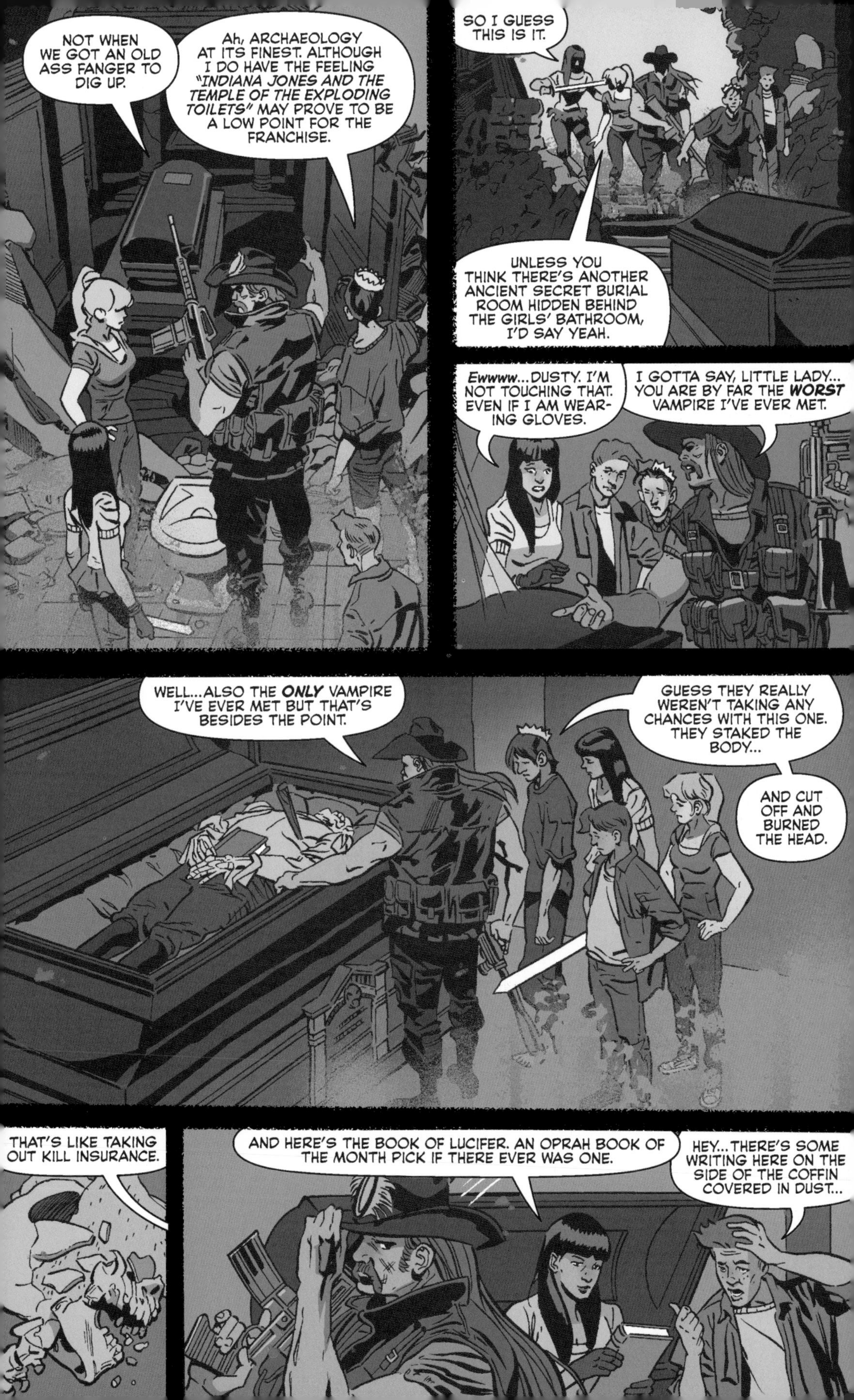
NOT WHEN WE GOT AN OLD ASS FANGER TO DIG UP.
Ah, ARCHAEOLOGY AT ITS FINEST. ALTHOUGH I DO HAVE THE FEELING *"INDIANA JONES AND THE TEMPLE OF THE EXPLODING TOILETS"* MAY PROVE TO BE A LOW POINT FOR THE FRANCHISE.
SO I GUESS THIS IS IT.
UNLESS YOU THINK THERE'S ANOTHER ANCIENT SECRET BURIAL ROOM HIDDEN BEHIND THE GIRLS' BATHROOM, I'D SAY YEAH.
Ewwww...DUSTY. I'M NOT TOUCHING THAT. EVEN IF I AM WEARING GLOVES.
I GOTTA SAY, LITTLE LADY... YOU ARE BY FAR THE ***WORST*** VAMPIRE I'VE EVER MET.
WELL...ALSO THE ***ONLY*** VAMPIRE I'VE EVER MET BUT THAT'S BESIDES THE POINT.
GUESS THEY REALLY WEREN'T TAKING ANY CHANCES WITH THIS ONE. THEY STAKED THE BODY...
AND CUT OFF AND BURNED THE HEAD.
THAT'S LIKE TAKING OUT KILL INSURANCE.
AND HERE'S THE BOOK OF LUCIFER. AN OPRAH BOOK OF THE MONTH PICK IF THERE EVER WAS ONE.
HEY...THERE'S SOME WRITING HERE ON THE SIDE OF THE COFFIN COVERED IN DUST...

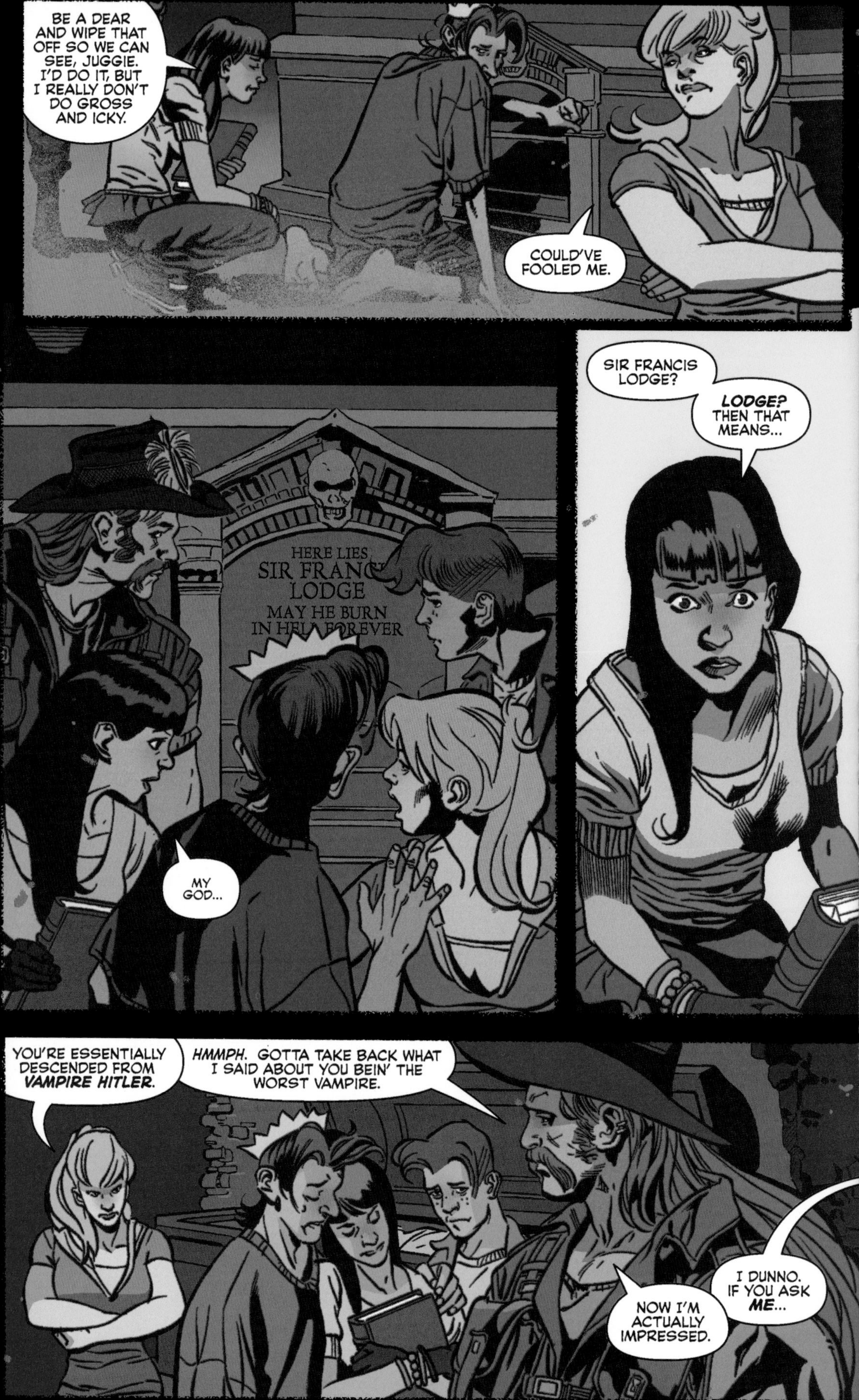
BE A DEAR AND WIPE THAT OFF SO WE CAN SEE, JUGGIE. I'D DO IT, BUT I REALLY DON'T DO GROSS AND ICKY.
COULD'VE FOOLED ME.
HERE LIES SIR FRANC LODGE MAY HE BURN IN HEL FOREVER
MY GOD...
SIR FRANCIS LODGE?
LODGE? THEN THAT MEANS...
YOU'RE ESSENTIALLY DESCENDED FROM VAMPIRE HITLER.
HMMPH. GOTTA TAKE BACK WHAT I SAID ABOUT YOU BEIN' THE WORST VAMPIRE.
NOW I'M ACTUALLY IMPRESSED.
I DUNNO. IF YOU ASK ME...

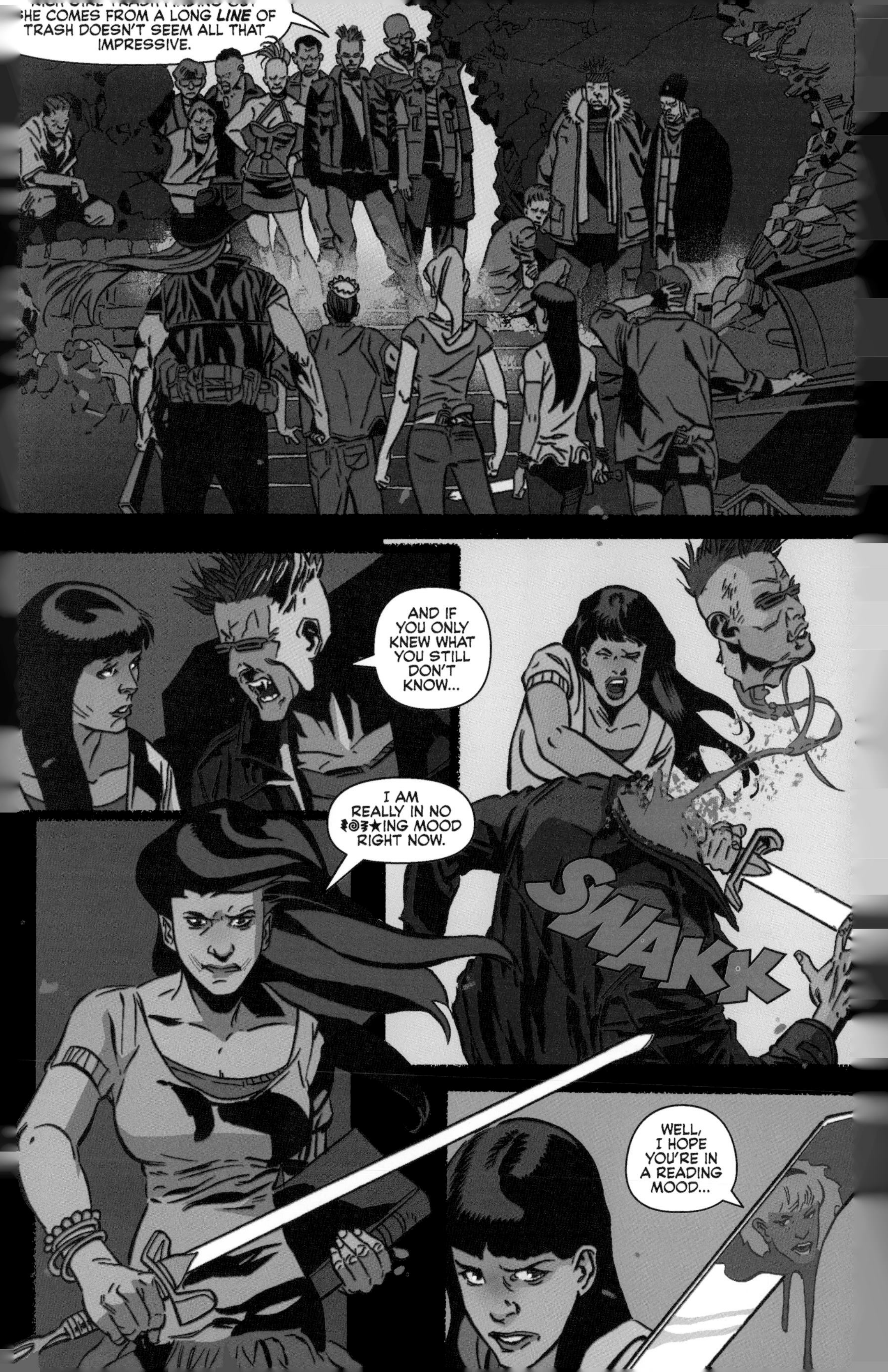
HE COMES FROM A LONG LINE OF TRASH DOESN'T SEEM ALL THAT IMPRESSIVE.
AND IF YOU ONLY KNEW WHAT YOU STILL DON'T KNOW...
I AM REALLY IN NO §@Ʒ★ING MOOD RIGHT NOW.
SNAKK
WELL, I HOPE YOU'RE IN A READING MOOD...

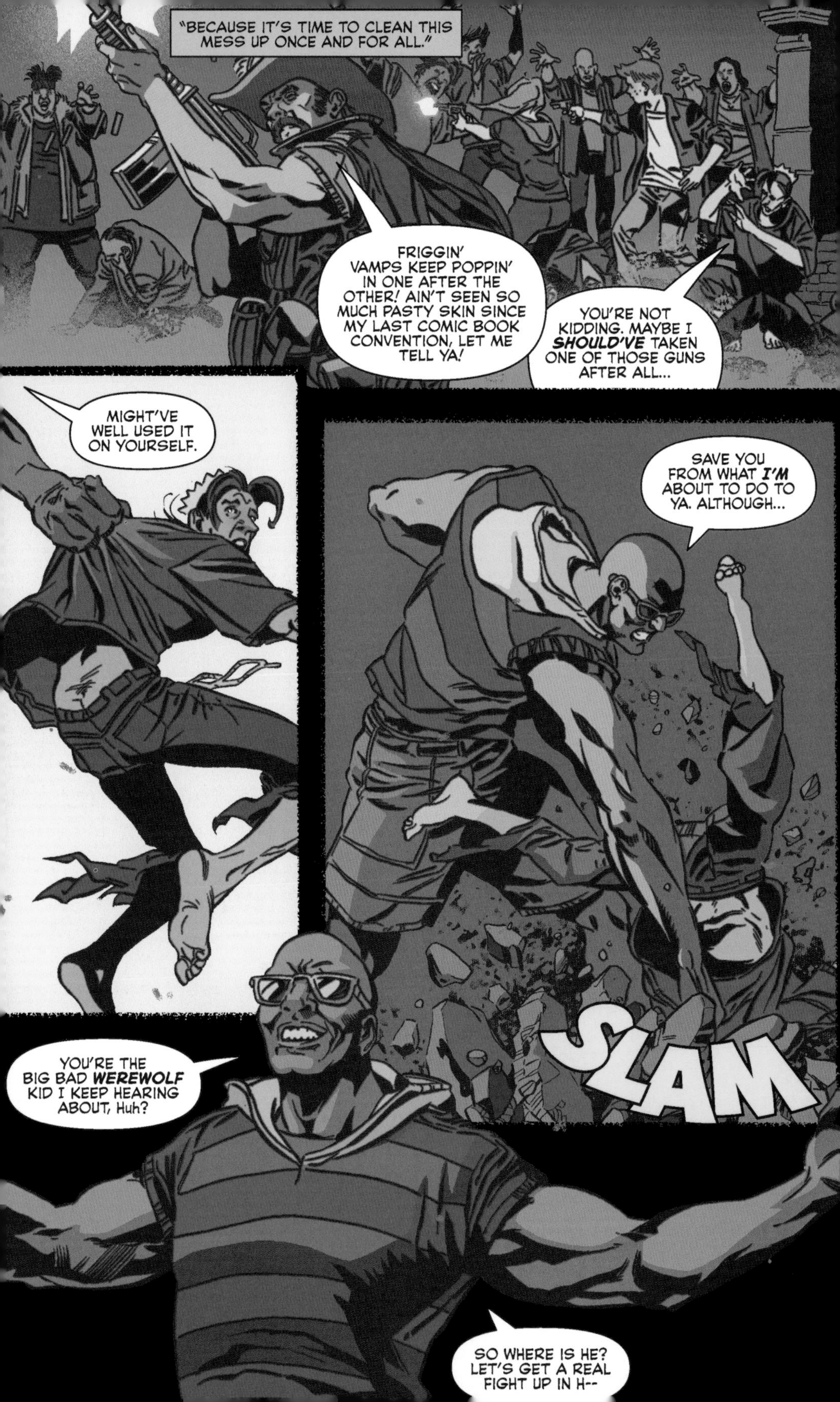
"BECAUSE IT'S TIME TO CLEAN THIS MESS UP ONCE AND FOR ALL."
FRIGGIN' VAMPS KEEP POPPIN' IN ONE AFTER THE OTHER! AIN'T SEEN SO MUCH PASTY SKIN SINCE MY LAST COMIC BOOK CONVENTION, LET ME TELL YA!
YOU'RE NOT KIDDING. MAYBE I SHOULD'VE TAKEN ONE OF THOSE GUNS AFTER ALL...
MIGHT'VE WELL USED IT ON YOURSELF.
SAVE YOU FROM WHAT I'M ABOUT TO DO TO YA. ALTHOUGH...
SLAM
YOU'RE THE BIG BAD WEREWOLF KID I KEEP HEARING ABOUT, Huh?
SO WHERE IS HE? LET'S GET A REAL FIGHT UP IN H--

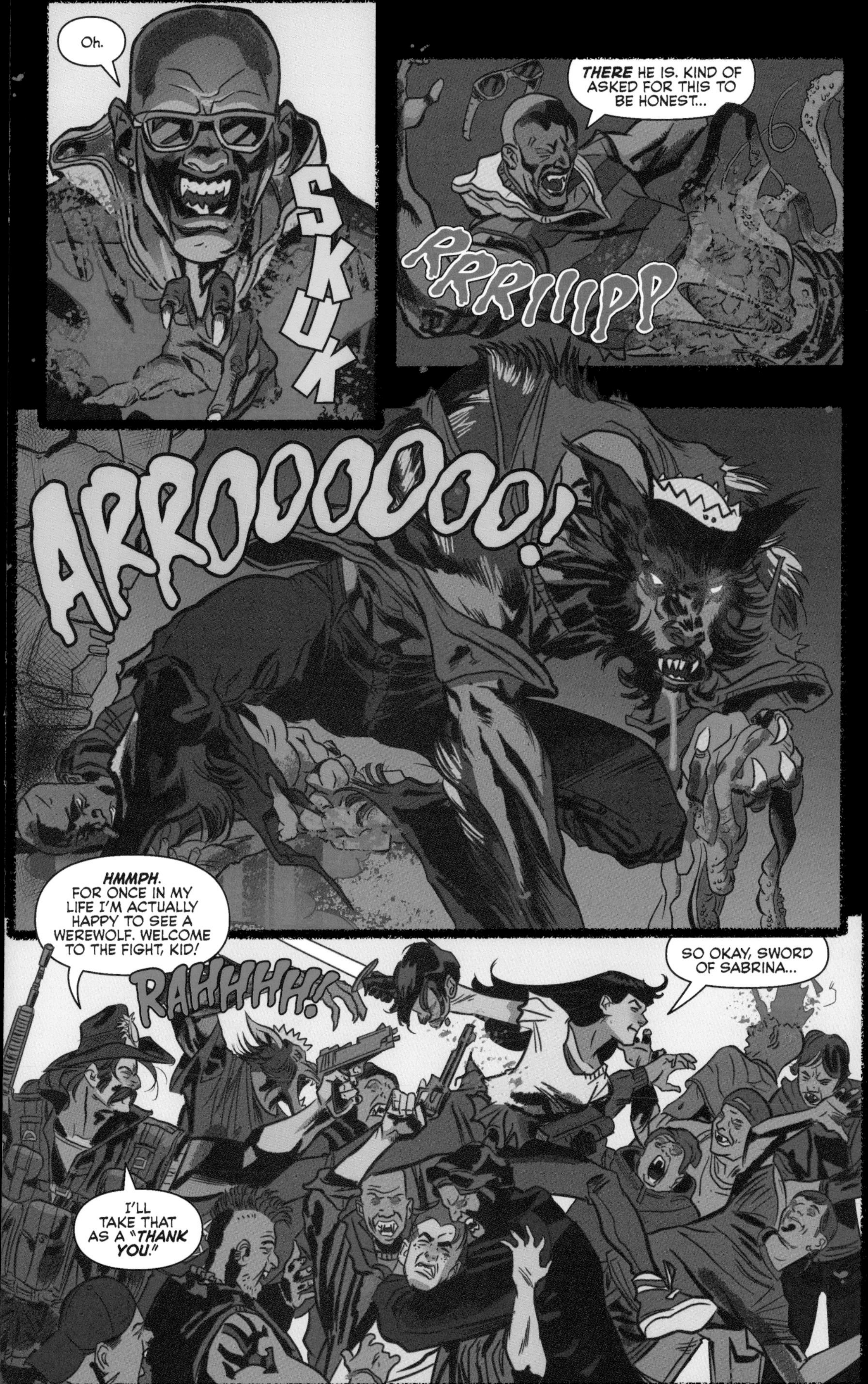

Oh.
SKUK
THERE HE IS. KIND OF ASKED FOR THIS TO BE HONEST...
RRRIIIPP
ARROOOOOO!
HMMPH. FOR ONCE IN MY LIFE I'M ACTUALLY HAPPY TO SEE A WEREWOLF. WELCOME TO THE FIGHT, KID!
RAHHHH!!
SO OKAY, SWORD OF SABRINA...
I'LL TAKE THAT AS A "THANK YOU."

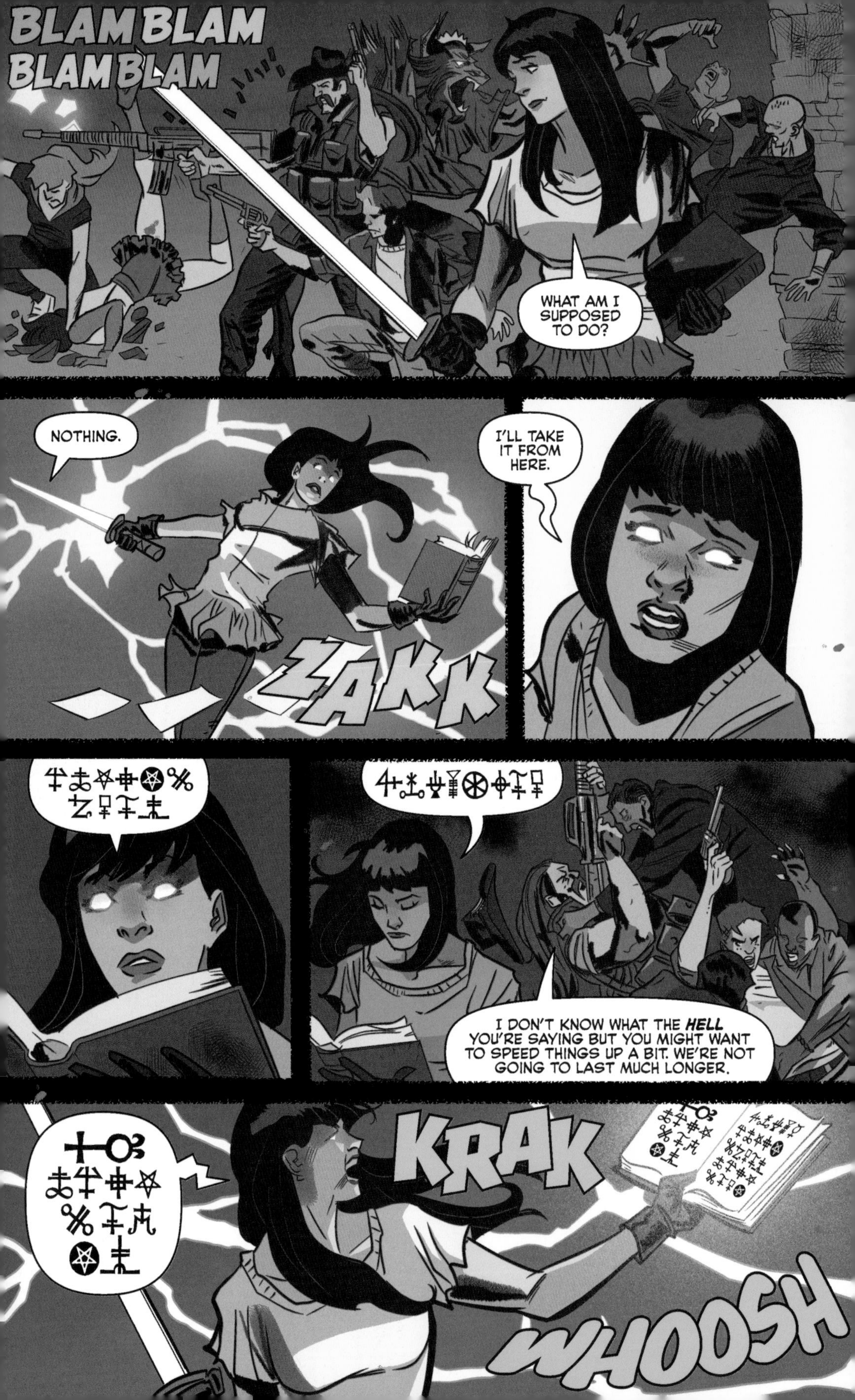
BLAM BLAM
BLAM BLAM
WHAT AM I SUPPOSED TO DO?
NOTHING.
ZAKK
I'LL TAKE IT FROM HERE.
I DON'T KNOW WHAT THE *HELL* YOU'RE SAYING BUT YOU MIGHT WANT TO SPEED THINGS UP A BIT. WE'RE NOT GOING TO LAST MUCH LONGER.
KRAK
WHOOSH

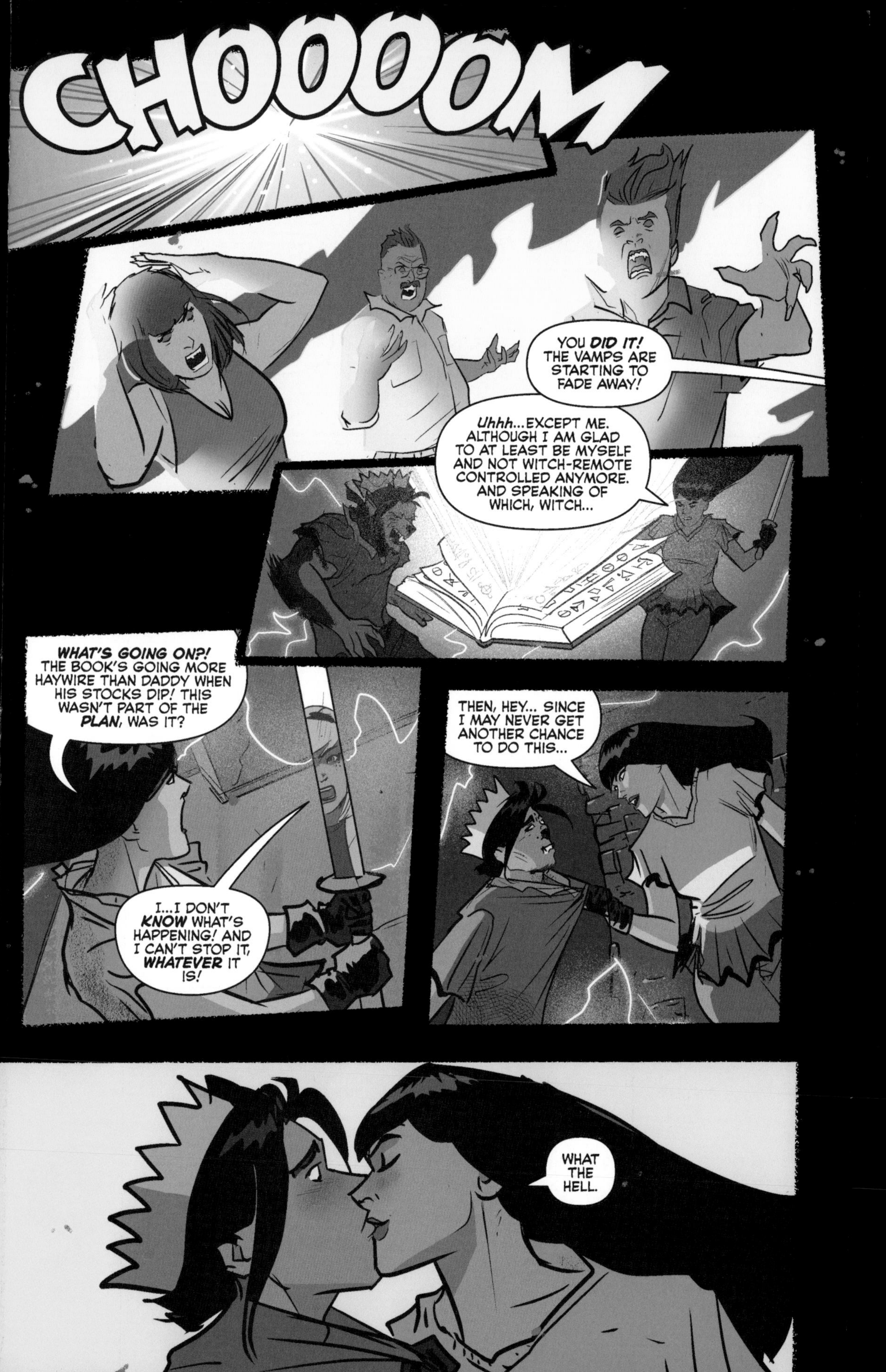
CHOOOOM
YOU DID IT! THE VAMPS ARE STARTING TO FADE AWAY!
Uhhh...EXCEPT ME. ALTHOUGH I AM GLAD TO AT LEAST BE MYSELF AND NOT WITCH-REMOTE CONTROLLED ANYMORE. AND SPEAKING OF WHICH, WITCH...
WHAT'S GOING ON?! THE BOOK'S GOING MORE HAYWIRE THAN DADDY WHEN HIS STOCKS DIP! THIS WASN'T PART OF THE PLAN, WAS IT?
I...I DON'T KNOW WHAT'S HAPPENING! AND I CAN'T STOP IT, WHATEVER IT IS!
THEN, HEY... SINCE I MAY NEVER GET ANOTHER CHANCE TO DO THIS...
WHAT THE HELL.

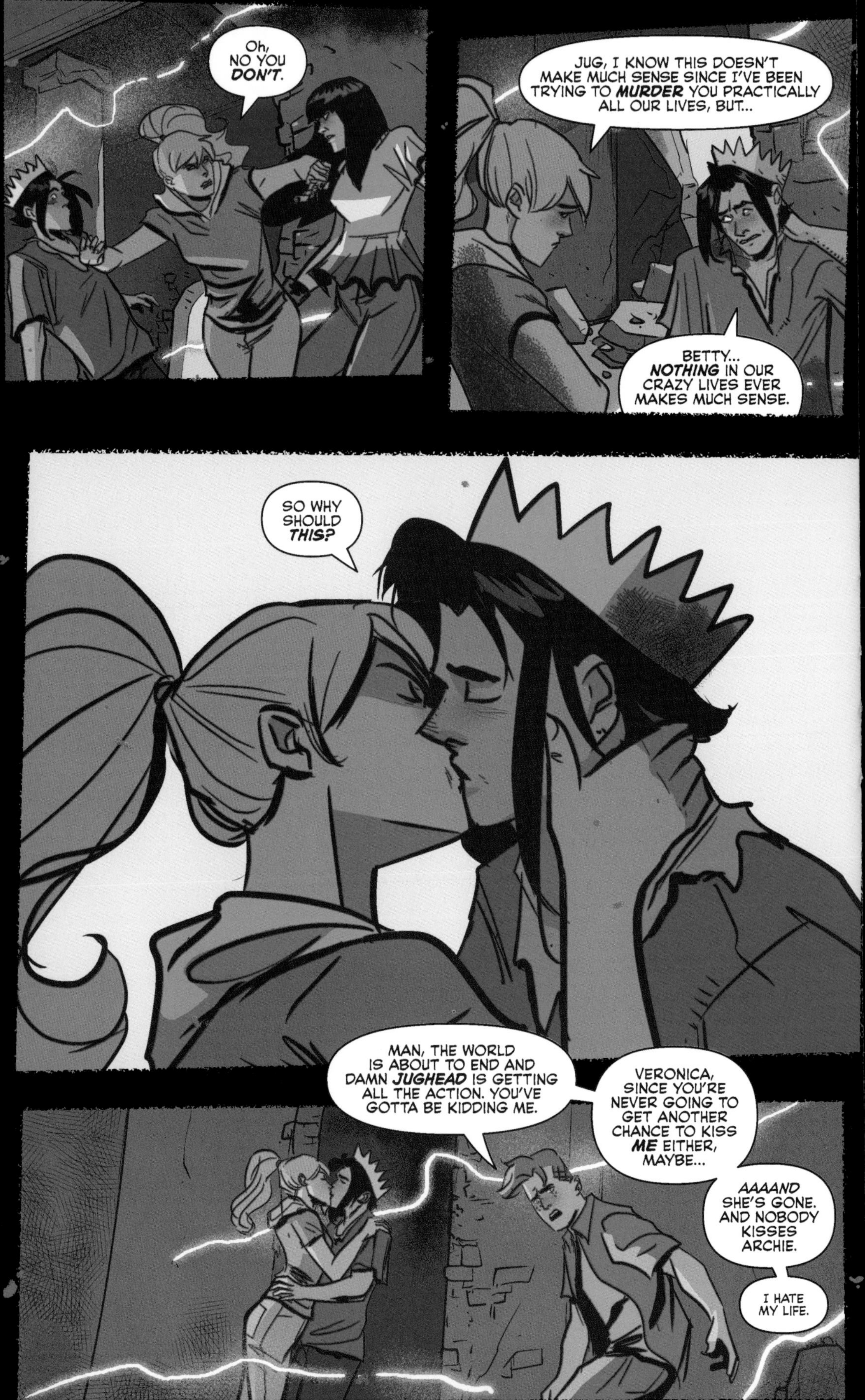
Oh, NO YOU DON'T.
JUG, I KNOW THIS DOESN'T MAKE MUCH SENSE SINCE I'VE BEEN TRYING TO MURDER YOU PRACTICALLY ALL OUR LIVES, BUT...
BETTY... NOTHING IN OUR CRAZY LIVES EVER MAKES MUCH SENSE.
SO WHY SHOULD THIS?
MAN, THE WORLD IS ABOUT TO END AND DAMN JUGHEAD IS GETTING ALL THE ACTION. YOU'VE GOTTA BE KIDDING ME.
VERONICA, SINCE YOU'RE NEVER GOING TO GET ANOTHER CHANCE TO KISS ME EITHER, MAYBE...
AAAAND SHE'S GONE. AND NOBODY KISSES ARCHIE.
I HATE MY LIFE.

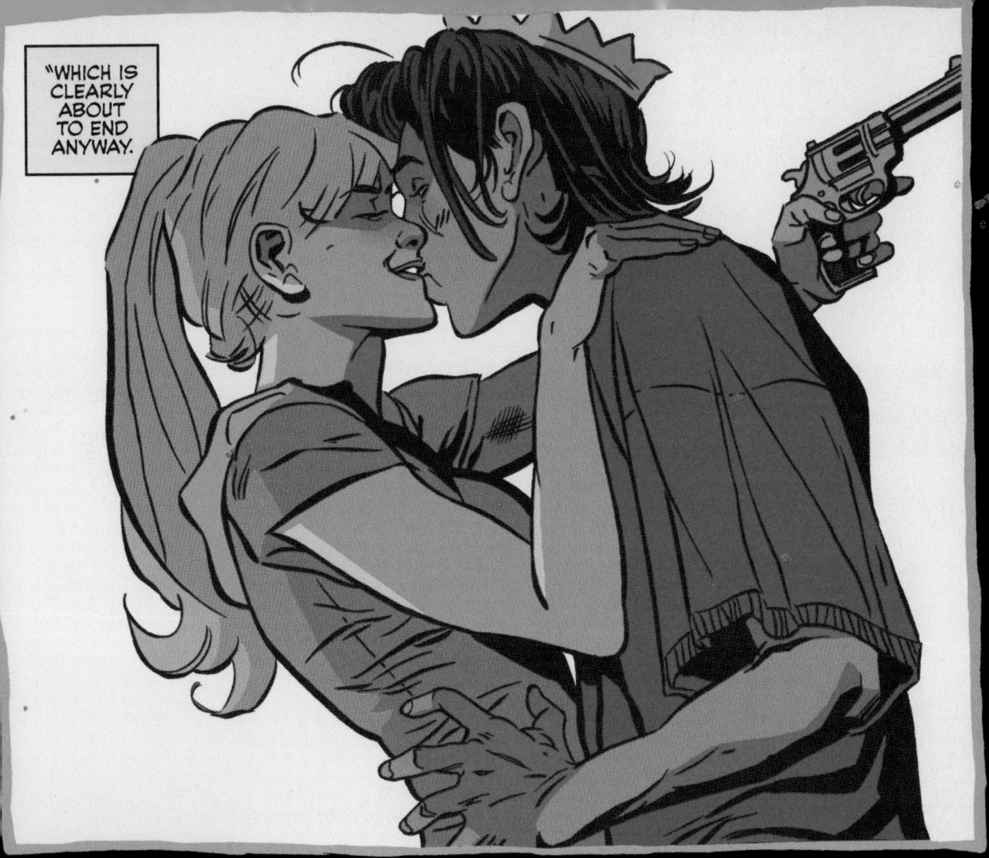
"WHICH IS CLEARLY ABOUT TO END ANYWAY.

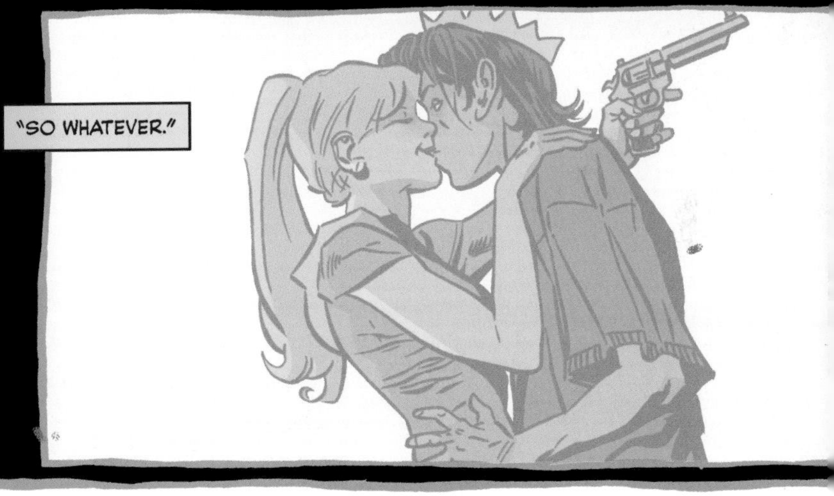
"SO WHATEVER."

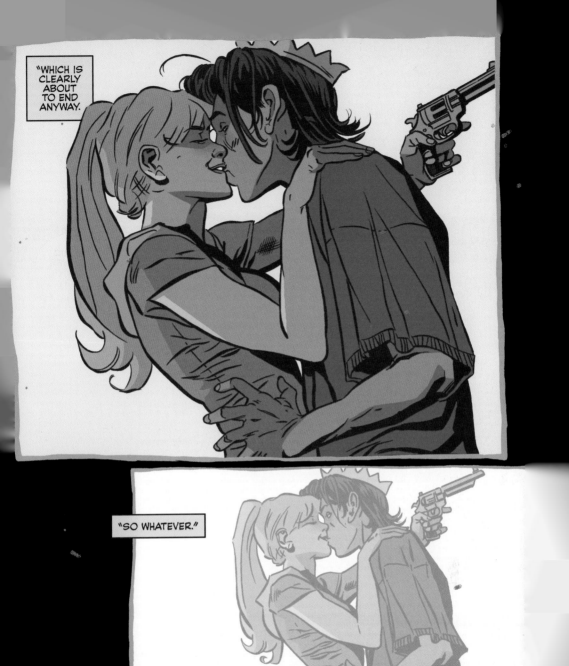

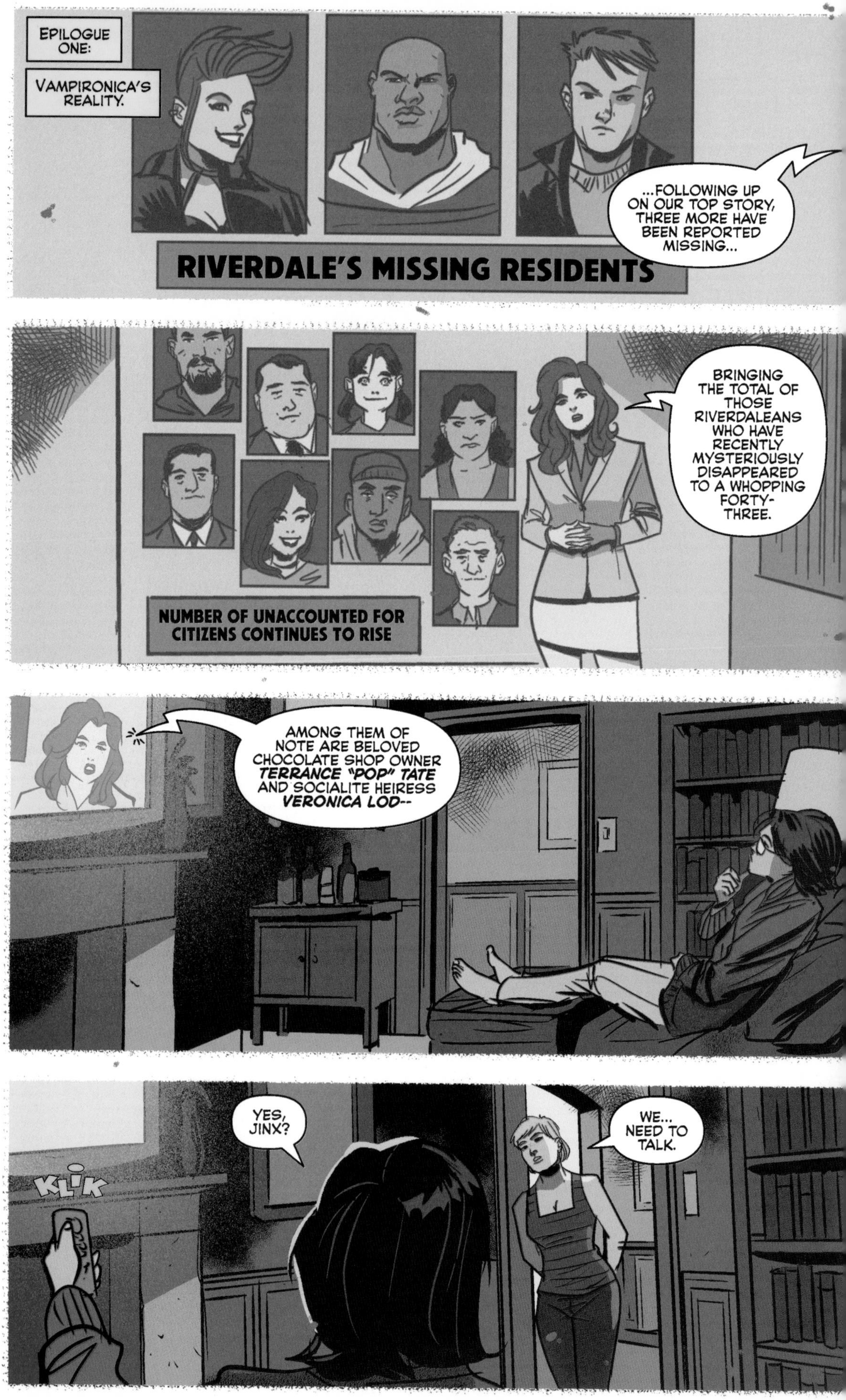
EPILOGUE ONE:
VAMPIRONICA'S REALITY.
RIVERDALE'S MISSING RESIDENTS
...FOLLOWING UP ON OUR TOP STORY, THREE MORE HAVE BEEN REPORTED MISSING...
NUMBER OF UNACCOUNTED FOR CITIZENS CONTINUES TO RISE
BRINGING THE TOTAL OF THOSE RIVERDALEANS WHO HAVE RECENTLY MYSTERIOUSLY DISAPPEARED TO A WHOPPING FORTY-THREE.
AMONG THEM OF NOTE ARE BELOVED CHOCOLATE SHOP OWNER ***TERRANCE "POP" TATE*** AND SOCIALITE HEIRESS ***VERONICA LOD--***
KLIK
YES, JINX?
WE... NEED TO TALK.

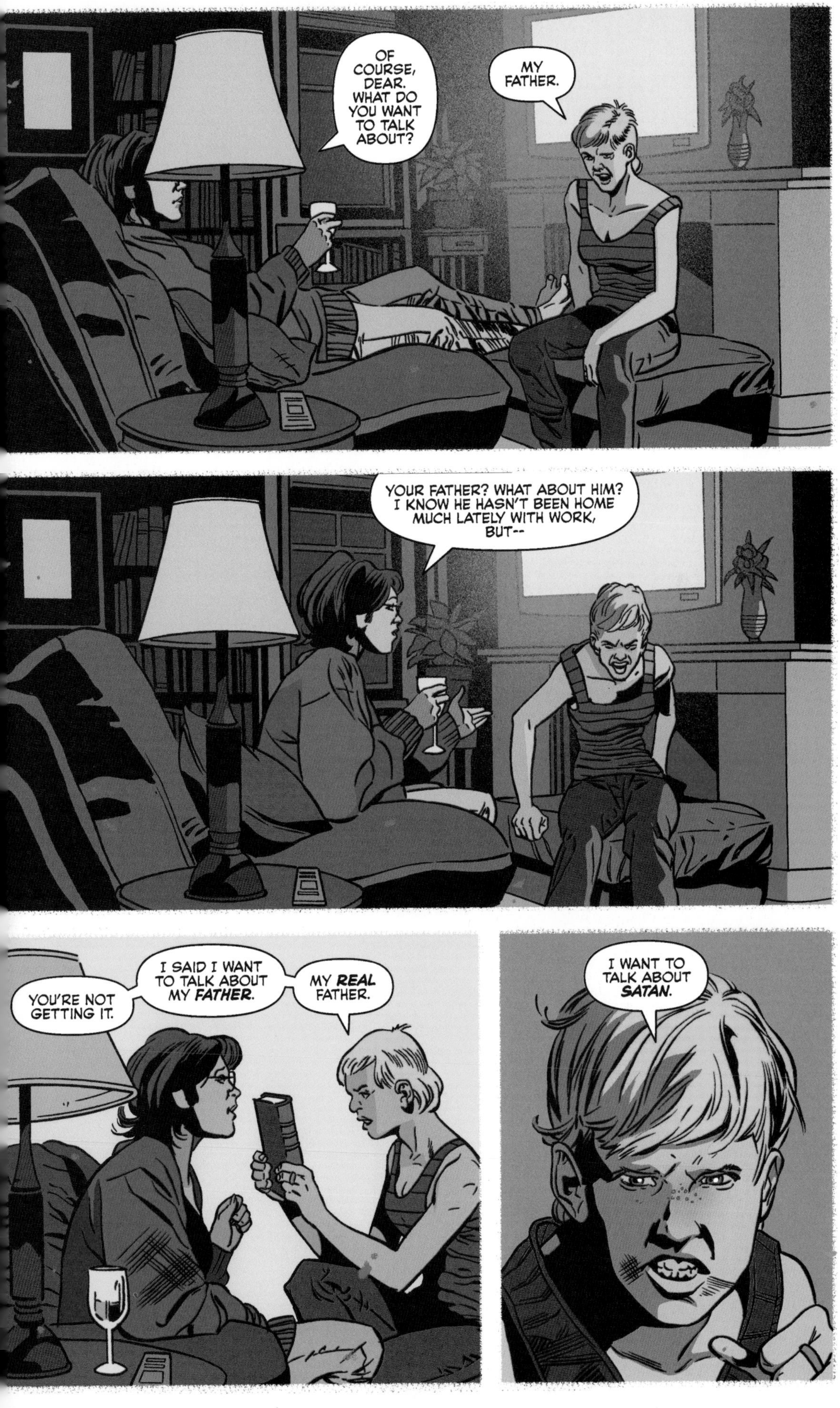
OF COURSE, DEAR. WHAT DO YOU WANT TO TALK ABOUT?
MY FATHER.
YOUR FATHER? WHAT ABOUT HIM? I KNOW HE HASN'T BEEN HOME MUCH LATELY WITH WORK, BUT--
YOU'RE NOT GETTING IT.
I SAID I WANT TO TALK ABOUT MY FATHER.
MY REAL FATHER.
I WANT TO TALK ABOUT SATAN.

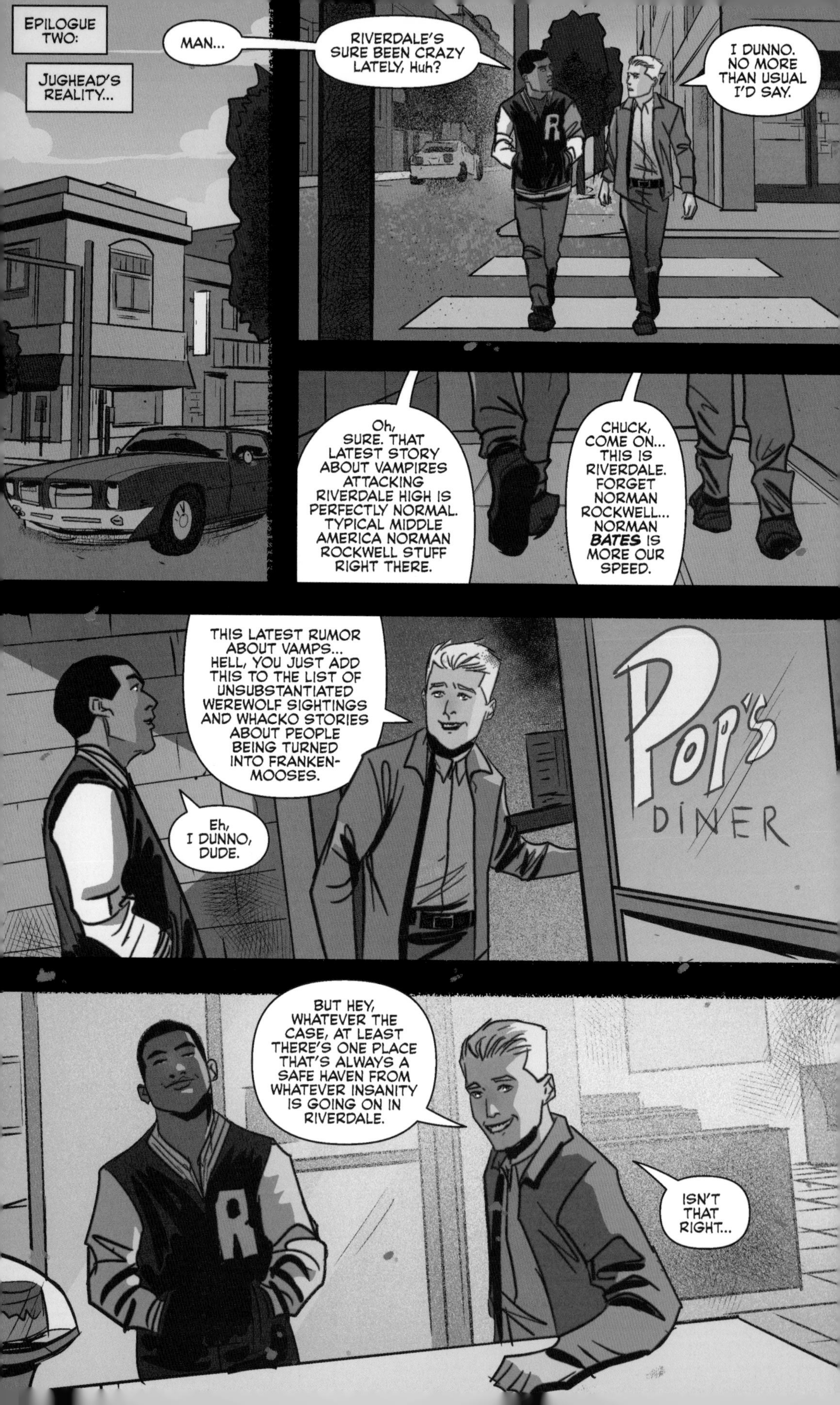
EPILOGUE TWO:
JUGHEAD'S REALITY...
MAN...
RIVERDALE'S SURE BEEN CRAZY LATELY, Huh?
I DUNNO. NO MORE THAN USUAL I'D SAY.
Oh, SURE. THAT LATEST STORY ABOUT VAMPIRES ATTACKING RIVERDALE HIGH IS PERFECTLY NORMAL. TYPICAL MIDDLE AMERICA NORMAN ROCKWELL STUFF RIGHT THERE.
CHUCK, COME ON... THIS IS RIVERDALE. FORGET NORMAN ROCKWELL... NORMAN **BATES** IS MORE OUR SPEED.
THIS LATEST RUMOR ABOUT VAMPS... HELL, YOU JUST ADD THIS TO THE LIST OF UNSUBSTANTIATED WEREWOLF SIGHTINGS AND WHACKO STORIES ABOUT PEOPLE BEING TURNED INTO FRANKEN-MOOSES.
Eh, I DUNNO, DUDE.
Pop's
DINER
BUT HEY, WHATEVER THE CASE, AT LEAST THERE'S ONE PLACE THAT'S ALWAYS A SAFE HAVEN FROM WHATEVER INSANITY IS GOING ON IN RIVERDALE.
ISN'T THAT RIGHT...

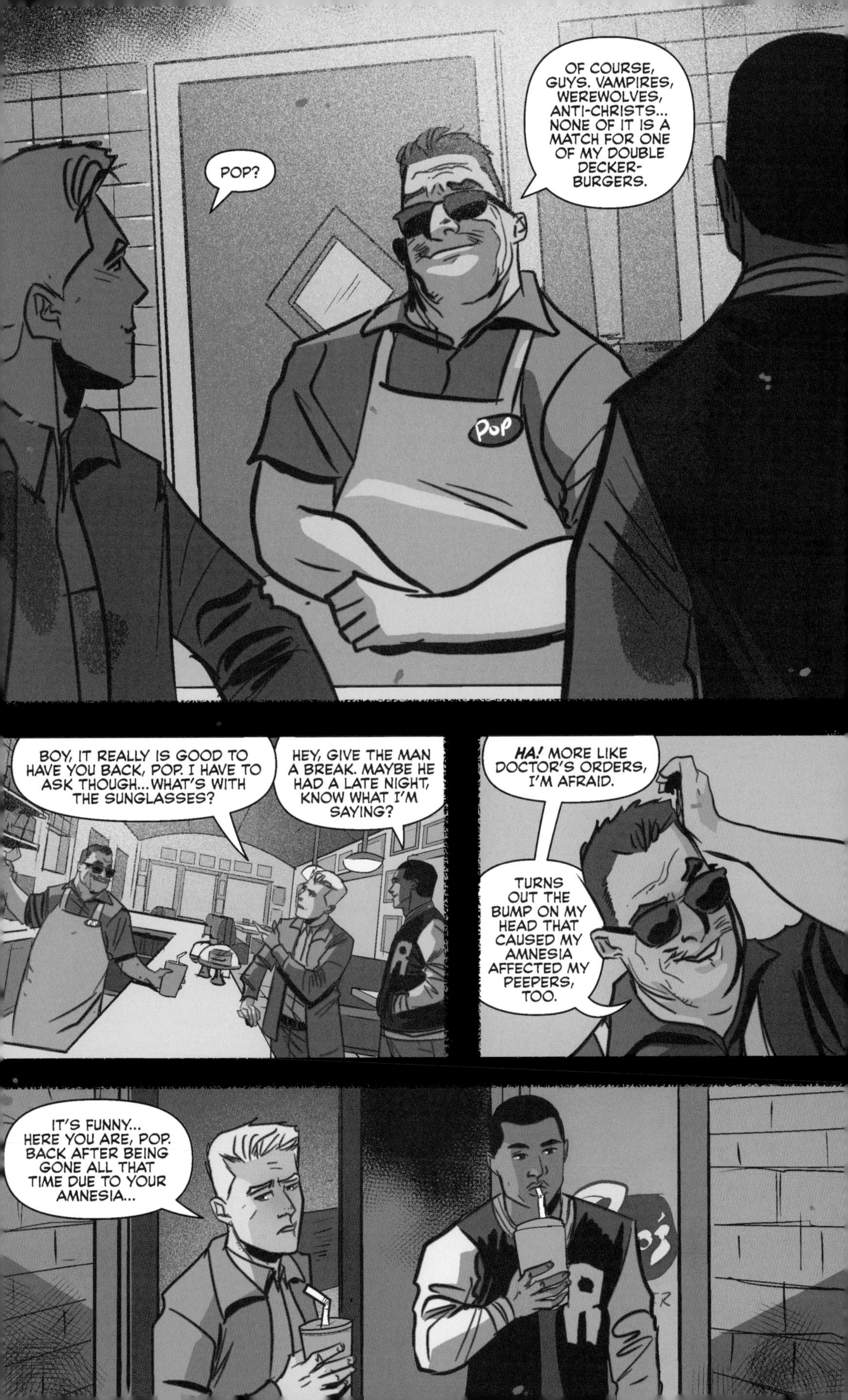
POP?
OF COURSE, GUYS. VAMPIRES, WEREWOLVES, ANTI-CHRISTS... NONE OF IT IS A MATCH FOR ONE OF MY DOUBLE DECKER-BURGERS.
POP
BOY, IT REALLY IS GOOD TO HAVE YOU BACK, POP. I HAVE TO ASK THOUGH...WHAT'S WITH THE SUNGLASSES?
HEY, GIVE THE MAN A BREAK. MAYBE HE HAD A LATE NIGHT, KNOW WHAT I'M SAYING?
HA! MORE LIKE DOCTOR'S ORDERS, I'M AFRAID.
TURNS OUT THE BUMP ON MY HEAD THAT CAUSED MY AMNESIA AFFECTED MY PEEPERS, TOO.
IT'S FUNNY... HERE YOU ARE, POP. BACK AFTER BEING GONE ALL THAT TIME DUE TO YOUR AMNESIA...

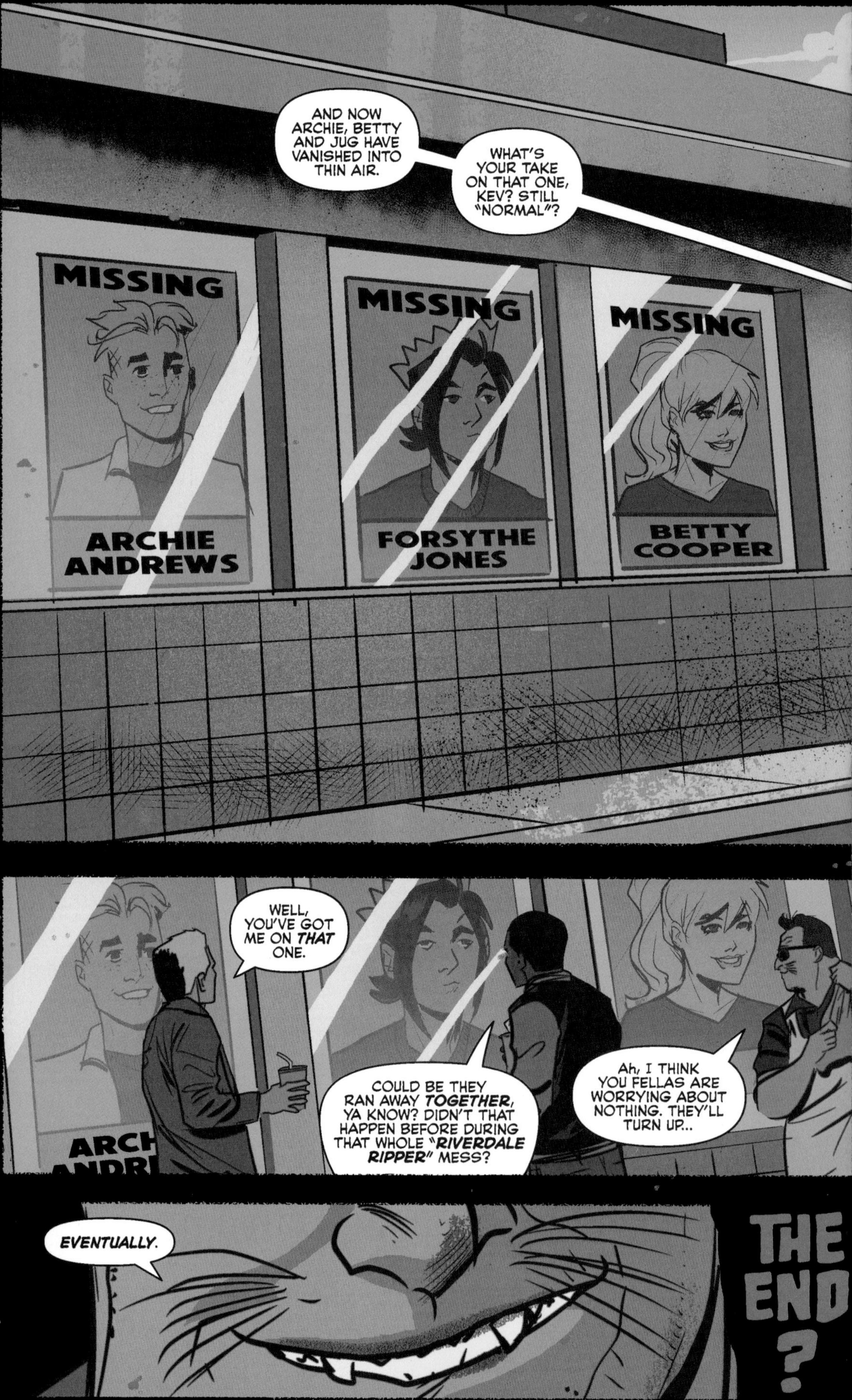
AND NOW ARCHIE, BETTY AND JUG HAVE VANISHED INTO THIN AIR.
WHAT'S YOUR TAKE ON THAT ONE, KEV? STILL "NORMAL"?
MISSING
ARCHIE ANDREWS
MISSING
FORSYTHE JONES
MISSING
BETTY COOPER
WELL, YOU'VE GOT ME ON *THAT* ONE.
COULD BE THEY RAN AWAY *TOGETHER*, YA KNOW? DIDN'T THAT HAPPEN BEFORE DURING THAT WHOLE "*RIVERDALE RIPPER*" MESS?
Ah, I THINK YOU FELLAS ARE WORRYING ABOUT NOTHING. THEY'LL TURN UP...
EVENTUALLY.
THE END?

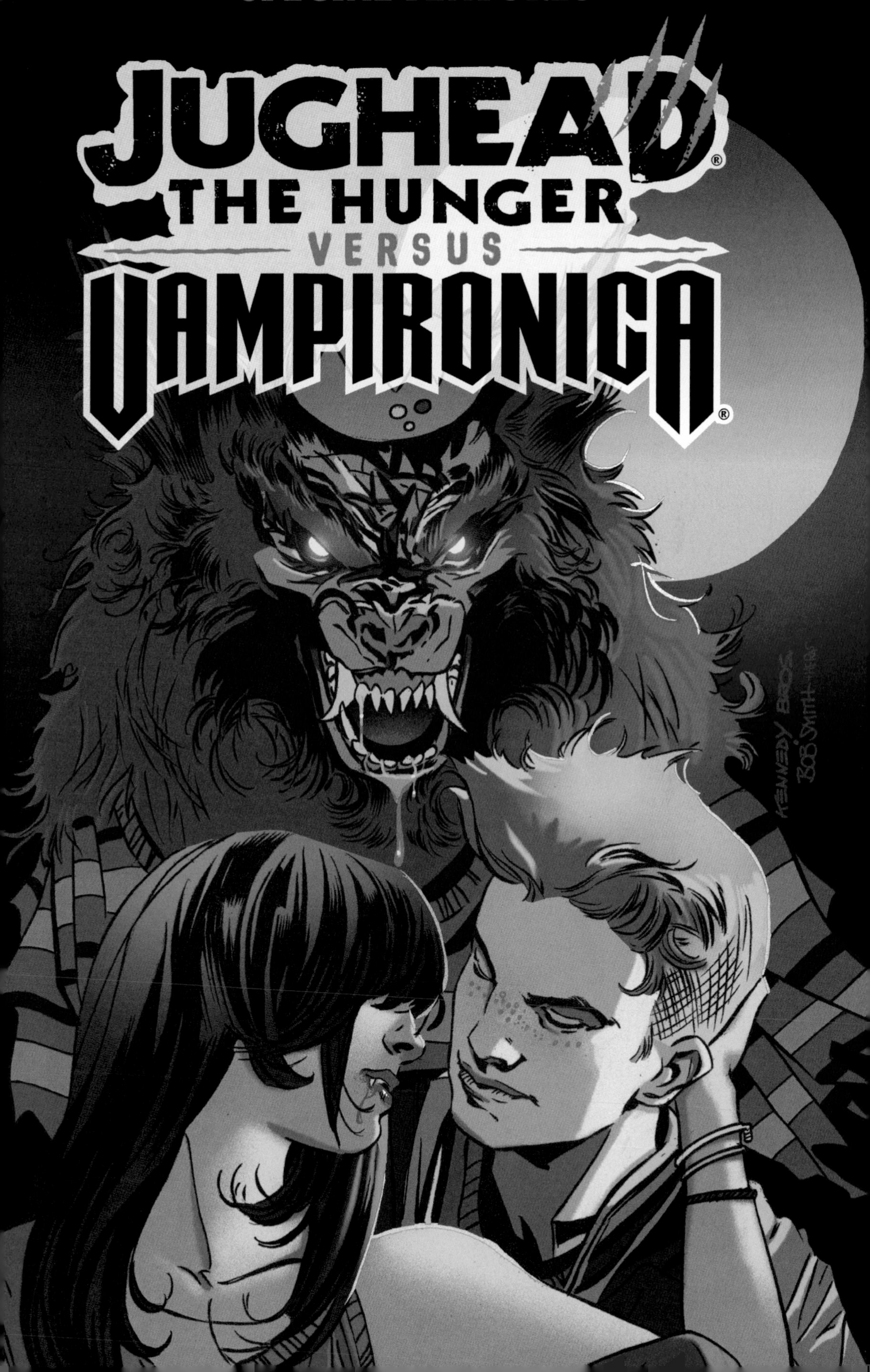
JUGHEAD®
THE HUNGER
VERSUS
VAMPIRONICA®

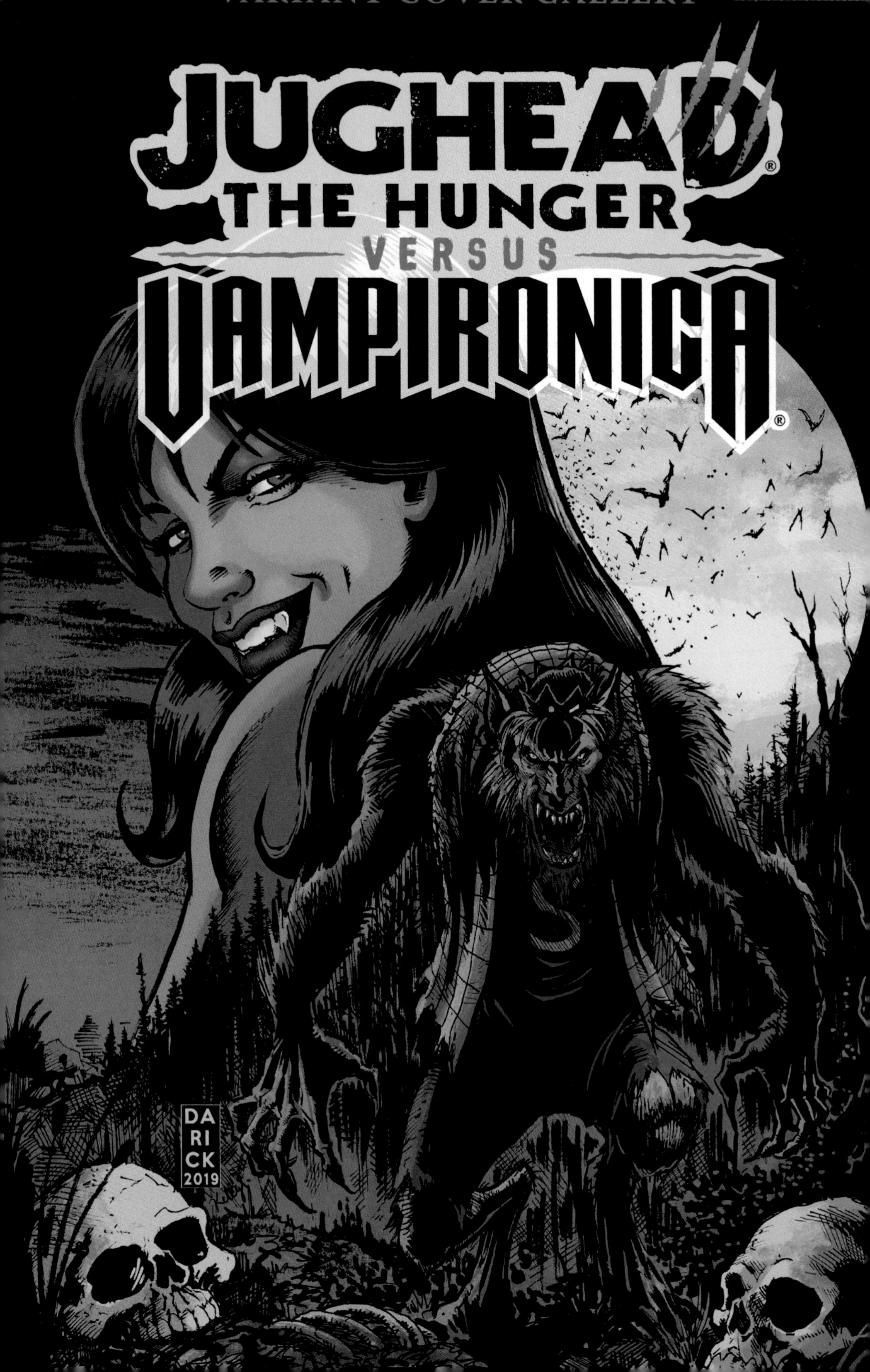
JUGHEAD®
THE HUNGER
VERSUS
VAMPIRONICA®
DARICK 2019

1.

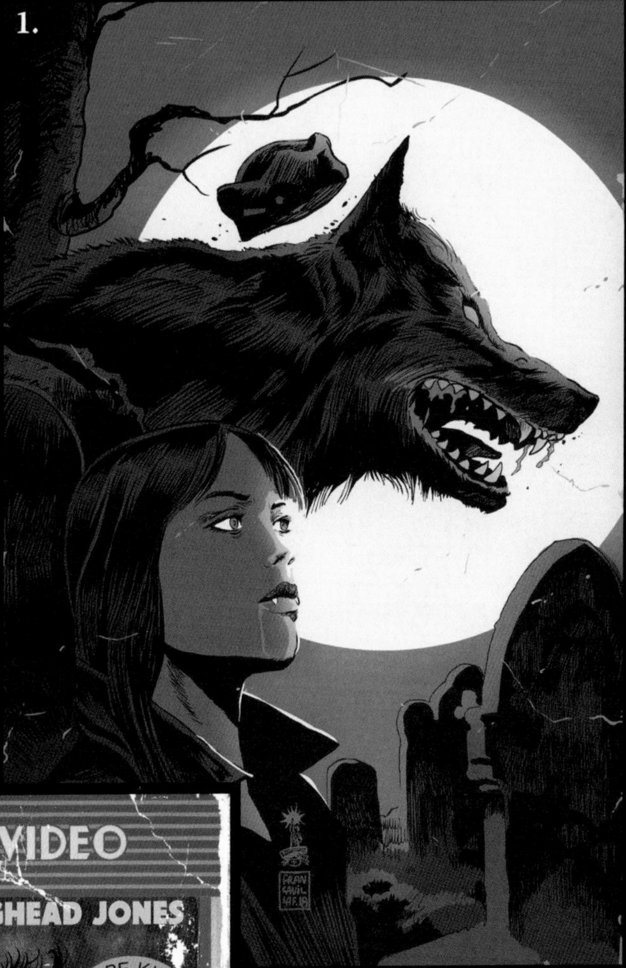

2.

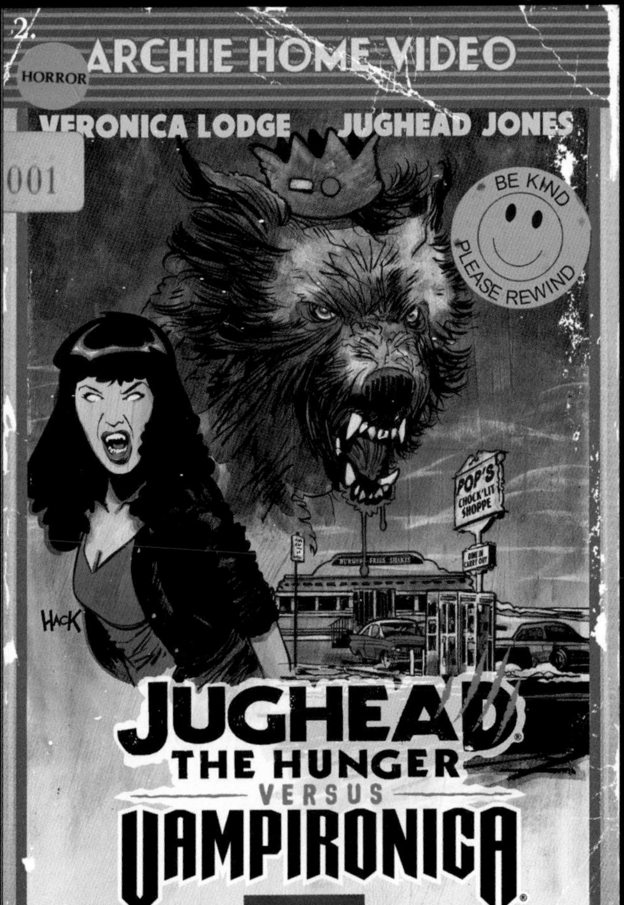
ARCHIE HOME VIDEO
HORROR
VERONICA LODGE
JUGHEAD JONES
001
BE KIND PLEASE REWIND
POP'S CHOCK'LIT SHOPPE
HACK
JUGHEAD THE HUNGER VERSUS VAMPIRONICA
VHS

ISSUE ONE

1. FRANCESCO FRANCAVILLA

2. ROBERT HACK

ISSUE ONE

3. JOHN McCREA

4. DAN PANOSIAN

3.

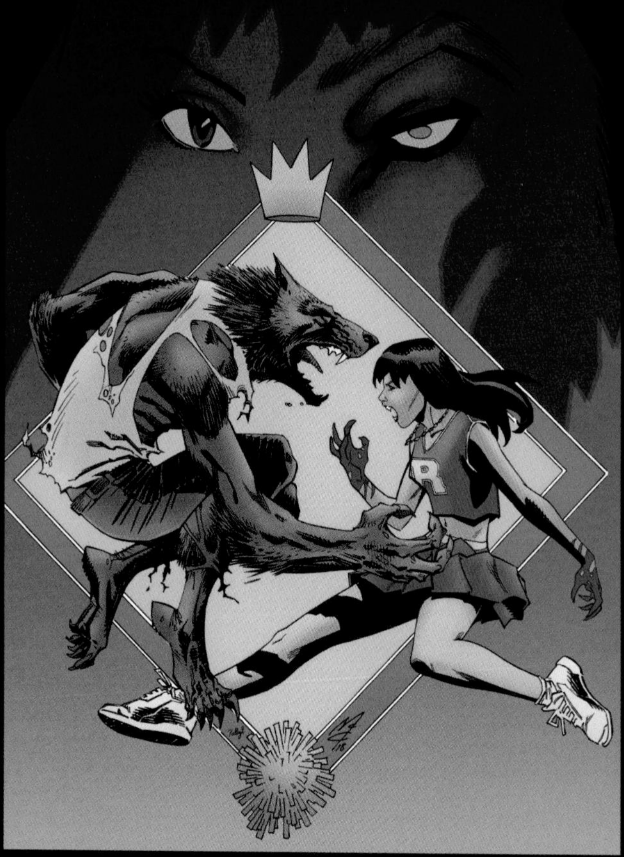

4.

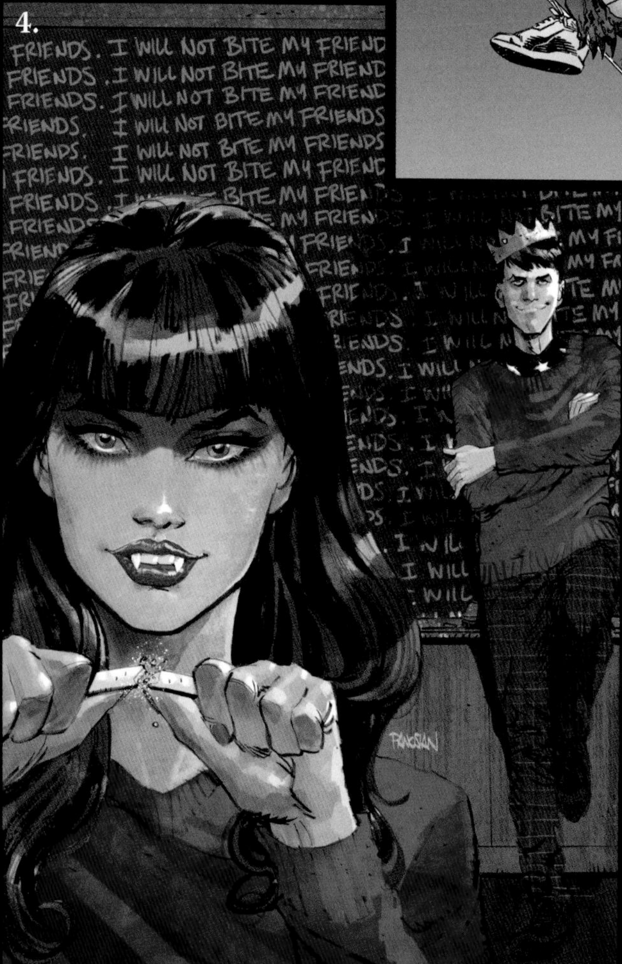
FRIENDS. I WILL NOT BITE MY FRIEND
FRIENDS. I WILL NOT BITE MY FRIEND
FRIENDS. I WILL NOT BITE MY FRIEND
FRIENDS. I WILL NOT BITE MY FRIENDS
FRIENDS. I WILL NOT BITE MY FRIENDS
FRIENDS. I WILL NOT BITE MY FRIEND
PANOSIAN

1.

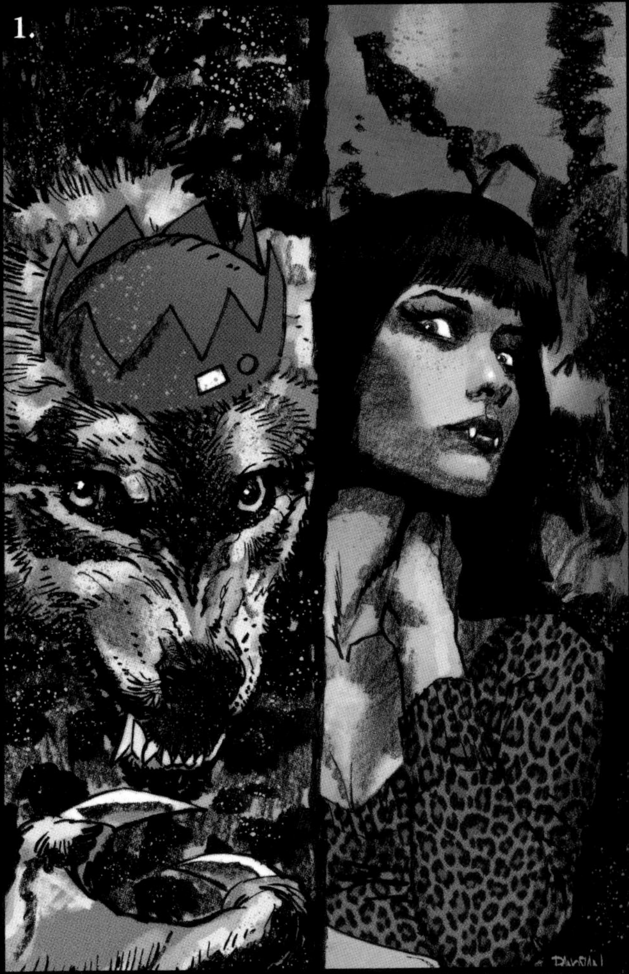

2.

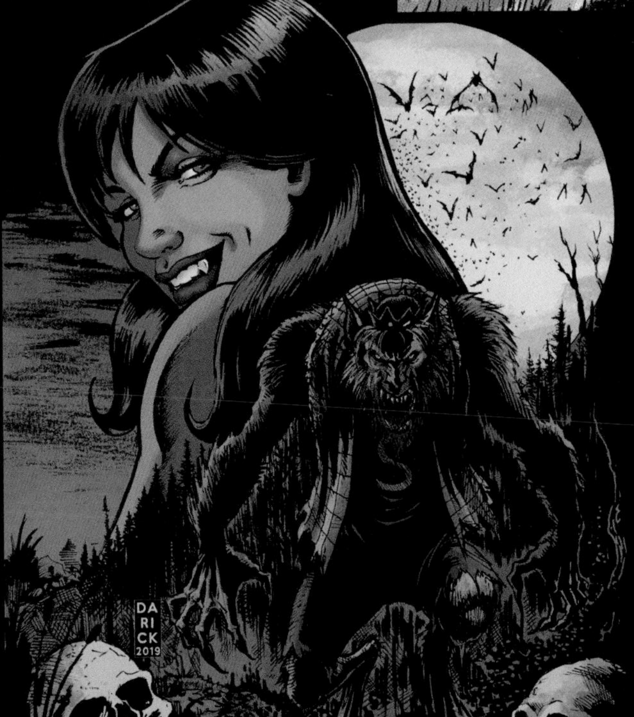
DA
RI
CK
2019

ISSUE TWO

1. DAN PANOSIAN

2. DARICK ROBERTSON

ISSUE THREE

1. DAN PANOSIAN
2. CAT STAGGS

1.
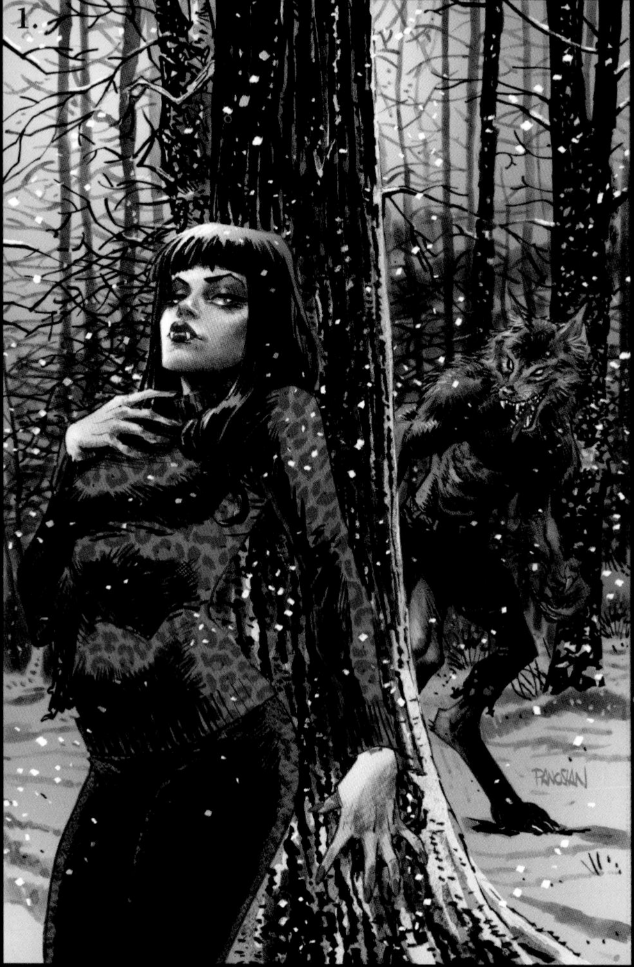
PANOSIAN

2.
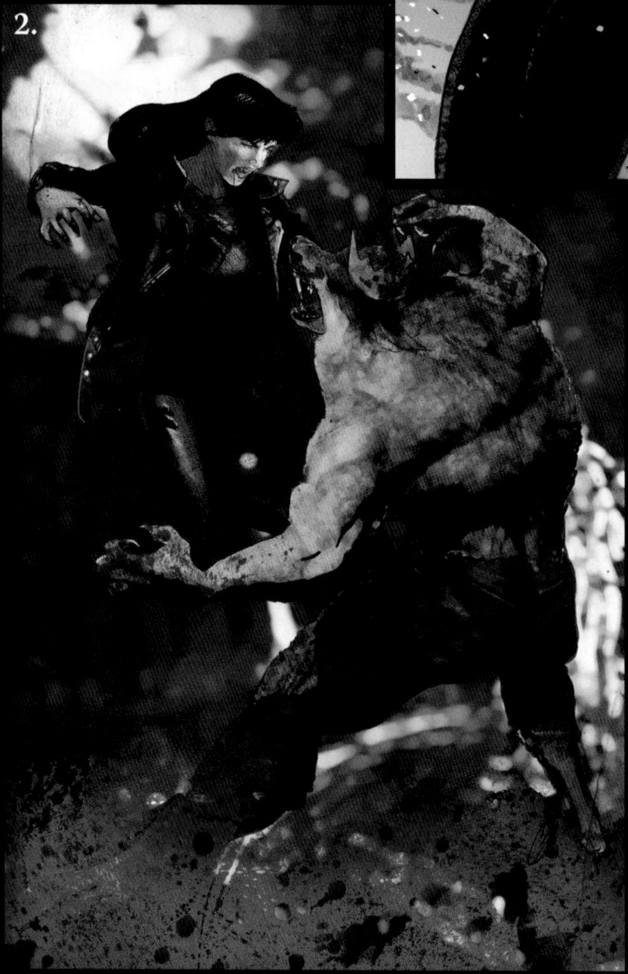

1.

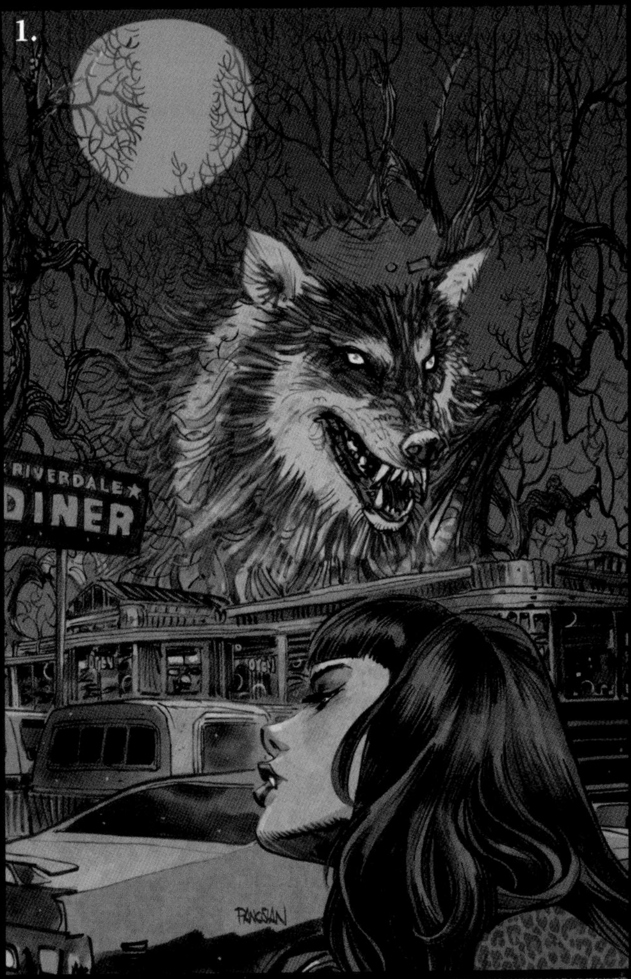
RIVERDALE
DINER
PANOSIAN

2.

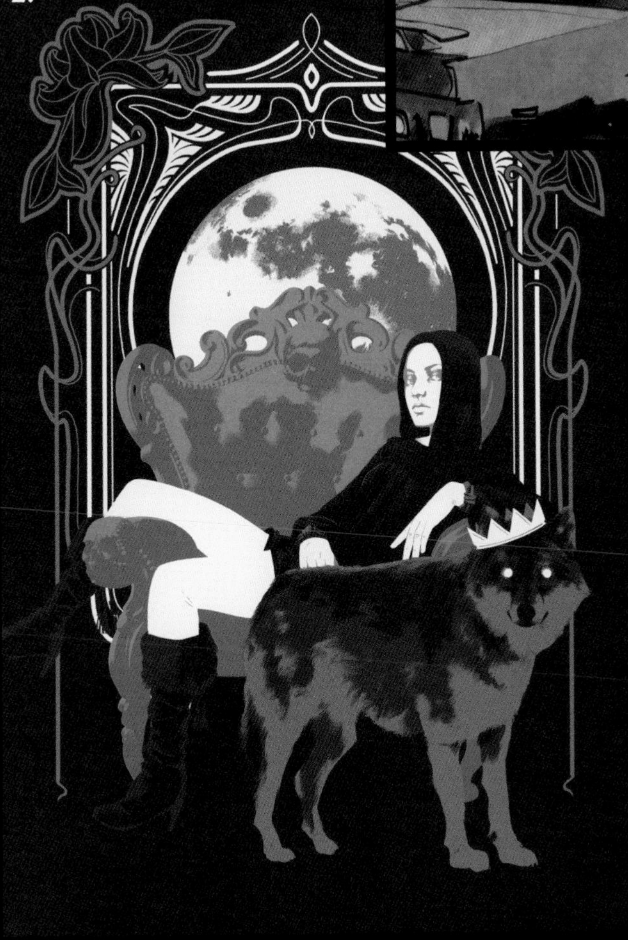

ISSUE FOUR

1. DAN PANOSIAN
2. MATTHEW TAYLOR

ISSUE FIVE

1. DAVID MACK
2. DAN PANOSIAN

1.

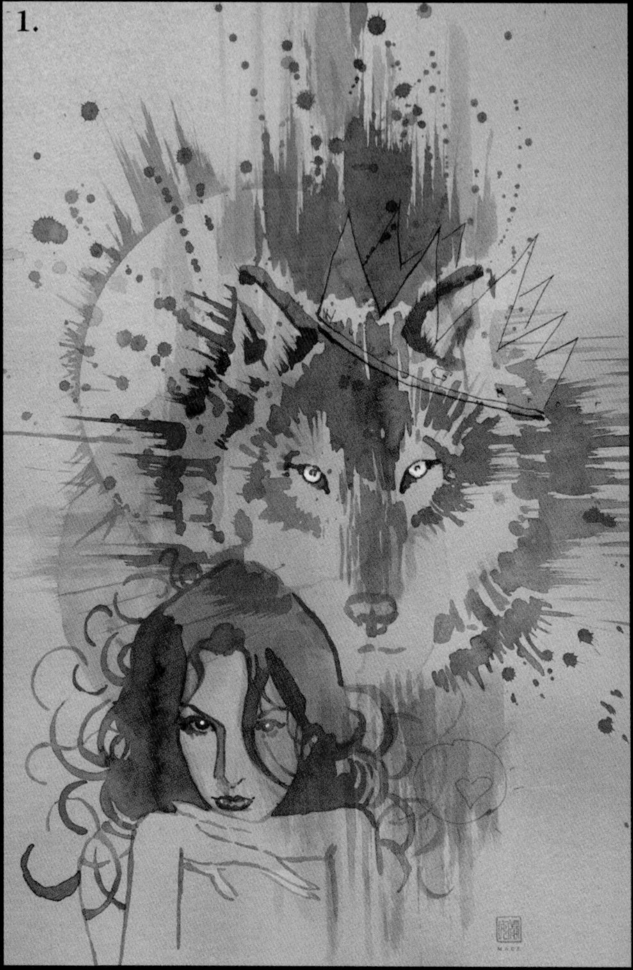

2.

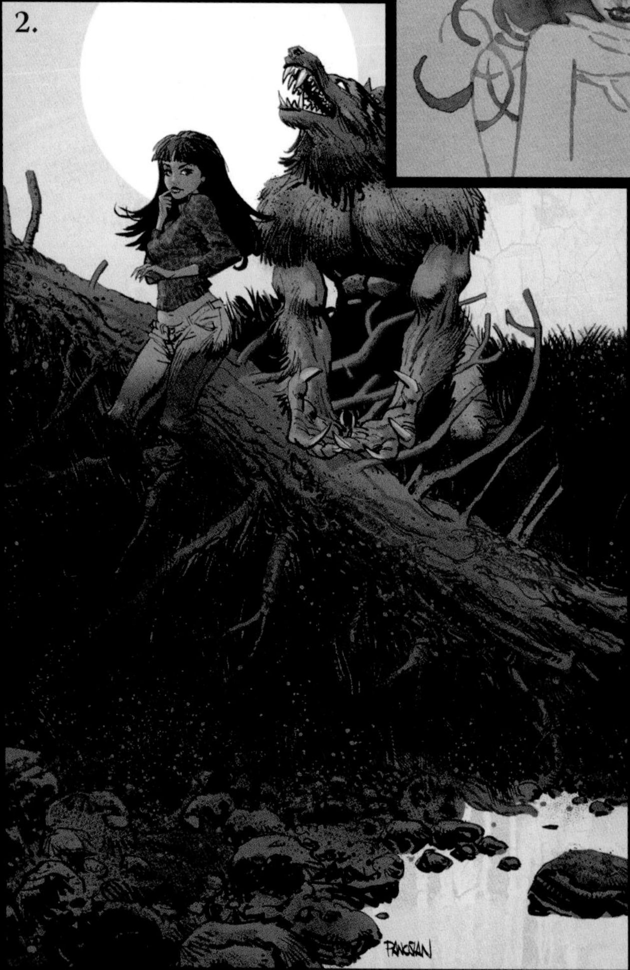
PANOSIAN

COVER PROCESS

Here's a behind the scenes look at the cover process for the *Jughead the Hunger vs. Vampironica* main cover. It starts with an original cover sketch by Pat & Tim Kennedy, the cover is then sent to Bob Smith for inks and Matt Herms for colors. Once the art is complete the logo and cover dress is added by the Archie Comics editorial team.

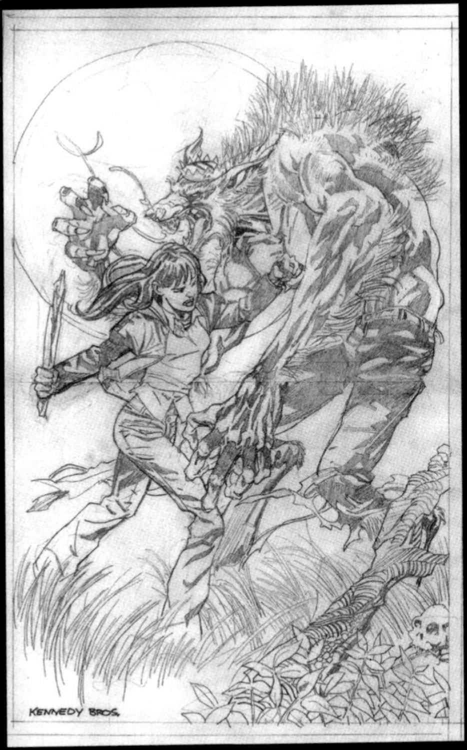
KENNEDY BROS.

PENCIL SKETCH

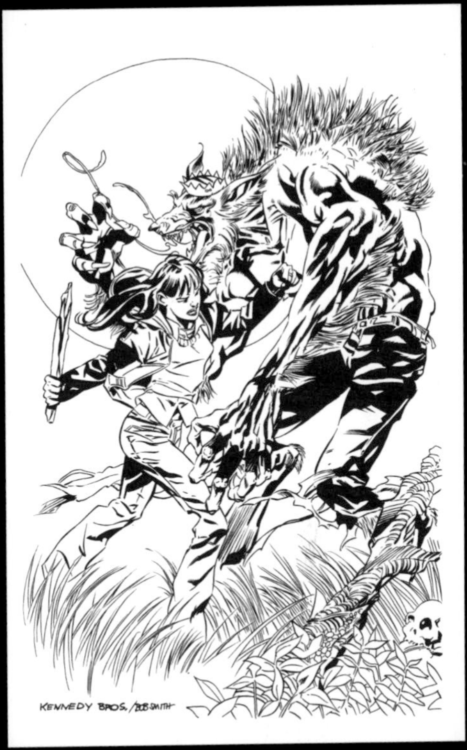
KENNEDY BROS./BOB SMITH

INKS

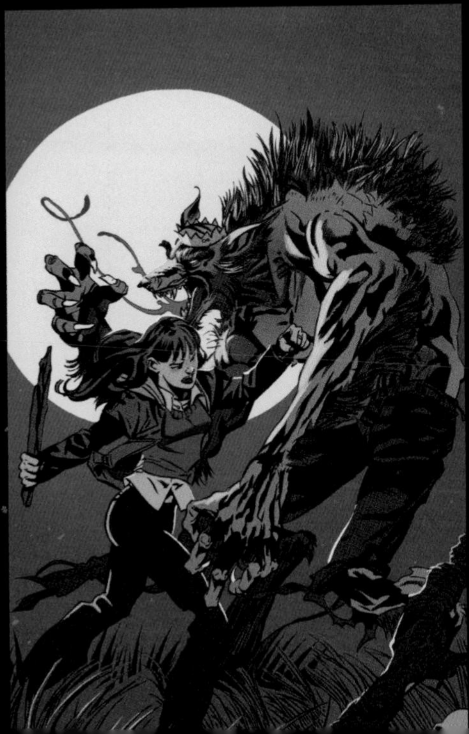

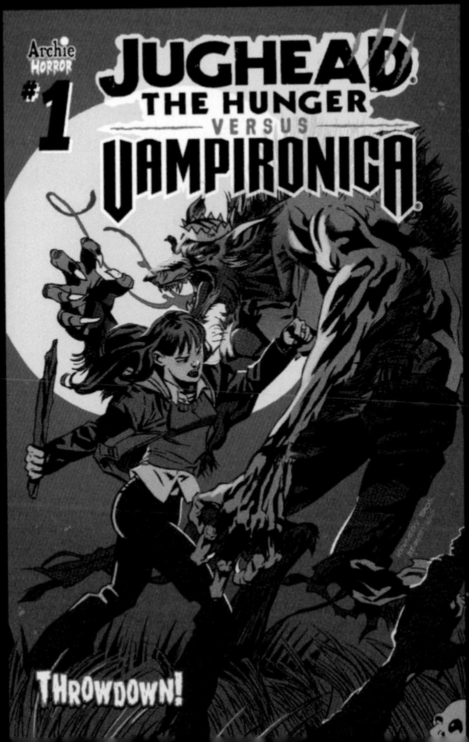
Archie
HORROR
#1
JUGHEAD
THE HUNGER
VERSUS
VAMPIRONICA
THROWDOWN!

PROMO SKETCHES

Check out these original sketches by Pat and Tim Kennedy. Before starting the *Jughead the Hunger vs. Vampironica* series the Kennedys sent in some sample pages of how they envisioned the book to look. They were able to pick up right where the *Jughead the Hunger* series left off with their gruesome details and horrific monsters.

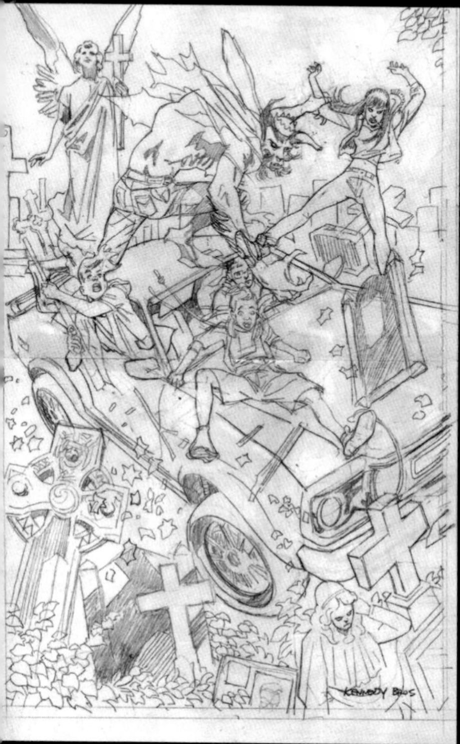
KENNEDY BROS

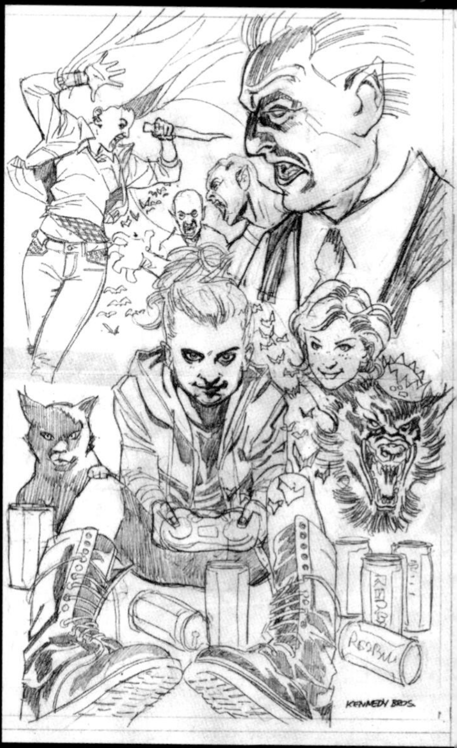
KENNEDY BROS.

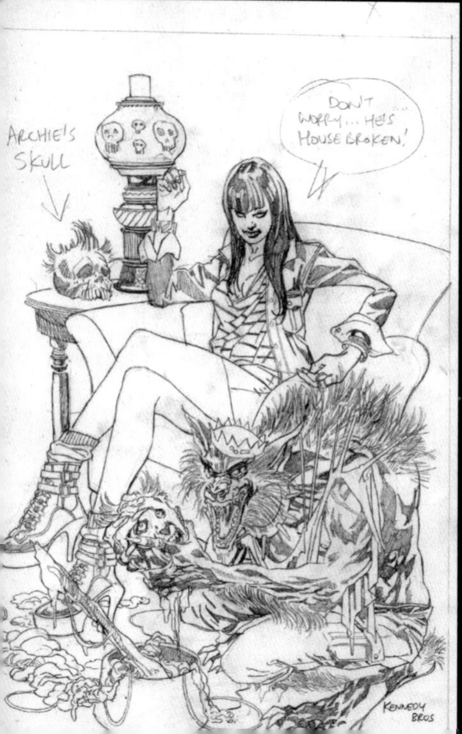
ARCHIE'S SKULL
DON'T WORRY... HE'S HOUSE BROKEN!
KENNEDY BROS

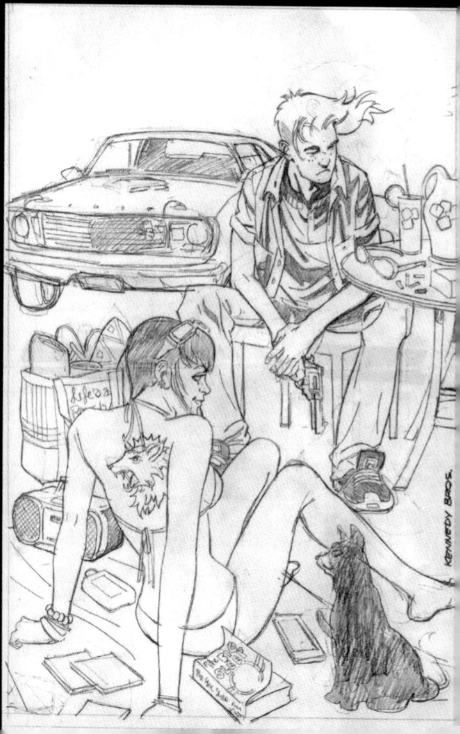
KENNEDY BROS.

Riverdale's own bombshell bloodsucker is back! Following the events of the *Jughead the Hunger vs. Vampironica* crossover, Veronica returns to her own universe, still a vampire. She's not the same, and she knows it. And now she needs answers. But she may not be ready for what she's about to discover!

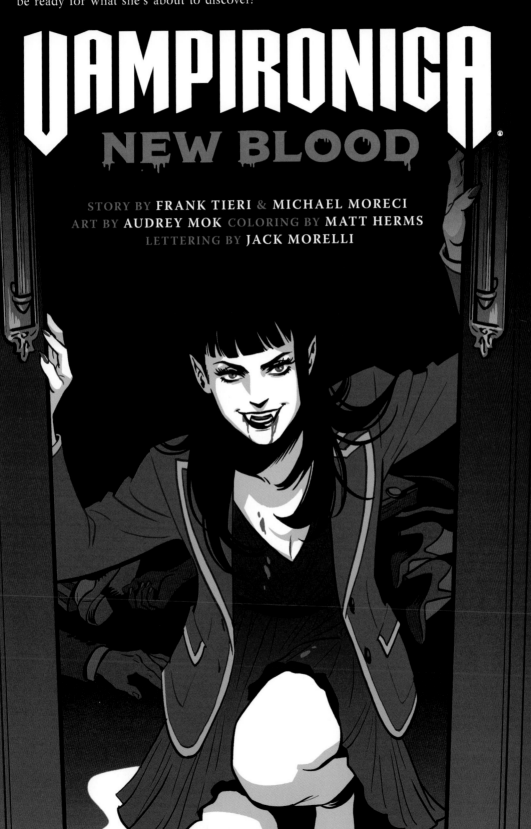

VAMPIRONICA
NEW BLOOD

STORY BY **FRANK TIERI** & **MICHAEL MORECI**
ART BY **AUDREY MOK** COLORING BY **MATT HERMS**
LETTERING BY **JACK MORELLI**

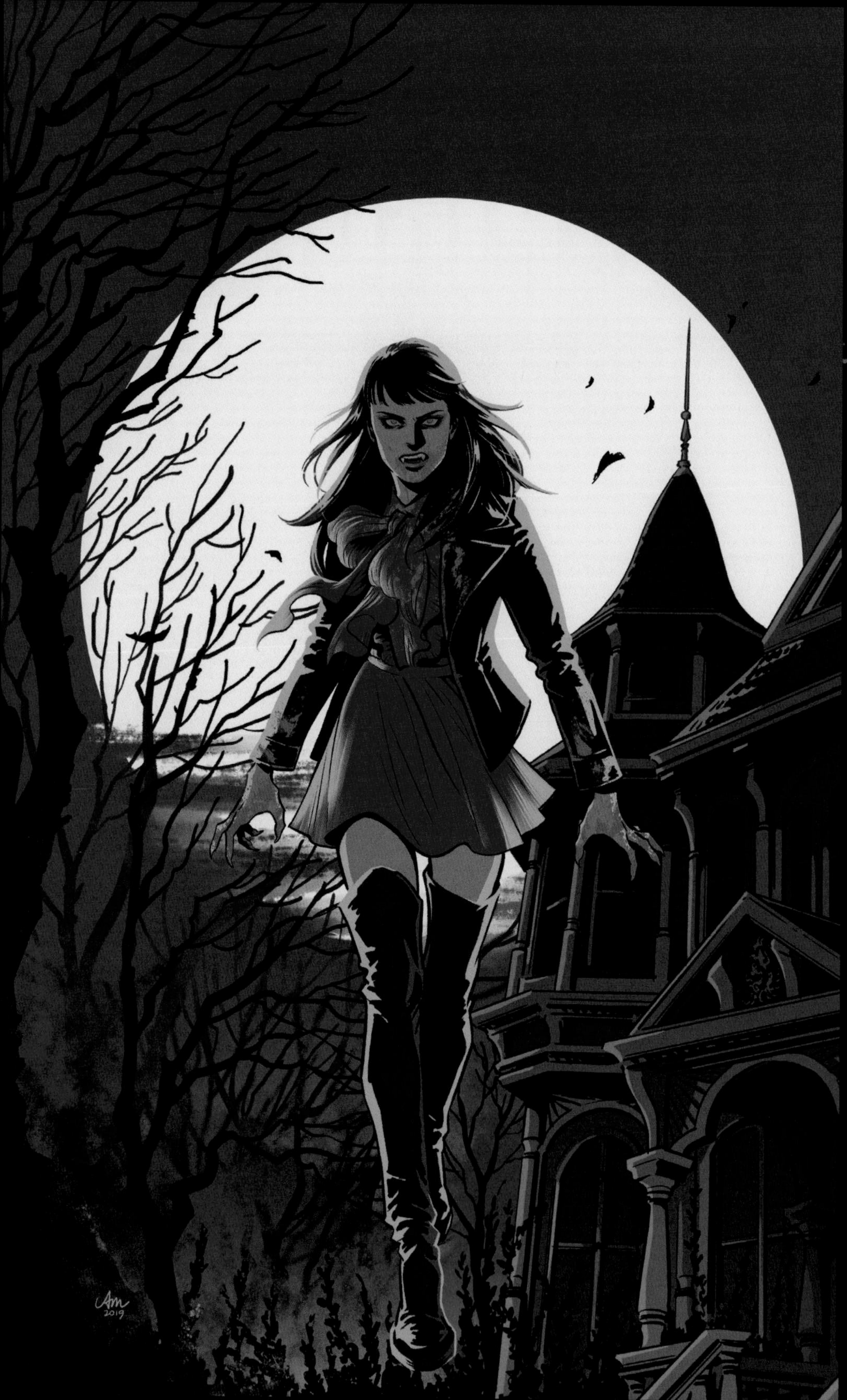
Am
2019

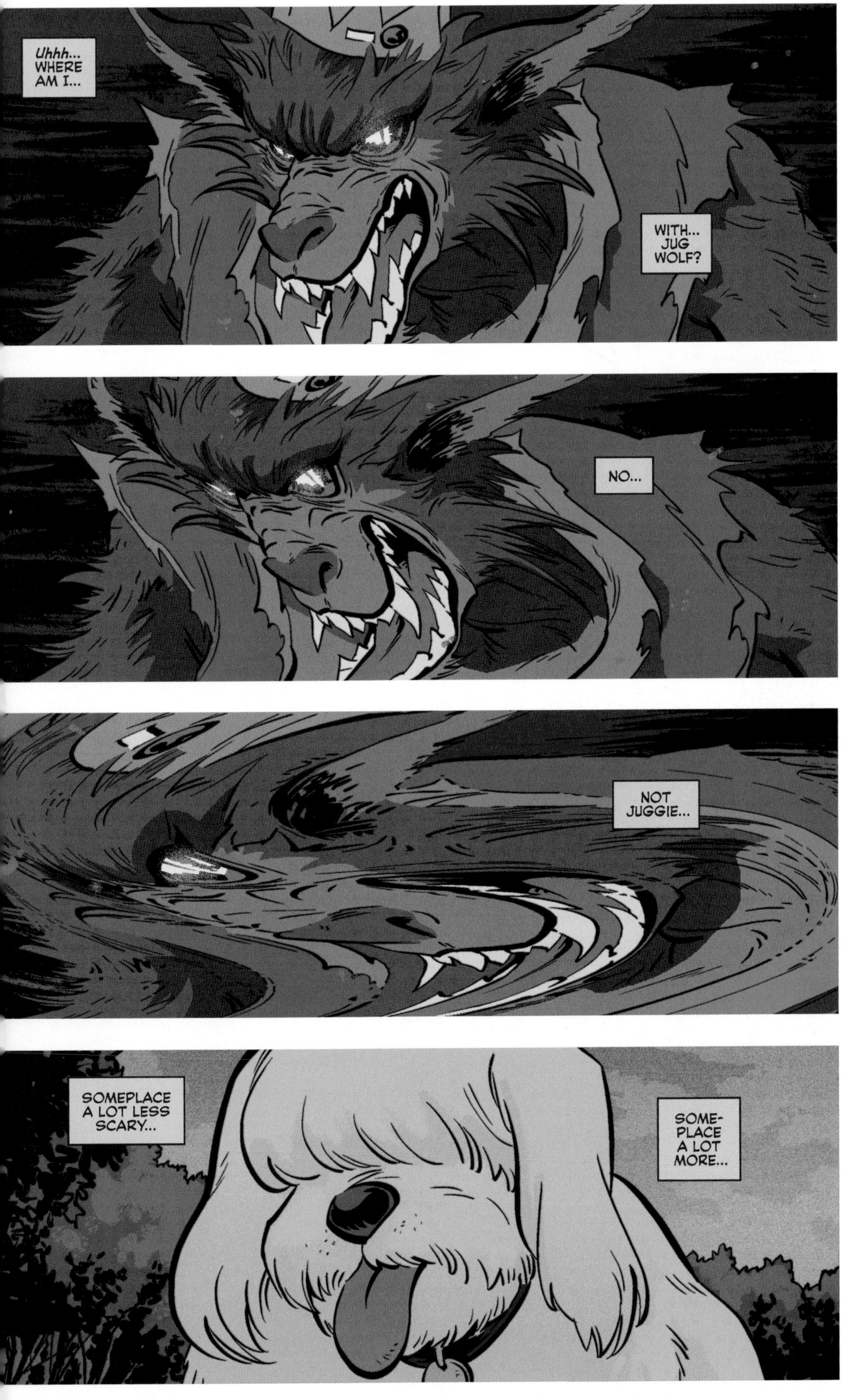
Uhhh... WHERE AM I...
WITH... JUG WOLF?
NO...
NOT JUGGIE...
SOMEPLACE A LOT LESS SCARY...
SOME-PLACE A LOT MORE...

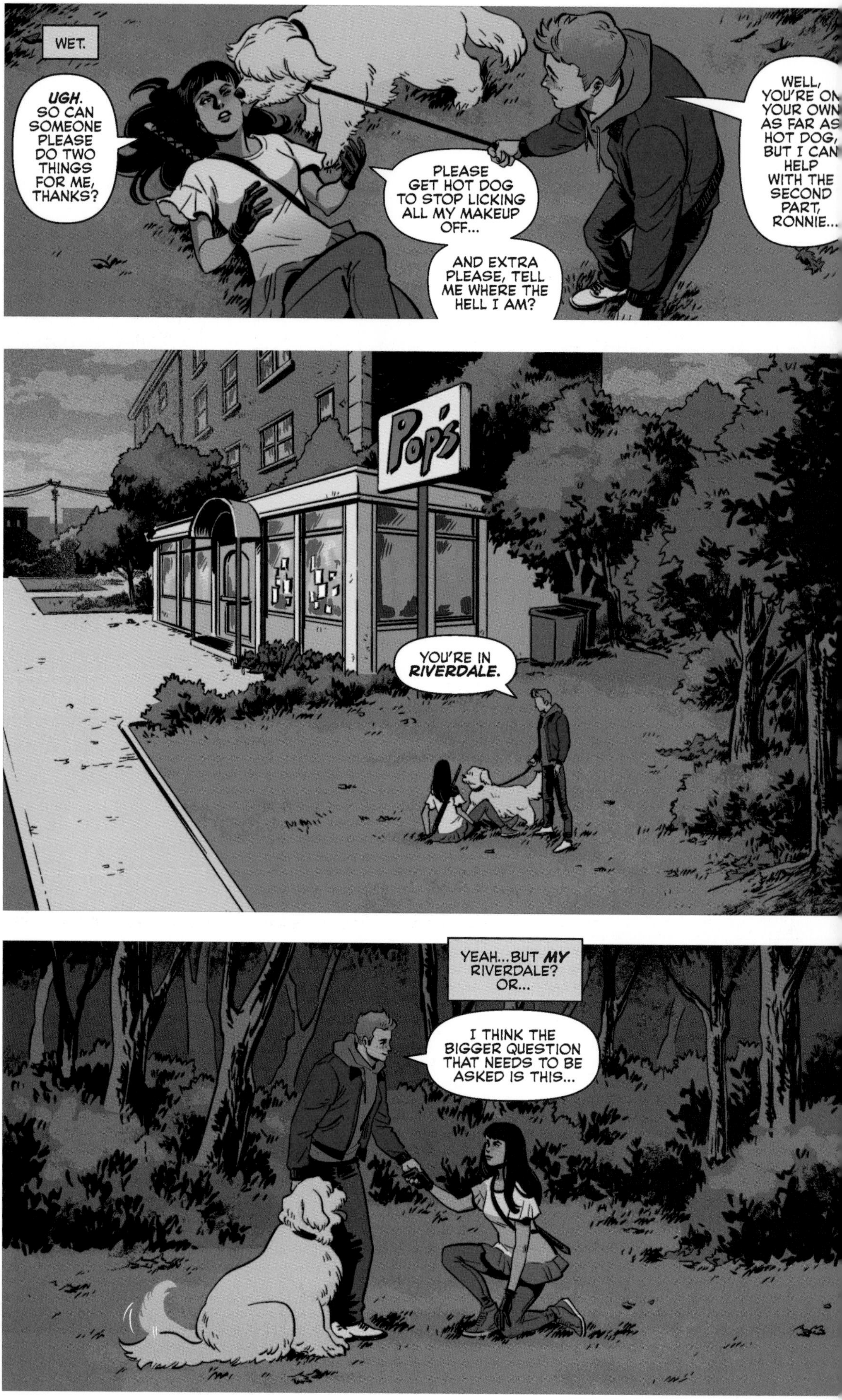
WET.
UGH. SO CAN SOMEONE PLEASE DO TWO THINGS FOR ME, THANKS?
PLEASE GET HOT DOG TO STOP LICKING ALL MY MAKEUP OFF...
AND EXTRA PLEASE, TELL ME WHERE THE HELL I AM?
WELL, YOU'RE ON YOUR OWN AS FAR AS HOT DOG, BUT I CAN HELP WITH THE SECOND PART, RONNIE...
Pop's
YOU'RE IN RIVERDALE.
YEAH...BUT MY RIVERDALE? OR...
I THINK THE BIGGER QUESTION THAT NEEDS TO BE ASKED IS THIS...

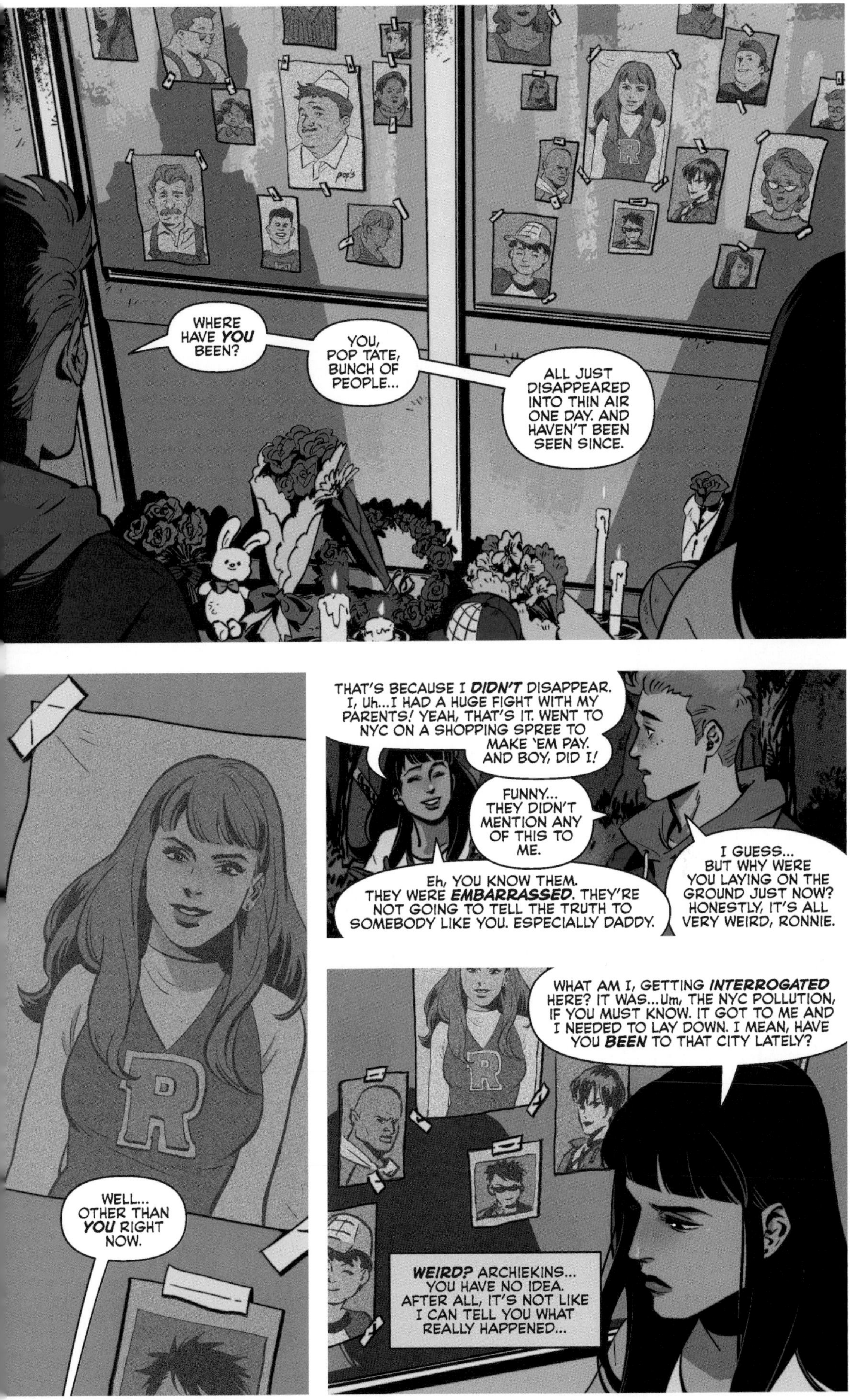
WHERE HAVE YOU BEEN?
YOU, POP TATE, BUNCH OF PEOPLE...
ALL JUST DISAPPEARED INTO THIN AIR ONE DAY. AND HAVEN'T BEEN SEEN SINCE.
WELL... OTHER THAN YOU RIGHT NOW.
THAT'S BECAUSE I DIDN'T DISAPPEAR. I, Uh...I HAD A HUGE FIGHT WITH MY PARENTS! YEAH, THAT'S IT. WENT TO NYC ON A SHOPPING SPREE TO MAKE 'EM PAY. AND BOY, DID I!
FUNNY... THEY DIDN'T MENTION ANY OF THIS TO ME.
Eh, YOU KNOW THEM. THEY WERE EMBARRASSED. THEY'RE NOT GOING TO TELL THE TRUTH TO SOMEBODY LIKE YOU. ESPECIALLY DADDY.
I GUESS... BUT WHY WERE YOU LAYING ON THE GROUND JUST NOW? HONESTLY, IT'S ALL VERY WEIRD, RONNIE.
WHAT AM I, GETTING INTERROGATED HERE? IT WAS...Um, THE NYC POLLUTION, IF YOU MUST KNOW. IT GOT TO ME AND I NEEDED TO LAY DOWN. I MEAN, HAVE YOU BEEN TO THAT CITY LATELY?
WEIRD? ARCHIEKINS... YOU HAVE NO IDEA. AFTER ALL, IT'S NOT LIKE I CAN TELL YOU WHAT REALLY HAPPENED...

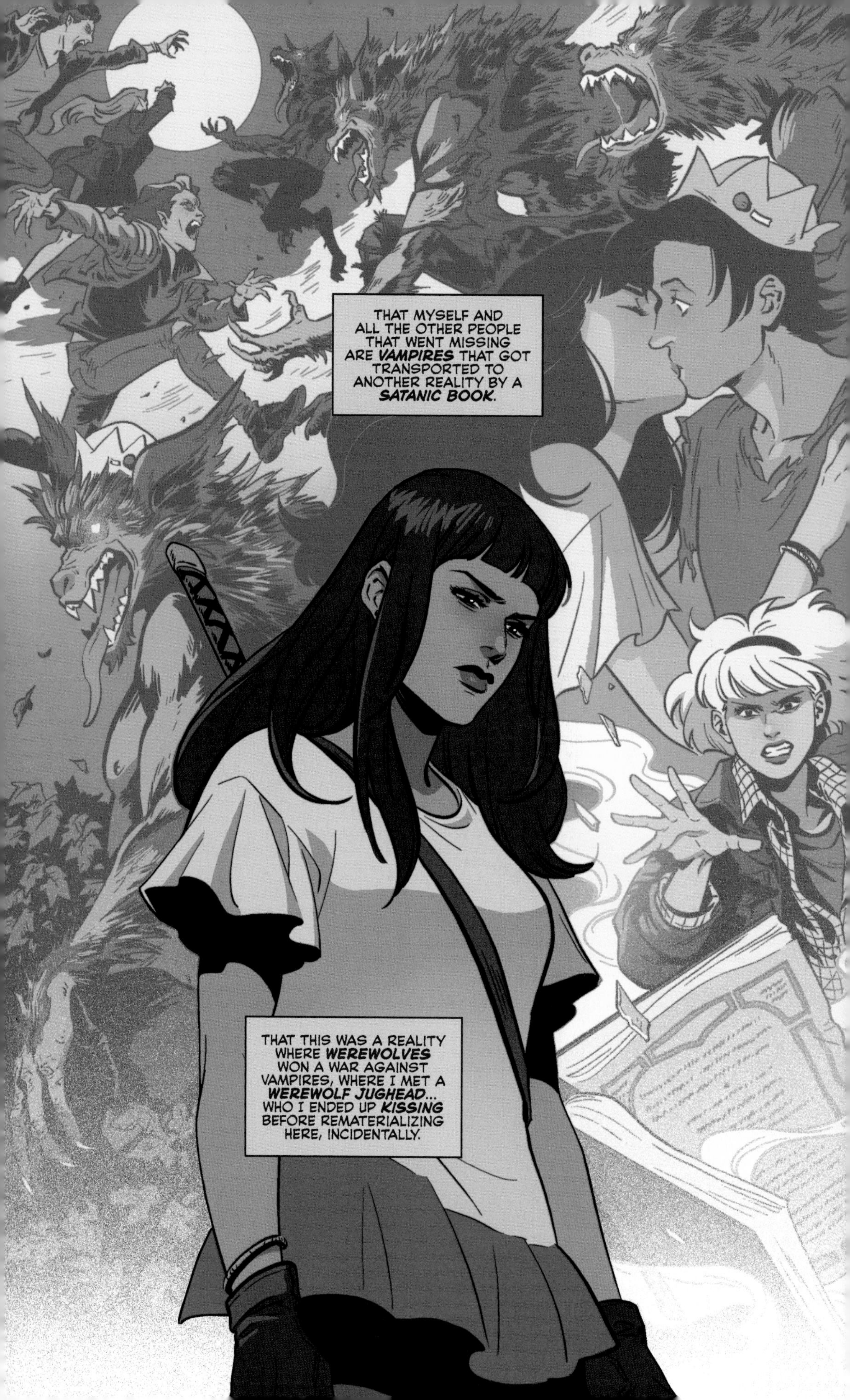
THAT MYSELF AND ALL THE OTHER PEOPLE THAT WENT MISSING ARE **VAMPIRES** THAT GOT TRANSPORTED TO ANOTHER REALITY BY A **SATANIC BOOK**.
THAT THIS WAS A REALITY WHERE **WEREWOLVES** WON A WAR AGAINST VAMPIRES, WHERE I MET A **WEREWOLF JUGHEAD**... WHO I ENDED UP **KISSING** BEFORE REMATERIALIZING HERE, INCIDENTALLY.

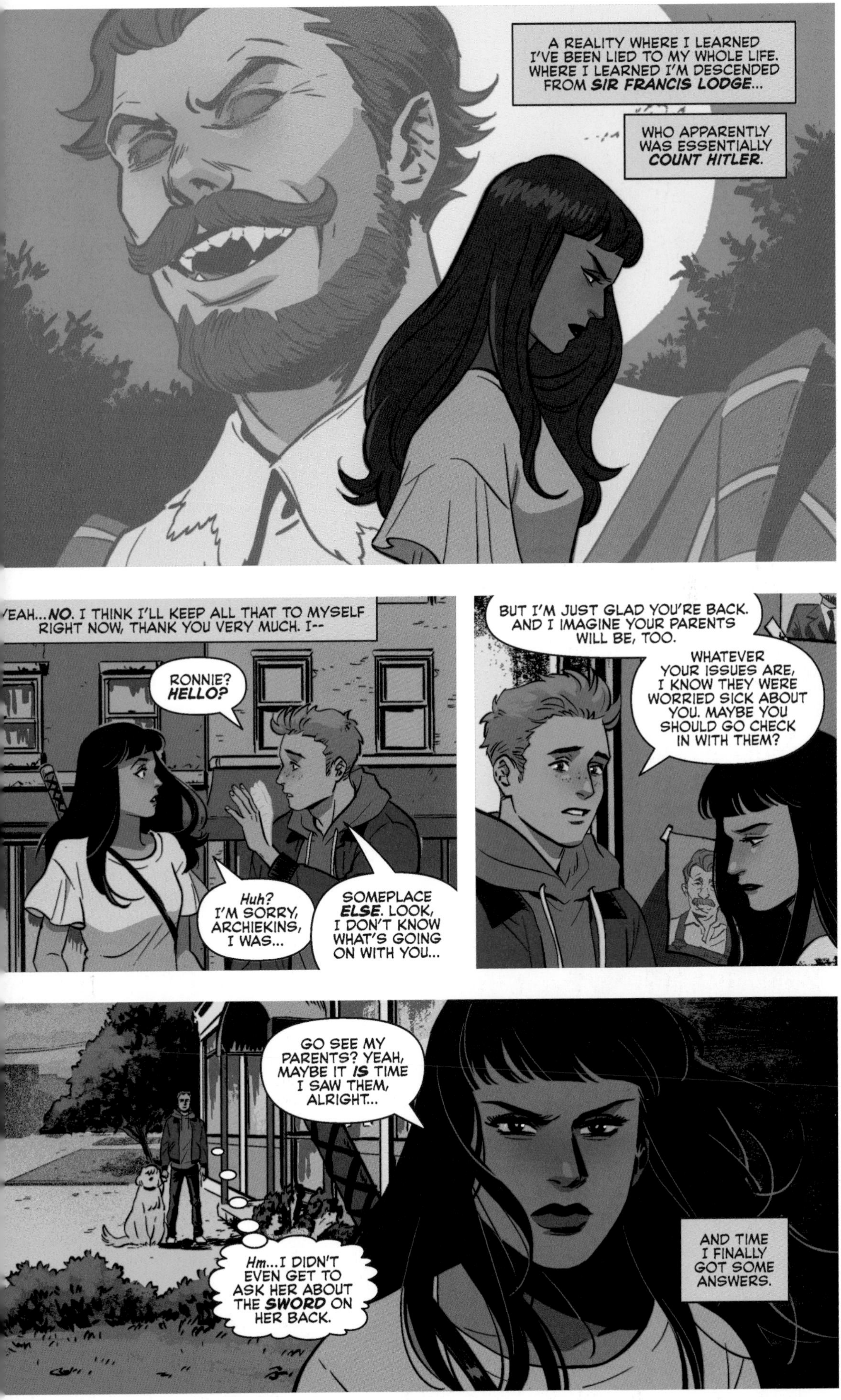
A REALITY WHERE I LEARNED I'VE BEEN LIED TO MY WHOLE LIFE. WHERE I LEARNED I'M DESCENDED FROM **SIR FRANCIS LODGE**...
WHO APPARENTLY WAS ESSENTIALLY **COUNT HITLER**.
YEAH...**NO**. I THINK I'LL KEEP ALL THAT TO MYSELF RIGHT NOW, THANK YOU VERY MUCH. I--
RONNIE? **HELLO?**
Huh? I'M SORRY, ARCHIEKINS, I WAS...
SOMEPLACE **ELSE**. LOOK, I DON'T KNOW WHAT'S GOING ON WITH YOU...
BUT I'M JUST GLAD YOU'RE BACK. AND I IMAGINE YOUR PARENTS WILL BE, TOO.
WHATEVER YOUR ISSUES ARE, I KNOW THEY WERE WORRIED SICK ABOUT YOU. MAYBE YOU SHOULD GO CHECK IN WITH THEM?
GO SEE MY PARENTS? YEAH, MAYBE IT **IS** TIME I SAW THEM, ALRIGHT...
Hm...I DIDN'T EVEN GET TO ASK HER ABOUT THE **SWORD** ON HER BACK.
AND TIME I FINALLY GOT SOME ANSWERS.

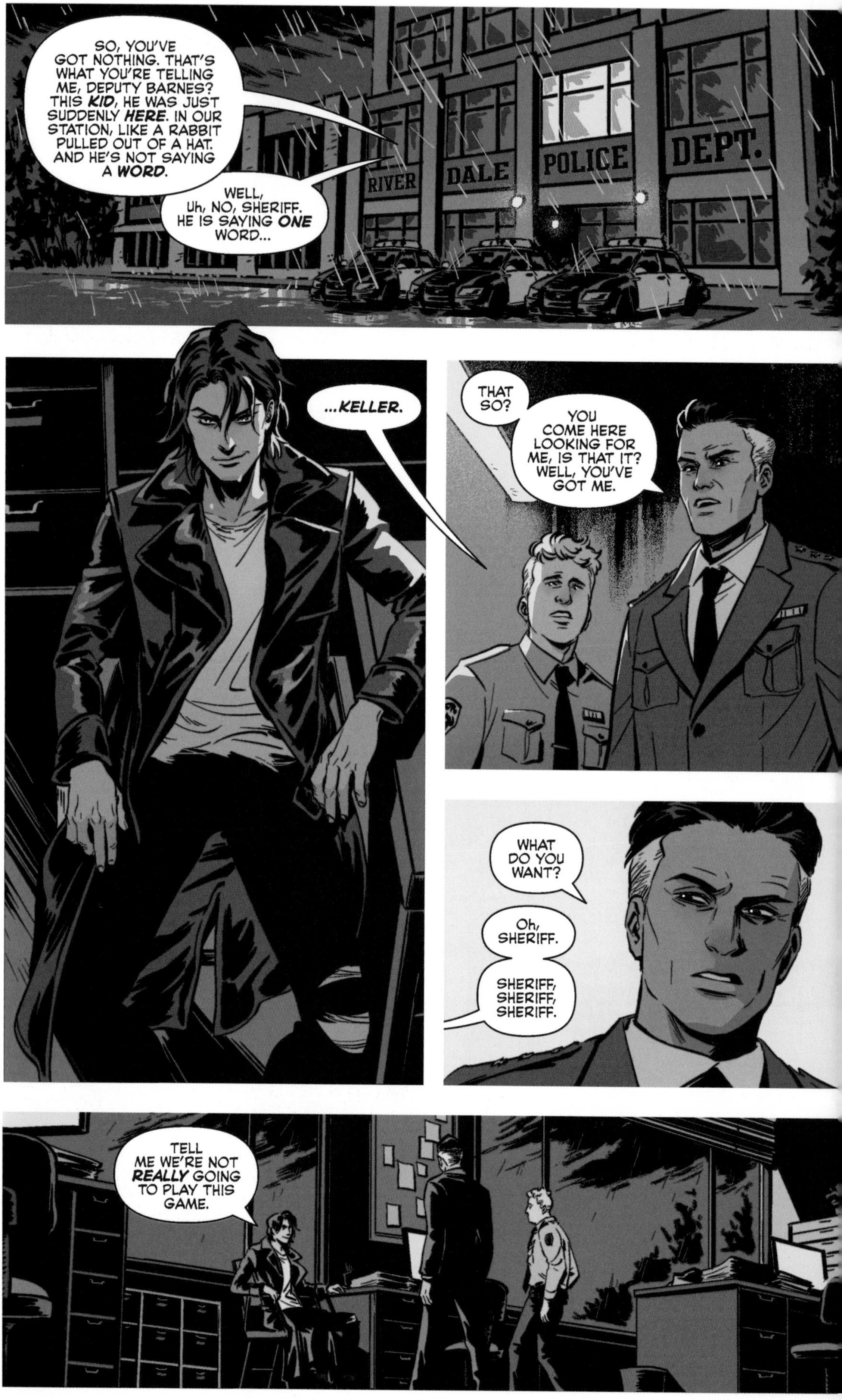
SO, YOU'VE GOT NOTHING. THAT'S WHAT YOU'RE TELLING ME, DEPUTY BARNES? THIS *KID*, HE WAS JUST SUDDENLY *HERE*. IN OUR STATION, LIKE A RABBIT PULLED OUT OF A HAT. AND HE'S NOT SAYING A *WORD*.
RIVER DALE POLICE DEPT.
WELL, Uh, NO, SHERIFF. HE IS SAYING *ONE* WORD...
...*KELLER*.
THAT SO?
YOU COME HERE LOOKING FOR ME, IS THAT IT? WELL, YOU'VE GOT ME.
WHAT DO YOU WANT?
Oh, SHERIFF.
SHERIFF, SHERIFF, SHERIFF.
TELL ME WE'RE NOT *REALLY* GOING TO PLAY THIS GAME.

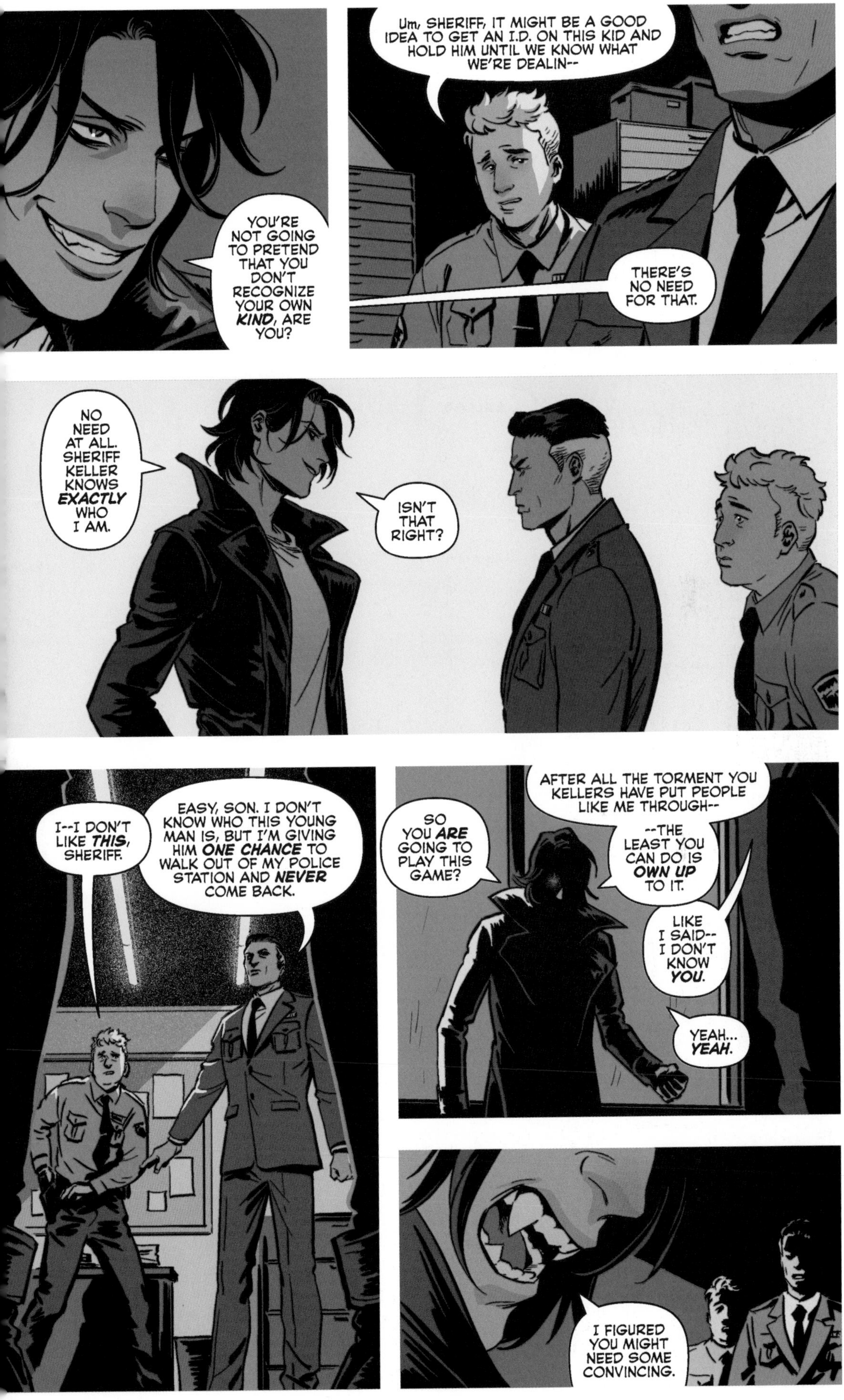
YOU'RE NOT GOING TO PRETEND THAT YOU DON'T RECOGNIZE YOUR OWN KIND, ARE YOU?
Um, SHERIFF, IT MIGHT BE A GOOD IDEA TO GET AN I.D. ON THIS KID AND HOLD HIM UNTIL WE KNOW WHAT WE'RE DEALIN--
THERE'S NO NEED FOR THAT.
NO NEED AT ALL. SHERIFF KELLER KNOWS EXACTLY WHO I AM.
ISN'T THAT RIGHT?
I--I DON'T LIKE THIS, SHERIFF.
EASY, SON. I DON'T KNOW WHO THIS YOUNG MAN IS, BUT I'M GIVING HIM ONE CHANCE TO WALK OUT OF MY POLICE STATION AND NEVER COME BACK.
SO YOU ARE GOING TO PLAY THIS GAME?
AFTER ALL THE TORMENT YOU KELLERS HAVE PUT PEOPLE LIKE ME THROUGH--
--THE LEAST YOU CAN DO IS OWN UP TO IT.
LIKE I SAID-- I DON'T KNOW YOU.
YEAH... YEAH.
I FIGURED YOU MIGHT NEED SOME CONVINCING.

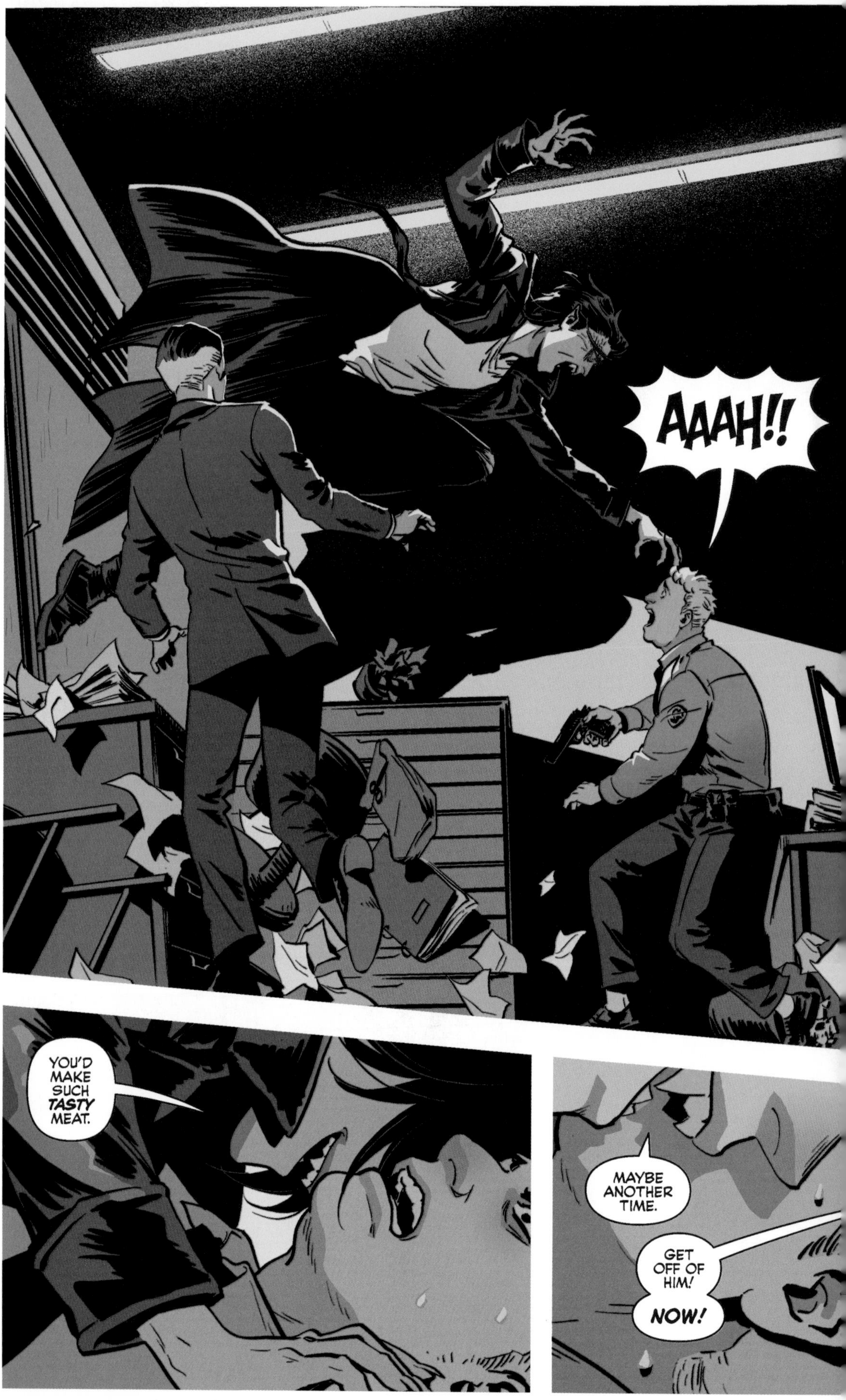
AAAH!!
YOU'D MAKE SUCH *TASTY* MEAT.
MAYBE ANOTHER TIME.
GET OFF OF HIM!
NOW!

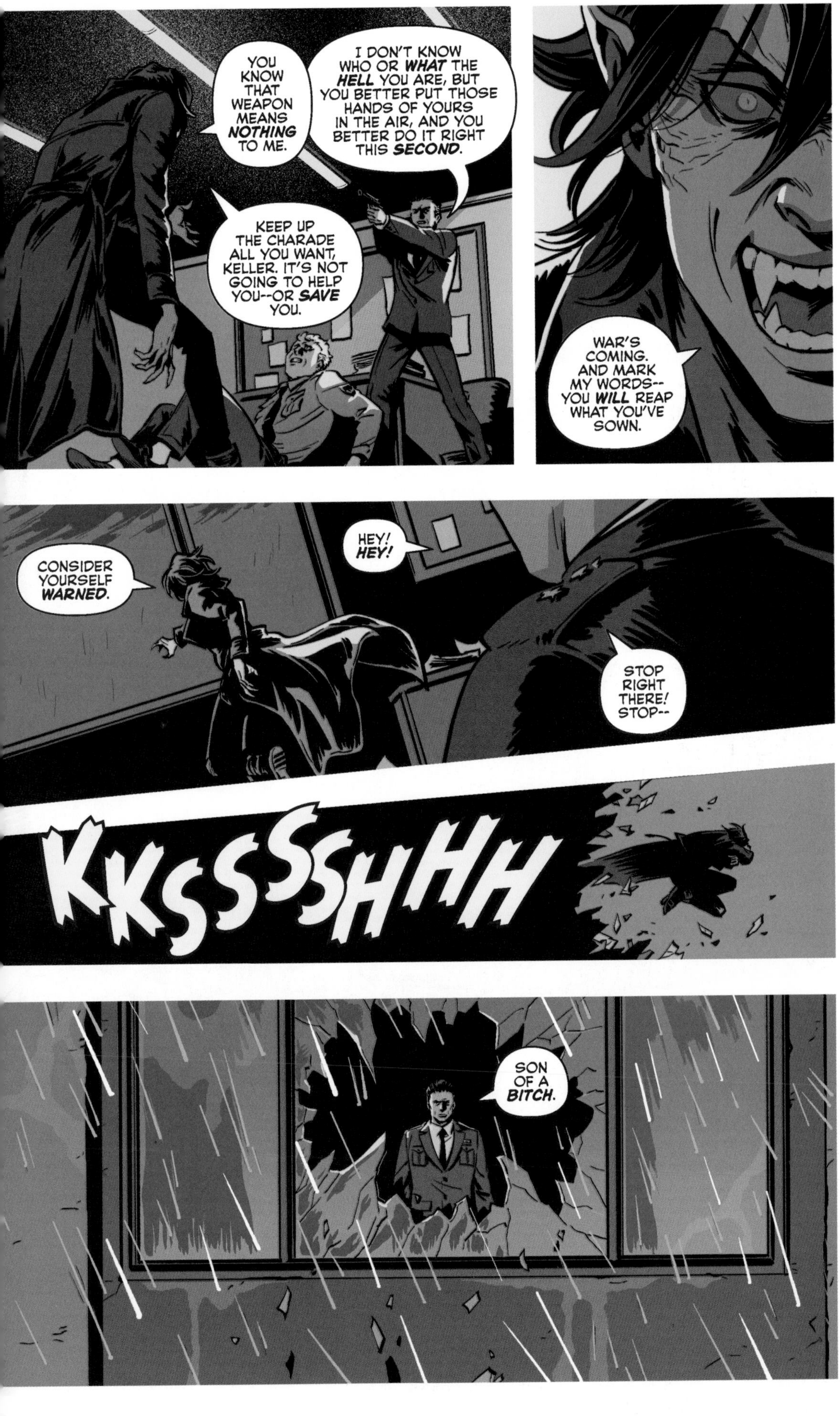
YOU KNOW THAT WEAPON MEANS NOTHING TO ME.
I DON'T KNOW WHO OR WHAT THE HELL YOU ARE, BUT YOU BETTER PUT THOSE HANDS OF YOURS IN THE AIR, AND YOU BETTER DO IT RIGHT THIS SECOND.
KEEP UP THE CHARADE ALL YOU WANT, KELLER. IT'S NOT GOING TO HELP YOU--OR SAVE YOU.
WAR'S COMING. AND MARK MY WORDS--YOU WILL REAP WHAT YOU'VE SOWN.
CONSIDER YOURSELF WARNED.
HEY! HEY!
STOP RIGHT THERE! STOP--
KKSSSSHHH
SON OF A BITCH.

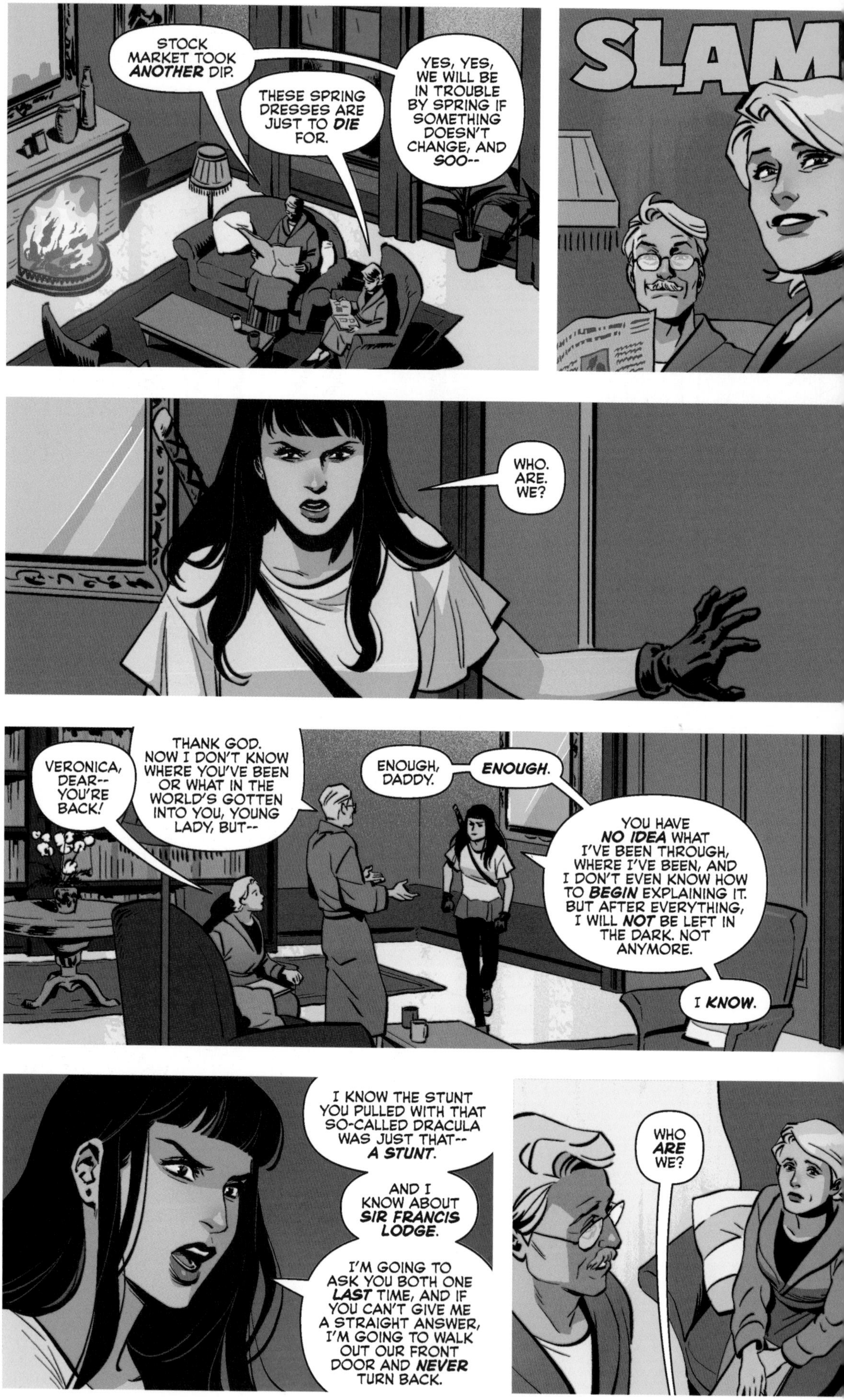
STOCK MARKET TOOK ANOTHER DIP.
THESE SPRING DRESSES ARE JUST TO DIE FOR.
YES, YES, WE WILL BE IN TROUBLE BY SPRING IF SOMETHING DOESN'T CHANGE, AND SOO--
SLAM
WHO. ARE. WE?
VERONICA, DEAR-- YOU'RE BACK!
THANK GOD. NOW I DON'T KNOW WHERE YOU'VE BEEN OR WHAT IN THE WORLD'S GOTTEN INTO YOU, YOUNG LADY, BUT--
ENOUGH, DADDY.
ENOUGH.
YOU HAVE NO IDEA WHAT I'VE BEEN THROUGH, WHERE I'VE BEEN, AND I DON'T EVEN KNOW HOW TO BEGIN EXPLAINING IT. BUT AFTER EVERYTHING, I WILL NOT BE LEFT IN THE DARK. NOT ANYMORE.
I KNOW.
I KNOW THE STUNT YOU PULLED WITH THAT SO-CALLED DRACULA WAS JUST THAT-- A STUNT.
AND I KNOW ABOUT SIR FRANCIS LODGE.
I'M GOING TO ASK YOU BOTH ONE LAST TIME, AND IF YOU CAN'T GIVE ME A STRAIGHT ANSWER, I'M GOING TO WALK OUT OUR FRONT DOOR AND NEVER TURN BACK.
WHO ARE WE?

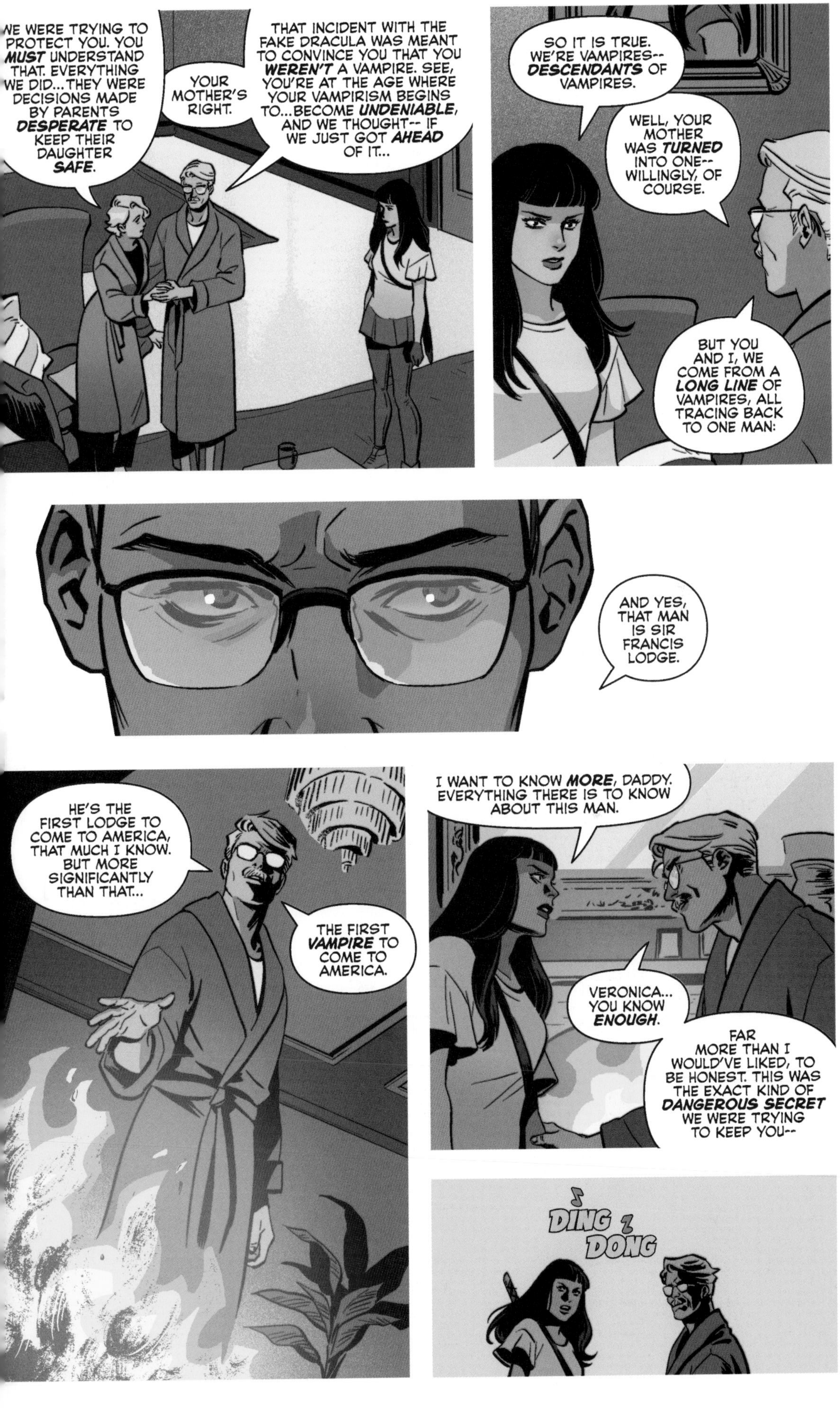
WE WERE TRYING TO PROTECT YOU. YOU MUST UNDERSTAND THAT. EVERYTHING WE DID...THEY WERE DECISIONS MADE BY PARENTS DESPERATE TO KEEP THEIR DAUGHTER SAFE.
YOUR MOTHER'S RIGHT.
THAT INCIDENT WITH THE FAKE DRACULA WAS MEANT TO CONVINCE YOU THAT YOU WEREN'T A VAMPIRE. SEE, YOU'RE AT THE AGE WHERE YOUR VAMPIRISM BEGINS TO...BECOME UNDENIABLE, AND WE THOUGHT-- IF WE JUST GOT AHEAD OF IT...
SO IT IS TRUE. WE'RE VAMPIRES-- DESCENDANTS OF VAMPIRES.
WELL, YOUR MOTHER WAS TURNED INTO ONE-- WILLINGLY, OF COURSE.
BUT YOU AND I, WE COME FROM A LONG LINE OF VAMPIRES, ALL TRACING BACK TO ONE MAN:
AND YES, THAT MAN IS SIR FRANCIS LODGE.
HE'S THE FIRST LODGE TO COME TO AMERICA, THAT MUCH I KNOW. BUT MORE SIGNIFICANTLY THAN THAT...
THE FIRST VAMPIRE TO COME TO AMERICA.
I WANT TO KNOW MORE, DADDY. EVERYTHING THERE IS TO KNOW ABOUT THIS MAN.
VERONICA... YOU KNOW ENOUGH.
FAR MORE THAN I WOULD'VE LIKED, TO BE HONEST. THIS WAS THE EXACT KIND OF DANGEROUS SECRET WE WERE TRYING TO KEEP YOU--
DING DONG

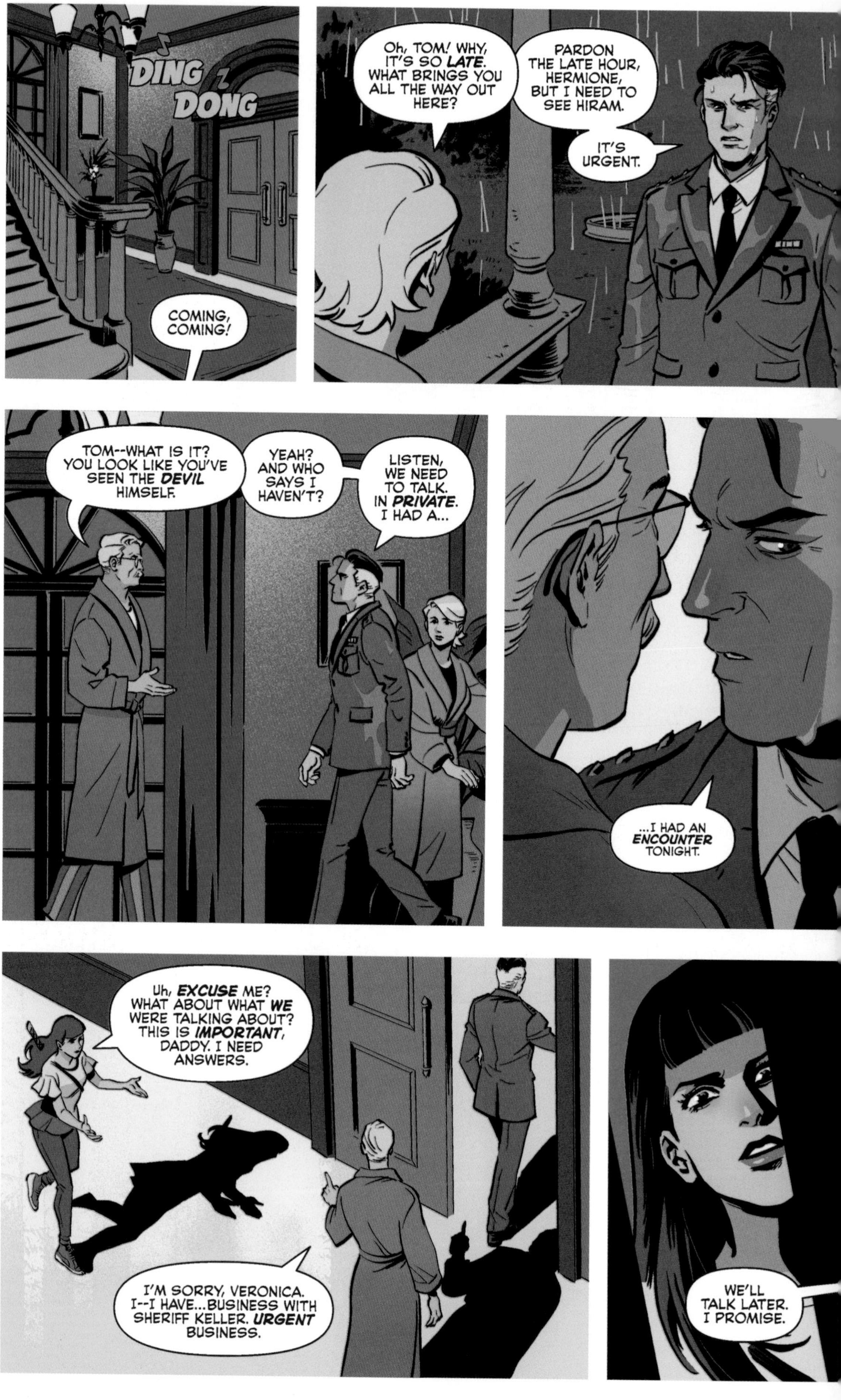
DING DONG
COMING, COMING!
Oh, TOM! WHY, IT'S SO LATE. WHAT BRINGS YOU ALL THE WAY OUT HERE?
PARDON THE LATE HOUR, HERMIONE, BUT I NEED TO SEE HIRAM.
IT'S URGENT.
TOM--WHAT IS IT? YOU LOOK LIKE YOU'VE SEEN THE DEVIL HIMSELF.
YEAH? AND WHO SAYS I HAVEN'T?
LISTEN, WE NEED TO TALK. IN PRIVATE. I HAD A...
...I HAD AN ENCOUNTER TONIGHT.
Uh, EXCUSE ME? WHAT ABOUT WHAT WE WERE TALKING ABOUT? THIS IS IMPORTANT, DADDY. I NEED ANSWERS.
I'M SORRY, VERONICA. I--I HAVE...BUSINESS WITH SHERIFF KELLER. URGENT BUSINESS.
WE'LL TALK LATER. I PROMISE.

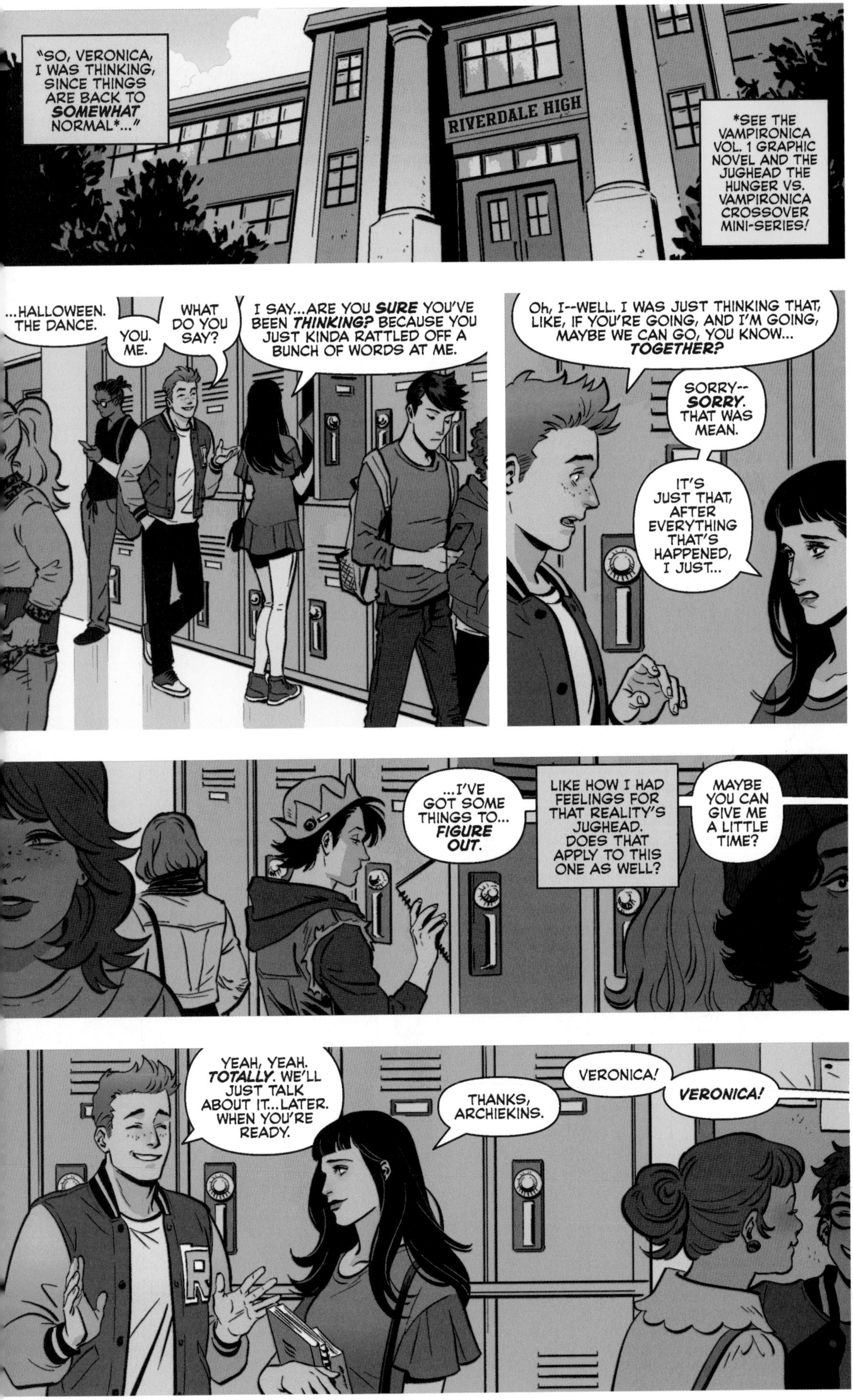

"SO, VERONICA, I WAS THINKING, SINCE THINGS ARE BACK TO SOMEWHAT NORMAL*..."
RIVERDALE HIGH
*SEE THE VAMPIRONICA VOL. 1 GRAPHIC NOVEL AND THE JUGHEAD THE HUNGER VS. VAMPIRONICA CROSSOVER MINI-SERIES!
...HALLOWEEN. THE DANCE.
YOU. ME.
WHAT DO YOU SAY?
I SAY...ARE YOU SURE YOU'VE BEEN THINKING? BECAUSE YOU JUST KINDA RATTLED OFF A BUNCH OF WORDS AT ME.
Oh, I--WELL. I WAS JUST THINKING THAT, LIKE, IF YOU'RE GOING, AND I'M GOING, MAYBE WE CAN GO, YOU KNOW... TOGETHER?
SORRY-- SORRY. THAT WAS MEAN.
IT'S JUST THAT, AFTER EVERYTHING THAT'S HAPPENED, I JUST...
...I'VE GOT SOME THINGS TO... FIGURE OUT.
LIKE HOW I HAD FEELINGS FOR THAT REALITY'S JUGHEAD. DOES THAT APPLY TO THIS ONE AS WELL?
MAYBE YOU CAN GIVE ME A LITTLE TIME?
YEAH, YEAH. TOTALLY. WE'LL JUST TALK ABOUT IT...LATER. WHEN YOU'RE READY.
THANKS, ARCHIEKINS.
VERONICA!
VERONICA!

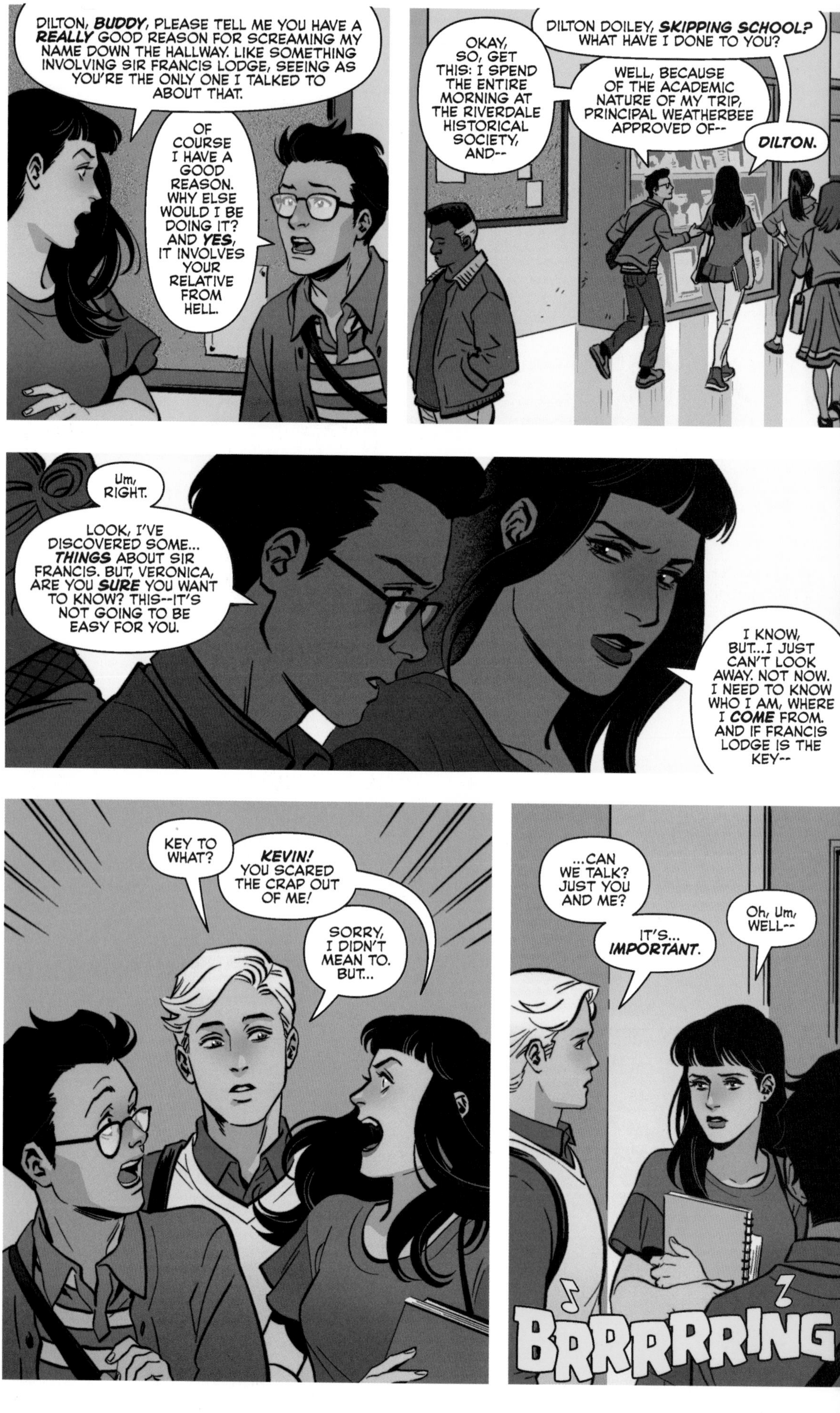
DILTON, BUDDY, PLEASE TELL ME YOU HAVE A REALLY GOOD REASON FOR SCREAMING MY NAME DOWN THE HALLWAY. LIKE SOMETHING INVOLVING SIR FRANCIS LODGE, SEEING AS YOU'RE THE ONLY ONE I TALKED TO ABOUT THAT.
OF COURSE I HAVE A GOOD REASON. WHY ELSE WOULD I BE DOING IT? AND YES, IT INVOLVES YOUR RELATIVE FROM HELL.
OKAY, SO, GET THIS: I SPEND THE ENTIRE MORNING AT THE RIVERDALE HISTORICAL SOCIETY, AND--
DILTON DOILEY, SKIPPING SCHOOL? WHAT HAVE I DONE TO YOU?
WELL, BECAUSE OF THE ACADEMIC NATURE OF MY TRIP, PRINCIPAL WEATHERBEE APPROVED OF--
DILTON.
Um, RIGHT.
LOOK, I'VE DISCOVERED SOME... THINGS ABOUT SIR FRANCIS. BUT, VERONICA, ARE YOU SURE YOU WANT TO KNOW? THIS--IT'S NOT GOING TO BE EASY FOR YOU.
I KNOW, BUT...I JUST CAN'T LOOK AWAY. NOT NOW. I NEED TO KNOW WHO I AM, WHERE I COME FROM. AND IF FRANCIS LODGE IS THE KEY--
KEY TO WHAT?
KEVIN! YOU SCARED THE CRAP OUT OF ME!
SORRY, I DIDN'T MEAN TO. BUT...
...CAN WE TALK? JUST YOU AND ME?
IT'S... IMPORTANT.
Oh, Um, WELL--
BRRRRRING

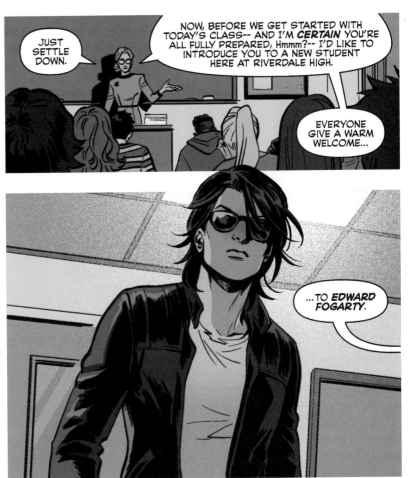

SORRY, KEV. GOTTA GET TO CLASS. MAYBE LATER?

ALL RIGHT, EVERYONE. SETTLE DOWN.

JUST SETTLE DOWN.

NOW, BEFORE WE GET STARTED WITH TODAY'S CLASS-- AND I'M *CERTAIN* YOU'RE ALL FULLY PREPARED, Hmmm?-- I'D LIKE TO INTRODUCE YOU TO A NEW STUDENT HERE AT RIVERDALE HIGH.

EVERYONE GIVE A WARM WELCOME...

...TO *EDWARD FOGARTY*.

HEY.

YOU KNOW ME? KNOW WHO I AM?

I USED TO *BE* RIVERDALE, SAME AS YOU. THEY NEVER TALK ABOUT ME?

MAYBE ONE DAY THEY'LL TALK ABOUT THE KID WHO GOT DETENTION IN HIS FIRST FIVE MINUTES OF SCHOOL.

COME ON. THINK *REAL* HARD.

THEY USED TO CALL ME *FANGS*.

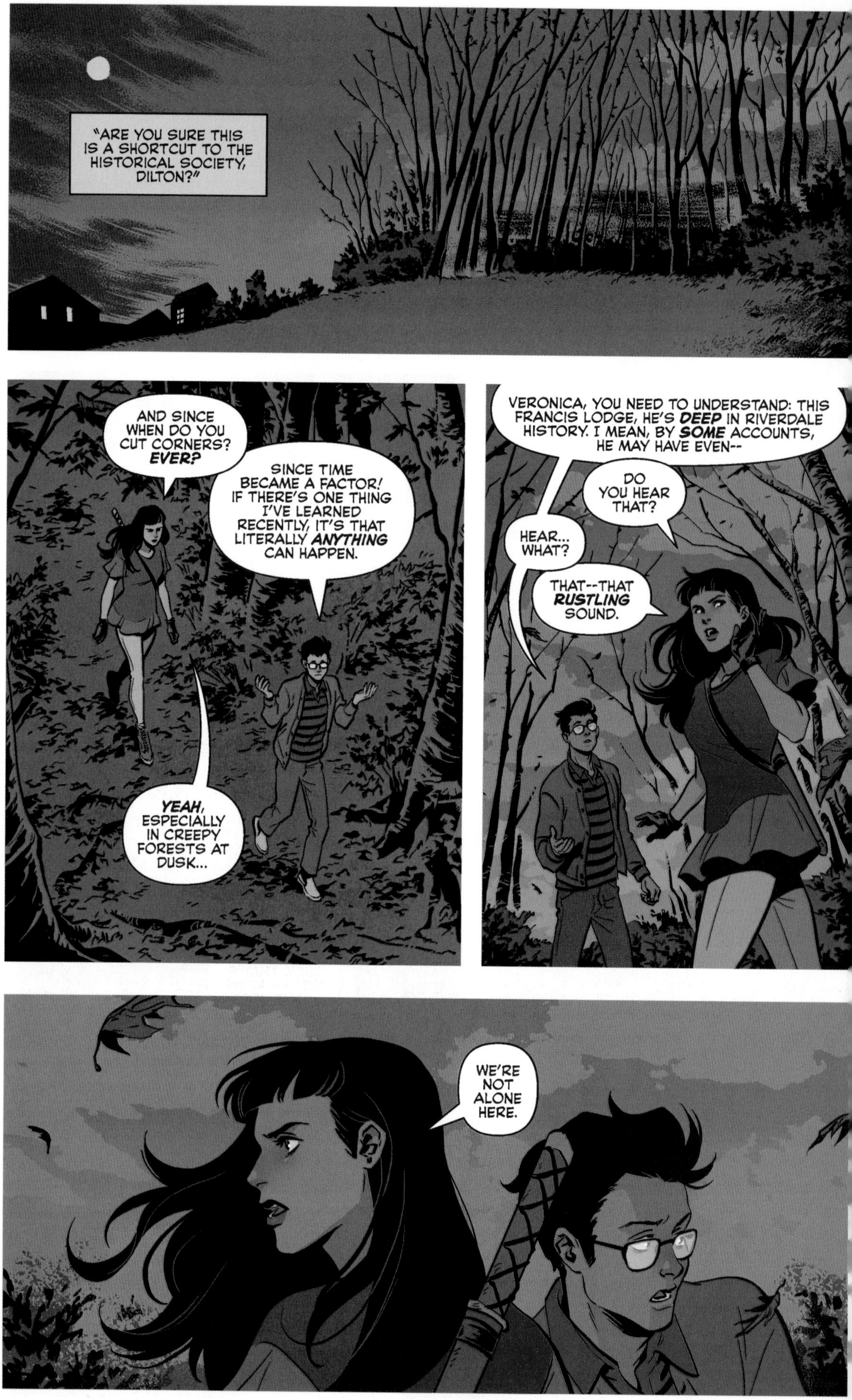
"ARE YOU SURE THIS IS A SHORTCUT TO THE HISTORICAL SOCIETY, DILTON?"
AND SINCE WHEN DO YOU CUT CORNERS? EVER?
SINCE TIME BECAME A FACTOR! IF THERE'S ONE THING I'VE LEARNED RECENTLY, IT'S THAT LITERALLY ANYTHING CAN HAPPEN.
YEAH, ESPECIALLY IN CREEPY FORESTS AT DUSK...
VERONICA, YOU NEED TO UNDERSTAND: THIS FRANCIS LODGE, HE'S DEEP IN RIVERDALE HISTORY. I MEAN, BY SOME ACCOUNTS, HE MAY HAVE EVEN--
DO YOU HEAR THAT?
HEAR... WHAT?
THAT--THAT RUSTLING SOUND.
WE'RE NOT ALONE HERE.

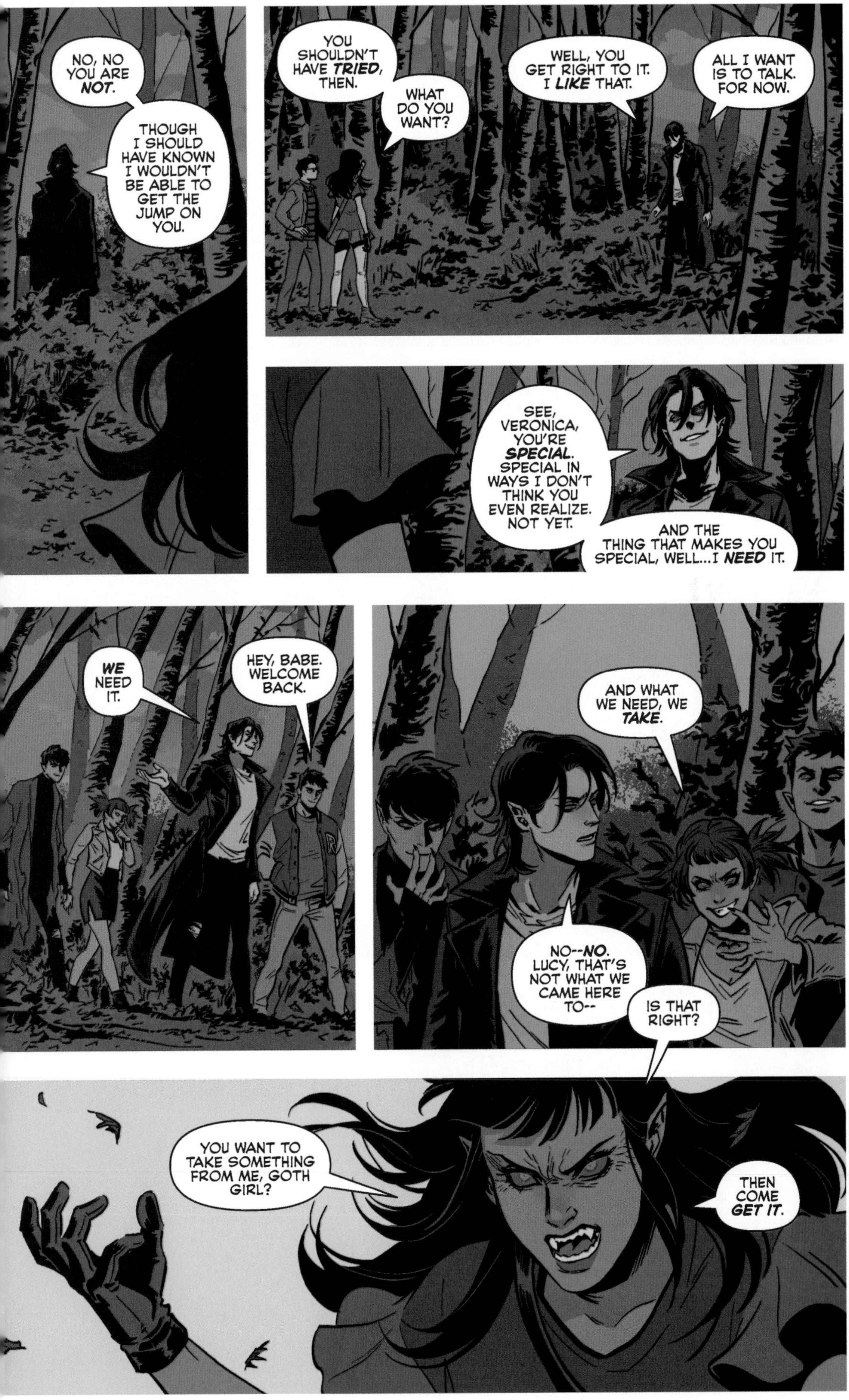
NO, NO YOU ARE NOT.
THOUGH I SHOULD HAVE KNOWN I WOULDN'T BE ABLE TO GET THE JUMP ON YOU.
YOU SHOULDN'T HAVE TRIED, THEN.
WHAT DO YOU WANT?
WELL, YOU GET RIGHT TO IT. I LIKE THAT.
ALL I WANT IS TO TALK. FOR NOW.
SEE, VERONICA, YOU'RE SPECIAL. SPECIAL IN WAYS I DON'T THINK YOU EVEN REALIZE. NOT YET.
AND THE THING THAT MAKES YOU SPECIAL, WELL...I NEED IT.
WE NEED IT.
HEY, BABE. WELCOME BACK.
AND WHAT WE NEED, WE TAKE.
NO--NO. LUCY, THAT'S NOT WHAT WE CAME HERE TO--
IS THAT RIGHT?
YOU WANT TO TAKE SOMETHING FROM ME, GOTH GIRL?
THEN COME GET IT.

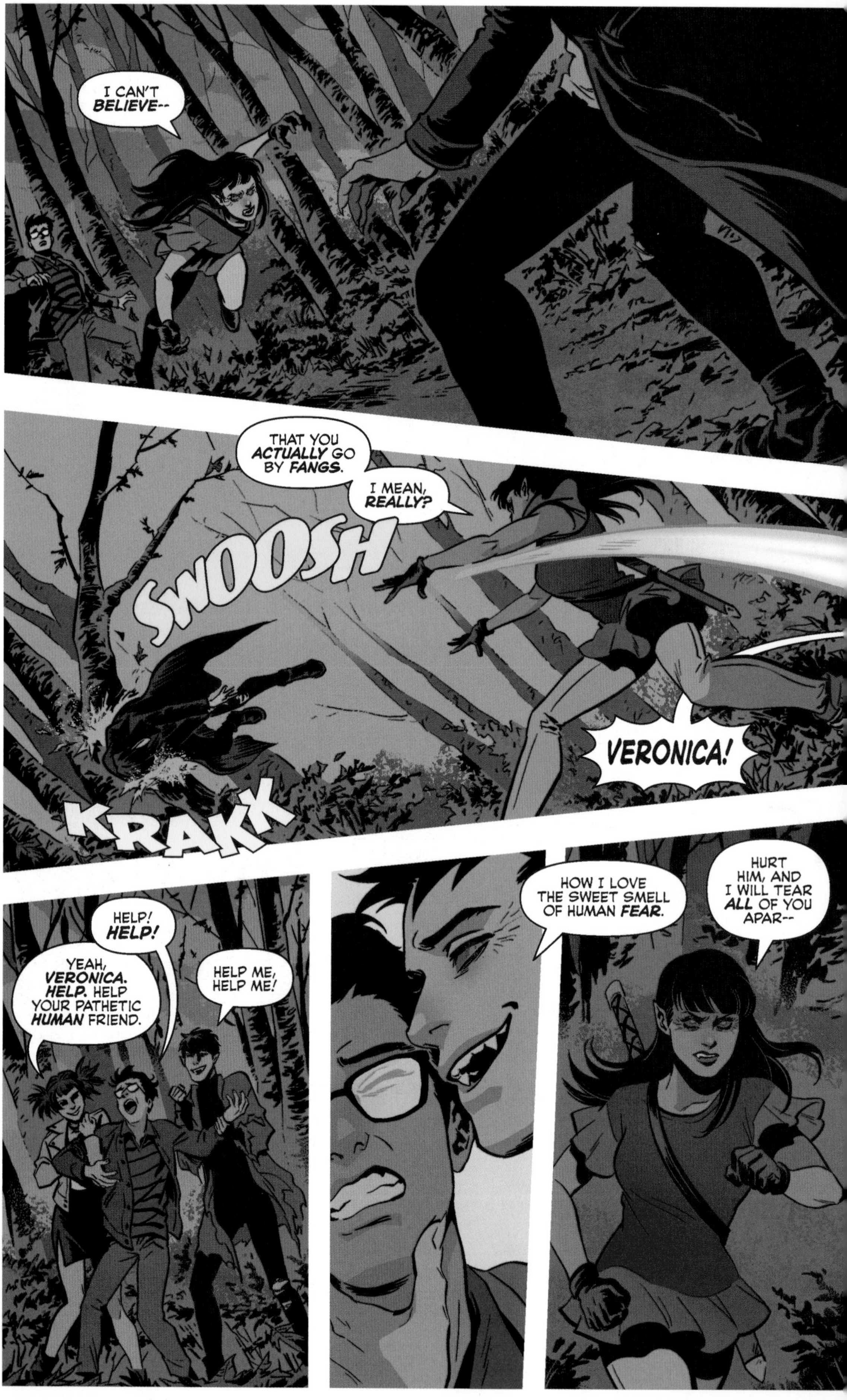
I CAN'T *BELIEVE*--
THAT YOU *ACTUALLY* GO BY *FANGS*.
I MEAN, *REALLY?*
SWOOSH
KRAKK
VERONICA!
HELP! *HELP!*
YEAH, *VERONICA. HELP.* HELP YOUR PATHETIC *HUMAN* FRIEND.
HELP ME, HELP ME!
HOW I LOVE THE SWEET SMELL OF HUMAN *FEAR*.
HURT HIM, AND I WILL TEAR *ALL* OF YOU APAR--

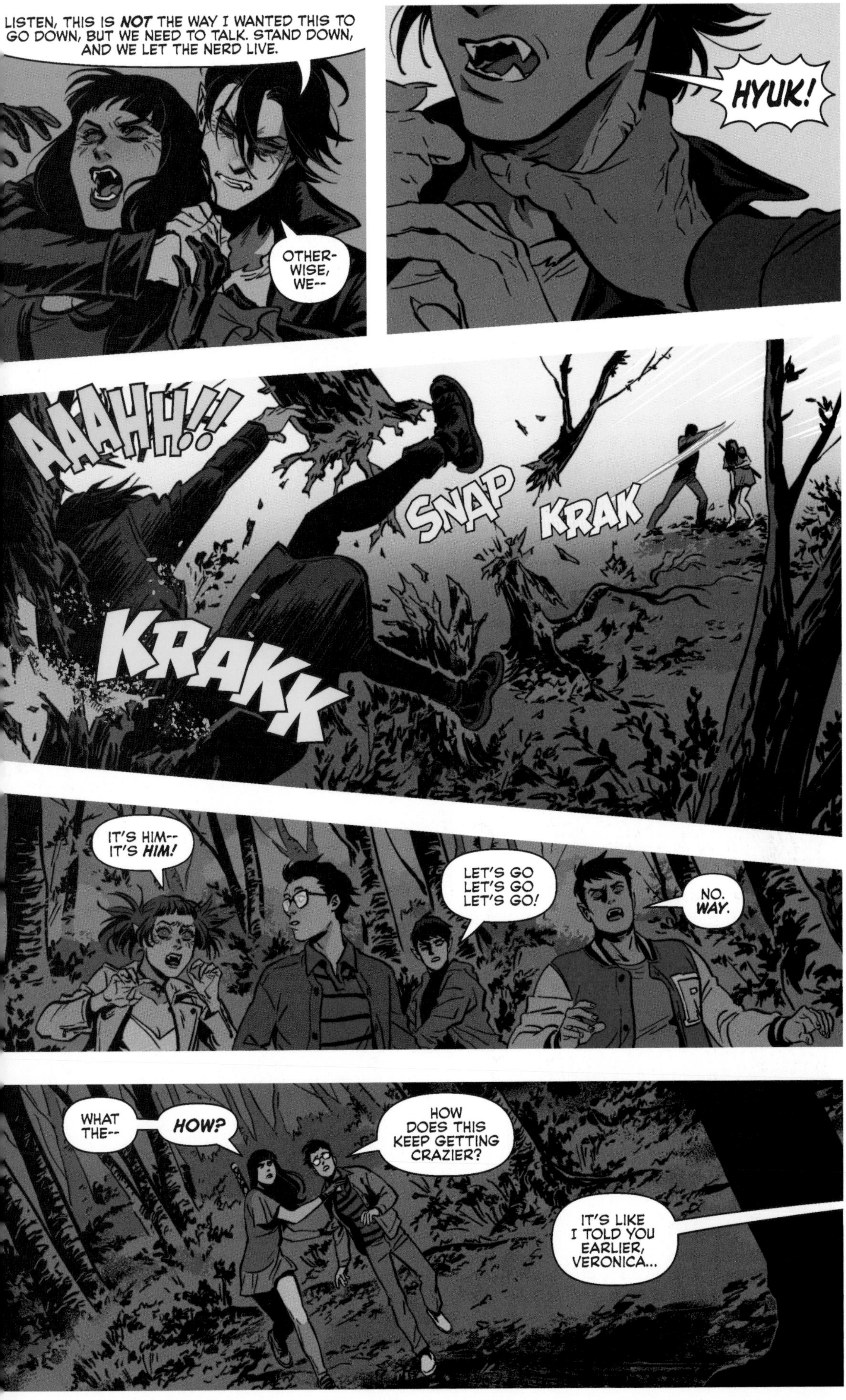

LISTEN, THIS IS **NOT** THE WAY I WANTED THIS TO GO DOWN, BUT WE NEED TO TALK. STAND DOWN, AND WE LET THE NERD LIVE.
OTHER-WISE, WE--
HYUK!
AAAHH!!!
SNAP
KRAK
KRAKK
IT'S HIM-- IT'S **HIM!**
LET'S GO LET'S GO LET'S GO!
NO. **WAY.**
WHAT THE--
HOW?
HOW DOES THIS KEEP GETTING CRAZIER?
IT'S LIKE I TOLD YOU EARLIER, VERONICA...

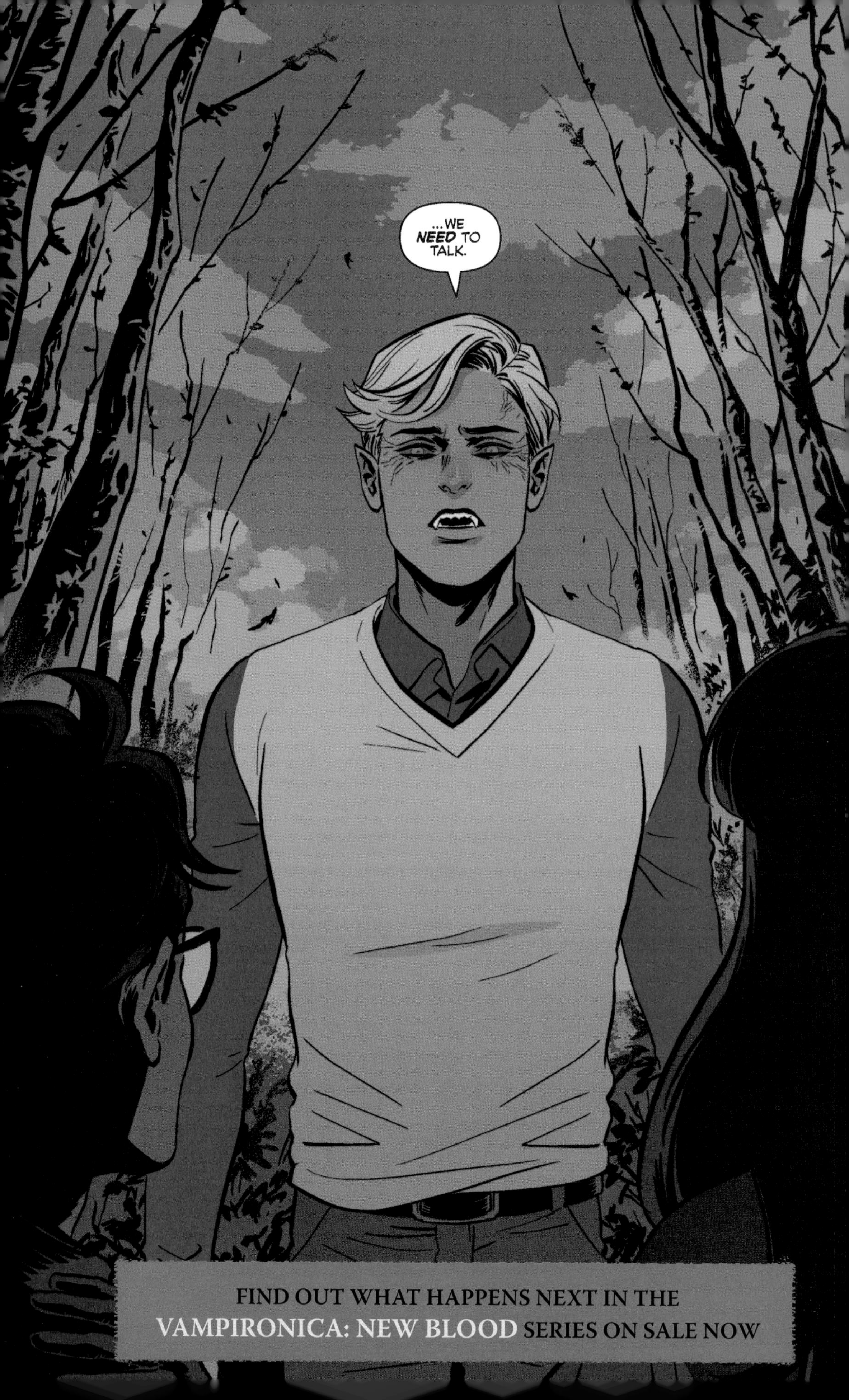
...WE NEED TO TALK.

FIND OUT WHAT HAPPENS NEXT IN THE
VAMPIRONICA: NEW BLOOD SERIES ON SALE NOW